Library Book Selection

Library Book Selection

M. Ram

RANDOM

RANDOM PUBLICATIONS
NEW DELHI (INDIA)

Library Book Selection

ISBN 978-93-5111-558-8

Published in 2015 in India by

RANDOM PUBLICATIONS

4376-A/4B, Gali Murari Lal, Ansari Road
New Delhi-110 002
Phone : +9111-43580356, 011-23289044, 011-43142548
e-mail: sales@randompublications.com,
info@randompublications.com, randomexports@gmail.com

Reprinted 2026

Type Setting by : Friends Media, Delhi-110089

Preface

Books assist in the dissemination of information by providing a convenient means of access to recorded knowledge. It is true that a medical book is out-of-date when it is published, but this does not invalidate its use as a digest of available knowledge in a physically handy form.

Libraries usually receive a lot of announcements from the publishers about the availability of new books. Moreover, many publishers produce various types of catalogues for their publications, sometimes including previously published editions which are still in print. It is necessary for the library to be on the mailing list of the publishers in the disciplines that concern the library. Visiting their web sites is now enabled as well.

As knowledge-based computer programmes in clinical medicine and other health care disciplines are improved and gain wider acceptance, they appear more commonly as library resources, especially if they can be accessed remotely from offices and clinical care sites. Selection of computer software by students, hospital staff, faculty, clinicians, or researchers should be guided by the library's collection development policy. The policy should address the criteria by which these resources are selected. Scope, depth and audience will define the boundaries.

The policy for reference collection should relate to the general collection development policy, whether it forms part of it or written separately. All selection criteria applied to books in general apply here as well. It remains to cover here the types of materials that form the reference collection and the selection sources of reference items.

The book will be found immensely informative and useful for all and for students and scholars.

I would like to thank my team for standing beside me throughout my career and writing this book. My special thanks go to "Random Publications" who have published the book.

– M. Ram

Preface

[illegible]

Contents

1

Serials and Book Selection

SERIALS SELECTION

From the eighteenth century, the journal has been an important mechanism for communicating scientific findings, advances in techniques, and changes in accepted practice in medicine and other health professions. Journals continue to constitute the core of health sciences library collections. But biomedical journals now face price increases, dwindling number of personal and institutional subscribers and the threat that print publications will be overshadowed by electronic forms of scientific communication. They also face various changes in the title, the publishers, emerging or splitting, editorship, supercession, ceasing, format or size, numbering, or frequency.

Responsibility for Selection

Because a decision to subscribe to a journal is often a long-term one, with a financial commitment over several years, selection is rarely left to a single person, although the final decision is often so.

Selection Committee

This is the practice in academic medical libraries and in large hospital libraries, as suggestions or requests are brought to the committee for review. Criteria for evaluation are agreed upon and an evaluation form is used to collect data for decision-making and to document decisions. The information should be recorded in a consistent manner on a standard form to allow comparisons.

The information may include the following: Title, publisher, frequency, starting date, cost, coverage of contents by standard indexing and abstracting services and online databases, published rankings or reviews, interlibrary loan data, information about purchase requests, information about other titles in the subject field, evidence of peer review of articles, assessment by faculty or hospital staff, availability in other affiliated library, relevance to the parent organisation's programmes. The frequency to committee meeting may vary from monthly to semiannually.

External Reviewers

These may be faculty or other health professional staff without forming any group. A form similar to the one used for selection committee may be used, preferrably with a sample issue of the journal. The library may use departmental representatives for this purpose. The librarian has to set a plan for follow-up.

SELECTION CRITERIA

Although selection criteria previously dealt with apply to all types of library materials, there are some unique characteristics of the journal format that need to be considered:

- *Quality*: Although no single measure will be sufficient to judge quality, there are several factors to be taken into account:
  - *Publisher*: Who is he? How reputable is he as a scientific publisher? Is the publisher a professional society or association? Is the membership of such society or association international? National? Regional?
  - *Editors*: Are they recognized? What is their institutional affiliation? are they themselves writers as well? Does the editorial board include prominent names?
  - Editorial review.
  - *Authors*: Are they members of the editorial board? What is there affiliation?
  - Content.
    - a. *Research Journals*: Research journals should publish articles that follow the accepted format for describing scientific research.
    - b. *Clinical Journals*: These may be evaluated by practitioners for selection.
    - c. *Review Journals*: These require more selectivity than the previous types because they do not report new information, and reviews on similar topics may cover much of the same ground.
- Writing and Style:
  - *Writing Style*: Articles should be readable. The writing should be grammatically correct, well organised and clear.
  - *Abstracts*: These should be informative.
  - *References*: These should be pertinent, thorough and up-to-date. Citations should be complete and accurate.
- *Accessibility of Content*: The inclusion of the journal in indexing services may be a criterion for selection. Inclusion in a selective database may also be used for this purpose.
- *Bibliometric Indicators*: Bibliometrics, or statistical bibliography,

analyses literature by numerically examining the publications of a discipline. Data can be used to identify journals with the greatest number of articles on a subject or that cover greatest percentage of the literature. But bibliomteric data must be used cautiously as a selection tool, as articles may be cited for multiple reasons and not necessarily to indicate useful research or clinical content.

- *Physical Quality*: It is to be noted here that not all countries have equal access to high-quality paper and printing.
  - *Illustrations*: Clarity and definition in reproduction of radiographs, photographs and other images. Use of colour may be important in some fields.
  - *Paper and Binding*: This may not be a factor to be considered as a factor for selection, although using acid-free paper is relevant for material preservation.
- *User Needs*: Patient care and current research needs are driving forces for selection. One indicator of need is the number of requests made to obtain copies of articles through interlibrary loan or document delivery services. The departmental representatives for selection may be a source for identifying department needs.
- Local Availability.
  - Whether the title is available in another library of the parent organisation.
  - Duplication is becoming less likely except for heavily used items.
  - Availability through a network to which the library subscribes.
  - Reliance on remote collections or document delivery services.
- *Cost:* The judgement on the benefit for cost may be difficult, and subject experts should be called upon for advice.

Electronic Journals

Electronic journals may be categorized either by availability of electronic and print parallels or by mode of access.

The first will result in:

- Electronic journals that have an electronic version only, such as Online journal of current clinical trials.
- Electronic journals that are versions of print journals, such as New England journal of medicine.

The second will result in:

- Electronic journals that are available through a commercial vendor.
- Electronic journals that are locally accessible through CD-ROM, floppy disk or other electronic format loaded on a library workstation or parent organisation's network.

The issues that electronic journals pose for libraries are not substantially different than those posed by print journals. Information on availability of electronic journals may be obtained from the Association of Research Libraries (ARL) in both print and electronic format.

SELECTION SOURCES

There are several sources or information about journals:

- *Advertising and Announcements*: Advertisements may be sent directly by publishers, or are published in library or medical journals. Vendors also alert libraries in various ways: through lists, order forms, and online information systems. Publishers' catalogues may also be used.
- *Sample Issues*: These are sent by the publisher as sample or trial issues, which often may be requested and sometimes purchased.
- *Core Lists:* Lists of key journals, sometimes together with some other library materials are compiled. The following are examples:
- *User Recommendations:* The library can encourage users to suggest new titles using request form available in the library, whether manually or electronically.
- *Interlibrary Loan Requests*: Repeated requests from users to obtain articles from a journal should prompt the library to consider a subscription.
- *Reviews:* There are scientific journals that publish reviews of new titles. Among these journals are Nature and Serials review.
- *Indexes*: Lists of journals indexed for major indexing services are used to make a judgement on titles already identified. Announcement of titles added can alert selectors to them. Examples of these lists are:
  - List of journals indexed in Index Medicus. New titles are announced in *NLM technical bulletin*.
  - Serial sources for the BIOSIS Previews Database.
  - Chemical Abstracts Service Source Index.
- *Other Sources*: There are general sources that cover a wide range of subjects. Among these are the following:
  - Ulrich's international periodicals directory. Bowker.
  - Standard periodical directory. Oxbridge.
  - New serial titles. OCLC.
  - Faxon's librarians' guide to serials.
  - EBSCO's librarians' handbook.
  - Computer databases such as OCLC, RLIN, SERLINE (an NLM database)
  - Serials review. Ann Arbor: Pierian. Quarterly

It has to be noted here that all such sources are also available in machine-readable form.

ACQUISITION OF SERIALS

The Anglo-American cataloguing rules, second edition defines a serial as:

- A publication in any medium issued in successive parts bearing numeric or chronological designations and intended to be continued indefinitely. Serials include periodicals; newspapers; annuals, the journals, proceedings, memoirs, transactions, etc. of societies; and numbered monographic series. Series is a group of separate items related to one another by the fact that each item bears, in addition to its own title proper, a collective title applying to the group as a whole. The individual items may or may not be numbered.

The indefinite continuation of a serial is important from the acquisitions point of view, as it continues arriving, which necessitates updating its record.

CATEGORIES OF SERIALS

Periodicals

Periodicals are serials characterized by the regularity of publication and frequency of issue. They are generally paid for in advance.

They include scholarly journals, popular magazines, newsletters and loose-leaf publications with a regular updating service:

- *Journals*: Journals constitute the majority of periodicals in the health sciences library. They are usually distributed unbound, bear a volume and issue number, and mostly have continuous pagination throughout the volume. A volume index and cumulated table of contents are common.
- *Magazines*: They are usually intended for a wider audience. Advertisements are interspersed with articles, each issue is paginated independently, indexes are uncommon, and article content is not generally subject to peer review.
- *Newsletters and Newspapers*: These are typically composed of folded sheets and frequently lack standard journal feature such as table of contents and index. Libraries keep simple records for them, and are most likely discarded when they are outdated. A microform copy may be kept instead. Some of them are now available electronically online or on CD-ROM.
- *Loose-leaf Publications*: These are issued in loose-leaf format, and are updated regularly with additional or replacement pages for an annual fee. Many of them are now offered on CD-ROM.

Annuals and Proceedings

Annuals are titles published on a more or less annual basis.

They can provide:

- Updating review of the literature in a specific discipline
- Compilation of standard data

- Directory information, or
- Proceedings of annual professional meetings

Many libraries establish a standing order for acquiring this category, and process items the way books are processed.

Numbered Monographic Series

These include series that are issued with a collective series title and a consecutive volume number, frequently with but not necessarily accompanied by a unique title for each work in the series. Publishing is generally irregular, and mostly processed like books after checking-in as serials. They, thus, have two records, one as serials, and another as books.

Pseudoserials

These are not strictly speaking serials, but are treated as such for acquisitions purposes. They include any publication that appears in separate parts or editions under a consistent title, and continues for more than a year or two years.

Examples of this category include:

- Encylcopaedias or dictionaries issued in parts over a period of several years.
- Successive editions of reference works, such as directories, cumulative bibliographies, biographical lists of 'who's who' type and handbooks for special disciplines.

SOURCES OF SERIALS

Publishers

Most publishers accept subscription orders for their serials, although a few make their publications available only through agents or exclusively through a general purchase arrangement, such as a standing order or a membership in the publisher's parent organisation:

- *Commercial Publishers*: Libraries may place a subscription directly with a publisher. Commercial publishers may provide some services useful to libraries, such as providing sample copies of issues before the library makes a subscription decision, and establishing standard terms for claiming missing or damaged issues and for purchasing backfiles.
- *Society Publishers*: These publishers publish their serials for the membership of the association or society, and for broader distribution to the scientific community. Some publishers will not sell their serials except to members, while others give discount or provide their publications as part of the membership perquisites. Some do not allow an agent to be involved in subscription.

- *Government Agencies*: Many government agencies publish serials. Procuring such publications present a challenge to the library in identifying and receiving them promptly. They may be obtained directly from the government central publishing house, from the individual issuing agency, or through a specialist vendor.

Gifts, Exchange or Deposits

Exchange or gift arrangement may be effective in the acquisition of serials published in other countries under the auspices of academic institutions or scholarly groups. Sometimes titles may be available only through exchange arrangement or gift. Deposits are much like gifts and exchange, except that they may not be officially the property of the receiving library. A factor that should be considered in accepting arrangements for exchange, gifts or deposits, is whether the library would be willing to pay for a subscription if the agreement were suddenly terminated.

Subscription Agents

At the most basic level, subscription agents accept subs-cription orders and forward them to the appropriate publishers with payment. The agent, in return, sends the library a consolidated invoice, which the library pays to him. The agent represents the library in communicating with the publisher when claims for skipped or late issues are necessary.

The library usually pays the agent the list price of the subscriptions plus a service fee, usually calculated as a percentage of the subscription costs. Some libraries may employ the services of multiple subscription agents. However, this number should be kept to a minimum in order to realise the full benefits of order and payment consolidation.

The following services provided by subscription agents are customarily covered by the service charge paid by the library:

- Place new orders with publishers
- Notify publishers of renewals
- Pay publishers for orders and renewals
- Notify publishers of cancellations
- Obtain refunds from publishers when due
- Transfer subscriptions from previous agents
- Notify publishers of non-receipt of issues, *i.e.* claims
- Notify library of publisher response to claims
- Intervene with publishers to resolve unsatisfied claims
- Provide consolidated invoices and account statements
- Provide information on changes of title, frequency, or publishing schedule affecting the library's subscriptions
- Notify publishers of changes in library ship-to address
- Provide standard and financial reports on the library's account.

Moreover, the following additional services may be covered by the service charge or may have to be paid for:

- Place orders for replacement issues and backfiles
- Supply sample issues of journals
- Provide a comprehensive catalogue of published serials, either in print or electronic format
- Provide custom reports on the library's account
- Provide online access to the agent's serials information databases

In addition, some agents may provide specialized services such as:

- Consolidated shipment of foreign publications
- Provision of machine-readable bibliographic records
- Software for automated serials control
- Union list products

A key person in the success of agent-library relationship is the account executive, or the customer representative designated by the agent, to coordinate services for the library's account. This person should be available to the library by telephone, fax and e-mail to respond to the queries of the library.

SERIALS CONTROL SYSTEM

Automated Systems

Automated serials control systems typically accommodate multiple simultaneous users, and provide rapid access to records by title, keyword and other identifying elements such as the ISSN. They can display current receipt information and summary holdings, both for the public and for staff, and provide automatic prediction of the next expected issue which enables routine claiming of skipped or delayed issues. They can accept electronic invoice information and create printed listings and online reports in a variety of formats. They can support related functions such as binding, routing and union listing. Library journal regularly publishes a review of the automated systems marketplace that profiles the systems and includes a directory of names and addresses for each. Some agents have developed stand-alone microcomputer-based serials control systems, such as Microlinx of the Faxon Company.

The functions of an automated serials control systems may be summarized as follows:

- Public search and display
- Order entry and payment processing
- Check-in
- Claiming
- Report production

Manual Systems

The most common manual system for serials control is the cardex, where the cards used are formated in a calender-like fashion so that receipts can be recorded in the appropriate chronological block and so that any skipped issues are obvious upon visual inspection of the cards. There should be room for: processing notes, routing instructions, summary statement of the library's holdings and payment information.

SERIALS RECORD KEEPING PROCEDURES

The records required for serials are basically similar to those for books, including copies of purchase orders, commitments records of the general budget and special funds, and accounts of receipts, billings and payments. However, many libraries find it useful to keep books and serials acquisitions responsibilities separate.

Record of the Subscription

New serials order requires instructions that apply to all titles, invoicing requirements, delivery address, starting year, ISSN, number of copies for each title ordered.

Elements of the standard instructions include:

- Ship-to address
- Invoicing requirements including:
  - Bill-to address
  - Required number of copies of invoices and credit memos
  - Batch vs. individual invoices
  - Inclusion of library assigned codes such as order number and department
  - Preferred handling of credit adjustments
- Policy on supplements
- Renewal policy
- Acceptability of multiple-year orders
- Order confirmation requirement

A requisition or purchase order is required to initiate an order which is forwarded to the agent or publisher. Some agents can accommodate on-line entry of orders. Once the new order has been placed, preparation for receiving the issues should be made. This includes check-in records, and payment record.

Check-in Record

Important elements of the check-in record include:

- Title
- Publisher
- ISSN
- Frequency
- Pattern of publication, and anticipated supplements

- Supplier
- Supplier's title number
- Notes for labelling and marking
- Other instructions: binding, special issues expected, retention policy, and volumes or issues that receive monographic cataloguing
- Routing instructions
- Availability of title pages and indexes
- Order reference number, if the check-in record is not otherwise linked to the payment record.

Procedures must emphasize accurate record-keeping and efficient processing of serials as they are received by the library. Check-in begins in the mail room where incoming mail is received, sorted and prepared for distribution. Mailing labels or envelopes are examined to avoid misrouted mail, and to assist in resolving delivery problems in case the issue turns out to be unwanted or duplicate. Backlogs in mail processing and check-in are unaccep-table. Maximum of twenty-four hours is reasonable to get the issue to the shelf.

The correct check-in record in most automated systems can be selected by entering the ISSN or keywords form the title. Some systems can use the bar code printed on the journal to call up the corresponding check-in record. If a manual system is used, it is advisable to sort receipts alphabetically before check-in. When a check-in record cannot be found for a received title, it should be reviewed by a supervisor before it is treated as unwanted or misrouted mail. When the record is located, the issue receipt is recorded. When check-in is completed, routine physical processing is carried in accordance with the instructions set by the library.

This processing includes:

- Stamping receipt date
- Stamping library name
- Placing a mark on the cover identifying the title for purposes of alphabetic filing
- Attaching special labels identifying locations, call numbers or circulation status
- Inserting a security strip
- Attaching a bar code
- Inserting date due slip

It has to be stressed that serials may have various changes that should be addressed. These typically include: title changes, change of publisher, frequency changes, combined issues, issuing supplement and other special issues, and delayed publication schedules.

Reasons for title changes usually include one of the following:

- Change in editorial board, sponsoring organisation, or publisher.
- Response to new concepts or terminology in the field.

- Change in subject scope or targeted audience.
- Change in language, frequency, or peer review status.

Payment Record

Payment records identify funds committed for new tittles not yet invoiced, and provide a retrospective listing of all payments and credit for each continuing title. They ensure not paying twice for the same purpose, and monitor price increases. Whether manual or automated the payment record must be linked to the check-in record so that claiming can be carried out with convenient access to relevant payment information.

The following data is included in a basic payment record of serial:

- Title
- Number of copies on order
- Name and address of the supplier
- Account number of the supplier
- Title number of the supplier
- Fund charged
- Ledger of payments and credits
  - Invoice number and date
  - Amount paid
  - Volume and Year covered

To be effective, the payment record should enable the library to renew or cancel subscription promptly. If the publisher is the direct supplier, it has to be noted that some do not send renewal invoice.

Claiming

Claiming is the process of notifying the publisher directly or through the subscription agent that an issue was not received or was received in unsatisfactory condition.

A notice is typically sent which includes the following essential elements:

- Library name and account number
- Title being claimed
- Enumeration, chronology or edition of the issue being claimed
- Reason for the claim
- Date of the claim
- Claim sequence
- Publisher
- Order reference number
- Alternative identifiers such as ISSN
- Explanatory notes

The most common reasons for a claim are:

- Skipped issue

- Overdue issue
- Issue damaged in transit
- Defective issue
- Incorrect number of copies

Claims forms are usually supplied by the supplier. Some may allow automated systems online claim. EDIFACT will facilitate automated claiming when it is widely adopted. Claims should be made within the time frame specified by the publisher and before the publisher's supplies of the issue are exhausted. In a manual system, the check-in card can be flagged at check-in with a coloured tab to indicate that an issue has been skipped. Claims are based on the flagged cards.

The bigger problem is with overdue issue as this needs reviewing every check-in card. In automated systems, skipped issue can be identified upon check-in of a subsequent issue. But overdue issues are identified based on the frequency of the serial, the number of days since the last issue was received and the title-specific grace period assigned by the library. Titles that are overdue based on this interval are flagged as potential claims by the system.

Such intervals may be as follows:

- Daily 10 days
- Weekly 14 days
- Monthly 60 days
- Quarterly 150 days
- All others 30 days after expected arrival

Premature and unnecessary claims may be caused by the library or by the publisher.

The causes of this may be:

- The system-supplied expected receipt date has gotten off track, or the grace period is too short.
- Delayed publication not reported to the library.
- Combined issues not noticed at check-in.
- Issue checked in as supplement or on wrong title record.
- Frequency change.
- Issue received but not checked in due to human error.
- Title changes.

From the publisher:

- Misnumbering of issues.
- Publishing out of sequence without notifying subs-cribers.
- Changing frequency without notifying subscribers.

For following up of unresolved claims, subscription agents usually send to the library a monthly claim report. The library has to review this report and return it promptly to the agent. Issues not received should be reclaimed and recorded as such in the library's files. It is important for the library to document that its first claim was sent within the time period acceptable to the publisher.

Renewals

Many publishers send subscribers renewal invoices about three or four months before the end of a subscription term. These invoices need to be paid six to eight weeks before the end of that term to guarantee continuous delivery. Needless to say that special care must be taken not to overlook renewal notices for titles ordered directly from the publisher. Subscription agents offer two methods for renewal, one automatic and the other requires manual reauthorization by the library. The second method is preferred by the library.

Listings are usually sent by agents between July and August. The library reviews the list, makes necessary changes, and returns it to the agent with payment by mid October.

The agent must make follow-up later with a supplemental invoice, covering the price increases. Renewal decisions in the library involve one of three options: renew, cancel or hold. They may also involve changing the number of copies. Hold option means that the final decision will be given later, because the library needs more time or when a title is substantially behind schedule and the library does not want to be invoiced for it until it has received what it has already paid for.

Payment by the agent to the publisher should be timely to avoid missing any issue. The future trends in serials acquisitions will deal with both print and electronic formats or a hybrid of both. This means that it may be difficult to separate purchase process from licensing of digital products. On the other hand a number of subscription agents are now offering serials check-in and records maintenance as an addition to their basic subscription services. The developments in electronic publishing is paving the way to the transformation from subscription to journals to article-level acquisitions. Moreover there is an increase in the efforts of creating standards applicable to serials.

Among these efforts the following may be briefly mentioned:

- *CONSER*: Is a cooperative effort which aims at establishing a core database of bibliographic information on serials titles.
- *ISBD*: International Standard Bibliographic Description for Serials, is issued by the *international Federation of Library Association and Institutions* (IFLA).
- *ISSN*: International Standard Serials Number is an eight digit code whose last digit is a check number, issued by ISDS.
- *ISDS*: International Serials Data System has respon-sibility for assigning ISSN and the key title of serials.
- *CODEN*: It is a unique five character code. The Chemical Abstracts Service is responsible for its maintenance since 1973.

BOOK SELECTION

Books assist in the dissemination of information by providing a convenient means of access to recorded knowledge. It is true that a medical book is out-of-date when it is published, but this does not invalidate its use as a digest of available knowledge in a physically handy form.

The main categories of books are:

- *Quick Reference Books:* Dictionaries, directories, pharmacopoeias, data book. These are essential items in every collection. Now many of these books are also available in CD-ROM format.
- *Standard Works of Reference*: These provide access to knowledge in depth in subject at an advanced level. They are usually too detailed to serve as textbook guides to their subjects.
- *Postgraduate Textbooks:* The need to specialize is paramount and the number of courses leading to future qualifications is numerous in medicine. This ensures a good market of textbooks at the postgraduate level. They are among the most heavily used materials in the medical library.
- *Texts for Basic Study:* There is virtually no topic in the undergraduate level which is not suitably covered by this type of material.
- *Monographs*: A monograph consists of a treatise on a single subject, and it is always an advanced level work. They may also appear in series.
- *Theses and Dissertations:* Most of the smaller medical libraries do not hold this type of material and larger one will onlyhold those originating in their own parent organisations. If required, it is usual to have them collected by a central body such as national or depository libraries.
- *Pamphlets and other Ephemera:* Pamphlets are short topical and written with a particular object in view. They may quickly lose their currency. They may be ordered and treatedas books. Many useful pamphlets are available free particularly from pharmaceutical companies.
- *Reports:* A report is a work written by a task force or particular group specially commissioned to study a particular issue or problem. They may be difficult to trace. Reports may also emanate from important bodies in the profession. Research reports in, for example, the pharmaceutical industry may be confidential. Another example of reports is the annual report of a research or teaching institution. Government departments generate a great deal of report literature, of which many are on social and medical subjects.
- *Conference Proceedings:* The quality of this type varies from carefully edited account of important meetings to mere photolithography of the authors' typescripts with little editing and no index.

Responsibilities

- Responsibilities for book selection should be formally agreed upon, and the flow of information and decisions clearly delineated. If most of the selection is distributed among several persons, a manual describing both the responsibilities and the process is useful. This manual promotes consistency and thoroughness in carrying out the functions
- In small libraries, there is little confusion regarding who has what responsibility. But in large libraries the situation is different as procedures need to document how selection tools are handled:
  - Who sees advertising materials, how they are divided, for instance by subject, how they are marked for follow up
  - If books reviews are used, the routing process should be established
  - Method of transmitting ordering information from the selector to the acquisitions unit
  - If interlibrary loan requests are to be reviewed, there must be a mechanism for receiving the information.
- The link between selection activity and the budget allocations must be established, whether the individual selectors have any fund management responsibilities or not.

SOURCES FOR BOOK SELECTION

Selection tools for book selection should be both alerting and evaluative to be convenient for selection. They may be in the form of bibliographies, review or advertising materials, and may be in print and/or electronic formats. Other sources are relevant for selection.

The various sources may be summarized as follows:

- *Publishers' Flyers and Catalogues*: Libraries usually receive a lot of announcements from the publishers about the availability of new books. Moreover, many publishers produce various types of catalogues for their publications, sometimes including previously published editions which are still in print. It is necessary for the library to be on the mailing list of the publishers in the disciplines that concern the library. Visiting their web sites is now enabled as well.
- *Vendors' Flyers and Catalogues*: Many vendors do the same thing as publishers. Make sure that you are regularly informed of their offerings. Some provide altering service, in print or electronically, of new titles.
- *Recommendations from Users*: This should be encouraged. Request forms must be readily accessible. Remember that they themselves receive flyers and catalogues from publishers and sometimes complimentary copies of new titles.

- *Interlibrary Loan Requests:* Although particularly appropriate for journal selection, they may be also relevant for selecting books that are not brand new.
- *Bibliographies and Library Catalogues:* Bibliographies are of several categories as there are national biblio-graphies, subject bibliographies both total and selective, author bibliographies, bibliographies of bibliographies, etc. Some of these bibliographies include health sciences while there is one devoted to medicine which is Medical books in print of Bowker.

Another tool that is considered here is what is usually called core lists:

- *British Council*: Core list of library materials: medicine.
- *EMRO*: List of basic sources in English for a medical faculty library. 8th ed. 1999.
- *Royal College of General Practitioners*: Books for general practice and primary health care. London, 1992. Regularly revised.
- *Royal College of Psychiatrists:* Lists of books suitable for a psychiatric library 1988-1993. London, 1993. Re-gularly revised and updated.
- *Royal College of Psychiatrists:* Key books for a psychiatric library. London. Regularly revised and updated.

Moreover, the most comprehensive catalogue of health sciences books is CATLINE.

This is NLM's online catalogue. NLM Locator, which includes CATLINE, AVLINE for audiovisuals, and SERLINE for information on journal titles, is now available on the Internet.

- *Book Reviews*: There are two types of book reviews:
  - Those published in professional and scientific journals. Examples of such journals are:
    a. *JAMA:* Journal of American Medical Association
    b. Lancet
    c. British medical journal
    d. British journal of hospital medicine
    e. Nursing times
    f. Journal of advanced nursing
    g. New England journal of medicine
    h. Bulletin of the Medical Library Association
    There are journals not limited to health sciences such as Nature, and Science, and Library journal:
  - Those that are fully devoted as journal to reviews. Some of these reviews cover medicine among the disciplines that they serve. Among them, are the following:
    a. *New Technical Books*: New York Public Library (10/year).
    b. *Technical Book Review Index:* JAAD Publications (monthly).

c. *Science Books and Films*: American Association for the Advancement of science (5/year).
d. *The Bookseller:* Whitaker (weekly).
e. *Contemporary Psychology*: A journal of reviews. American Psychological Association (monthly).
f. *Directory of Published Proceedings*: Series SEMT-Science, Engineering, Medicine and Technology. InterDok (10/year)
g. *Choice:* Association of College and Research Libraries (11/year).
h. *British Book News*: The British Council (monthly).
i. *American Book Publishing Record*: Bowker (monthly).
j. *Cumulative Book Index*: H.W. Wilson (11/year).

The outstanding example of book reviews is the new publication of Doody Publishing set up in 1993. This publication is entitled Doody's journal: health sciences book reviewing, issued bimonthly and evaluates about 250 titles in each issue. It can be accessed on Internet.

A British version is under discussion:

- *Approval Plan*: Although approval plans are concerned with acquisition. The selection function of the approval plan is summarized as follows:
  - The library supplies the vendor with a detailed profile of its requirements in specific fields, together with any budgetary limits, and the publishers to be considered;
  - The supplier selects and regularly supplies the materials as specified in the profile;
  - The library monitors the materials supplied and have the right to return any item received;
  - If the percentage of returns is high then the library should review the plan and take required action, which may include changing the supplier.
  - The approval plan does not fit with small medical libraries.

SELECTION IN SPECIAL SETTINGS

ELECTRONIC RESOURCES

Selection decisions of electronic resources parallel those of print materials in many ways, but they are treated separately, because their unique characteristics introduce additional factors to collection decision-making and because these formats can affect information delivery, budgeting, equipment, and staffing. Electronic resources play an essential role in every health sciences library. But they are usually expensive, and thus may consume a great portion of a library's budget. So a greater degree of care should be taken in making decisions regarding what the library will provide to its users.

As knowledge-based computer programmes in clinical medicine and other health care disciplines are improved and gain wider acceptance, they appear more commonly as library resources, especially if they can be accessed remotely from offices and clinical care sites. Selection of computer software by students, hospital staff, faculty, clinicians, or researchers should be guided by the library's collection development policy. The policy should address the criteria by which these resources are selected. Scope, depth and audience will define the boundaries.

There are several types of software that may be acquired by health sciences libraries:

- Bibliographic
- *Full Text*: Books and journals
- Numeric or factual databases
- Clinical assist programmes for diagnosis or treatment decisions
- Educational software
- Applications software, such as word processing, analytical or statistical packages, file management, telecommunications, authoring software, graphics software (note here that such software is general pur-pose not resources)
- Administrative functions or staff support
- Criteria of Resources for Selection
  - *Scope*: The resource must fit the subject scope of the library.
  - *Depth*: The intensity of collecting in a discipline will dictate how many resources the library will acquire, or the degree of specialization needed.
  - *Audience*: The selection should answer the question whose needs should the library intend to serve with the software? Different clientele will require different resources. Computer-based resources for student use should usually be selected with advice and recommendation from faculty or potential users.
- Selection Principles:
  - The resource should fit the mission of the library, and the scope and depth defined in the collection development policy, it should meet users' needs;
  - Specific criteria should address the content, the user interface retrieval software, the format, and the hardware and software required by the resource;
  - Careful investigation and evaluation of the cost-effective-ness of different formats should precede any decisions. An information policy both for the library and for the parent organisation will help guide these decisions.
- Selection Criteria:

- Content:
  a. Quality of the material presented.
    i. Authoritiveness of content
    ii. Expertise of the authors
    iii. Reputation of the producer
    iv. Comprehensiveness of the information
    v. Quality of the images, if important
  b. *Currency*: Regular updates should be provided.
  c. *Content Usefulness*: Such as:
    i. Interactive capabilities of testing
    ii. Simultaneously hear and see as required
    iii. Combine text and images, sound and movement
    iv. Highly accurate and up-to-date knowledge
    v. Able to show relationships and probabilities, and suggest possibilities
  d. Relationship to Print Publications.
    i. Whether additional material is added
    ii. Convenience of access, amount of demand, need for permanent presentation
    iii. Are updates offered electronically through networks?
- User Interface:
  a. Ease of use.
  b. Software functions.
    i. The search engine or other control functions should be powerful enough to support the resource;
    ii. Response time should be snappy;
    iii. Use of Boolean operators, adjacency feature, saving searches or search strategies are enabled.
  c. Printing and Downloading Capabilities.
  d. Duplication of Print Publications. When the software duplicates to a large extent a print publication, the library must determine whether the electronic version offers additional features, such as easier search, use hypertext, reformat information, manipulation or animation of illustrative material, extraction and manipulation.
  e. Compatibility with Other Resources.
  f. Documentation and Guides.
- *Format*: The library has several formats to choose from:
  a. In print
  b. On stand-alone CD-ROM
  c. On CD-ROM on a LAN
  d. By tapes mounted on local institutional network

e. By various routes to a remote utility through a gateway
The following factors should be considered in making this choice:
a. *Users*: Consider the likely users; if they are very few, the cost and support may not be justified.
b. *Expected Use*: The number and frequency of use.
c. *Accessibility*: Convenient access.
d. *Content*: Whether formats differ in comprehen-siveness or specialized contents. Compare the interface and performance characteristics. Updating.
e. Costs.
f. *Equipment*: Compatibility with local systems.
g. Legal Issues:
  i. Licensing
  ii. Restrictions to making backup copies, downloading, and printing
  iii. Possibility of sharing

– Hardware, Software, and Space Requirements.
a. Space:
  i. The facilities should be conducive to the types of use that will be made of them.
  ii. Whether the workstation has to be an open area.
  iii. Whether the resources can be used effectively in the available setting.
b. Workstation Configuration.
  i. Networking is to be provided.
  ii. Adequate number of workstations to ensure effective use of the resources.
  iii. Avoid workstations dedicated to single resource, except for those that will be heavily used, such as MEDLINE, or the library's catalogue.
c. Compatibility.
  i. Is the resource compatible with existing equipment?
  ii. Is the memory sufficient and the machine fast enough for the type of content, such as images?
  iii. Does the new software conflict with any other resources on the same equipment?
d. Additional Software.
  i. Does the resource require specific software such as operating system or database loader?
  ii. Audio and video require additional component.
  iii. Is the existing hardware adequate to accommodate the required software?

Reference Collections

The policy for reference collection should relate to the general collection development policy, whether it forms part of it or written separately. All selection criteria applied to books in general apply here as well. It remains to cover here the types of materials that form the reference collection and the selection sources of reference items.

2

Selection of Library Book Materials

S.R. Ranganathan's five laws of librarianship:

- Books are for use
- Every book its reader
- Every reader his book
- Save the reader's time
- The library is a growing organism

These laws provide the ideas that decide the principles of effective selection. Such principles may be summarized as follows:

- The selection process is related to other professional activities and is dependent on them both for policy decisions and practical procedures. Selection is part of the overall collection development process and must be viewed in this perspective;
- One should update professional competence by regular reading in the literature concerning the principles and practices of collection building, selection, publishing, reviewing and acquisitions;
- One must have an intimate knowledge of the library's purpose, its collections and its user groups. These are the key factors in effective, responsible selection of library materials;
- A good selector will develop over time a sound under-standing of how the publishing industry and the book trade operate; this includes how library materials of all types are generated, distributed and sold;
- One should become familiar with the publishing policies, advertising media, publicity outlets, names of senior editors and general reliability of those publishers whose lists are most directly relevant to the library's collection building requirements;
- One should become fully familiar with the key reviewing media and should read reviews regularly in order to keep abreast of critical opinion on books and other library materials;
- One should become fully familiar with trade and national bibliographies, and should understand their strengths and weaknesses with regard to the library's collection-building requirements;

- One should always make independent but well-informed judgement about what materials are to be selected for a library, as the competent professional is in the best position to determine the right materials for the specific collection and its users.

THE SELECTION ENVIRONMENT

Selection of library materials occurs within a set of common factors:

- It is done on the basis of existing collection require-ments and user needs and wants with regard to subjects, formats and level of content;
- It proceeds within a carefully determined budget, with funds may be allocated to specific areas or other categories to the library;
- It involves a structured approach to the identification and evaluation of potentially suitable library materials.

Within this set of factors there are many permutations, depending largely on the specific variables which apply to the different types of medical libraries:

- In medical libraries within an academic setting, disciplines are being studied at specific levels, from basic undergraduate to advanced research, and both disciplines and levels can be determined accurately from the parent organisation's clearly defined teaching activities. There is generally substantial documentation upon which selectors can draw for information about user interests and needs. Academic libraries use a broader and more detailed range of selection tools, such as trade publications, national bibliographies, reviewing journals, scholarly journal, indexing services.
- Moreover, selection is not restricted to professional librarians, as academic staff are expected to have significant input in the process, particularly if the funds are allocated by departments and schools. This situation is challenged by professionals.
- In non-academic medical libraries, in which collections range from small collection in a single room to large collections in a multi-branch library. In such libraries the subject focus is relatively narrow and emphasizes currency. Here, a high proportion of the collection is devoted to serials. Such libraries are also characterized by the following features:
  - It is most likely for there to be a single professional in charge of the library operation, or at least for collection development not to be the responsibility of professional appointed for this specific purpose.
  - Selection relies heavily on information from publishers and suppliers, and on indexing and abstracting services.
  - Reliance on intimate requirement, because libraries normally build up user profiles, particularly when they offer special dissemination services.

SELECTION PROCEDURES STATEMENT

Selection criteria, as a component of collection develop-ment policy. This part does not repeat the information given there, but rather elaborates and complements it. It is looked at as an administration device designed to facilitate implemen-tation of decisions about materials based on collection development policy guidelines. All administrative matters requiring consistency over time, require procedures formalized in a written statement.

The following reasons for advocating the adoption of a formal selection procedures statement, and many of these echo the rationale for having a written collection development policy:

- It sets standards for procedures to be followed;
- It reduces the likehood of bias and personal influence;
- It provides continuity despite staff changes;
- It serves as an orientation device for new staff;
- It provides guidelines for complaint handling;
- It assists in weeding.

SELECTION RESPONSIBILITIES

This addresses two questions:

- Who shall do the selecting?
- How shall the procedure be organised?

The answer to the first question is a combination of library staff and users. Within the library it may be done by:

- The chief librarian;
- Division or department heads engaged specially for this task (collection development librarian, acquisitions librarian);
- Subject or area specialists; or
- Other professional staff as part of their general duties (re-ference librarians, technical services librarians).

Whichever applies, it should be stated clearly in the written document. Outside the library, selection should involve input from users from all types, and these should be specified clearly: administrators, parent organisation staff, students, teaching staff, general public, etc. To facilitate and encourage participation of these groups, a request form is provided.

This form should have space for all essential information needed to identify an item: author, title, number of volumes or pages, place of publication, publisher, date of publication, series and price, as well as the name of requester. This form is usually an attachment to statement. Copies should be made readily available and accessible to selectors both within and without the library.

HOW SELECTION IS ORGANISED

It should indicate clearly and precisely who has responsibility for what and who is responsible to whom. If a selection committee is used: who chairs the committee, and who appoints the members? How often does the committee meet? What are its terms of reference? If selection is the responsibility of individuals outside the library: How is this responsibility allocated and monitored? What resource does the librarian have if his external selectors fail to perform adequately? If selection is done jointly by external and internal selectors, what are the lines of demarcation? Who selects reference materials, serials, decides on multiple copies, etc.? All such questions should be addressed in the statement so that there is no doubt about responsibility and so that the newest member of staff has a clear grasp of procedures.

GENERAL GUIDELINES FOR SELECTION

This part turns to what to select. It presents only general guidelines derived from and based on the collection development policy. It lists here general selection sources, together with categories of more specific types of sources (publishers' catalogues, scholarly journals, indexing services, etc.). These listings help ensure that the named sources are used by selectors, and remind selectors of the other types of sources that they ought to be using.

Some libraries may actually name specific sources within each type, but this cannot be done in libraries selecting across a broad range of subjects and types of materials.

This part may list languages in which materials are selected, or other limitations which apply across the range of materials. In other words, all selection criteria derived from, or at least compatible with, the collection development policy should be stated here. This will enable all selectors to operate within the same set of guidelines.

HANDLING OF GIFTS AND DONATIONS

Basically, a donated item has to be taken into the collection according to the same criteria applied to purchased item. Therefore, the statement says this and indicates that gifts are received on the understanding that they may be disposed of in a manner deemed appropriate by the librarian. The statement also indicates acceptable conditions of gifts.

CRITERIA FOR WEEDING

The library may well have included a part on weeding in its collection development policy; if so, this needs to be taken into account at this stage. Weeding, often termed 'deselection' in USA and 'relegation' in the UK, involves a number of decisions that should be outlined in the selection procedures statement, involving criteria for weeding, scope of weeding procedures, frequency and purpose, together with a general allocation of staff responsibilities, so that there is no confusion about who is responsible for what and when.

HANDLING OF COMPLAINTS

Complaints about and censorship of library materials have been controversial issues for many years. although this case is less likely to occur in medical libraries than in other types of libraries such as public and school libraries, but it could happen. This part contains a statement of complaint-handling procedures and a standard form to be completed by potential censors. The written statement should be made available, together with a copy of the collection development policy, at the first hint that an item in the collection is being challenged.

The complaint-handling form should be completed only if a formal complaint is lodged. The exact procedure, who is to be involved and the documentation to be utilized must all be stated clearly in this part. The entire statement should be readily accessible not only to selectors, but also to all users, as this often alleviates the need for complaints to go beyond an informal discussion.

ACQUISITIONS OF BOOKS AND BOOK-LIKE MATERIALS

A successful book acquisitions operation depends upon a well-structured and wellmaintained record keeping system. This system should allow staff to issue purchase orders and other communications to suppliers and to track the status of all outstanding and recently received orders. Whether manual or automated, the system aims at avoiding redundant data entry by establishing a single unit record for the order, which is updated as the order moves through the various stages of various order entry, claiming, receipt, payment and cataloguing and processing.

In an automated system ordering process is speeded up; bibliographic records can be downloaded from bibliographic utilities as order records; can provide information needed for mana-gement decisions; and can assist in vendor performance. Manual records are still used in small libraries. It involves typing individual orders onto preprinted multipart order forms. These forms are then separated, with one copy sent to the supplier, and the rest kept in one or more files arranged to provide different access points-title, author, budget fund, supplier, number, date, or even card catalogue. Carbonless multipart order forms are available in the market both in standard and customized formats. The format of a basic form may look like figure.

THE ACQUISITION PROCESS

There are three types of purchasing agents for ordering

- *Jobber:* He is a wholesaler who anticipates what his customers are going to buy, and stocks those items in advance. By buying large stocks from publishers, the jobber obtains a maximum discount. Part of this discount can be passed on to his customers. Many factors are considered when selecting a jobber:

- Discount
- Handling rush orders, telephone, fax, electronic orders
- Stocking of titles
- Publishers handled
- Reporting
- Payment method

- *Dealer*: The dealer can handle a wider range of materials than the jobber. They have variant specialties. Discount offered is usually lower than that of the jobber. So acquisitions staff should know the discount and fee policies of the various dealers, as well as their repu-tation for good service. Many medical libraries rely on dealers to solve the problem of hard currency in their respective countries.
- *Publisher*: There are sometimes compelling reasons to order directly from the publisher. This may be because of:
  - The book is only available from the publisher and orders through vendors or dealers are not accepted;
  - It is sometimes quicker to receive a book directly from the publisher;
  - Ordering from the publisher keeps the library on his mailing list.

Some libraries arrange approval plans with a jobber or publisher as previously mentioned. Having selected the purchasing agent, the following processes are performed.

Bibliographic Searching

This process is sometimes called 'preorder searching' or 'preorder verification'. It aims at preventing the ordering of something that the library has already ordered or received, and at verifying that the item actually exists by confirming its biblio-graphic description in an authoritative source.

A third aim has been added: obtaining reliable cataloguing information to initiate a bibliographic record with complete and accurate information. This searching may be manual, if the library is not yet automated or if it has no access to automated sources. otherwise the relevant databases whether in-house or external have to be searched. Although requestors are encouraged to use request forms, selection may be from dealers' lists, photocopies of bibliographies, publishers' catalogues and similar materials.

The process goes as follows:

- *Sort the Request Forms*: This may be by age of materials, country, language, form, or completeness of the citation.
- *Check the Libraries Records*: The catalogue, on-order file and in-process file. If the system is automated, one check of the bibliographic database will be required.
- *Check Bibliographic Sources:* The sources that may be used for this checking are:

- *Publishers' Catalogues:* These must be the most up-to-date versions. But be careful some mistakes may be present, such as misspelling of author's name, ISBN, date, and price. Some publishers have their catalogues on Internet.
- *Books in Print and Related Tools*: This is authoritative in the bibliographic information it contains. Its updating is done through: Books in Print Supplement and bimonthly Forthcoming Books. PIB Plus is a CD-ROM of Books in print. In addition Bowker publishes: Medical and health care books and serials in print. The British parallel of books in print is Whitaker's Books in Print.
- *Vendors' Lists and Databases*: These may be print or electronic. Normally the library which is customer is allowed free access online.
- *Bibliographic Networks*: Most academic libraries use the major bibliographic utilities, such as OCLC, RLIN, BLCMP, for cataloguing purposes, but they can be used for verification purposes as well. Downloading from them is enabled in most of them. When CIP records are used, the information may be incomplete or inaccurate.
- *NLM CATLINE:* The medical libraries that have no access to other bibliographic utilities, may use this online catalogue of NLM.

Assigning Internal Ordering Information

Additional elements are required for the order record. They provide necessary or useful information for payment, processing and statistics:

- *Purchase Order Number:* This is required unless the size of acquisitions is so small. Assigning this number may be:
  - Through the purchasing department of the parent organisation
  - Assigned automatically by the automated system
  - By obtaining order forms with sequential number preprinted on them
  - By using a sequential numbering stamper
  - By assigning sequential numbers manually
- *Budget Account*: The correct account name or code should be given in the order form, if there is more than one budget account.
- *Subject Code*: Some libraries assign a broad subject heading or code to each order. This breakdown may be useful for collection development and budget preparation. An automated system allows the library to maintain a list of controlled subject terms that can be assigned to orders.
- *Type of Order*: This is used when the library likes to know cases

when there is a need for additional copies or replacements of lost or damaged items to be ordered.

- *Name of Requester*: When the item is requested by a library user, there may be a need for notifying him of the availability of the requested item in the library, or that it has been received and ready for him to use. His name, address and telephone number are recorded in the order form.
- *Information for Cataloguing*: During the verification process some information that cataloguers may require is added. This information should be passed to the cataloguing unit. Such data includes:
  - Previous editions of the item in the collection
  - Other copies of the item in the collection
  - Whether the item is a replacement or added copy
  - Shelving location of item
  - Circulation restrictions of the item
  - Name of requester to be notified
  - Special funding source or name of donor

This information has fields in the order form in an automated system, which can be produced after the book has been received; otherwise this production is done manually.

Returning Requests

If a request for acquisition is submitted without a supporting citation, the acquisitions staff proceeds according to the policies of the library. In some instances, incomplete requests may be returned to their initiator with a form requesting the needed information. If this is the case, the staff member should not return a request merely because it lacks a technical detail not likely to be available to the initiator, as he is not skilled in identifying or using the sources that provide it.

Sending Orders

Orders may be sent through the following means:

- *By Mail*: Large libraries may batch their orders to consolidate processing time and reduce mailing expenses. Small libraries may send an order out as soon as it has been completed. Rush orders have to be taken care of,
- *By Telephone*: This can be used for rush orders. Telephone orders should be documented for future reference. The problem here is that orders have to be prepayed with a credit card, which is not possible in many libraries.
- *By Computer*: EDIFACT Standard. Many libraries with automated systems still send their orders by mail. With the progress in electronic

communications it is now possible to transmit orders from computer to computer, particularly when a standard for *electronic data interchange* (EDI) has been created by the UN *Economic Commission for Europe* (ECE). This standard will allow the library to send its address to any vendor, dealer or publisher electronically. All operations required will be dealt with without human intervention.

- *By Vendor System*: Many vendors have already automated their internal systems for ordering, invoicing and inventory. They provide access to them for their customers, to browse the inventory, enter new orders and enquire about outstanding orders. Some vendors may even allow downloading their online records, and the table of contents of individuals books if provided. For libraries with manual systems, many vendors offer dial-in service and confirm orders on multipart forms by mail. Acquisition staff have to learn each vendor's system when they deal with more than one.
- *By Fax and E-Mail*: Using fax speeds up ordering, and guarantees accurate records to be transmitted. Many book vendors have also set up Internet electronic mail accounts, which is relatively inexpensive to use, and the order records are accurate. Anyhow, some libraries may request a confirmation of receiving the order, as they do not consider faxed or e-mailed documents as legal documents.

Receiving Materials

When receiving materials ordered, the following actions must be performed:

- Boxes are unpacked
- Books are sorted
- Items are matched to the original order and to the invoice or packing slip
- Each book should be examined briefly and checked for blank or damaged pages, broken binding or any other imperfection
- The status of the item must be changed in the on-order file, whether manually or electronically. Date of receipt is recorded.
- The invoice is approved for payment. If the library is authorized to make payments, this payment is done. If not, an internal document called a payment voucher is filled out and sent to the department concerned of the parent organisation. This voucher contains, as a minimum, the supplier's name and address, invoice number and its date, the amount to be paid, and the fund to be used. It should be accompanied with the original invoice. It must also have an authorized signature. A copy of the voucher and invoice is retained by the library. The library should make every effort to pay the supplier promptly.
- If any problem is found in the invoice, it has to be solved before

authorizing payment. This may be handled as follows, provided it is agreed upon.

- Credit memo issued by the supplier that can be deducted from the invoice if not yet paid; otherwise it can be deducted from a later invoice.
- Striking from the invoice, by cancelling the items concerned and subtracting the amount from the total.
- Requesting a new corrected invoice. This may be preferr-ed by the parent organisation.
- Returning the invoice with the item. This can be done if the invoice is for a single item.

- Recording the payment for each item in the individual order record. The completed record will have:
  - All of the original order information
  - The date the item was received
  - Invoice number and date
  - The amount paid
  - The payment voucher number
  - The date the payment was processed

In a manual system, this information is recorded on purchase order form which is then placed in the completed orders file. In automated system, it is in recorded the order record.

The amount committed for each item is automatically zeroed and the amount paid is deducted from the account charged:

- The library has better to keep the order records after the item is received and its payment sent. Some libraries do this until the books are shelved and the catalogue records are made available to the public. Others may retain them to enable staff to compile information required for various reportings; while others may never destroy their order records.
- Once the order record is cleared from the current file some libraries alert a staff member or library user that the item has arrived and is available for use.
- If a library uses an acquisitions/cataloguing form, this form is inserted into the book before it is sent forward to cata-loguing. Automated systems that produce such processing forms may allow batch printing of the forms for books received that day, or can print out forms for each book as soon as its status changes from ' on-order " to ' received ".
- Acquisitions may be responsible for adding property stamps, book plates, security strips, etc. or sending paper backs for binding.
- The library has to report its purchase to other libraries or bibliographic agencies for cooperative purposes. This reporting may be in the form of a paper record sent by mail or messenger, or as an electronic message to a centralized, computerized database.

- Receiving materials in an approval shipment requires slightly different procedures, since they arrive with no preorder searching or records preceding them. Most libraries follow procedures similar to the following for receiving:
  - Verify the package contents against the invoice or packing list.
  - Check the approval items against the catalogue and on-order file to detect duplicates.
  - If previous editions of a book exist, check as to whether the library owns any.
  - Assign purchase order number, budget account, subject code and type of order.

Returns

Vendors and publishers sometimes send the wrong item, or send two copies of a book when only one was ordered. The book sent may be defective or damaged during transit. Such books must be returned. Most vendors allow returns with a note explaining the problem.

Publishers may:

- Require returned items to be sent to a special address;
- Require returned items to be identified with a special shipping label which they supply;
- Require postal insurance.

Claims

Orders that remain outstanding too long, require the library to send claims. Timing of claims is essential, as they are made when the waiting periods exceeded the time schedule agreed upon. In a manual system the order file has to be examined for possible claim. An extra copy of the order form may be used for this purpose, or a claim form is sent to the supplier. A typical claim form looks like figure.

Sometimes, there is a need for sending more than one claim, in which case the claim number should be mentioned on the form. Automated systems can produce claim forms on demand. When EDI is operational, it will enable sending claims electronically to which suppliers will respond electronically too. Moreover fax and e-mail are already used for speeding up claims.

In addition to responding to specific claims, suppliers send out periodic reports indicating the status of all outstanding orders. The information provided in such reports is entered into the order records, so that the library does not claim for a book that has been reported as delayed.

Most suppliers use standard abbreviations or phrases for their claims responses and status, among which are:

- NYR-Not yet received, the order remains active

- OS-Out-of-stock, the order remains active
- OSI-Out-of stock indefinitely, the order is cancelled
- NYP-Not yet published, the order is mostly cancelled Claiming-Claiming from the publisher, the order is active
- OP-Out-of-print, the order is cancelled
- NOP-Not our publication, the order is cancelled Cannot Supply-the supplier cannot supply the item, the order is cancelled. It has to be ordered from another source.

Many libraries cancel an order if it has been outstanding for too long, say over one year, with no predicted delivery date. Others cancel all outstanding orders at the end of a fiscal year in compliance with the requirements of the parent organisation. Libraries usually use a cancellation form to identify the items being cancelled.

Direct Orders

Direct ordering is ordering directly from the publisher.

This may be for one or more of the following reasons:

- Publications are not available through book vendors. Publishers may not have business relations with book vendors because they demand prepayment, do not offer attractive discounts, or because the publisher feels the need for a direct relationship with the library customers.
- The library may find it preferrable to deal with the publisher directly: the publisher may offer a special sale or the library needs the item.

Direct ordering includes ordering from professional societies and associations. This requires prepayment as well.

But there are two unique aspects for this ordering:

- *Deposit Accounts:* This is done when the library places a standing order of the society's publications. In return the society will offer a discount and exemption of shipping and handling expenses.
- *Membership Pricing:* Many associations offer special discounted pricing for their members.

ACQUISITION OF SPECIAL BOOK-LIKE MATERIALS

Microforms

Microforms are included here because they are always reproductions of books and booklike materials. They range in format, size, reduction and storage media. This means that microforms require different types of readers and copiers. Microforms are usually acquired directly from publishers. Micro-publishing is often on demand publishing process. The types of materials covered include: out-of-print books, current serial subscriptions, backfiles of journals, working copies of rare books and manuscripts, government or international organisation documents and dissertations. Among the best guide to microforms is: Guide to microforms in print, published annually by K.G. Saur. It has to be noted that libraries are themselves main sources of microforms, as they hold negative films that another library may want copied.

Government Documents

Government documents are either issued by a central government publisher or by government agencies. They are mostly difficult to acquire from book vendors. They are ordered directly either prepaid or charged to a deposit account. Some countries distribute all or some of such documents free or on exchange. Care should be taken in verifying bibliographic information of the ordered items. International organisations documents are normally included here.

The source may be the individual agency which usually publishes its catalogue of publication or provides access to its data base, a local sales agent in the respective country, or the Interna-tional bibliography published quarterly by UNIPUB, New York. Of special interest to health sciences libraries is WHO, which issues publications from both its headquarters and from regional offices. It also distributes publications of the *International Agency for Research on Cancer* (IARC), the *Council for International Organisations of Medical Sciences* (CIOMS) and the English Language publications of *Pan American Health Organisation* (PAHO).

Out-of-Print Books and Reprints

Health sciences books stay in-print for short periods. This means that unless a book is ordered within a few years of its publication, it is likely to be out-of-print when it is ordered.

The ways to obtain this type of books are:

- Borrowing the title through interlibrary loan service.
- Publishing a list of desiderata or want list, and either publishing in the Library bookseller or Antiquarian bookman's weekly, sending it to OP book dealers, or to search services, individuals or companies who take desiderata from libraries and attempt to find the items using their own contacts.
- Contacting authors or editors directly.
- Obtaining reprints. The library can use Guide to reprints, published annually by Microcard Editions. UMI produces reprints of OP books in hard-cover, paper back, or microfilm. Their ' books on demand " service covers many subjects including the medical subjects. Subject catalogues and an author guide are available upon request from UMI.
- Exchanging OP materials.

Remember the following when handling OP materials:

- It is time consuming

- The desiderata lists should be reviewed periodically
- Acquiring OP books in microform or in a photocopied version should be considered
- Prices should be considered carefully.

Dissertations and Theses

It is rare that a health sciences library has to acquire a dissertation or thesis produced at another institution. If any need arises, the right sources for selection should be used.

Among these are:

- UMI dissertation abstracts international
- UMI master abstracts
- Index to theses
- Some countries include them in their national biblio-graphies
- In the Arab world the Jordanian University Library is a depository library for dissertations of the universities that are members of the Union of Arab Universities. Some libraries published bibliogrãphies of Arab disser-tations as onetime publication.

One negative aspect of this type of material, is that some universities place restrictions on acquiring their dissertations. These may include the time limit preventing even the use of them before, say, five years; some do not allow reproduction completely or provided the author authorizes it.

SPECIAL PROBLEMS

But they are given here as a summing-up:

- *Item Not Supplied*: Unsupplied items should be claimed. Sometimes the vendor may fail to report. Some libraries, to avoid claiming process, specify that orders not supplied within a stated period of time are automatically cancelled.
- *Wrong Item Supplied*: The library may accept the loss, or return the item for credit.
- *Defective Item Supplied*: The item must be returned for replacement. Complications may arise if the vendor does not have access to another copy, or if his staff misunderstand the reasons for an item's return.
- *Incomplete Order*: Some of the items in the invoice were not supplied. This is likely to occasion written or oral communication with the vendor, sometimes over an extended period of time.
- *Missing Order Record*: The order record cannot be located in manual system, a lost record in one file may be found in another. But in automated system, the record is actually lost unless a backup file is maintained.
- *Duplicate Item Ordered or Received*: The library may accept the item

and absorb the loss, or return the item for credit. If the item is to be returned, it should not be marked with the ownership stamp. If the item is accepted, it may be used for exchange.

- *Incorrect Item Checked In*: An item is received but incorrectly checked in against a wrong purchase order. When the correct item comes, it appears to be duplicate although in fact it is not. This may result in a mix-up as the item was considered duplicate and returned, or the library may claim it and the vendor reports that it was sent.
- *Unavailable Items*: An item is reported as not available and the order is cancelled. This resulted in many disagreements between libraries and suppliers. Some vendors are not careful in reporting the item as out-of-stock or even out-of-print inaccurately. It may be wise for the library to initiate further checks on the status of the item and confront the supplier with evidence of incorrect reporting. Repeated wrong reports can justify terminating the relationship with the supplier.
- *Unexpected Prices of Items*: An item may be priced far higher than the library expected, and payment either cannot be made or will severely unbalance the budget if it is made. Libraries, to solve this problem, state a limit when the supplier should not send item until agreement is reached. This precaution is vital for libraries with low budgets, and those in which overspending is not permitted.
- *Invoice Errors*: Among these errors are:
  - The item on the invoice are in disagreement with the item sent;
  - The discount may be computed erroneously, or omitted;
  - The invoice total is not in agreement with the sum of the prices listed on it;
  - The number of copies for which the library is billed is incorrect.

Such mistakes should be corrected before payment is made:

- *Improper Payment Made*: Improper payment may have been made by the library, or the supplier has incorrectly credited a payment. This has to be corrected by the library.
- *Incorrect Accounting Records*: A mistake may be made in keeping the financial records. Among such mistakes are:
  - Failing to deduct a payment from the budget
  - Deducting the amount from the general budget rather than the specific fund
  - Debiting payment against the fund account but not against the general budget
  - Failing to remove the committed price when the actual cost is entered.

Such errors are substantially reduced when an automated system is used. But it has to be remembered that even the most sophisticated automated system cannot prevent staff from entering figures incorrectly or failing to enter them at all.

TYPES OF MATERIALS

Reference collections are used to locate the following:

- *Directory Information*: Brief factual information about people, institutions, organisations, programmes.
- *Data:* Compilations of such information as statistical data, biological facts, chemical compositions, drug descriptions.
- *Definitions:* Collections of medical terminology, foreign language, specialized nomenclature.
- *Descriptions:* Short or encylcopaedic summaries of diseases, procedures, biological processes, historical events.
- *Bibliographic Information:* References or abstracts by subject, author, citation, historical period, or source.

To enable this, the following types of materials have to be provided:

- *Bibliographies:* Examples include the various core lists and other sources for selection of books, journals and electronic resources mentioned previously.
- *Business or Corporate Information about Health Care Industry:* Examples: The medical and health information directory; the Patersons guides series; Research centres directory; World of learning; Encyclopaedia of associations; the Medical and health care marketplace guide; the Foundations directory; Directory of medical and health care libraries in the United Kingdom and Republic of Ireland.
- *Dictionaries: Examples*: Dorlands illustrated medical dictionary; Stedman's medical dictionary; the International dictionary of medicine and biology; Taber encyclopedic dictionary; Segen's dictionary of modern medicine; the encyclopaedia and dictionary of medicine, nursing and allied health; Jablonski's dictionary of syndromes and eponymic diseases; Mangalini's directory of syndromes; Encyclopaedia of human biology; Sloane's medical abbreviations and eponyms; the Acronyms, initialisms and abbreviations dictionary; Mosby's medical, nursing and allied health dictionary.
- *Directories and Biographical Sources:* Examples are the various medical directories published in many countries of the world, such as the UK Medical directory.
- *Drug and Chemical Information:* Examples are the various pharmacopoeias published in many countries.

- *Funding Sources:* Some are listed under the second type mentioned.
- *Handbooks and Manuals:* This also includes style manuals. Examples: Merck index; CRC handbook of chemistry and physics.
- *Health Legislation, Regulations and Standards:* These are published and documented in various countries.
- *Indexes and Abstracts*: Many are available in both print and electronic formats. Examples include:
  - Index Medicus (Medline);
  - Science citation index (SCISEARCH);
  - Current contents;
  - Excerpta medica (EMBASE);
  - Cumulative index to nursing and allied health (CINAHL);
  - Hospital literature index (Health Planning and Administration);
  - Biological abstracts (BIOSIS Previews);
  - Chemical abstracts (CA Search);
  - Psychological abstracts (Psych-INFO);
  - CANCERLIT;
  - PDQ;
  - TOXLIT.
- *Statistical Compilations:* Many countries and health associations publish statistics on different aspects of health. WHO publishes World health statistics annual.
- *Tests*: Examples include: Mental measurements yearbook; stromborg's Instruments for clinical nursing research.
- Yearbooks and annual reviews.
- *General Works:* Most reference collections include a small number of general reference works such as an encyclopaedia, dictionary, almanac, directories of local organisations, an atlas.
- *Textbook Collections:* If the library does not maintain a reserve collection. A representative collection of textbooks in the reference collection may provide convenient access to students who need information for assignments or patient care questions.
- *Electronic Resources:* There is an increasing number of electronic reference sources covering the range of print sources, including bibliographic and fulltext databases, handbooks, encyclopaedias, directories, and textbooks. The data is stored on CD-ROM, floppy disks, hard drives and mainframe or minicomputers. Some are duplicates or enhancements of printed sources or mainframe sources, such as CD-ROM versions of MEDLINE, others incorporate several publications or resources. Another electronic resource is the OPAC (Online Public Access Catalogue) were one or more workstations are dedicated for them.

- *Ephemeral Materials*: Collection of pamphlets, information sheets, brochures, and even reprints or bibliographies are maintained as adjuncts to reference collections. This collection may also include press clippings. A policy for selection criteria and guidelines for weeding and retention should be developed and followed.

Audiovisual Collections

Audiovisual materials comprise an important segment of many health sciences libraries. But they usually have requirements (such as space, equipment and funding) that make them different from collections of other materials.

Collection development for audiovisuals is different from those for other materials in the following aspects:

- Selection of audiovisuals is more user-driven than that for other formats;
- Previewing is required in the selection process, whether this takes place in the library or at the supplier's place.

Audiovisuals supports all aspects of educational programmes in both academic settings and hospitals (whether for staff or patients).

Selection Criteria

In addition to the general criteria of selection previously discussed, the following additional criteria may be considered:

- *Audience:* The library's interest in the audience which may be professional, academics, or general public including patients and patient families, should be documented in the collection development policy and taken into account in the selection process.
- *Equipment Availability*: The following questions have to be answered: Does the library already own the proper equipment so that users can view or listen to the programme? Are users likely to have access to compatible equipment at home or in their departments? Can the item be used on patient to other broadcast networks?
- *Appropriateness of Format*: Is the format in which the material is presented the most useful one to convey the information? Slides *vs.* videotapes, audiovisual *vs.* print, motion *vs.* still images, audiotape *vs.* printed description.
- *Origin of Format:* does the audiovisual conform to national standards: slides may differ in size.
- *Rental or Permanent Acquisition*: Can the need be satisfied through rental? Is there sufficient recurring demand to justify a purchase? Is it possible to borrow particular items from other library or institution?
- *Restriction on Use:* Are there special guidelines which must be

followed regarding the use of the title, such as prohibition on group showings? If it is difficult to monitor and enforce such restrictions, it may not be advisable to procure the item.

- *Cost*: Is the item worth the investment?

Grey Literature

Grey literature is defined as the " literature which is not readily available through normal bookselling channels, and therefore difficult to identify and obtain". Examples of grey literature include reports, technical notes and specifications, conference proceedings and preprints, translations, official publications, supplementary publications and data, trade literature. It has to be noted that not all materials in all these categories are grey.

Grey materials are characterized by the following:

- Poor availability
- Poor bibliographic information and control
- Non-professional layout and format
- Low print run

Types of Grey Literature in Health Sciences

- Government Information.
  - The grey titles issued by government departments. These may outnumber the other normal publications in some countries.
  - The health agency documents, including circulars.
  - Documents produced by national statutory and non-statutory bodies, academic units and voluntary sector.
  - *Health Authority Literature*: This includes:
    a. Minutes and agenda papers
    b. Annual reports
    c. Public health reports
    d. Strategic plans
    e. Working party plans
    f. Statistical series and bulletins
    g. Medical audit plans
    h. Policy documents
    i. Research and surveys
    j. Health needs assessment surveys
    k. Public opinion surveys
    l. Financial statements
  - Documents of other relevant authorities, such as the ministries of interior, housing, transport, labour, sports and even police service.
  - Grey literature of health service providers in both public and

private sectors. This literature also includes research activities and statistics.

Operations Require Careful Planning and Adequate Personnel and Materials

Salvage operations require careful planning and adequate personnel and materials. It is a good idea to develop a list of potential volunteers if the situation is too large for the staff to handle within a reasonable time.

Keep in mind that the library can count on only about 72 hours of assistance from volunteers—that is, 72 hours from the time the first request for assistance goes out. Thus, there should be planning for what to do after 72 hours, if the disaster is major.

Water damage is a potentially destructive problem, as is the development of mold and mildew. Mold can develop in as little as 48 hours, depending on the temperature. What basic steps should one follow in a water emergency?

The best way to handle large quantities of water-soaked paper is to freeze it and process the material as time and money allow. Planners should identify companies with large freezer facilities and discuss with them the possibility of using or renting their freezers in case of emergency.

Often, such companies are willing to do this at no cost, because of the good publicity they gain from such generosity. Large grocery store chains and meat packing plants are possible participants. Refrigerated trucks can be most useful, if costly to rent. Getting wet materials to the freezing units is a problem: milk crates, open plastic boxes, or clothes baskets work well, because they allow water to drain.

Cardboard boxes absorb water. Plastic interlocking milk crates are ideal, because they are about the right size for a person to handle when three-fourths full of wet material. Sometimes, local dairies are willing to assist by supplying free crates for the duration of the emergency. Freezer or butcher paper is best for separating the materials; never use newsprint, because it tends to stick and the ink comes off. Finally, find some drying facilities. There are three primary methods of drying wet books: (1) freezing freeze-drying, (2) vacuum drying, and (3) vacuum freeze-drying. Vacuum freeze-drying is the best way to handle wet items. Often, vacuum drying facilities are difficult to locate and can handle only a small volume of material at a time, so materials may be in the freezer for a long time while a small quantity is done whenever the source and funding permit.

Two other steps are important when designing a disaster preparedness plan. One is to identify the nearest conservation specialist(s). Most are willing to serve as a telephone resource, and often they will come to the scene. A second important step is to arrange for special purchasing power. Although some groups, organizations, and companies may be willing to assist free of charge, many will not, and the library may need to commit quickly to a specific expense. Having to wait even a few hours for approval may cause irreversible damage. Although most disasters are minor—a few hundred water-damaged items-a large disaster is always possible. One example was the April 1986 fire that struck the Los Angeles Public Library. For more than 10 years, there had been concern about the fire danger, but the hope that a new building would be constructed forestalled major modifications in the existing building.

According to *Library Hotline*, it took 1,700 volunteers working around the clock to shrink-wrap and freeze the 400,000 water-soaked books (about 20 per cent of the Central Library's collection). In addition, the city paid a salvage contractor $500,000 for his firm's services. One can only speculate what the costs and problems might have been with no disaster preparedness plan.

Preservation

By having the collection properly stored and handled in a controlled climate, and with sound security practices as well as a disaster preparedness plan in place, the library will lengthen the useful life of its materials and reduce preservation problems.

However, if the library fails to employ good preservation methods, much of what it gains from those practices will be lost as items fade, decompose, or become unusable. Conservation should start with the purchase decision (which ought to include consideration of how well the material will stand up to the expected use) and should end with the question of what to do about worn, damaged materials and items identified in the weeding process.

One element in a library's conservation programme is the basic binding and repair programme. In-house repairs are fine as long as they employ good conservation methods and use materials that will not cause more harm. Repairers should do nothing that cannot be undone later, if necessary. For example, one should avoid using any adhesive tape other than a reversible adhesive, non-acidic tape to repair a torn page.

Most commercial binderies follow sound practices and employ materials that will not add to an already serious problem of decomposing books. An excellent overview of library binding practices, in a commercial setting, is Paul Parisi's "An Overview of Library Binding."

Selecting a commercial binder should involve the chief collection officer, if the bindery operation is not under the supervision of that person. Most libraries spend thousands of dollars on bindery and repair work each year, and having a reliable and efficient binder, who uses the proper materials, benefits the library and its customers.

Knowing something about bindery operations and the process the materials undergo can help the library staff responsible for selecting materials for binding to make better judgements about the type of- binding to order, given the probable use of the material. Most commercial binders are pleased to explain their operations and give customers and new library employees tours of their plant. At present, the source of many conservation and preservation problems is acidic wood pulp paper. William J. Barrow is the person most often associated with identifying acid as the cause of the deterioration of wood pulp paper.

The problem is not new, but people are now seeing the full implications of the findings of Barrow and other researchers. Estimates vary as to just how big the problem is. One project estimated that there were more than 600,000 brittle or moderately brittle books in a collection of 2 million books in the UCLA library system in 1979. (*A brittle book* is one in which a corner of a page breaks off when folded back and forth two or fewer times.)

The estimate was based on a random sample of books in the collection. An estimated 1 million volumes in Widener Library (Harvard University) are in similar condition. In the early 1980s, the Library of Congress estimated that it had 6 million brittle volumes." According to Richard Dougherty, the Commission on Preservation and Access estimated that more than 25 per cent of the world's greatest monographic collections are already embrittled beyond redemption." The problem grows with each passing day and nothing is done to stop the process. Unfortunately, few libraries have sufficient funding to do more than address a small percentage of the items needing attention.

Deanna Marcum published a short article in the *New York* Times in 1998 about the ever-growing problem of preservation. She outlined the stark facts and made a strong case that technology may be a greater problem than acidic paper.

In the article, she noted that the U.S. National Archivist had advised government agencies that they "could delete certain computer files *if they kept paper copies*" (emphasis added). She also noted that the acidic paper issue was still a problem.

In the case of brittle books, short fibres and chemical residues from the paper manufacturing process are the culprits. The longer the fibres in the paper, the stronger it is. When ground wood pulp became the standard source for paper manufacturing, the long-term strength of paper dropped sharply.

A weak paper combined with the acidic residue from sizing and bleaching, as well as lignin (a component of the wood used for paper), creates self-destructing material. At one end of the scale is newsprint, which is very acidic; at the other end is the non-acidic paper that more and more publishers are using in books.

The Council on Library Resources' efforts to establish some guidelines for publishers, manufacturers, and librarians regarding the use of alkaline paper in book production are paying off. The CLR report stated that "alkaline paper *need not be more expensive* than acidic paper of the quality normally used in hardbound books." The guidelines provide standards for both performance (acid content) and durability (folding and bending), as well as long-term book binding for the initial commercial binding. Though the guidelines will reduce future problems, they cannot help the present situation.

Each year, the number of brittle items already in the collection increases. What can be done about materials that are self-destructing in the stacks? Maintaining environmental factors (temperature, humidity, and light) at the recommended levels slows the chemical processes; thus, this is a first step to take. For the already-brittle materials in the collection, the two concerns are permanence (shelf life) and durability (use). Permanence is the first issue, and there are several ways to stop the acidic activity. After the acidic action is under control, several options exist to enhance durability. Several mass deacidification systems on the market are designed to process large numbers of books at one time.

The only one with a reasonably long history of use is the Wei T'o process developed by Richard Smith. Probably the second best known system is the DEZ system. Developed with the support of the Library of Congress, the process received widespread press coverage after it encountered several problems, the most notable being an explosion at the test site. A good review of the history of deacidification systems is found in Michale V. Cloonan's "Mass Deacidification in the 1990s."

Options for Handling Brittle Materials

Given the magnitude of the acid paper problem, almost every library will be faced with a variety of decisions on what to do. Here, if nowhere else, collection development staff must enter the preservation picture. When an item in the collection deteriorates to the point that it cannot be rebound, what should one do? Ten options exist:

- Ignore the problem and return the item to storage.
- Withdraw the item from the collection and do not replace it.
- Seek a reprint edition on alkaline paper.
- Convert the material to microfilm and decide what to do with the original.
- Convert the material to an electronic format.
- Photocopy the material on alkaline paper and decide what to do with the original.
- Seek a replacement copy through the out-of-print trade.
- Place it in an alkaline protective enclosure made for the item and return it to the collection.
- Withdraw the item from the main collection and place in a controlled access storage facility.
- Deacidify and strengthen the item and return it to use.

Ignoring the problem is the most reasonable alternative for materials about which one is confident that long-term retention is unnecessary or undesirable and only a limited amount of use is probable. If there is little or no probability of use in the near future, withdrawing the item is probably the most effective option.

Seeking a reprint edition printed on alkaline paper is the least expensive option for materials that are worth long-term storage and probably will experience moderate to heavy use. Reprints are not available for all the items that are self-destructing; only the high-demand titles are reprinted.

Several companies exist to serve the reprint market, for example, AMS, Scholarly Reprints, Kraus, Harvester Press Microform Publications, and Research Publications.

Guide to Reprints (Guide to Reprints, Inc.), *Books on Demand* (University Microfilms), and *Guide to Microforms in Print* (Microform Review) are three sources of information about a broad range of titles. (*Note*: Just because an item is a reprint does not mean that it is printed on alkaline paper. Be certain to specify alkaline paper when ordering.)

Microformat and electronic storage of the brittle material are other options. Until the mid-1980s, microfilming was the most common way of storing the content of brittle materials in a secondary format. The cost of making the master negative is high, but once made, duplicate copies are relatively inexpensive to produce.

Thus, if the primary collection development concern is with preserving the intellectual content of the brittle material and not with the item as an artifact, a microformat is a good solution. It may be possible to locate a master copy of an item, thereby reducing costs. Two places to check are the *National Register of Microforms Masters* (Library of Congress) and *Guide to Microforms in Print* (Meckler). The *Register* covers more than 3,000 library and publisher holdings worldwide and is produced by the Library of Congress. *Guide to Microforms in Print* is similar to *BIP*; it lists titles from commercial publishers around the world.

The Directory of Library Reprographic Services (Meckler) can be of assistance in identifying libraries with the capability of making a master. The Library of Congress has the most experience in working with analog videodisc technology as a preservation format. The advantages of the technology are high-density storage (54,000 graphic images stored on one disc) and random access to those images.

In contrast, optical discs are used to store print material. A disc can hold about 3,000 pages of text or 200,000 catalogue cards. Both technologies have potential for assisting in solving preservation problems.

As one might expect, there is a relatively high cost associated with these systems, but as more organizations use optical or analog disc technology, it is reasonable to expect the cost to decline. However, it is now clear that digitization does not necessarily translate into long-term preservation. Some publishers (and even the Copyright Office) have questions about the legality of converting copyrighted material to a disc format: How this differs in principle from microfilming, which no one seems to question, is unclear. Under U.S. copyright law (§ 108(e)), it is legal for a library to make a single complete copy of an out-of-print item after making a reasonable search for the item.

A photocopy of the original may be the best option when the library anticipates moderate use and cannot locate a reprint. There are commercial firms that will produce a bound photocopy on alkaline paper from an individual volume on demand. This is an especially good alternative when it is not necessary to preserve the original item. Photocopying and microfilming cause physical wear on bound materials, and a bound item may have to be taken apart to be duplicated properly. Generally, in the photocopy process, there is some loss in image quality; obviously, this may not be acceptable for items with high-quality photographs and illustrations. Several paper manufacturers (for example, Hollinger, Process Materials, and Xerox) offer buffered (alkaline) paper for use in photocopy machines. When binding the photocopies, it is necessary to specify that the binder use buffered materials. If alkaline paper or deacidified paper comes into contact with acidic material, the acid will migrate into the alkaline paper and start the process all over again.

The staff should think carefully before going to the out-of-print market for replacement copies. Although a replacement copy may be available at the lowest price of any of the options, will the replacement be in any better condition than the one it is to replace? Unless the replacement copy had better storage conditions than the library's copy, both will be in about the same state of deterioration.

It is probable that the replacement copy will be less worn (as long as it is not an ex-library copy), but there will be little difference in the acidic state.

Normally, the replacement copy's storage history is worse than the library's copy, and thus the replacement copy will be in greater need of preservation. Locating a replacement copy in the out-of-print market will take months or even years. During the search, the library must decide what to do with the item in hand. If it is brittle, should customers continue to use it while the library is waiting for a replacement copy that may or may not exist? Additional use may make it difficult, or perhaps impossible, to exercise other options, if the library fails to find a replacement. Although the out-of-print market is a frequent first choice, it is probably the least suitable for long-term preservation purposes.

Protective enclosures or containers provide a stopgap treatment. Enclosing the brittle item in an alkaline container (made of paper, plastic, or cardboard) protects it from unnecessary handling and light. This is a common method of storage for the original (hopefully deacidified) item when a surrogate copy is available for general use. The most common approach is to make custom-sized phase boxes for the item using alkaline cardboard. Bindery/archival supply firms and commercial binderies offer a wide range of prefabricated standard-sized phase boxes, as well as materials for constructing custom-sized boxes. Unfortunately, the materials, including alkaline mending tapes and adhesives, are expensive. To save a small amount of money, some libraries decide not to use the proper materials. Certainly, there is no need to use expensive mending materials on items that the library is likely to discard in time, but, all too often, librarians do not know which items will be kept and which will be discarded.

Secondary storage is a stopgap measure in most cases. It may become the most common first option when the quantity of brittle materials escalates beyond the library's ability to handle it. A controlled environment with limited handling would slow the destructive process and buy some time to determine which of the more permanent solutions to implement. The essential element is controlling the storage environment; merely placing the materials in a remote storage area with the same or worse climate control accomplishes little and may cause further deterioration. Another danger of remote storage is that the adage "out of sight, out of mind" frequently applies. Without a preservation officer or someone on the staff charged with supervising preservation activities, the storage area can become a dumping ground for materials that no one wants to think about. Even in a controlled environment, the disintegration continues day and night until something is done to stop it. The following are some basic guidelines for preparing materials for storage:

1. Remove extraneous materials, such as paper clips, rubber bands, wrapping material, old folders, and any other material that is not pertinent. If foreign matter, such as pressed flowers, must be saved as documentary evidence, place it in a separate enclosure.
2. Unfold and flatten papers wherever possible without causing damage to the folds. If the paper is brittle or inflexible, it may have to be humidified before unfolding. Remove surface soil with a soft brush.
3. Isolate newsprint because it is highly acidic and will stain adjacent paper. Newspaper clippings can be replaced with photocopies on alkaline paper or placed in a separate envelope. Fax copies are similarly unstable and should be reproduced or isolated, unless they are plain-paper faxes.
4. Note any badly damaged items; place them within individual folders and set them aside for professional conservation treatment. Do not undertake any first aid unless you have received training and are qualified to do so.
5. If it is necessary to place identifying information on the object itself, use a soft (no. 2) pencil and write on the verso or in the lower right margin. Repeat the identification on the storage folders and envelopes in pencil or typing. Never use ballpoint or felt-tip pens that might stain or bleed.

6. Identify boxes with labels that contain adequate information about the contents. This curtails unnecessary browsing and rifling through documents.

If materials should be humidified, consult Mary Lynn Ritzen-thaler's *Preserving Archives and Manuscripts*.

Restoration is expensive, and libraries will never be able to restore all or even most of the brittle items they own.

As noted earlier, the deacidification process is also expensive, and added to that are costs of restoring strength to the individual pages and binding. For a good description of the advantages and disadvantages of the various methods of preservation, see Robert Mareck's "Practicum on Preservation Selection."

SOURCES FOR SELECTION

There are services concerning grey literature in various fields. They are normally with national covering although some may be international.

The following are examples:

- *Government Reports Announcements and Index. Virginia*: NTIS. This publication has three major headings related to health sciences in its subject categories:
  - Biomedical technology and human factor engineering
  - Health planning and health services research
  - Medicine and biology
- Scientific and Technical Aerospace Report (STAR). NASA. This has the following parts concerning health sciences:
  - Life sciences
  - Aerospace medicine
  - Behavioural sciences
  - Man/system technology and life support
  - Space biology
- Energy research abstract (ERA). US Department of Energy. It has:
  - Biomedical sciences, basic studies
  - Biomedical sciences, applied studies
  - Health and safety
- British reports, translations and theses. Boston. Spa: The British Library Document Supply Centre. It has: 06 biological and medical sciences.
- System for information on grey literature in Europe (SIGLE). The European Association of Grey Literature Exploitation (EAGLE). It is a bibliographic database holding contributions from 9 European countries.
- For librarians seeking German language grey literature in medical and health care, there are two publications:

  - FTN (Forschungsberichte aus Technik und Nat-urwissencha ften). Weinheim: VCH Verlag. This is a bibliography of projects sponsored by the German Federal Ministry for Research and Technology.
  - Bibliography of medicine. Munich: K.G. Saur. This is a bibliography of German-language publications outside the book trade, and includes literature from Switzerland and Austria.
- PASCAL Bibliographies internationales. Paris INIST. This is an international bibliography with French emphasis covering science and medicine.
- Ethnic minorities health. Bradford: Bradford Community Quarterly bulletin covering conference proceeding, theses and much useful grey literature.
- The Cumulative index to nursing and allied health literature (CINAHL). It is useful for dissertations, standards and conference proceedings.
- *Health Service Abstracts. Oldham:* Department of Health Leaflets Unit. Monthly. It includes books, book chapters, NHS executive publications, reports and periodical references.
- *The European Union Biomedical and Health Research. Brussels:* European Commission. 3/year. It concentrates on national research into medical and health problems in Europe.
- Health Care Literature Information Network (HECLINET). Berlin: Institut für Krankenhausbau, Dokumentation Krankenhauswesen. Bimonthly. It covers the entire range of European literature, both grey and white, on hospitals and health care. It includes conference reports, theses and company publications.
- Conference papers index. Louisville, NY: Data Courier. Monthly. It covers published and unpublished papers.
- WHODOC. Geneva: WHO. Bimonthly. It lists all WHO publications, including periodicals, technical and policy documents, as well as documents emanating from WHO funded programmes.

Other disciplines, such as food and environment, are covered in international databases.

They include:

- *AGRIS. Rome*: Food and Agriculture Organisation (FAO). It has a print version, AGRINDEX.
- CAB abstracts. London: Commonwealth Agricultural Bureau.
- AGRICOLA. US National Agricultural Library. It has a printed version: bibliography of agriculture.
- International register of potentially toxic chemicals (IRPTC). Nairobi: United Nations Environment Programme (UNEP).

- Environmental Chemical Data and Information Network (ECDIN). European Communities at Ispra (Italy) Establishment. This is a factual database.

CONSUMER HEALTH COLLECTIONS

During the 1980s and 1990s, increasing attention has been given to the provision of information on health care issues to patients, relatives, carers and wider public. The information provided is called "Consumer Health Information (CHI)'. Deve-lopment of consumer health information is now a necessity dictated by law in some countries.

It has significant benefits:

- It leads to more truly informed consent
- It leads to increased patient's understanding and satisfaction
- It leads to increased compliance with treatment
- It leads to quicker and less stressful recovery from illness and surgery.

The increased availability of health information for lay people has also been influenced by the WHO declaration of " Health for All by the year 2000 " which says:

- "Health for all will be achieved by people themselves. A well informed, well motivated and actively participating community is a key element for attainment of the common goal".

Consumer health collections exist to serve library users seeking authoritative information, in clearly understood language, about normal anatomy and physiology, diseases, conditions, treatments and other health care topics. Besides the general public users of these collections include medical school students seeking materials to help explain health and disease concepts to patients and their relatives. Others include primary care physicians, nurses and faculty members. It may be part of the reference collection, or on its own. But it is not always the responsibility of the medical library to contain consumer health collections. In some cases it is the responsibility of the parent organisation's public relations unit, while in other cases the responsibility rests with a variety of statutory and voluntary agencies, as it is rather common for the ministries of health and other health authorities to provide this information. Yet in other cases, the responsibility rests with public libraries.

Selection Criteria

The general selection criteria previously mentioned apply here.

But further criteria may be given:

- *Presentation of Information*: This includes the writing style, easiness of use, presence of index and table of contents, illustration, presentation of alternatives and presence of citations and sources.

- *Audience*: The collection development policy should document the audience to be served, to be taken into account in the selection process.
- *Pathway to Additional Information:* The item should have bibliographies, reading list, referral sources and resource organisations.
- Qualifications of the Author and Publisher.
- Currency.

Rare Book, History of Medicine and Archives Collections

Rare book, history of medicine and archives collections, are not found in all health sciences libraries. The difference between collection development in general, and that of rare books derives from the nature of the books themselves. Thus policies governing it are frequently singled out for special consideration in overall collection development policy statements. A distinction is often made between rare book collections and history of medicine collections, under the assumption that the latter are generally comprised of secondary works, the materials are collected in the same manner as other books for the medical library collections, and they are kept in open stacks with the rest of the library's collection.

Rare books are primary research materials, require more proper storage and security controls than the general stack collection, and may also be used as showplace for the parent organisation. The archives collection of the parent organisation is different and is not common in medical libraries as it may be under the responsibility of another department of the parent organisation.

If it exists, it may include: official correspondence, minutes, books of account, publications of the parent organisation, books by and about staff and students including alumni publications, theses from the parent organisation or its staff, records of parent organisation's clubs, associations, and societies catalogue, newsletters, personal papers of the more eminent members of the staff, and photographs. It may also contain records from other local health-related organisations, such as affiliated hospitals.

Selection Criteria

Additional to generic criteria, there are further ones that need to be considered:

- *Presence of other Editions of the Same Work*: In addition to availability of other editions or printings, there may be need for specific edition with special features. Some large libraries may require that all editions of a work be acquired for comparison.
- *Availability of a Facsimile Edition*: Facsimile editions may be useful as reading copies.
- *Physical Condition*: The physical condition may be the reason for

selection as the item may be different from modern works. Items that need restoration are not usually acquired.

- *Cost:* This must be appropriate.
- *Research Value of the Artifact over Content:* This concerns signed or annotated copies, special bindings and illustrations. Works of particular publishers may be of interest.
- *Provenance*: Previous owners of the copy. Whether the copy is a stolen copy.
- *The Subject in Context*: This means that the copy may show whether the discipline changed over time.
- *Format:* Formats other than books may figure prominently in rare book and history of medicine collections.
- For archives there must be a policy for retention and disposal of the materials rather than a selection policy.

TRADITIONAL LIBRARY MATERIAL

PROCESSING LIBRARY MATERIAL

Written Notations

Written notations such as cataloguing and foliation inscriptions should be made as neatly and unobtrusively as possible with a soft (B) pencil, applying light pressure to prevent indentations. It is worth considering enclosing notations within brackets to indicate that the information was added by the institution. Inked notations (and accidental markings) are often permanent and cannot be removed. Many inks are acidic; others are water-soluble and will bleed and run when exposed to moisture, such as that encountered in a water-related disaster.

Shelfmarks (Call Numbers)

Shelfmarks should not be painted on books, nor should they be typed onto labels which are attached to books with pressure-sensitive tape or adhesive. Paint is unattractive and disfiguring; tape and adhesive may discolour, stain or otherwise damage the binding. For antiquarian material, shelfmarks should be written on the first fly-leaf with soft pencil.

When using self-adhesive labels, care should be taken to ensure that the adhesive will remain effective over time. It is especially important that the adhesive does not desiccate, causing labels to come loose or fall off, and does not ooze, which will attract dirt and may damage other materials that come into contact with it. Ideally, labels should be on permanent paper.

Bookplates

If bookplates must be used in books, they should be made of low-lignin, alkaline paper, and should be attached with a stable, reversible adhesive, preferably riceor wheat-starch paste, or methyl cellulose; or polyester film jackets should be made and the bookplates attached to them. Circulation card pockets should be treated the same way, although books of special value usually should not circulate.

Inserts

All acidic inserts, such as loose bookmarks, scraps of paper, and pressed flowers, should be removed from books, assessed, documented, photocopied, and, if to be saved, then encapsulated in polyester. This is to prevent staining and acidity in the inserts from migrating into book pages and damaging them.

Fasteners

No attempt should be made to separate documents that are attached with lines or dots of paste or glue. If such items must be separated to allow for the safe handling, use, or filming of the records, a conservator should be contacted. Great care must be exercised when removing old fasteners such as staples, paperclips, etc.

Fasteners that have rusted or become strongly adhered to paper surfaces must be gently lifted; before removal, the line of contact between the paper and any encrusted rust must be broken. When removing fasteners, the document should be fully supported on a table, and one hand should be placed on the document to hold it in position and support the paper while the fastener is being removed. If the procedure is conducted in mid-air, documents are likely to be torn and damaged. Staple removers should not be used on fragile or brittle documents, as they can easily remove an entire weak or brittle corner along with the intended staple.

READING ROOM PRACTICE

Reading rooms should have sufficient numbers of staff to ensure security against theft, mutilation, and vandalism.

Supporting Books When in Use

Books are complex composite objects which open in a variety of ways and require different methods of support when opened. Very few books can be opened at 180° without being damaged. It is strongly recommended that no book is opened more than 120°, and tightly bound volumes no more than 90°. Bindings are far more vulnerable and fragile than is presumed and need to be handled with great care.

Board attachments are often precarious, with extremely thin leather over the joints. Such books should always be supported when in use and boards should never be flipped back 180° from the text-block. The traditional wooden lectern or reading stand has caused many volumes to be damaged by presenting the book at a steep angle which strains the sewing and does not support the joints, which will soon weaken and eventually split. Moreover, such steep lecterns are not comfortable for readers to use. For fragile and rare material, the foam book supports designed by Christopher Clarkson provide the most suitable way of supporting both tight- and hollowback volumes. A book can be set up at a comfortable reading angle of 20°, with an opening not greater than 120°, the joints fully supported, and the leaves restrained with strips of weighted fabric. As the reader progresses through the volume, the blocks can be adjusted to retain optimum support for the book's vulnerable joints. With a thicker book, the reader should add or remove one or more of the flat pads to fit the volume's changing profile as it is opened in different places. A larger wedge may be placed beneath the two side-supports, to form the base of the book-rest and provide a more comfortable reading angle.

Notices to Readers

Reading rooms should have notices clearly directing readers NOT to:

- Drink, eat, or smoke in the library except in designated areas
- Handle library material with unwashed hands
- Use ink of any kind
- Use correction fluid or highlighters
- Annotate texts, or write on paper placed on top of the pages of an open book
- Lean on library material
- Touch illuminations, painted images, manuscript or printed text areas
- Insert slips or notes in the gutter of a book
- Leave items in direct sunlight
- Leave out items not in use
- Have more than a limited number of items out at a time for consultation
- Pile items on top of each other
- Shuffle loose items to fit them in an enclosure, but to handle them individually (in order to prevent hidden edge tears from interlocking and causing further damage).

Assistance for Readers

Reading rooms should provide readers with:

- Information to encourage a regard for the welfare of library material
- Guidelines on how to handle library material
- Book supports and guidelines on how to use them
- Guidelines on how to remove and replace books on shelves
- Adequate space for the viewing of large items
- Cotton gloves for handling valuable material and photographs

- Clean work surfaces
- Polyester sheets for tracing maps
- Assistance with handling large items
- Clean, smooth weights to restrain unrolled plans.

Photocopying

Photocopying raises serious preservation issues. Flat-bed photocopiers and poor handling can cause severe damage to the structure of books and documents. Photocopy machines specifically designed for bound material and not office photocopiers should be provided.

Overhead photocopiers, which allow a book to be copied face-up, are ideal but expensive. Ideally, photocopying should be carried out by the library's own fully trained staff, with each item being examined for its suitability. The criteria for restricting certain material and copyright regulations must be thoroughly understood by all staff members.

Training parts in good handling practice and good copying practice should be mandatory for all new staff, with refresher parts for existing staff at frequent periods.

If it is not possible to allocate staff to carry out copying, there are some factors which can help to reduce wear and tear:

- Position the machines where they are within clear sight of staff.
- Post clear and concise guidelines on careful handling prominently by the machines. It is worth considering posters illustrating that the spine of a book should never be pressed down with the hand or the cover of the copier to ensure a good quality image.
- Make criteria for restricting material clear to users and discourage practices such as photocopying an item for the sake of a few sentences.
- Keep a record of what has been photocopied so that items which are frequently requested can be microfilmed.

The following material should not be photocopied:

- Fragile or damaged items
- Tightly-bound volumes
- Rare books and photographs
- Books stapled or stitched through the sides
- Fine bindings
- Vellum and parchment
- Items with seals attached
- Perfect bindings (books which rely on adhesive to keep the pages together and are not sewn)
- Oversize items that would have to be excessively manipulated to obtain a complete image.

STORAGE METHODS AND HANDLING

Storage methods have a direct effect on the useful life of material. While proper storage can extend life, slovenly, haphazard, overcrowded conditions soon result in damage to collections. Moreover, poor-quality storage enclosures can accelerate the deterioration of the material they are intended to protect. Handling by staff and users also directly affects the useful life of library collections. Damage to books is cumulative. Repeated poor handling can quickly transform a new book into a worn one, and a worn book into an unusable book that requires costly repair, rebinding, or replacement. By following the guidelines presented here, the library can make significant strides towards improving the welfare of the collection.

Shelving and the Shelving of Books

- Shelving should be designed to provide smooth, secure, clean, and convenient support. Any protrusions and sharp edges should be attended to. Ideally, book cases should be constructed of steel with a baked enamel finish.
- Volumes should be shelved a minimum of 10 cm off the floor to reduce the risk of damage from flooding or passers-by. When possible, use shelving units that have a 'canopy' on top, as this will deflect water, dust, and some damaging light.
- Good air circulation should be maintained in storage areas and around shelving.
- Book cases should be at least 5 cm away from walls and the books another 5 cm away from the back of the book case. This is especially important when book cases are positioned against the outside walls of a building.
- When books are stored in steel cabinets, ensure the cabinets are adequately ventilated. Holes should be in the sides and not on the top of the cabinets to avoid dust and debris falling on the books.
- Books kept on mobile shelving must be shelved carefully to avoid any possibility of them falling off or being crushed when the shelves are moved.

For the maximum protection of books, the following rules should be enforced:

- Shelve books so that they are not difficult to remove or replace. Books which are tightly shelved will soon be damaged when they are removed or replaced.
- Use bookends to support books when shelves are not full. Allowing books to lean will distort and strain the structures and eventually cause their breakdown. Bookends should have smooth surfaces and broad edges to prevent covers from being abraded and leaves torn or creased.

- Do not let books extend beyond the edges of shelves into aisles because they can be damaged by passers-by and trollies.
- Shelve books by size whenever possible. Avoid keeping large books next to small ones because the large book will be inadequately supported.
- Box, or at least separate with a piece of card or board, bindings with metal furniture (clasps, bosses, studs, etc.), which are shelved next to unprotected books.
- Separate paper and cloth bindings from leather bindings. Acidity and oils in the leather migrate into paper and cloth and hasten their deterioration. Furthermore, degraded powdery leather will soil paper and cloth.
- Shelve small, structurally sound books upright.
- Move the books or rearrange the shelves if books are too tall to stand upright. Do not store books on their fore-edges as this will damage the structure of a book and loosen the binding.
- Store oversize, heavy, structurally weak, or damaged books horizontally to give them the overall support they require. Additional shelves may need to be inserted at narrow intervals to avoid having to stack these books.
- When oversize books that are stored flat are removed, the upper volumes should be transferred to an empty shelf or book trolley. The desired volume should be removed by lifting it with both hands, and the removed volumes should then be transferred back to the shelf. Replacing the book on the shelf is done in the same way.
- Avoid stacking books in piles on shelves or tables as the books can easily topple over. Ensure the stacks contain no more than two to three books.
- Take special care to ensure that shelfmark flags or titles of books that are stored flat are visible so the books can be identified without moving them.
- Do not place a large book on a small book.
- When the binding must remain on view, such as in a period room in a historic house, the use of book-shoes (supports that cover the sides but leave the spines of books visible) or placement of a piece of polyester film between the books.

Poor handling procedures can cause irreparable damage to books.

- They should not be pulled off the shelves by the headcap, a practice that causes the headcap to fail, tearing the spine of the binding.
- If there is room above the book, reach over the top of the book to the foreedge and then pull it out.
- If there is no room, push back the books on either side of the one to

be retrieved, to expose enough of the spine to allow for a firm grip on either side of the spine with the thumb and fingers.
- The book should be removed, and the remaining books on the shelf and the bookends readjusted.

Carrying and Transporting Books

- Do not carry more books than can be comfortably held firmly in both hands.
- Pack books flat in tough boxes when moving them out of a room.
- If necessary, pad the box with polystyrene or foam so that the books do not slide around.
- Transport individual books in card boxes. Carry the box in a polythene bag when going outside.
- Use water-resistant polypropylene containers with securely fitting lids when moving books out of a building.
- Whenever possible use two people to move containers.
- Avoid leaving library material in vehicles.

Book Trollies and Books on Trollies

Use book trollies that:
- Have large rubber wheels, for this helps stability, and manoeuvrability, and reduces vibration
- Have wide shelves or protective rails to secure the items in transit
- Have bumpers on corners to minimize damage from inadvertent bumps.

When putting books on trollies ensure that:
- They are shelved upright on the trolley and are properly supported as in the stacks
- Volumes do not protrude beyond the edges of the trolley
- The trolley is loaded so that it has a low centre of gravity.

ENCLOSURES FOR BOOKS AND PAPER MATERIAL

Enclosures should be lignin-free, sulphur-free, alkaline buffered, and have a high cellulosic content (above 87 per cent). Enclosures include boxes, envelopes, and folders and are available commercially in a range of shapes and sizes.

Enclosures are crucial to library preservation, for they:
- Provide protection from over-handling
- Provide protection in transit
- Provide protection on the shelves
- Provide protection against fire, smoke, and flood damage
- Keep out light

- Keep out dust
- Act as a buffer against fluctuations in the ambient environment
- Act as a buffer against atmospheric pollution.

Types of Enclosures for Books

- Tailor-made boxes of bookboard and cloth are ideal but are expensive and require time and skill to make. They can be justified only for extremely rare, unique, and valuable material. They have the advantage of being able to provide all round support and are more robust than other types of enclosures.
- Phase-boxes are a cheaper alternative, which provide adequate short-term (15-20 years) protection, and are much quicker and simpler to construct. They can be made in-house or commercially.
- Commercially made, archival-quality boxes and four-flap folders come in a wide range of sizes and can be purchased in small and large quantities.
- Book-shoes are appropriate for books that require structural support while being displayed on shelves.
- Slipcases should be avoided because they often abrade the surface of the binding and damage the text-block when the book is slid in and out.
- Envelopes are sometimes used for the storage of books. These generally do not provide the support books need and should be replaced with boxes.
- Wrappers of a permanent durable paper or card can be used to protect books that are infrequently used, if enclosures are too expensive or take up too much space on shelves.

Selecting Material to be Boxed

When prioritising books for boxing the following should be considered:

- Books with fragile and important bindings.
- Vulnerable and damaged books – books with loose or torn leaves, and books with loose covers.
- Books bound in vellum or with vellum text-blocks. Vellum responds readily to changes in relative humidity by expanding and contracting. This can result in warped covers and cracked joints. Boxing helps restrain vellum bindings and thereby minimizes warping.

Shrink-wrapping and Vacuum-packing

Shrink-wrapping and vacuum-packing, adapted from the food and packaging industry, are economical ways of protecting material. Both processes involve placing an item between sheets, or into pouches, of polyester/polyethylene film.

The film is either shrunk using heat, as in shrink-wrapping, or a vacuum is created around the item and all air expelled, as in vacuum-packing. While they seem to be stable in the short term, further tests have yet to be carried out on the effects of long-term storage. Material which is to be moved and fragile items, in particular those with brittle paper, can be placed between boards and protected in one of the ways; the result is a rigid and strong enclosure. Shrink-wrapping and vacuum-packing are also being used as means of combatting insect and fungal attack and creating a stable micro-environment. Space can be saved as the process expels most of the air, thereby reducing the thickness of the item.

Newsprint

Commercially made, archival-quality boxes and vacuum-packing are both ways of preserving newspapers. However, because much of the newsprint produced after 1840 is made of short-fibred paper that contains lignin and other impurities, its long-term preservation is difficult at best and, consequently, microfilming has become the most common method of dealing with newspapers. Collections of newsclippings are usually important because of the information they contain and not because of the value of the clippings themselves. For this reason, again, photocopying and microfilming are the most practical preservation options. All photocopying should be done on low-lignin, buffered paper using an electrostatic copier with heat-fused images. Newsclippings that must be retained should be treated and then physically separated from better-quality papers in a folder or in an enclosure made of polyester film.

Periodicals and Pamphlets

Periodicals and pamphlets can be stored in boxes, folders, or card envelopes. Several items of the same cover size can be stored together in commercially made boxes. Items that differ in size can be placed in card envelopes and then boxed. If a single periodical or pamphlet must be shelved between books, it should be placed in a card envelope.

Scrapbooks and Ephemera

Many historical collections include scrapbooks and ephemera (*e.g.,* trade cards, valentines, patterns, paper dolls, etc.). These items pose challenging preservation problems because they often contain a variety of components and media. They may have raised surfaces, three-dimensional decoration, or moving parts.

They are frequently unique, fragile, damaged, and of significant associational value. They should never be interfiled with other categories of library and archival material because damage may result from the different sizes, shapes, weights, and materials represented. Scrapbooks that are of special historic value in their original form should be individually boxed. Unbound ephemera should be grouped by size and type (*e.g.,* photographs, printed material, manuscripts, etc.), individually enclosed to protect items from acid migration and mechanical damage, if needed, and stored in a way that will support them structurally.

Single-sheet Material

- For paper collections, only objects of the same size and category should be stored together.
- Differences in bulk and weight are potentially damaging, so it is not advisable to store single sheets in the same box with books or pamphlets.
- Generally speaking, heavy objects should be stored separately from lighter ones, as should bulky objects (which cause uneven pressure inside boxes).
- As acid migrates from paper of inferior quality to any other paper with which it comes into direct contact, it is important to separate poor-quality papers from those that are better. Newsclippings and other obviously inferior-quality papers must be removed from direct contact with historical documents and manuscripts on better-quality paper.
- Documents and manuscripts should be unfolded for storage, if this can be done without splitting, breaking, or otherwise damaging them. If unfolding may result in damage, a conservator should be consulted before proceeding.
- Documents should be stored in file folders. Ideally, no more than ten to fifteen sheets should be placed in each folder.
- Folders should be placed in document-storage boxes.
- All folders inside a box should be the same size and should conform to the size of the box.
- Boxes should not be overfilled because this can cause damage when items are removed, replaced, or reviewed.
- Boxes can be stored flat or upright. Flat storage will give the documents overall support and will prevent crumbling edges, slumping, and other mechanical damage to which upright storage might subject them. Flat storage, however, causes documents on the bottom of the box to suffer from the weight of those above. If boxes are stored flat, they should be stacked only two high in order to facilitate their removal from, and replacement onto the shelves.
- Upright storage is acceptable when documents and folders are well-supported to prevent slumping and edge damage. 'Spacer' boards made out of stable materials can be used to fill out boxes that are not quite full.

- Vellum documents and maps, etc., are highly susceptible to fluctuations in temperature and relative humidity and should be placed in an enclosure. Suitable enclosures include encapsulation, folders, mats, and boxes, or a combination of these.

Fascicules

Rare and unique single-sheet items, such as letters, have been traditionally bound into guard books. These are satisfactory if they are kept fairly thin and allow a support sheet for each manuscript page to ensure that the support and not the manuscript is handled. A simpler method is to make up fascicules. A fascicule is a single-section, pamphlet-sewn binding comprising support sheets of bifolia and hooked leaves (acting as compensation guards) with an acid-free stiff paper cover. Sizes are made to fit commercial boxes. All items are foliated and placed loosely in the fascicules by librarians. The leaves on which the items are to be attached are also foliated. A Japanese paper hinge is pasted onto the edge of the item. The hinges are then pasted and the items attached to the recto of the support sheets.

The fascicules are then boxed. Fascicules have several advantages:

- Each item is kept flat and supported.
- Items can be easily removed and replaced if necessary (*e.g.,* for exhibition).
- Flexing of the object is reduced.
- Abrasion between items is reduced.
- Handling is reduced.
- A variety of materials within a standard format can be accommodated.
- The contents are protected from light and airborne pollutants.

Oversize Single-sheet Material

Oversize material includes architectural drawings, blueprints, maps, large prints, posters, and wallpaper samples. These items are best stored flat in plan chests. They should be placed individually in folders cut to fit the size of the drawer. If several items are placed in one folder, interleaving with acid-free tissue paper is desirable, especially if the items have colours or are of special value. There should be sufficient space between chests to facilitate the safe removal and replacement of oversize material. There should also be an adequate surface on which to place items once they are removed or prior to replacement.

If they are not brittle or fragile, oversize material can be rolled when flat storage is not possible. Some items need to be rolled individually; others can be rolled in groups of four to six similar-sized items, the exact number depending on the size and weight of the paper.

A tube several inches longer than the largest item being rolled and at least four inches in diameter (larger diameters are preferable) should be used. If the tube is not made of low-lignin, pH-neutral materials, it should be wrapped in neutral or buffered paper or polyester film. Alternatively, place the items between two sheets of polyester film or acid-free tissue cut several inches larger in both dimensions than the largest item being rolled. Roll the item or items onto the tube. Wrap the assembly with neutral or buffered paper or polyester film to protect it from abrasions. Using flat linen, cotton, or polyester tape, loosely tie up the wrapped roll. This assembly can be stored inside a larger rectangular box for added protection if desired. Tubes should be stored horizontally.

Handling and Transporting Oversize Single-sheet Material

- Use both hands when handling large items.
- Take care that large pendant seals are supported and turned with the document.
- Consider the route and destination before setting out, even if simply moving items from one room to another.
- Place maps, plans, and large single-sheet material in a portfolio or purposemade folder.
- Use two people for carrying large portfolios.
- Carry portfolios vertically.
- Use waterproof portfolios when moving items outside.

EXHIBITIONS

When exhibiting library material, special attention should be paid to the following:

- Selecting items which are fit for display.
- The security of the exhibit-cases should have locks, shatter-proof glass, be alarmed, and the room should be invigilated at all times.
- Materials used for case construction should be chemically stable and checked for offgassing.
- The climatic factors of temperature, relative humidity, light, UV radiation, and atmospheric pollutants should be tightly controlled and monitored by appropriate equipment.
- Materials used for mounting exhibits should be chemically stable and pose no detrimental threat to the artefact.
- Books should be strapped with polythene to tailor-made card or acrylic cradles which acurately follow the profile of the opened or closed book. Books generally should not be displayed at an angle greater than 20° from horizontal, nor opened wider than 120°, and should be provided with a text-block support when appropriate.
- Acid-free card with an alkaline reserve should be used for window mats and mounts.

- Exhibits like paintings, not in cases, should be secured to walls or floors and cordoned off for security reasons so that visitors cannot touch them.
- A record of all items exhibited should be kept.

Loans to other institutions for consultation or for exhibition may involve risk or damage. The librarian has a duty to see that such requests, if granted, involve the borrower's making adequate provisions for safekeeping. All items should be protected against wear and damage in transit, and for security reasons the lending library may require such items to be carried both ways by personal courier, preferably a conservator or librarian.

The mounting of the exhibit should also be carried out or supervised by the courier. Loan items must be adequately insured, on an all-risks basis, again at the borrower's cost. The librarian needs to be satisfied that the conditions for exhibiting the item are appropriate on conservation grounds, and also that the security arrangements for the exhibitions are dependable.

Travelling exhibitions pose particular problems for conservation, because the likelihood of damage is multiplied. Lending institutions should make condition reports, including photographic records, of items being sent away for exhibition; they also should consider making a complete microfilm of each loan, for the sake of security.

3

Planning for Book Collections

INTRODUCTION

One of the keys to the success of any library project is to provide enough shelving to meet the requirements for planned collections. There are various ways of calculating the shelving requirements for a project, ranging from using a simple mathematical calculation based on an average number of volumes per shelving unit to using sophisticated software applications, such as Libris Design, which will calculate the shelving requirements on a collection-by-collection basis. To plan the shelving for a project, a number of decisions must be made once the size of the planned collections has been determined.

These decisions should be made during the programming phase in order to allocate enough space in the building for collections. The criteria which determine the number of bookstack units and the space required include: shelf capacity or number of volumes per shelf, shelf depth, stack height and/or number of shelves per unit, selection of single or double-faced shelving units, and aisle width.

The width, depth and aisle requirement for the stack unit will determine the footprint or amount of space required for each stack unit. The net square footage allocated for each shelving unit is the amount of space that is necessary to house the shelving unit plus space in front of the unit for a person to stand.

The net square footage typically includes regular (side) aisle space, which is shared with the adjacent shelving unit and an allotment of space for main and end aisles. Space allocation for single-faced units ranges from 10 to 14 square feet per unit and for double-faced units, from 18 to 22 square feet. The number of stack units required will be determined by the size of the collections divided by the capacity per unit.

For example: if the capacity for fiction volumes is 336 volumes per full height double-faced unit and the on-shelf collection size is projected at 3,360 volumes, then the number of stack units required will be ten. The total collection space required will be the sum of the space requirement for each individual collection. This equation is the number of units required x net square footage per unit = stack area required. The space requirement for fiction collection of 3,360 volumes is:

- 10 (units) x 18 (square feet per unit) = 180 (assignable square feet)

CAPACITY

Capacity is defined as the number of volumes capable of being shelved on a linear foot of shelf. The horizontal running length of a shelf is its linear length or width. A typical standard 3' wide section of shelving has shelves that provide three linear feet of storage per shelf. Typically, the published capacity for a collection will use volume numbers that will produce 25 per cent of excess space per shelf. The shelves will not be full using these calculations. Optimum capacity for a working collection requires shelves that are only 70 to 75 per cent full.

This extra space is not considered future growth space, but is the space required for collection management, efficient reshelving, interfiling of new acquisitions and multi-volume sets. The capacity per shelving unit will vary based on the collection being housed. The factors involved in determining the capacity are volumes per linear foot (by collection type) and number of shelves per shelving unit.

Capacity of a shelving section is then an arithmetic calculation of volumes per foot x shelf length (width) x number of shelves. A 90" high x 36" wide, single-faced shelving section, consisting of one base and six adjustable shelves would have a total of seven shelves. The equation illustrating the capacity for fiction books at eight volumes per linear foot housed on a single-faced shelving unit is:

- 8 (volumes per linear foot) x 3 (linear feet) x 7 (shelves) = 168 (volumes)

SHELVING HEIGHT

One of the most critical decisions to be made in planning for shelving is the height of the stack unit. The height of the unit will determine the number of shelves per unit, which, in turn, will determine the capacity for each unit and the number of units required to house the planned collections. Manufacturers offer shelving units in various heights. The most common standard heights are 42", 66", 78", 84" or 90" high. This height refers to the height of the vertical (upright) component of the shelving unit. Units hold from two to seven shelves per side for storing collections.

Other *non-standard* heights including 36", 45" and 60" are also available. Frequently 60" high units are substituted for 66" high units to exempt the units from the seismic requirements in the State of California which refer specifically to units *over* 60". The height of the shelving selected will depend on the type of material housed. Younger children's materials are typically shelved on 42" and

66" high units and adult and young adult materials are typically housed on higher units. The shelving height selected will vary from library to library and often depending on the requirements for supervision of a particular area with shelving over 66" high blocking sight lines. In specific cases accessibility requirements will affect the height of the shelving selected.

Accessibility

Shelving height in most collection areas is unrestricted unless an attendant will not be available, and then it is limited to 54" above the finished floor. The exception is current periodicals, which must be accessible with a maximum side reach of 54" above the finished floor (48" preferred), and a front reach of no more than 48" above the finished floor. To accommodate this reach, shelving units can be no higher than 66" inches, or three sloped display shelves high. Additionally, collections such as the large print collection should reflect the physical challenges of the elderly and the visually impaired, with shelving that is not too high or too low. Heavier materials such as automotive repair manuals, oversized books, or telephone books might also be shelved on lower units.

SHELVING DEPTH

Along with the width and aisle requirements, the shelving depth will determine the footprint or amount of space required for each stack unit. Since stack units are available in various depths, library planners must select the proper size shelf for the materials being stored.

- Flat bookshelves 8" deep are still available as standard, but are virtually never used.
- Most collections can be accommodated on a flat 10" deep bookshelf.
- The use of a 12" deep shelf is common for reference, technical or scientific collections and pre-school collections, where some substitution of a 12" divider-type shelf is desirable.
- Periodical display shelving is always designed as being a minimum of 12" deep due to the use of a 12" deep flat shelf for back issue storage.
- Most manufacturers will have available a 16" deep shelf section, which has application for oversize book storage, but may be used for flat newspaper storage, or may be outfitted with hinged periodical display shelves on a 16" deep flat storage shelf for extra deep back issue storage facilities.

STACK AISLE REQUIREMENTS

In addition to the width and depth of the shelving, the aisle allowance is the third determining factor in the amount of space allocated for each stack unit. Stack aisles are pedestrian paths located in stack areas. Stack aisles include Main Aisles, Side Aisles, Range Aisles, and End Aisles. Aisle requirements for libraries in California are found in Section 1106B.6 of Part II of Title 24 of the California Code of Regulations.

- Cross aisles that run parallel to the stack aisles, which are intended to break up the side aisles into increments, are also known as range aisles. These are required to be 36" wide to meet accessibility requirements.
- End aisles run perpendicular to side aisles and may have books on one side. These must also be a minimum of 36" wide; 44" is required in some cases.
- Main aisles are those aisles, which are the principle accessible routes, and must be a minimum of 44" wide in California.

Stack Aisles and the Americans with Disabilities Act

Aisles in stack areas must comply with accessibility requirements. Side aisles, which run parallel to stack sections, can be no longer than 20 to 21 feet (6 to 7 stack sections) without a cross aisle (range aisle) provided to break up the side aisles. Both side and range aisles are required to be 36" wide. Main aisles are principle access routes which run perpendicular to side aisles and must be a minimum of 44" wide. End aisles run perpendicular to side aisles and must be a minimum of 36" wide. They can serve a single-faced section of stacks and in certain instances 44" may be required. Range and side aisles in magazine and other display area must be a minimum of 44" wide.

Stack Aisles and Column Spacing

In addition to planning the space required to house collections, determining the aisle requirements early in the project can provide valuable information to the architect and structural engineer. The stack aisle requirement and the column spacing should be coordinated to create a satisfactory stack layout. Without this advance coordination valuable space can be lost when aisles are blocked or valuable stack units lost to unexpected columns. In planning the structural requirements, a bay or module is the space between four columns and with good planning this dimension should equal some multiple of the stack unit width and the shelving aisle requirement.

A 2' base shelf with a 3' aisle requirement would indicate an ideal column bay of some multiple of 5' in at least one direction. This would typically be a distance of 25' from one column to another. Including the column dimensions for a 6" square column, the measurement is taken from mid-column to mid-column to produce an ideal module of 25'6". If 4' aisles are requested, then the column bay would be based on a 6' module and 24'6" or 30'6" might be the ideal module. The dimension in the other direction might be based on multiples of 3' with a 6" column at the end of every 5th or 6th range depending on the structural requirements of the facility.

SINGLE-FACED OR DOUBLE-FACED

The decision to use single-faced or double-faced units is usually a design decision made when the furniture, equipment, and shelving are being drawn onto the floor plans. Occasionally libraries will require that certain collections, such as genre fiction, be housed on perimeter shelving, thus requiring single-faced units. Unless called out for a specific reason, this decision can be deferred until the schematic design phase and units can be calculated in either single-faced or double-faced equivalents. The only advantage to specifying double-faced units is that in a normal design condition, there can be a slightly more efficient use of space when double-faced units are utilized

BOOKSTACK DIMENSIONS

Manufacturers of wood library shelving follow a standard format of overall section heights and depths. The same is true for manufacturers of steel cantilever-style shelving; however, it is a different dimensional format from that adopted by wood shelving manufacturers. A critical difference between wood and steel shelving manufacturers occurs when dimensions are published.

- Wood Shelving: Industry-standard width for wood shelving section is: 36" wide. All other widths are generally considered custom widths, and are factory-manufactured to actual field dimensions and carry a price increase.
- Cantilever-style Steel Shelving: Industry-standard width for a steel shelving section is: 36" wide, with 30" and 24" wide widths available. It is very rare for a steel shelving manufacturer to factory-build shelving to custom widths.

CANTILEVER-STYLE STEEL SHELVING DIMENSIONS

Cantilever-style steel shelving manufacturers dimensions are considered to be nominal. A double-faced, Cantilever-style steel shelving that is described as " a section is 84" high x 24" deep" is, in fact, 84" in overall height, but actually somewhere close to 24-." in depth. A singlefaced, cantilever-style steel shelving that is described as " a section is 84" high x 12" deep" is, in fact, 84" in overall height, but actually somewhere close to 13-." in depth. When developing shelving space plans utilizing Cantilever-style steel shelving, this is a critical concept to master, especially where space is tight and one must struggle to maintain adequate legal and accessible aisles. Growth is a dimension concept used in applying actual stack unit dimensions to actual plan layout and physical building spaces. Conceptually, growth is the factoring in of actual stack unit depths that are greater than published nominal dimensions, plus the growth in length of assembled ranges due to the insertion of reinforcing gussets between frames, as their thickness increases the length. Often, architectural floor plans are drawn using nominal dimensions, therefore, it is important to realize that the aisle will be diminished in width by the amount of growth which results from factoring in the oversize actual shelving dimensions. One should also add from ö." to 2" to the shelving width dimension when including decorative end panels at range ends, as aisle width will be determined by clearance between end panel edges at the entrance end of the aisle.

WOOD SHELVING DIMENSIONS

Wood library shelving dimensions are considered to be actual dimensions. Wood shelving that is described as "a section is 82" high x 24" deep" are exactly, and actually, those overall height and depth dimensions.

SEISMIC ISSUES

Due to the frequency and potential severity of seismic activity throughout the State of California, this study on the design, features, and use of shelving must accordingly address these seismic forces and their potential impact on both the construction and installation of library shelving. The task of attempting to resist the vertical and lateral forces created in an earthquake requires structurally enhanced shelving structures and special anchoring procedures in installation.

This requirement originates in the Uniform Building Code which identifies structural performance standards for any shelving over 5'-0" high. In seismic zones 2B-3-4, bolt type, 3/8" diameter sway braces are utilized, 1 pair every fourth section zone 2B; 1 pair every third section zone 3; and 1 pair every other section zone 4; a pyramidal shaped 13 gauge web stiffener 6" wide at bottom and 3" wide at the top, welded to base brackets and uprights 60" high and higher is utilized.

Floor anchors, ICBO approved, are required. Only in recent years have most shelving manufacturers fabricated the special reinforcing components needed to satisfy California Seismic Code compliance. These special components must be specifically ordered along with standard shelving structures, and are fitted into the assemblies at the time the shelving is installed. The installation process not only includes the assembly of such specially reinforced structures, but also the requirement to anchor all assemblies in place.

In this process, wall shelving would be secured to some structural element in the walls at the tops of the sections, plus, floor anchored to resist vertical forces. Freestanding, or island sections, usually double-faced, must be floor anchored. The anchoring hardware is heavy-duty, with specific size, content and insertion details determined by a structural engineering evaluation. The structural nature of cantilever-style steel shelving is unique and as such, all manufacturers follow a nearly identical retrofitting concept to enhance the standard shelving structures in longitudinal and lateral strength.

LIBRARY SHELVING INSTALLATION

As compared with a typical Midwestern state where a manufacturer's standard shelving unit is assembled, ganged into a range and perhaps levelled in place but left truly free-standing with wall shelving only anchored into drywall at the top, a California library shelving installation is much more demanding:

- A floor-anchored installation requires additional use of shims to produce a level and plumb shelving range installation.
- Because shelving is required to be anchored in place, it is considered to be part of the building structure, which results in the requirement that the shelving installation contractor be licensed to perform this specialty work. Installation of shelving in California requires a minimum C-61 Specialty Contractors License on the part of the organization doing the work.

Professional Review

Shelving installations in new construction fall under the responsibility of the architect, and are pursuant to all applicable Federal, State and local codes, plus, any local governing control responsibility, such as Fire Department review. A complete set of documents consisting of floor plan layout and product engineering drawings, including structural calculations carrying the stamp of a licensed structural engineer are required. A less-extensive installation may require only written documents from the vendor/installer verifying that the installation meets commonly accepted standards.

CANTILEVER-STYLE STEEL SHELVING

Cantilever-style, or bracket, steel shelving systems are the most widely used book shelving and multimedia storage and display. This type of shelving, when installed to meet California seismic standards is very strong, very flexible, and the most economical solution for library shelving. The individual components are manufactured of 16-gauge to 18-gauge cold rolled carbon steel sheet. The uprights have elongated holes or slots in one-inch increments to allow for the easy adjustment and relocation of the shelves. As standard, this type of shelving will not include a canopy top or end panels. Such items along with many other features are considered accessories to be specified separately. Cantilever-style steel shelving is available as both single-faced and double-faced in a wide range of unit heights and depths. Standard width is generally 36", but 30" units can also be purchased. Standard heights are 42", 66", 78", 84" or 90", but custom heights can be fabricated by changing the dimension of the vertical support column.

Cantilever-style Shelf Dimensions

Shelf depth is typically described as a *nominal* dimension and shelving height and width are typically described as an *actual* dimension. Because the structural framework is an open-centered frame, in most cases, 2" deep, a 2" void exists behind the adjustable shelves. To calculate shelf depths, the centerline of this void (1" deep) is considered the rear edge line of the shelf space. In its definition, a shelving section would be specified to have a nominal 10" deep shelf, for example. In fact, the shelf itself if measured with a tape measure is actually 9" deep, with 1" of the rear void attributed to shelf depth, thus totalling 10" deep. This concept applies whether single-faced or double-faced construction. In the case of single-faced shelving, there will actually be the full 2" deep void into which materials can penetrate. This translates into an actual 9" deep shelf producing 11" of storage depth. Again, this 2" void space seems like "found" space, and it affords flexibility in shelving odd-sized or some oversized materials.

The exception to this is slotted divider type shelves. Since the adjustable dividers require a high back edge on the shelf for engagement, the divider shelf, when described as being nominally 12" deep, would be actually 11" deep due to the loss of access into the void space. The disadvantage of this void space is that books are often carelessly pushed back into this void, with the potential for small books to become dislodged, falling down into the void. To overcome this, there are two options:

- Option #1: Substitute an integral back-style shelf for the standard flat shelf. The integral back shelf has an "upturned" lip along the rear edge, resulting in the net actual depth of the shelf being the total storage depth.
- Option #2: Add a shelf space backstop accessory, which hooks into the frame above the flat shelf surface, thereby resulting in the net actual depth of the shelf being the total storage depth.

Cantilever-style shelving – Components and Options

Base Shelves

The impact of this 2" frame void carries into the base shelf as well. Most manufacturers produce a one-piece flat base shelf, which bridges the 2" void to produce a closed, flush shelf surface. In addition, the flat shelf usually will be of one-piece construction, including the toe kicks formed along outer edges. A manufacturer may choose to make a two-piece base shelf that butts against and is flush on the topside, with an infill piece 2" wide at the frame, providing an essentially flush base assembly. An integral back type base shelf becomes a two-piece base, and the upturned lip on the rear edge fits against the frame with the open void left inside the frames at the bottom.

Optional Sloped Base Shelf

Sloped base shelves serve the purpose of canting the books such that the spine titles and call number can be more easily read. Most manufacturers offer an optional two-piece sloped base shelf that also fits flat against the frame face leaving a void in the frame opening at the bottom. Some manufacturers construct their base assemblies using a flat base shelf component used in conjunction with a mechanically attached toe kick as a separate piece. Regardless of the design used, a closed base shelving system always provides the benefit of concealing all attaching brackets and anchoring hardware that are a necessity in California shelving installations.

Canopy Tops

Other than on case-style shelving where a canopy top is integral to the structure, this component is an accessory. A canopy top is a finish detail available for stack sections of all heights. Typically canopy tops are specified for sections under 72" in height, or below eye level, but they can be used for units of all sizes.

The canopy top can be used as an additional worksurface, storage shelf, as a means of keeping the collection dust free, and as a means of producing a limited amount of added strength to the shelving range. Canopy tops are available in a variety of materials, including laminated particleboard, solid wood or metal, with unlimited options available in colour and finish material. Typically the architect or interior designer specifies the finish material for canopy tops as part of the design process. The preferred style of canopy top is one which is made as a one-piece special component which completely covers the top of the supporting structure, and is designed to have a good size dropped edge fascia along the front edge. This achieves as close to a flush-enclosed top as possible. Some canopy tops are made up of parts which cantilever from the vertical columns, and butt against the top horizontal cross spreader of the structure. This style may not have the benefit of as large a dropped-edge fascia on the front edge.

End Panels

End panels, whether a structural part, such as on wood or metal case-style shelving, or, as a finished range end closure, on Cantilever-style shelving, are, as standard, very plain in appearance. In most library installations, a decorative end panel is applied on range ends to add a design element and likely, a functional feature where range signage can be applied.

Typically the architect or interior designer on the project would design these decorative end panels. There is usually a design scheme being followed which ties together the finest points in architectural millwork, the design statement followed through in furniture, and a related expression in the design of decorative end panels. Such end panels will be custom, and it is often advisable to include their manufacture as a millwork item from the Subcontractor on the job or, as an extension of the furniture contract from the supplier of the library furniture. Decorative end panels might involve the use of furniture woods and veneers, laminates, or a combination that results in a need for furniture grade finishes. Such finishes vary with wood species and depend on colour choices required, which is why decorative end panels are frequently considered to be furniture rather than shelving.

Filler Units

Frequently either the architectural design or the interior layout will require the use of filler units. These units are required to fill an architectural void, which is created when one of several conditions exists.

Corner Fillers

When wall shelving ranges meet at an inside corner, a void is created. A twosided, panel-type enclosure obscures this visually, and would be furnished with a top panel to prevent debris from getting inside the closed off void.

Intermediate Filler

When a double-faced unit is placed perpendicular to a wall mounted singlefaced shelving range, a large void occurs.

End Filler

When wall shelving ranges do not completely fill a wall area from end-to-end, it adds to the overall finished appearance of the installation if two-sided, panel-type enclosures are added at one or both ends of the range to obscure the void and close off the front and top of the opening. These voids can be furred out and filled in with drywall and/or plaster by the general contractor instead of utilizing a fabricated piece provided by the shelving manufacturer to enclose the void.

ACQUISITION OF LIBRARY SHELVING

THE MARKETPLACE

The marketing practices of shelving manufacturers may have some effect on how shelving is selected or specified for a library. Manufacturers of wood shelving, or wood-and-steelcombination shelving, are predominantly library furniture manufacturers, and distribute their products through furniture vendors. Distribution of cantilever-style steel shelving may or may not be through a furniture vendor.

The demands for quality installation performance is evident in all categories, but reaches critical importance when confronting the assembly and installation of cantilever-style steel shelving in the State of California. Cantilever-style steel shelving manufacturers will typically appoint a single distribution vendor for their product in any given market area. That distributor is responsible for bringing the value-added elements of local sales support, customer service, product service, provision of engineering documents, and finally, the skilled labour familiar with the product being used. Local representation for a shelving manufacturer can be located by calling the manufacturer directly, usually at their toll free number.

PRODUCT UNIFORMITY

Considering the limitations on the number of shelving products applicable for use in the State of California, and, in an analysis of each individual construction feature, one will find great uniformity in specification. When installed to meet the mandates of California seismic requirements, there is little difference among shelving products fabricated by different manufacturers.

SPECIFICATIONS AND BIDDING

The prime purpose for following a bid procedure when procuring shelving is to be able to make the purchase at the lowest possible cost. In that context, this procedure has merit for most initial purchases. A separate document, *Furniture and Shelving: Specification and Bidding,* available on the Libris Design web site details the various options for a bid process, sole source and proprietary specifications, detailed specification writing, and specific bid conditions and requirements. The vendor will be required to submit a shelving layout plan, which is similar to a furniture plan. This submittal must include a seismic calculation report and a stamped original signed by the structural engineer who performed the calculations. The cost of this engineering study is typically included in the shelving bid.

The vendor will also provide shop drawings showing the installation details as well as any details required for lighting installation or custom end panels or canopy tops if included in the shelving package. In addition to the stamped installation plans and the shop drawings, the shelving vendor will submit a shelving *schedule*, which will outline the quantity and location for each specific shelving type, included in the contract. At this time, it will be wise for the librarian to "check it twice." With plans, shelving schedule, building programme, and calculator in hand, the librarian should count the shelving units on the plan. This can often be the last chance to avoid a serious mistake.

SHELVING INSTALLATION

Closed base shelving in a new installation should be installed over the fully carpeted floor. To have carpeting installed around already-installed shelving will greatly increase the carpet installation cost, and will achieve no significant cost savings on the carpet. There is no cost difference in either option (over carpet or over floor), although installing over carpet places a heavy responsibility on the shelving contractor to avoid soiling or damaging the carpet during the installation process. For open base shelving installations, the installation will always be done over finished, carpeted floors. Typically the installer will lay out the entire installation using chalk marks or strings to outline the locations of stack units and aisles. The vertical frames are uncrated and positioned in their future locations. Since freestanding units over 60" high will require bolting to the slab to meet the seismic zone requirements, most installers will "burn" or "melt" a small patch of the carpet for each bolt before they begin drilling to avoid pulling zippers and damaging the carpet material.

It will be important for the librarian or project manager to instruct the shelving installers on any specific shelf spacing requirements or adjustments to the number of shelves to be installed in each unit. Specifying which units will have six shelves and which will have seven shelves will save countless time making these adjustments later. The installer will have a complete set of shop drawings with the location and shelving type for the entire job, but any special requests or changes to this should be made before the installation begins.

The Owner's final responsibility will be to perform a punch list, or thorough inspection of the shelving installation. Usually minor nicks or dings to the paint can be touched up on site, and the shelving vendor should leave behind some of this touch up paint for future nicks and dings. Occasionally however, units will be poorly manufactured, painted, or damaged in transit. These defective units must be rejected and a specific deadline for replacement must be agreed upon.

A small percentage of final payment may be withheld until this has been accomplished.

SHELVING RELOCATION

Relocation of shelving is a complicated task in California because all shelving must be anchored in place. As a result, any relocation becomes a significant task. Because a properly installed shelving installation is considered part of the permanent building structure, a specialty contractor must be hired to do the work.

Relocating shelving within an existing facility may provide an unexpected and expensive surprise if the building at some point has been re-carpeted and now after the shelving has been moved, well-preserved strips of the original unfaded carpet appear where the old shelving once stood. If re-carpeting the area had not been part of the scope of work, it may now become a necessity. Relocation of shelving in long ranges as assembled is not possible. If relocated within the same large area, the ranges may be broken down into manageable groupings for reassembly in new locations. Parts should be carefully labelled and stored. Other than this, relocation must be interpreted as disassembly, moving and reassembly.

CANTILEVER-STYLE SHELVING ACCESSORIES

Stack (range) Signage

Stack or range finding signage decisions should be made at the earliest planning stage. An interior designer who has responsibility for the furniture design and specification and the signage design would provide an added benefit in coordination. Sign manufacturers can produce custom designed and fabricated stack signage. Manufacturers offer range finder components and cardholders as accessories that can be attached to the end panels.

Multimedia Storage and Display Shelving

The broad diversity in multimedia materials makes their storage and display complicated. All shelving manufacturers offer several types of accessory shelves or other inserts such as browser bins and sliding trays which connect into their standard framework. It will be necessary for the library shelving specifier, knowing the nature of materials to be housed, to consult with the selected shelving vendor to determine the best possible solutions. Planners should pay special attention to required shelving depths for multimedia shelving units which can range in depth from 6" to 16" for browsing bins.

Further, it is critical to note that a full height unit may not be desirable, since patrons may prefer not to browse on the bottom shelf, or above eye level height. In cases where specific multimedia shelves are specified, decisions about the shelving height and depth are critical. These restrictions must be taken into consideration when calculating the number of stack sections required for multimedia units. In many cases, separate, freestanding furniture or display units specifically designed for media may prove to be superior solutions for the task, but they will not provide the flexibility of the Cantilever-style steel shelving unit.

Book Supports

The most popular type of book support is the plate-type book support. These are available in two heights (6" & 9") and are selected according to size of books or materials being shelved. The simplest design is one formed from sheet metal and is only the thickness of the metal material, which is approximately 1/16" thick. This style can be easily lost between books, or knifed inside of books as patrons re-shelve after browsing in the stacks. A second plate-type book support design is manufactured as a stamped part. This is strong and durable and has the added design feature of folded "flanges" towards the outside.

This creates a support surface which is."-." or more in thickness and is more easily findable when sandwiched between books which is why these are called *findable* book supports. Findable book supports are also manufactured in molded plastic. These are less durable and will support less weight than the steel findable supports. All of the plate-type book supports have an add-on option of a cork-surfaced bottom. The cork surface increases the grip against the shelf while protecting the shelf from being damaged. These findable book supports are available from either the shelving vendor or from library product catalogs. Wire-type book supports are another option available for cantilever-style shelving. The simplest is a formed wire bail, which is either long or short in the vertical dimension. This piece connects into the underside formed edges of the metal shelf. There is a similar formed bail that is attached by a compression fit into only one of the underside formed edges of the metal shelf above. These two types of book supports hang from an upper shelf to support books or materials on the shelf below.

Unless the topmost shelf in a section has a canopy top outfitted to receive the wire book support, one substitute plate-type support must be specified for each topmost shelf. These are the least popular type of book support as they frequently bend from the weight of the collections. Many manufacturers of metal shelves provide an adjustable shelf option with an upturned edge at the back of the shelf or *integral back shelf*. A wire-type book support that has a connector for attaching and sliding along this raised edge is available for this type of metal shelving. Some cantilever-style shelving includes a wire-type book support that attaches to and moves within a formed metal track that attaches to the shelving frame at the back of individual shelves.

Retractable Reference Shelves

Pullout reference shelves are available as an accessory option from manufacturers of metal shelving. They are provided as a convenience to patrons browsing in the reference bookstacks. These shelves are installed by being connected to the underside of an adjustable shelf, rather than attached to the shelving structural elements. It is important to critically evaluate the design and construction of this component, particularly as to the underside operable details where unfinished or sharp fabrication elements could result in damage to bookbindings or personal injury when accessing materials on the immediate shelf below.

Newspaper Shelves

The least popular method for display of newspapers is the old traditional wood newspaper sticks, which can hang into the shelving structure on special inclined brackets. The simplest display method is to stack the half-folded newspapers on a flat (minimum 12" deep) shelf. The most costly and most satisfactory method of display is to place the half-folded Newspaper on a typical sloped periodical shelf having the J-shaped lip at the bottom, installed on lower sloped brackets. This would accommodate two or three editions per shelf, and the special installation instructions must be called out in written specifications. The ultimate enhancement is to equip the sloped shelf with a pair of hinged, clear acrylic (plastic) covers to hold down the individual newspapers displayed on the shelf.

Periodical Display Shelving

Periodical display shelving provides a display surface for current periodicals with back issue storage below. The display shelves are sloped and are either fixed in position or hinged to side brackets allowing them to be lifted for better access to the back issue storage shelf. All sloped shelves should have a J-shaped retaining lip at the bottom edge. This is generally standard on hinged-typed periodical shelves, but not generally standard on fixed-type periodical sloping display shelves. The J-shaped feature should be specifically called for on fixed-type periodical display shelves. The J-shaped retaining lip feature allows for the installation of signage labels on the face of the upturned lip. An optional signage attachment fitting can be specified for this purpose.

Slotted Divider Shelves

Divider-type shelving is an optional accessory shelf, which comes with a number of adjustable vertical support members that fit into slots in the surface of the shelf. These metal dividers can be used to create contained compartments on the shelf area providing extra support for heavy use or larger format collections which might typically fall over; or they can provide space management to control storage space for items such as back issues of periodicals or telephone directories. These are most frequently used for picture books, small bound materials such as literacy materials, or heavy materials such as reference collections. These are among the most desirable types of shelves available, but the cost per individual unit makes extensive use cost prohibitive.

Top Tie Struts and Stack Lighting

Top tie struts are horizontal overhead beams that connect a bank of stack ranges. They are a manufactured accessory and are more widely used outside of Seismic Zones 3 and 4 than in the State of California. In these areas outside of California, top ties are used to add stability and eliminate shake due to the fact that sections are installed as truly freestanding stacks, having no internal added reinforcement and are not anchored in place. They do not meet the seismic requirements for Seismic Zone 4 and in some cases their use has been determined to be the cause of stack failure in a seismic event. These top tie members are sometimes used as supports for bookstack aisle lighting fixtures. This approach to stack aisle lighting though very simplistic, has several shortcomings:

- The resultant installation usually lacks finesse in its aesthetic detail.

- Unless the light baffles are narrowly spaced there is the possibility that removal of a book from a top shelf can break the lamp.
- It leaves the fixture so low that, it does not adequately distribute light to the top row of shelves, and being so low, it allows exposure to tampering.

These points can be corrected by fabricating a riser structure above the shelving frames, onto which top tie members are attached, leaving the light fixture high enough to distribute light to the top shelf area, and placing fixtures out of normal reach.

Stack-mounted Light Fixtures

The incorporation of stack attached light fixtures is neither simple nor inexpensive in California seismic zones. The addition of such structures adds a weight load to the shelving systems, and impacts the structural engineering and design of reinforcement and installation. Because there is no standard solution to this problem, the architect or designer needs to carefully design the details to avoid an unsatisfactory installation. Unless bookstack-supported lighting is the only design solution, this approach should be thoroughly analysed in comparison with strategically placed building lighting. While it takes coordination between building trades, the careful placement of pendant-supported fixtures can work well as aisle lighting.

Bookstack Aisle Lighting

Bookstack aisle lighting is typically a central aisle fixture distributing light to stack faces on both sides of an aisle. Once the bookstack space plan has been finalized, the services of a lighting consultant are essential in specifying the proper light fixture. Many shelving manufacturers have standard light fixture accessories that hook into the shelving systems at the top of the support columns. These are cantilevered canopy-type assemblies which either function like display case lighting, or, others cantilever outward far enough to provide down light on the whole face of the section. These are expensive components, and one must use two of these accessories to light both faces of a double-faced stack section.

It is important to remember that whenever using any style of stack-supported lighting, that a number of electrical stub-in locations (rough-ins) must be accurately determined. Coordination of dimensioned drawings must take place between the shelving vendor and electrical contractor early on in the construction process, unless the architect accepts the responsibility of detailing these placements. There are many issues related to stack lighting including the widely disagreed upon foot-candle requirement, the debate of direct and indirect lighting, and the pros and cons of parallel vs. perpendicular lighting installation.

CASE-STYLE SHELVING PRODUCTS

Case-style shelving refers to any type of shelving system that uses a full panel, vertical component from floor to top with adjustable shelves or supports which engages at ends into these vertical panels. This style of shelving will always have a closed base shelf assembly, and a canopy top. Case-style shelving is available in plastic laminate on chip core or particleboard, wood or metal. Such shelving is constructed in single-faced and doubled-faced versions, and may be used with or without back panels however; if double-faced models are used without back panels, some longitudinal bracing members must be added.

Case-style shelving is generally considered to be finished in appearance, and, for that reason, is most frequently used in meeting rooms, workrooms or offices, where an aesthetics override the structural, cost or flexibility requirements. An architect or interior designer will typically specify such shelving for what is referred to as a *contract interior*. When built-in case-style shelving is specified by a design professional for new or renovation construction, they will often refer to the shelving as casework or millwork.

Millwork shelving would be described as being of wood material, or, plastic laminate material construction, and built by a custom-fabricator for specific application to the construction project. Specifications for millwork construction are taken from published standards in casework construction. These standards are available from the Architectural Woodworking Institute or the Woodworking Institute of California. Under these standards, the shelving is considered to be a form of cabinet, and is built using general casework standards.

These specifications would be published as part of the project construction specification document. A review of the millwork shelving specifications should be made to insure that the adjustable shelf material provides load bearing strength to support a full shelf of books (approximately 100 pounds) without significant sagging. Library staff should also review the methods and hardware proposed for shelf adjustability for their practical use as well. When case-style shelving is specified as a manufactured shelving system in either wood or metal, it will be published under a *Special Equipment* category in the project specifications, and the exact requirements for the product and its use will be published.

Manufactured Wood (Case-style) Shelving

Wood shelving systems, by furniture manufacturers, will be offered according to their printed product specifications. Products will vary, as with millwork shelving, and again, the most important component is the adjustable shelf. Traditionally, all quality manufacturers have offered a solid hardwood lumber shelf, glued up in strips according to published woodworking standards. This produces a planked shelf that may or may not use the same hardwood species as that used for the case enclosure. The solid hardwood lumber aspect is critical. Adjustability is also important. Wood shelving products have evolved, in light of market competition, to being constructed more along the lines of custom millwork. The prime result of this move towards custom millwork is that shelf adjustability now tends to follow the 32mm spacing (1-.") that results from the use of European woodworking machinery.

This spacing, fine for cabinetry, presents problems in efficient book shelving spacing. Specifiers and librarians should be alert to this nuance when evaluating products for potential use. Wood library shelving systems, being a furniture manufacturer's product, will be offered in that manufacturer's standard wood species. These most likely are red oak or hard maple. When other wood species, such as walnut, cherry or ash are specified, the manufacturer applies price premiums that greatly increase the cost of wood shelving. Manufactured, modular-shelving systems will have basic accessory options available, such as periodical display, newspaper stick display and divider-type shelves. Back panel options for this type of wood shelving can be of wood veneer plywood, or, painted hardboard. The back panel in double-faced shelving serves as a structural component as well; thus when double- faced sections are installed without back panels, an added longitudinal brace option must be installed.

Metal (Case-style) Shelving

Case-style metal modular shelving systems have become the least popular shelving type and are now available from only a few sources. The most important feature in metal case shelving is that the upright end panels are flat on the inside shelf space, thus eliminating the ribs that books can be jammed against, potentially breaking the bindings. This type of shelving will have accessories for periodical display, divider-type shelves, retractable reference shelves and perhaps, newspaper display. The back panels in metal case-style shelving are also made of sheet metal and are not costly. In the installation of double-faced shelving, the back panel serves as a structural component as well as a separator between faces. Without the use of a back panel, an additional longitudinal brace must be added.

COMPACT SHELVING STORAGE

Compact shelving, which is also referred to as High Density, Moveable Aisle or MAC shelving, is a shelving system that rides on moveable carriages over floor-installed rails. The rails can be either surface mounted or set in the concrete when the slab is poured. Compact shelving units are now available with both manual and electrically operated chassis and with safety devices which cause the movement of the carriage to stop if it makes contact with an object (book truck) or a human. The benefit of compact shelving is to maximize use of floor space by having one access aisle, which is relocatable by moving the carriage mounted shelving to open an access aisle at a desired location. This arrangement can eliminate as many as five or six side aisles for an enormous space savings. By decreasing the aisle width requirement to one single relocatable accessible aisle, the amount of space required to house collections can be cut in one-half, at a minimum, and up to one-third for a larger installation. Because of the cost of the installation and the equipment, small installations are not recommended.

The benefits of cantilever-style steel shelving as a strong yet flexible system is reinforced in its use on moveable carriages for compact shelving installations. In this context, a storage shelving system appropriate for that use is furnished on the moveable carriages. When specifying systems for library use (book shelving), it is specify the cantilever-style steel shelving rather than storage shelving, which a compact shelving vendor might otherwise be predisposed to recommend.

The installation of compact shelving requires advance planning if the rail upon which the carriages ride is to be imbedded in the concrete slab. This installation provides a smooth flat floor and the carpet can be installed right up to the edge of the rail.

When the rail is installed later and surface mounted on the concrete slab, it will be necessary to create mini-ramps using plywood or other flooring material in order to provide a smooth, flat, and accessible path through the compact shelving units. Because of the increased load bearing requirements, the architect and structural engineers should be informed early in project of any planned or future compact shelving installation.

MULTI-TIER STACK CORE

Multi-tier stack cores are specially-engineered and constructed steel shelving systems which are assembled as two or more tiers of shelving sections in which the upper level support members are integral to the stack system and separate from any building structural elements. Extremely popular a number of years ago, the system incorporates floors for upper level access aisles and stairwells for passage between tiers. Because of the extreme California seismic structural demands, this type of system is generally not used in California.

This type of shelving construction can also present difficulty in meeting disabled access requirements due to narrower aisle widths. The low ceiling heights (typically 7'6" high) can make installation of fire sprinklers difficult as well. An existing multi-stack tier can usually be *grand-fathered in* when a full update to current code is required, but the low ceiling heights and requirements of a multi-stop elevator will often make demolition a necessity.

SECURITY AND DISASTER PLANNING IN LIBRARY

SECURITY

It is the responsibility of the library manager to intitiate, coordinate, and implement the development of a security policy within the library. When drafting such a policy other libraries, police, and staff should be consulted.

Securing Perimeters and Buildings

- Library perimeters and grounds should be kept tidy.
- Building exteriors should be assessed for ease of access by criminals. An alarm and closed-circuit television system should be seriously considered. All areas should be well-lit.
- Close attention should be paid to doors and windows in respect of locks, security glass, or film.
- The interior of the building should be kept tidy. It will present an image of care and supervision which will deter the potential criminal.
- All entry/exit points and routes should be kept separate if possible and staffed at all times.
- Any staff areas should be locked when not in use.
- Expensive equipment should be chained or bolted down and marked with security markings.
- All contractors should sign in and out of the library and wear passes at all times.
- The need for an alert attitude should be instilled in staff.
- All storage areas should be kept secure and clear policy guidelines provided on who has access to what areas.
- Specific measures, like the use of vaults, should be taken for the security of rare/valuable material.

Preventing Criminal and Anti-social Behaviour

Criminal and anti-social behaviour ranges from the rowdy visitor to the determined thief. Staff, books, equipment, and personal property are all at risk.

Starting-points in deterring criminal and anti-social behaviour include:

- Having a calm and ordered library
- Creating an environment which the genuine reader regards as helpful and efficient, but in which the villain feels anxious and wary
- Having prominent notices which clearly define what is unacceptable behaviour
- Training staff in how to deal with an awkward or aggressive user or a suspected book thief.

Security in Reading Areas

Points to consider:

- How are loose items issued and how are they checked on return?
- How well are reading areas invigilated?
- Are security devices in place?
- Are bags allowed in these areas and are they checked on exit?

Security of Library Material

All library material should be stamped in a way that clearly identifies it as belonging to a particular institution. Library stamps should be fast-drying, non-fading, stable, and indelible. Security tagging systems, if present, should be regularly inspected.

Emergency Information Booklet

It is useful for all staff to have easy access to an emergency information booklet which lists only the immediate steps to be taken, key personnel, and how they can be contacted in the event of:

- Accidents to staff and visitors
- Vandalism, theft, and assault
- Incidents like power failures, lift failures, loss of security keys
- Emergencies which threaten the welfare of people, the collections, and the fabric of the buildings – *e.g.* bomb threats
- Hurricane, earthquake, and flood warnings.

DISASTER PLANNING

It is vital for any library, no matter what its size, to take every precaution possible to prevent the occurrence of an avoidable disaster. Of equal importance is having measures in place to cope with the consequences of disasters, whether they be natural or man-made.

Natural:

- Hurricanes
- Floods
- Earthquakes
- Volcanic eruptions
- Sandstorms

Man-made:

- Acts of war and terrorism
- Fires
- Water (broken pipes, leaking roofs, etc.)
- Explosions

Numerous resources have been published to aid institutions in implementing disaster avoidance measures and formulating a disaster response and salvage plan. Only the key points are listed here.

It should be mandatory for every library to have a written plan in which all these elements are fully developed. A 'phased' approach can be used in disaster preparedness (as it can in preservation activities in general). That is, it is acceptable, as a first phase, to begin with a few parts (even in outline form), particularly if the institution focuses first on those issues that are of greatest concern.

In a subsequent phase, the planners can gradually add more detail and other parts as they become better educated, have time to pursue the plan, and are able to develop consensus on how the institution should organize its preparedness activities.

Disaster planning usually involves five phases:

- Risk assessment ascertaining the dangers to the building and its collections
- Prevention implementing measures which will remove or reduce any danger
- Preparedness developing a written preparedness, response, and recovery plan
- Response procedures to follow when disaster strikes
- Recovery restoring the disaster site and damaged material to a stable and usable condition.

RISK ASSESSMENT

Try to identify any external and internal threats that might cause problems for the collections and assess any shortcomings of disaster prevention measures which are already in place. Consulting with fire departments will help to find any potential hazards which are not immediately obvious.

Identifying External Environmental Threats

- Describe the district where the collections are housed (residential, industrial, shopping centre, rural, recreational).
- Are there any major industrial or natural hazards very close to where the collections are housed (airport, railroad/motorway, natural waterways such as the ocean, lakes, rivers, natural vegetation or bushland, other buildings)?
- What are the immediate surroundings or perimeters to the building (fences and gates, natural barriers such as rivers, lakes, ocean front, dark corners, overhangs, areas providing cover)?
- Are the surroundings secure (regular patrols, effective lighting, gates secured and access controlled, separate access for staff and visitors/ users)?
- Is pollution (dust, gaseous pollutants) from factories, traffic, or the environment a problem?
- How safe is the building from fire and flood – are there hazards in the vicinity, either natural as in woodland and river or man-made, as in petrochemical plants?
- Have any major incidents or disasters occurred in the past five years (bomb threats and bombing, civil disturbances, riots, wars, natural disasters – flood, earthquake, fire, dust storm, vandalism)?

Identifying Internal Environmental Threats

- What materials are used in the structure of the building?
- Is the external and internal fabric of the building fire-resistant?
- Are there fire-resistant walls separating parts of the building and are there fireresistant doors?
- Are collections stored at a safe distance from plumbing, electrical and mechanical installations-water pipes, radiators, air conditioning, kitchens, laboratories?
- Is the area where collections are stored susceptible to leaks or flooding?
- Is smoking allowed in any areas?
- Are large amounts of flammable material (like chemicals in laboratories) other than books stored on site?

Assessing Current Preventive Measures

- Has the building a smoke, fire or water detection system?
- Is there an automatic fire extinguishing system in the area?
- What sort of manual fire fighting systems are in the area (extinguishers – water, foam, CO_2, fire hoses etc.)?
- Are the fire detection and/or extinguishing systems inspected regularly?
- Does the building have lightning conductors?
- Are special precautions taken when potentially dangerous activities are undertaken, such as rewiring and refurbishing of the internal and external fabric of the building?
- Is the building security system (if there is one) connected to fire/police departments?
- Does a written disaster preparedness and response plan exist for the library? Elements it should contain: description of emergency procedures; disaster response outline; emergency supplies list; recovery priorities; conservation experts; supplies stored off-site; list of staff volunteers; other.
- Are staff trained in emergency response procedures (delegated officer-in-charge, regular training, emergency evacuations)?
- Is computer data backed up daily?
- Are manually accessed catalogues, registration and accession records duplicated and stored off-site?
- Are electronic catalogues and records duplicated and stored off-site?

PREVENTION

Once the risks have been assessed, take all the necessary precautions to make the library buildings and their holdings secure. Consult with the emergency services (fire, police, and hospital).

Fire Alarm Systems

All parts of the building should be provided with a fire and smoke detection system, which simultaneously alerts occupants and the local fire brigade. Smoke detection equipment can provide early warning of a developing fire, thereby giving an opportunity of manual suppression prior to the activation of a sprinkler system. Manually operated fire-alarm call points, which can be used by occupants to indicate the presence of fire or smoke, should also be present throughout the building.

Manual Extinguishing Systems

If an automatic fire extinguishing system is not present, the following should be installed:

- Hose reels or racks so as to ensure that all parts of the building are within 6 m of the nozzle of a fully extended hose.
- Hydrant systems or rising mains on all buildings more than 30 m in height or where a single floor exceeds 1000 m^2.
- The hydrant or rising mains should be located so as to permit the fire brigade to pressurise the pipework from outside the building.
- Portable fire extinguishers should always be available, even if an automatic fire suppression system has been installed. There should be a suitable number of hand-held extinguishers (CO_2, water, or foam according to the likely cause of fire, *i.e.,* electrical or chemical) strategically placed.

Automatic Extinguishing Systems

Consideration should be given to the benefits offered by an automatic fire extinguishing system.

- A CO_2 gas system is only suitable for smaller compartments, *i.e.,* spaces which can be made airtight and which are not normally occupied by people.
- Halon gas systems are no longer produced as they are environmentally damaging, particularly towards the earth's protective ozone layer.
- Wet-pipe sprinkler systems are a reliable and safe extinguishing method and are relatively easy to maintain. Contrary to popular belief, the activation of one sprinkler does not cause all sprinklers to operate; and so danger of accidental discharge should not be over-estimated. The average sprinkler discharges 15-20 gallons per minute (90 litres per minute) while typical fire hoses release 120-250 gallons per minute (540-1125 litres per minute). It is important to remember that the environmental and human safety aspects of water are known, unlike the possible impact from various chemical agents. Furthermore, the recovery techniques for water-damaged material are also known.

- Dry-pipe sprinkler systems are essentially the same as wet-pipe systems except that the pipes in the protected area contain pressurized air. When the sprinkler is activated a valve opens allowing water to flow into the pipes. This lessens any threat of water leaking into collection areas.
- Micromist systems are being developed which discharge limited quantities of water at very high pressures, resulting in exceptionally efficient cooling and rapid fire control with significantly little water. Tests have proved that water saturation, often associated with standard firefighting procedures, is avoided. Other anticipated benefits include: lower installation costs, minimal aesthetic impact, and known environmental safety.

Routine Maintenance

Fire alarms and suppression systems, the building fabric, plumbing, electric, and gas supplies and fittings, etc., should be maintained and routinely tested. All reports should be kept and any maintenance work documented.

PREPAREDNESS

The following should be prepared, reviewed, and updated regularly:

- Building floor plans which indicate storage areas, windows, entrances, and exits; fire extinguishers; fire alarms; sprinklers; smoke/fire detectors; water, gas, and heating pipes; elevator controls; electrical and water supply and cutoff points.
- Priority rescue lists made by departments, stating which items are to be salvaged from individual rooms. The fire services may allow entry into a building for salvage purposes for a limited time, and it is essential to know what items are to be saved and where they are located.
- Selecting and training an emergency response team comprising voluntary members of staff who live near the library. The team should be rehearsed in removing material and confident in making decisions about salvage techniques. It is essential for them to have participated in disaster workshops, where a disaster site is simulated and techniques can be practised.
- Detailed, step-by-step instructions on all phases of salvage operation, covering a range of incidents that are possible (*e.g.,* roof/plumbing leaks, flooding, and fire) and the various media included in the collections, such as books and journals, manuscripts/records, coated vs. uncoated stock, sound recordings, photographic media, computer/electronic media, etc.
- Instructions for long-term rehabilitation: procedures for activities

including identification and labelling, smoke/soot removal, cleaning, sorting and rehousing, repair and rebinding, etc.

- A list of external contacts and names, addresses, and home and work telephone numbers of personnel with emergency responsibilities.
- Areas which could be used for recording and packing material.
- Locations for temporarily rehousing staff and material.
- Contracts with local freezer services.
- Contracts with vacuum-drying services.
- Arrangements with transportation services.
- Supplies for transporting, cleaning, and sorting material.
- *Record-keeping forms*: Multiple copies of all forms that may be needed in the salvage operation, including inventory forms, packing lists, requisitions, and purchase orders, etc.
- *Accounting information*: Description of institutional funds available in a recovery effort and procedures/authorization for access to them.
- *Insurance information*: Explanations of coverage, claim procedures, recordkeeping requirements, restrictions on staff/volunteers entering a disaster area, and information on state/federal disaster relief procedures.

RESPONSE

- Follow established emergency procedures for raising the alarm, evacuating personnel, and making the disaster site safe.
- Contact the leader of the disaster response team to brief and direct the emergency response team.
- When permission is given to re-enter the site, make a preliminary assessment of the extent of the damage, the equipment, supplies, and services required.
- Correct the environment, if necessary, to prevent mould growth.
- Photograph damaged material for insurance claim purposes.
- Set up an area for recording and packing material which requires freezing, and an area for air-drying slightly wet material and other minor treatments.
- Transport water-damaged items to the nearest available freezing facility.

Drying Wet Material

As part of the preparation for a disaster plan it is essential to be familiar with the various procedures for drying different types of library material.

The following drying methods all have advantages and disadvantages:

- Air-drying
- Dehumidification

- Freeze-drying
- Vacuum thermal-drying
- Vacuum freeze-drying

If time must be taken to make critical decisions, books and records should be frozen to reduce physical distortion and biological contamination.

Air-drying

Air-drying is the simplest technique for drying damp-not totally wet-material. A damp book can be stood on its end and its pages fanned out or interleaved with blotting paper. Although this is an effective technique which does not require expensive equipment or materials (fans and interleaving paper), it is labour intensive, time-consuming, and generally results in some dimensional distortion.

RECOVERY

- Determine priorites for conservation work. Consult with conservators as to the most appropriate methods for cleaning and repairing material. Obtain cost estimates.
- Develop a phased conservation programme when large quantities of material are involved.
- Select items to be discarded, replaced, or rebound from those justifying special conservation treatment.
- Clean and rehabilitate the disaster site.
- Replace treated material in the refurbished site.
- Analyse the disaster and improve the plan in light of the experience.

It is worth liaising with local and district authorities/councils about the availability of temporary storage facilities and other services they may be able to provide. Cooperating with other libraries, museums, and galleries in the area can save time, money, and resources.

4

e-Books and e-Audio Books Selection

e-BOOKS AND e-AUDIOBOOKS FROM THE LIBRARY

Medicine Hat Public Library pays a company called OverDrive to provide access to copyrightprotected eBooks and eAudiobooks for Library patrons. Anyone with a valid library membership and a PIN number can access these resources from home. Currently, patrons can have up to 5 electronic titles checked out at once and each title can be kept for a maximum of 3 weeks. At the end of the lending period, each title will automatically expire. There are no late fees! While the file will still be visible on your computer or portable device, you will not be able to open it and it can be deleted. Due to restrictions imposed by book publishers, only one person may have an electronic title checked out at once. So when someone checks out The 9th Confession by James Patterson, that book is unavailable to everyone else until it is returned.

A FEW THINGS TO KNOW ABOUT e-BOOKS

Library eBooks come in two formats: ePub and PDF. The main difference between the two formats is that ePub books have reflowable text: as you increase the text size, the words automatically shuffle to fit your screen. PDF books do not have this feature, so when you increase the text size you may need to scroll from left to right to read everything on the page. Both formats are compatible with PCs, Macs, and most portable eReaders like the Sony Reader, Kobo and Nook. The iPad, iPhone and iPod Touch are also compatible with ePub files when downloaded directly to the device using the OverDrive Media Console App. In order to read an eBook on your computer or to transfer it to an applicable eReader, you must first install Adobe Digital Editions which is freely available from the Library to Go web site.

A FEW THINGS TO KNOW ABOUT e-AUDIOBOOKS

eAudiobooks from the Library come in two formats: MP3 and WMA. Both formats will work on PCs and most portable audio devices. Unfortunately, WMA files are not compatible with Mac computers. Depending on the type of software your Apple device is running you may be able to transfer a WMA file through a PC. In order to download an eAudiobook and transfer to a portable device, you must first install OverDrive Media Console which is freely available from the Library to Go web site.

LIBRARY TO GO

Library to Go is the library's catalogue for finding and downloading eBooks and eAudiobooks.

BEFORE YOU START BROWSING: DOWNLOAD THE REQUIRED SOFTWARE

In order to read and transfer eBooks you must first download the Adobe Digital Editions software. For eAudiobooks you must first download OverDrive Media Console.

Both are freely available on the Library to Go web site below the green menu on the left-side of the page:

ACTIVATING THE SOFTWARE

After you have installed the software, you need to take steps to activate it before downloading digital materials.

Adobe Digital Editions Requires Activation

You must create an Adobe ID in order to transfer eBooks from a computer to an eReader.

When you open Digital Editions for the first time click 'Get an Adobe ID online' and follow the prompts to create your Adobe ID. You can then enter your Adobe ID and password in the relevant boxes in Digital Editions to activate.

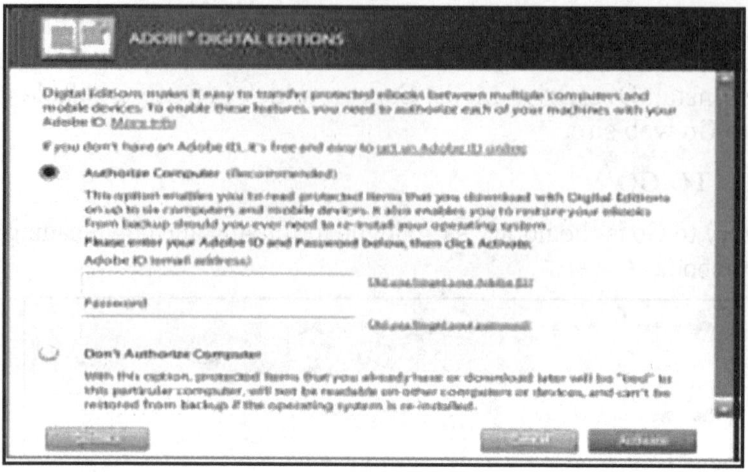

OverDrive Media Console Requires a Security Update

The first time you open an eAudiobook with OverDrive Media Console, a message will appear saying that a security upgrade must be performed before the file can be opened. Simply follow the on-screen instructions to perform the quick upgrade.

FINDING TITLES USING LIBRARY TO GO

You can search for a particular title or author using the 'Quick Search' box near the top of the Library to Go page.

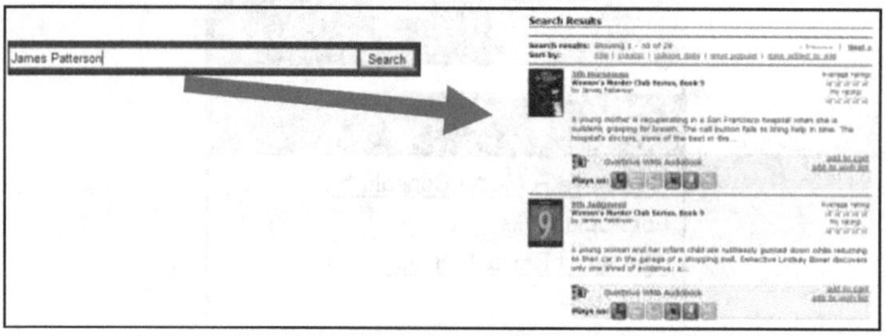

The 'Advanced Search' option to the right of the 'Quick Search' box can be used to perform a more specific search. You can also browse for titles using the green menu on the left side of the page or the categories in the centre of the main Library to Go page.

DOWNLOADING AN e-BOOK

When you have found an eBook that interests you, simply click on its title for more information:

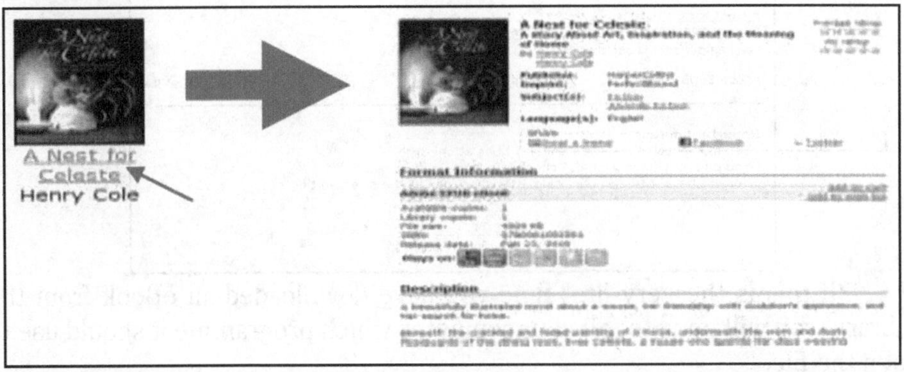

If the 'Add to Cart' option is visible in the grey bar under 'Format Information', then the book is available to download and you can click to move to the next step.

If you see 'Place a Hold' instead, then the item is checked out by someone else and you can click to enter your e-mail address and receive notification when the item is available.

Once the item is available for download, you will have three days to complete the checkout. After you click 'Add to Cart' you are given the option to 'Continue Browsing' or 'Proceed to Checkout'-if you 'Continue Browsing', your items will stay in your cart for 45 minutes.

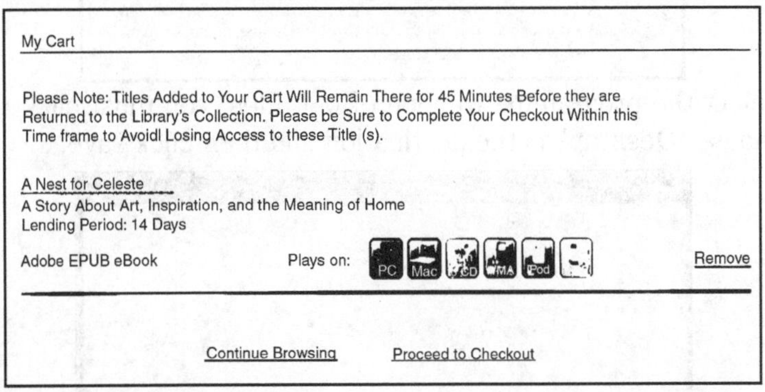

Clicking 'Proceed to Checkout' brings you to a screen asking for your Library card number and PIN number.

When you have entered this information, you will be brought to the Check Out screen:

From here you can choose your lending period and see how close you are to your 5 item limit. When you're ready to download, click 'Confirm Checkout' and then the 'Download' button on the next screen that appears.

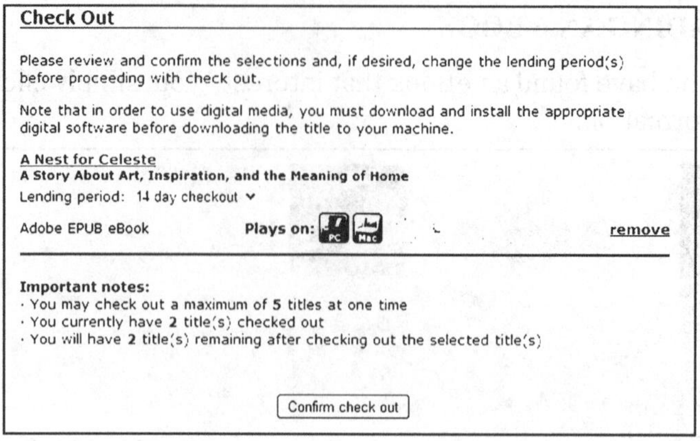

**If this is the very first time you have downloaded an eBook from the Library, you will need to tell your computer which programme it should use to open the file.

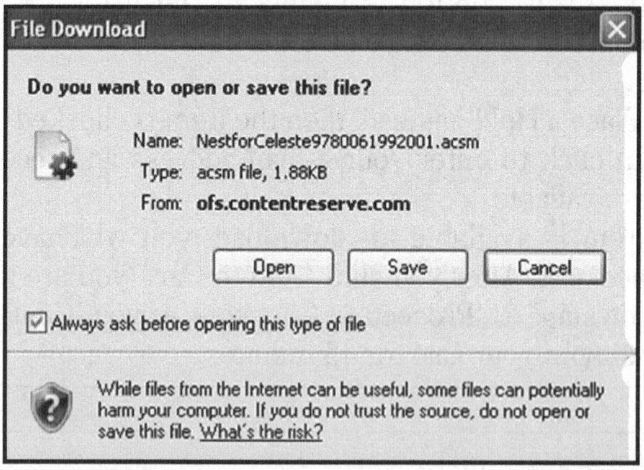

To select the programme to open eBook files, you must click the 'Save' button, choose 'Desktop' as the destination and then click save.

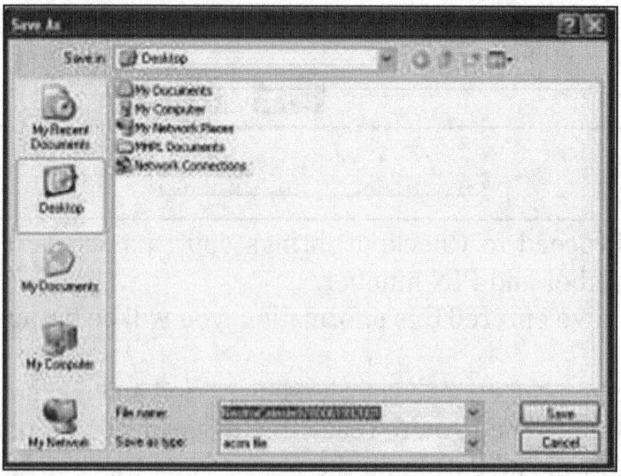

Next, find the file on the Desktop, right-click the icon, go to 'Open With' and click 'Choose Programme'.

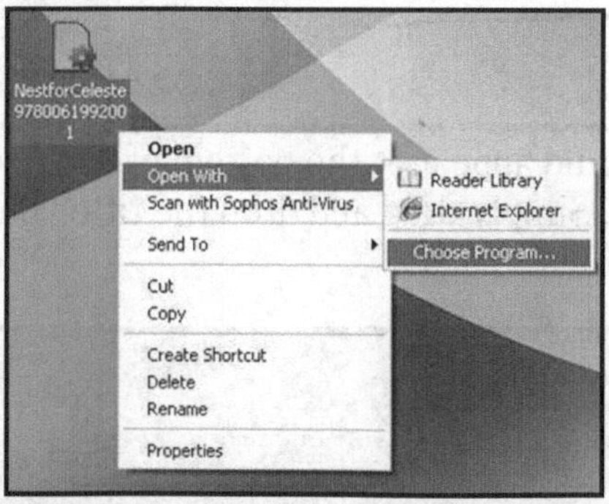

Choose Adobe Digital Editions from the list of programmes, click the box next to "Always use the selected programme to open this kind of file' and click 'OK'.

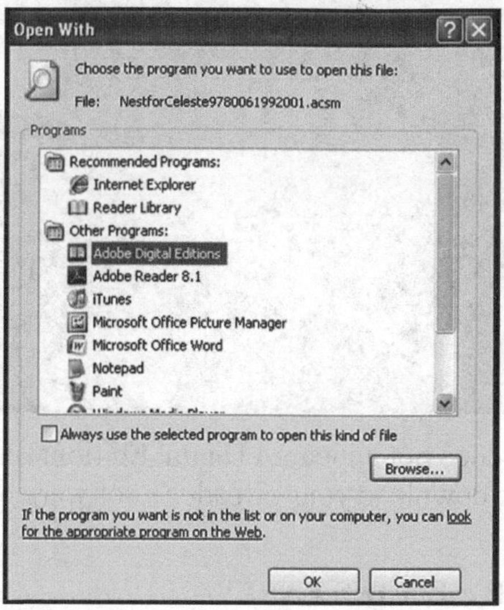

If Digital Editions does not appear in the list of programmes, you will need to find it using the 'Browse' button. Usually, it is saved under Programme Files \ Adobe \ Adobe Digital Editions \ digitaleditions.

TRANSFERRING AN e-BOOK TO AN e-READER

To transfer an eBook from Digital Editions to an eReader such as the Kobo Touch, you must first connect your eReader to your computer. If a window opens asking what Windows should do with the connected device choose 'Take No Action'. Then open Digital Editions and follow the steps to authorise your reader if you are using it for the first time. Click on the icon for Library View in the top-left corner of the screen.

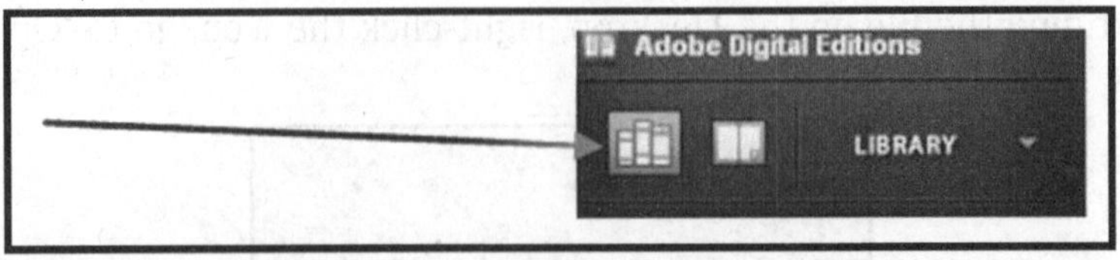

Your eReader should appear at the bottom of the Bookshelves area on the left side of the screen. Simply drag and drop the title you wish to transfer onto your eReader.

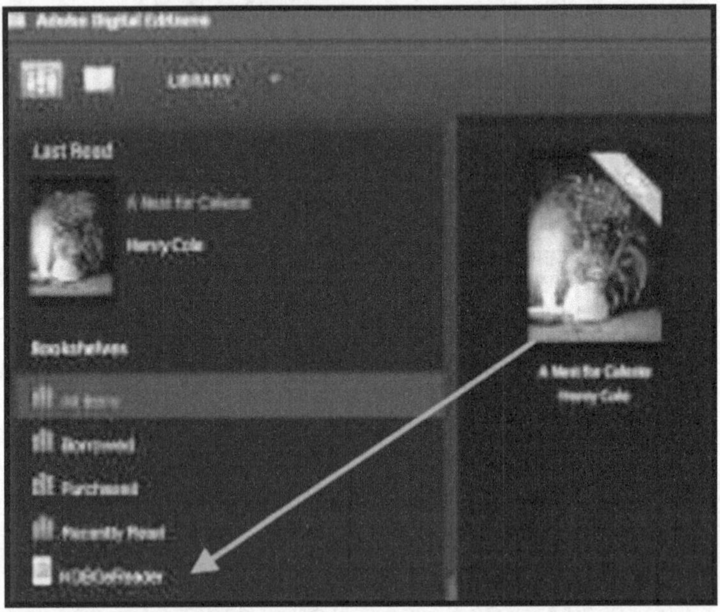

If your eReader does not appear in Digital Editions after you have plugged it in, you may need to download your eReader's software before your computer will recognise it.

RETURNING YOUR e-BOOKS EARLY

Any eBooks you borrow through the library system will automatically return themselves at the end of your borrowing period but if you finish an eBook early, you can also return it yourself.

In the Adobe Digital Editions software on your computer, click the 'Go to Library View' button in the top left corner:

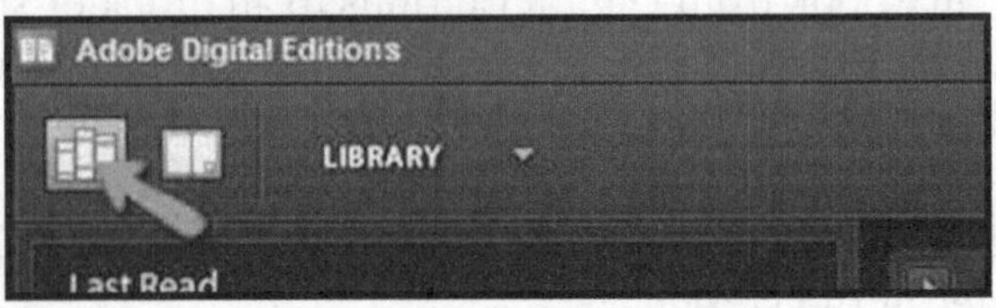

Next, click the 'Item Options' button for the book you wish to return:

Finally, click the 'Return Borrowed Item' in the Item Options menu:

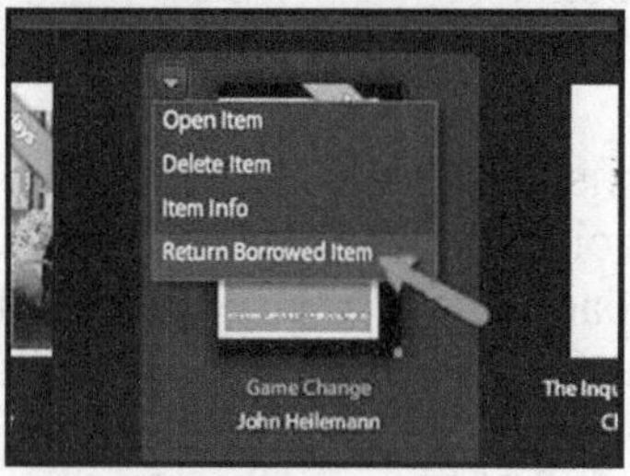

DOWNLOADING AN e-BOOK DIRECTLY TO A SONY WIFI e-READER

The Sony WiFi eReader will allow you to borrow eBooks from the library directly on your device without the use of Adobe Digital Editions or any external applications.

To download books onto your device, use the following procedure:

- Turn on your device.
- Go to page 2 and select the 'Public Library' icon.
- If you are asked to set up an account in the Sony eReader store, follow the prompts to do so. This will authorize your eReader to open the library books you borrow.
- In the 'Public Library' section, select the option to 'Discover More' or 'Find a Library'.
- Type in 'Medicine Hat' into the search area and press the small magnifying next to it.
- Select the 'Medicine Hat Public Library System' and then select the 'Library to Go' option—this will take you to the Library to Go homepage where you can login, search for, and download your eBooks.

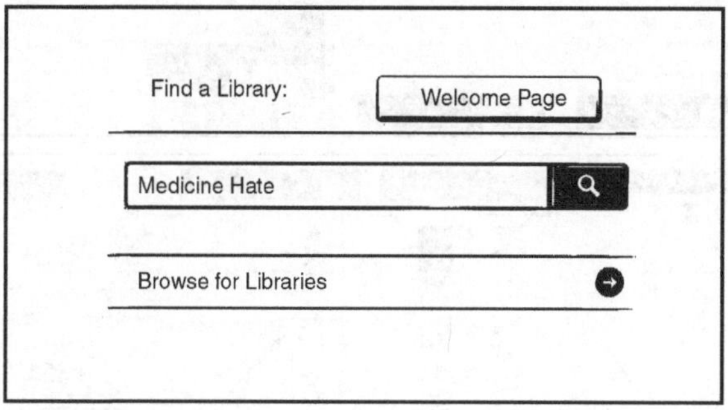

RETURNING e-BOOKS DIRECTLY ON A SONY WIFI e-READER

To return your eBooks directly from your Sony Wifi eReader use the following procedure:

- Select the 'Books' icon on your eReader screen.
- Press the Menu button.
- Select 'Return Books.'
- Select which books you'd like to return by checking the appropriate boxes.
- Press 'Done'.

Overdrive Media Console Mobile is a free app available for most iPad/iPhone/iPod Touch, Android, Blackberry and Windows Mobile devices. This app allows you to download titles directly to your device over Wi-Fi or 3g. However, not all file formats are currently compatible. Apple devices, for example, only support eBooks in ePub format and eAudiobooks in MP3 format. You can download the app from the app store for your device or the Library to Go web site. You must register your Adobe ID with the Overdrive Media Console Mobile app and you will be prompted for your library card number and PIN before you can download an eBook or eAudiobook.

HOW TO DOWNLOAD e-BOOKS AND e-AUDIOBOOKS WITH OVERDRIVE MEDIA CONSOLE MOBILE

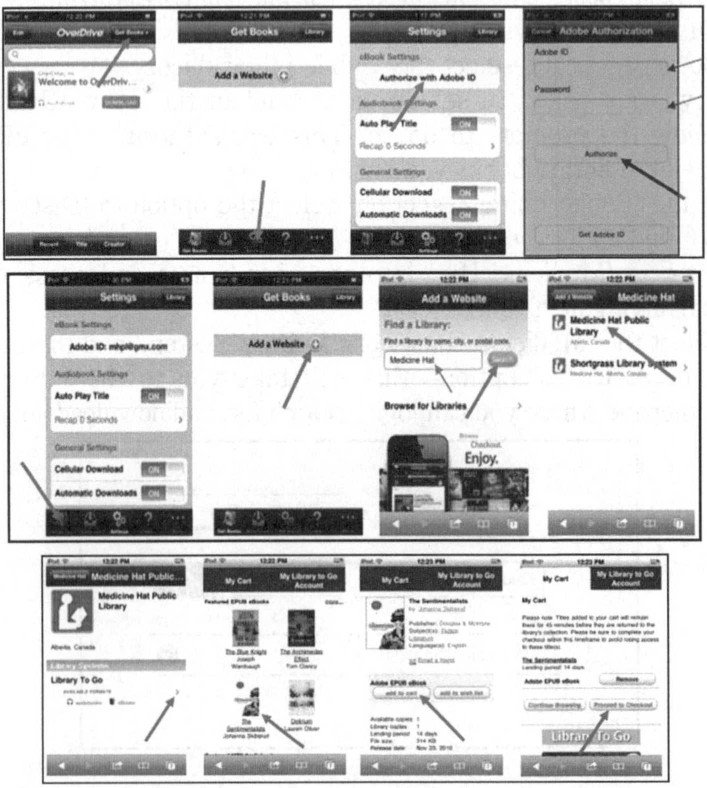

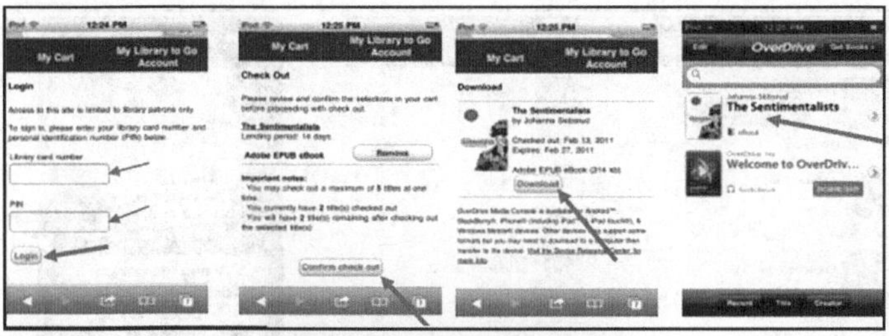

Note

Library books borrowed through the OverDrive Media Console app will always be found by opening that app on your device. For example, if you downloaded a title on your Kobo Vox using OverDrive, the next time you wanted to go and read it, you would open the app instead of looking for the title in your library.

RETURNING e-BOOKS DIRECTLY FROM YOUR PORTABLE DEVICE

You can also return your eBooks directly from your portable device by using the OverDrive Media Console app. By swiping your finger across the title on the main page you will be shown a button to delete the book. When you click that button, you will then be given the option to delete only, or delete and return the book.

Deleting the book only will free up space on your device, while deleting and returning the book will also free up space for another title in your Library to Go account.

Each device is different but most do offer you the option to return items early. To find out if your device has this feature, try to delete the item and see if you are asked whether you want to return the item as well. If you are not given the option, then look in the settings section for each borrowed item.

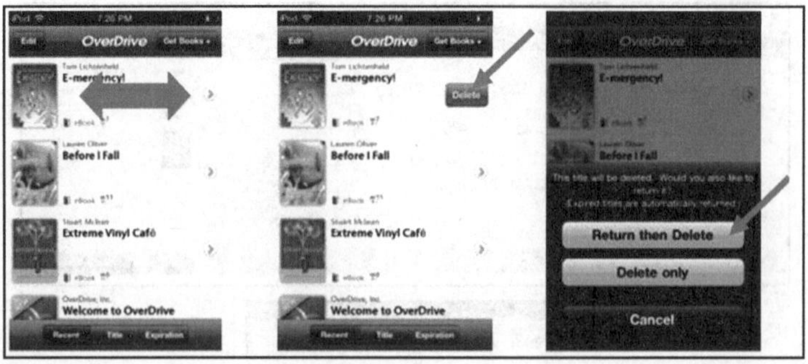

DOWNLOADING AN e-AUDIOBOOK TO YOUR COMPUTER

The process for finding and checking out titles is the same for eAudiobooks and eBooks. After checking out an eAudiobook click Open in the File Download window.

Overdrive Media Console will open automatically. eAudiobooks are divided into parts to facilitate faster download times. You will need to tell Overdrive Media Console which parts to download by checking the boxes beside the parts you want.

The default option is to download all parts. Once you have checked the parts you want, you can click the 'OK' button to download.

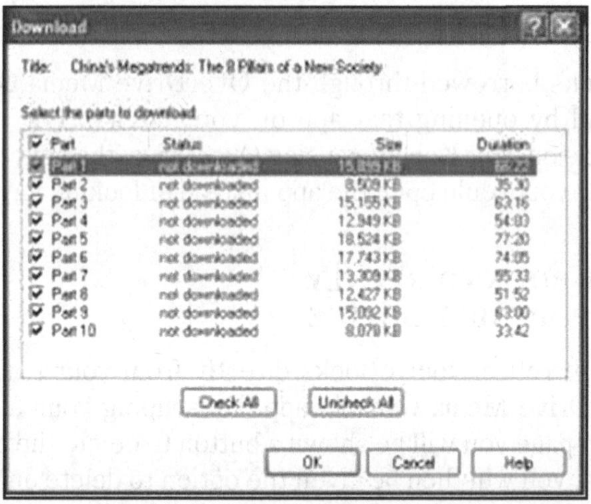

It could take a while to download depending on the speed of your Internet connection and how many parts you choose to download at once After the eAudiobook has downloaded, it will appear in Overdrive Media Console.

From here, you can click the 'Play' button in the top-left corner to listen to the eAudiobook on your computer. The 'Download' button lets you download any parts of the eAudiobook that you missed.

TRANSFERRING AN e-AUDIOBOOK TO A MOBILE DEVICE

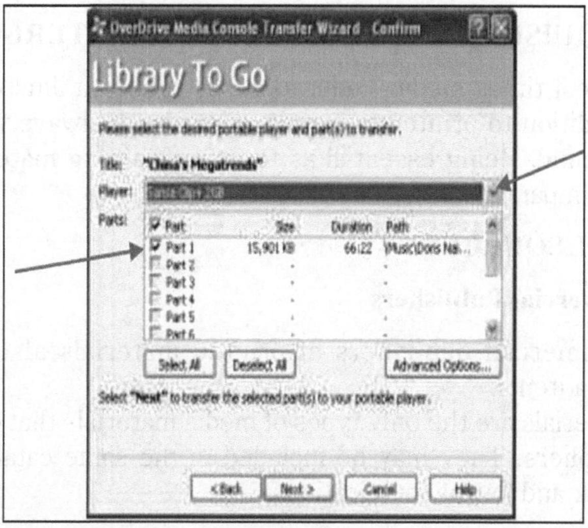

- Connect the device to your PC.
- Open Overdrive Media Console.
- Click the title of the eAudiobook you wish to transfer and click the 'Transfer' button in the topleft corner of the screen.
- Select your player and which parts of the eAudiobook you wish to transfer and click 'Next' to begin the transfer.
- Click 'Finish' and remove your player from the PC.

Special Considerations if Transferring to an iPod

- Some titles are not compatible with Apple devices st have iTunes v9.1 installed on your PC to transfer to an iPod.
- The iTunes setting 'Manually manage music…' must be enabled for Apple devices. Adjust this setting as follows.
  - Connect the device to your computer.
  - Open iTunes.
  - In iTunes, locate the device in the left vertical navigation panel and click the device.
  - If it is not already checked, place a checkmark next to the option 'Manually manage music…'and
  - Click the 'Apply' button.

Please note that at this time transferring WMA audiobooks to an Apple device running iOS 5 is not recommended due to compatibility issues between

OverDrive Media Console and Apple iTunes. If you do attempt to transfer WMA files to an Apple device then please be sure to back up your files before starting the process. If you are still experiencing difficulty transferring an eAudiobook to your Apple device, please consult the Help section on the Library to Go web site for other possible solutions.

ACQUISITIONS OF AUDIOVISUAL MATERIALS

Since earliest times medical education has relied on illustrative teaching materials in addition to printed materials. They were always visual and then incorporated sound. Being essential as teaching/learning materials, they are expected to form part of library stock.

AUDIOVISUAL SOURCES

General Commercial Publishers

Many commercial publishers of printed materials also produce and distribute media items.

These materials are the only types of media materials that can be ordered from book suppliers. They may be included in the same catalogue with the publisher's book and journal publications.

Specialized Commercial Media Publishers

There are many commercial publishers or distributors that deal only with media materials, with some producing a variety of formats, and others limited to one format.

Educational Consortia

National and regional consortia and other membership organisations are also sources of media materials. Membership organisations provides the library with catalogues of available materials, as well as discounted prices. Special acquisitions procedures may be required for such materials to ensure that member discounts are correctly applied.

Non-commercial Materials

Health sciences faculty, their schools and universities are also sources of media materials, as they sometimes develop media materials for use by teaching staff and students and may agree to make them available in the library. Some academic institutions have media centres and close cooperation with them will offer fast acquisition of their products.

Pharmaceutical Companies

Some pharmaceutical companies offer media materials such as slides free of charge to medical schools and hospitals.

Professional Societies and Organisations

Many professional societies and organisations, such as the Radiological Society of North America and the American Society of Clinical Pathologists, sell educational media materials. Their marketing efforts are most likely to be aimed towards members, so requests for purchases may often originate from health professionals and faculty. The ordering process is straightforward, although prepayment is frequently required.

ACQUISITION PROCESSES

Communication with Selectors

Because media materials are used for a variety of reasons within the library—such as reference information, as educational materials and as office productivity tools—requests for them may originate from various departments of the library, as well as from departments outside the library, such as patient education or continuing education department.

In addition to the standard order entry elements, such as title, date of publication, publisher, price, the media acquisitions request should include:

- Format
- Whether or not a preview copy is required, and who will do the previewing
- Full address of the producer or distributor, if available
- Notes on any special publisher/distributor policies already ascertained or negotiated by the selector
- Notes on special processing requirements

Bibliographic Searching

In addition to the usual preorder check of library files to avoid duplication, some preorder research is frequently required to verify or complete the item identification. An essential element is the publisher address as many titles have to be ordered directly from producers or distributors.

It has to be noted here, that bibliographic verification is often difficult because:

- Comprehensive bibliographies and directories are not available for audiovisuals
- Records in bibliographic utilities, such as OCLC and RLIN, can be unreliable
- Records of the Library of Congress and NLM AVLINE may be slow to appear or unavailable.

For these reasons, the library has to maintain bibliographic resources of its own for audiovisuals. These include commercially published directories, individual producer and distributor catalogues, media listings compiled by vendors and listings of media holdings compiled by other libraries. If all these fail, it is advisable to contact the producer or distributor directly, preferably by telephone, where the responses have to be documented.

Order Entry and Record Keeping

Whether the tracking system of media orders is manual or electronic, consideration should be given to accommodating data elements unique to media items, such as format, version and notes on handling preview copies. The order form itself has to be as clear and explicit as possible. Larger acquisitions operations may want to have a higher level supervisor do a final signoff on all media orders, or at least those with an estimated cost above a specified amount.

Ordering Items on Preview

Many media items are available on a preview or on approval basis. There are many factors in determining the suitability of an item by seeing and using it. A faculty member, for example may want to view a videocassette to determine its appropriateness and quality of the visuals. In health sciences libraries, it is usual to buy one item that most closely matches local needs, rather than a spectrum of viewpoints on a specific topic. Placing preview orders are similar to entering firm orders, except that the order itself must specify the preview nature of the request. Although a standard form for preview requests simplifies the process, the policies of publishers are different. Once the preview item is received, it must be sufficiently processed, the evaluator contacted, the item reviewed, and a purchase decision made within the specified preview period. If the item is to be returned, it has to be mailed and insured according to the publisher's instructions. When a decision is made to purchase the item on preview, it is better to return the preview copy and enter a new firm order to guarantee obtaining a new copy rather than the one used. Alternatively, the library keeps the preview copy and requests an invoice. Some previews are charged for, while some publishers may waive the fee if the copy is retained. Some publishers, instead of providing a preview option, do provide 'satisfaction guaranteed' allowing an item to be returned, if it is not satisfying, within a specified period of time.

Receipt and Precataloguing Processing

Items, once received are first checked to determine that the correct title and version have been received and that all the pieces are included. Additional check of completeness may be required by the requesting department. A thorough quality review to ensure that the item is not defective is required.

e-READERS

e-BOOK FORMATS

eBooks come in a variety of formats. Some publishers and sellers also place

DRM protection on the books so they cannot be copied, viewed on multiple devices, or restricted to specific readers.

There is no consistent licensing as each licence is an agreement between author, publisher and seller:

- ePUB is an open source format and continues to develop. ePUB books can contain video and active links which make the books dynamic. ePUB is the most versatile of all eBook formats. Textbooks developers are looking to this format as it will allow for content and media rich books, moving away from what can be done with traditional text and print media. ePub can be read by most popular devices except Amazon's Kindle. Amazon currently offers an e-mail service that lets you convert ePUB documents and books into the AZW format for a fee, though formaang and interactivity may be lost.
- MOBI also known as MobiPocket is owned by Amazon and is similar to the AZW format for Kindle. The MOBI format can be read by most of the popular readers except the Nook. MOBI was once the most popular format but is losing ground to ePUB.
- PDF is a format that is commonly used to publish documents and images. PDFs are essentially images of pages and therefore do not allow text to flow between pages or to fit the screen size. PDFs are best read on larger computer screens and not mobile devices. PDFs can be viewed in most readers except the first edition Kindle.
- Plain Text formaang allows for a very small file size, allowing large books such as the Bible to be distributed in this format. Plain text is read by major readers except Nook.
- HTML is the markup language for web pages and most eBooks that use HTML can be read in a web browser. Some other eBook formats include HTML in their packaging of books.
- Kindle/ AZW is a version of MOBI and is exclusive to Amazon Kindle. It can be read on a variety of mobile devices with the Kindle App. It cannot be read on other readers such as the Nook or Sony reader.
- eReader was originally developed for Palm. This format supports hyperlinks and images. The Nook can read pdb files while the Kindle cannot.

WHERE TO FIND e-BOOKS

Before you go out and make a purchase for a dedicated reader it might be worth your while to explore what books are available in eBook format. Take some time to read a few books on the devices you already have access to such as your computer or smart phone if you have one. eBooks are not quite the same as print. Some eBooks contain images and some do not. Some free versions were entered by volunteers and may contain a typo or two.

Let's explore a few places to find eBooks:

- Google eBooks puts the power of the Google search engine to work scouring the web for eBooks. Some books are hosted by Google, others from major publishers and distributors. If you are not tied to a particular reader Google books is a good place to start to find the books in a variety of formats. You can find many free books from the public domain, as well as books for purchase.
- Project Gutenberg has a large collection of books in the public domain. Currently there are over 33,000 free eBooks available. The eBooks on Project Gutenberg are found in 3 main formats plain text, ePUB, and MOBI.
- eBooks.com has a wide range of eBooks for purchase including many academic titles for colleges. eBooks.com sells books in PDF, for computer based reading; ePUB, Mobi and MicrosoV reader for mobile devices. eBooks has an eReader app for iPod/iPad/iPhone devices. eBooks from eBooks.com can also be read on a computer
- Amazon Kindle eBooks Books sold at Amazon for the Kindle are primarily in the AZW format, though some may be in MOBI depending on agreements with the publisher. AZW format is proprietary to Amazon and includes DRM protection. Amazon also offers some free ebooks that are in the public domain. Amazon offers the Kindle app for iPod/iPad/iPhone and other mobile devices.
- Barnes and Noble eBook store sells NookBooks formaXed for the Nook. They currently have over 2 million eBooks available. NookBooks are in the ePUB format, eReader and some PDF, though most books have DRM protection on them. Barnes and Noble offers an app called the Barnes and Noble e-Reader for iPod/iPad/iPhone and other mobile devices.
- Borders has adopted the ePUB, PDF and Mobile format for its books; most have DRM protections. Like other book sellers, they also have free books in the public domain. Unlike Amazon and Barnes and Noble, Borders does not sell its own reader but recommends seven different readers on its web site. These are described in the last section on eReaders. Borders also offers a free eReader app for many mobile devices.

The Apple iBookstore currently sells books for reading only on Apple mobile devices, through the iTunes interface. Rumours persist that Apple will release its iBooks app for the Mac and PC in the future but there are always rumours surrounding Apple. Apple prefers the tactile sensation of 'turning pages' with the touch screen on its mobile devices that current desktop and laptops do not have. Apple iBooks are in the ePUB format and allow for interactivity such as viewing embedded video and active web links. Apple also sells fully illustrated books and magazines because of the colour planorm provided by its devices.

e-READERS

Reading eBooks can be done on a variety of devices with a range of apps and programmes. As suggested, begin with a look at reading on computers and multifunctional devices and end with a look at some of the major dedicated readers.

e-READING SOFTWARE FOR COMPUTERS

If you own a computer you can read almost anything though you may need more than one programme to do so. Reading on your computer is not as comfy as reading a book curled up on the couch or siang in your back yard, but you do have access to a vast library of books. Each of the major eBook sellers provides a version of their reader for your computer. If you use a Windows based PC you can choose from Kindle for PC, Adobe Digital Editions, Nook for PC, or Borders eReader for PC. If you are a Mac user you have a similar selection of choices Kindle for Mac, Adobe Digital Editions, Nook for Mac, or Borders eReader for Mac.

EREADING ON MULTIFUNCTIONAL MOBILE DEVICES: iPODS, iPADS, AND MOBILE PHONES

Multifunctional mobile devices are just small computers, some with an added phone. These include iPods, iPads, iPhones, Android Phones, Blackberries and an increasing number of small tablets. Most of these mobile devices have LCD screens which make reading in bright light a bit of a challenge; most are colour and many have touch screens and support the interactivity of the ePUB format. Velocity Micro offers Android based tablets, Borders recommends two, these are described later on.

The device that offers the richest media content support for eBooks is currently the iPad. If you already have a number of gadgets in your bag you may wish for a multifunctional device so you have fewer devices to deal with. Similar to the computer, the devices can have a variety of e-reader apps installed so they can handle a large variety of book formats and work with all the major eBook distributors. Kindle Reading Apps, Nook Apps and Borders eReader Apps are available for mobile devices including apps for iPods/iPads/iPhone, Android and Blackberry phones. Adobe Digital Editions which reads PDF and ePUB can be used on a variety of mobile devices.

DEDICATED e-READERS

When it comes to dedicated eReaders the ones that get the most coverage are the Amazon Kindle and the Barnes and Noble Nook. These two major book sellers have developed their own eReaders. Borders has taken a more open approach and does not market to a particular eReader allowing the reader greater choice. As suggested, begin with a brief summary of the Kindle and Nook readers currently available and then look at the 7 that Borders recommends. Amazon currently offers the Kindle 3 and Kindle DX. The two models each come in two flavours—wifi or wifi and 3G. 3G is provided free allowing you to purchase books and download them whereever you are.

The more recent release of the Kindles uses pearl e-ink which allows for crisper images and text, and reading in bright light. The screens are not touch screens, navigation is carried out via a keyboard and side buXons. The kindle 3 has a 6 inch screen and the DX 9.7 inch screen. Kindle supports; AZW, PDF, MOBI, TEXT formats. It does not support ePub, but a programme called Calibre can convert epub to MOBI. Amazon currently offers an e-mail service for a fee to convert files. The Barnes and Noble Nook now comes in two models the original in black and white and the new Nook Colour. Both have two flavour; wifi or wifi and 3G.

As with the Kindle the 3G is free. Both devices use e-ink and can be read in bright light. Nook Colour has a touch screen and designed for those who love reading magazines. The traditional black and white e-ink did not do justice to the visual images found in many magazines. Nook colour also has extras including some web browsing, e-mail access and games. It is clearly aimed at the iPad, though the Nook colour is not yet a true multifunctional device. The Nooks support the following formats: EPUB, PDB, PDF, MP3, JPG, GIF, PNG, PMB. It does not read Mobi, AMZ, LRX/LEZ, or Text

There are other eReaders on the market that are not tied to a specific vendor. Borders offers a comparison chart for a variety of readers it recommends.

Below is a brief summary of each:

- Aluratek Libre Pro supports books in the ePub, PDF, TXT, RTF, FB2, MOBI, PRC formats. It can play mp3 files and uses an LCD screen that is black and white.
- Kobo Wireless eReader support eReader, ePUB and PDF formats. It uses e-ink and has a 6 inch screen.
- Sony offers 3 models of eReader; the Pocket edition, Touch edition and the Daily Edition. The Sony models all have touch screen navigation and use e-ink. The pocket edition is not wireless and requires a computer to sync books to. They support ePub, PDF, TXT, RTF, and BBeB formats. Sony also has its own eBook store.

Finally rounding out our look at eReaders the Cruz reader and Tablet from Velocity Micro. The Cruz Reader is not a standalone eReader, it more a multifunctional device. It is a colour eReader with 7" screen that also browses the web, plays mp3 files, watch movies, play games and has some productivity apps. The Cruz Tablet is a true multifunctional Android colour tablet. There are two versions of this device—one with Borders eReader and the other with Amazon's Kindle soVware.

There is a great deal of variety in this very fluid technology. It is apparent that eBooks are here and are gaining more and more ground. eBook readers continue to improve as time goes on. Just as with computers, change is inevitable. Reading is a very personal experience therefore each person should make the choice that works for them. It is clearly not a one size fits all experience. Do your research and make the choice that works for you.

BOOKS, LIBRARIES, AND THE SOCIALLY DISADVANTAGED

Today, the long-standing three-way tension between the commercial interests of publishers, the needs of society and information users, and the social mandate of public libraries, is being pulled and stretched as never before. First, the very notion of a "book" is evolving in many different directions: books become more interactive; publishers rent content; books are distributed under restrictive conditions that mechanically prohibit sharing.

While it would be premature to make specific predictions, it seems likely that these trends will further disadvantage the disadvantaged—particularly those in poorer countries who have yet to benefit from ready access to ordinary books. Second, a huge body of information is becoming freely available on the Internet.

Much is of questionable quality, but some is very good indeed. In many cases the information is provided for the "public good" rather than for commercial profit, and the redistribution of such information is likely to be encouraged, rather than prohibited, by those who make it available.

Initiatives like UNESCO's "Information for all" programme and the upcoming World Summit on the Information Society highlight the importance of public information; they are founded on the belief that information literacy will help alleviate many of the problems confronting human societies.

Third, the implications for libraries are mixed. Whereas new controls by publishers over how the content they own may be used presents libraries with significant problems, the ready availability of "public good" information meshes well with library philosophy. A new role is emerging for information professionals who can select material, index it, add appropriate metadata, and redistribute it in added-value form for the good of society. Suitable technological infrastructure is being provided by the open source movement, which is making available high-quality software for repackaging and distribution of information (and not just on computer networks).

BOOKS

What future has the book in the digital world? The question is a complex one that is being widely aired. Authors and publishers ask how many copies of a work will be sold if networked digital libraries enable worldwide access to an electronic copy of it.

Their nightmare is that the answer is *one*: how many books will be published online if the entire market can be extinguished by the sale of one electronic copy to a public library? To counter this threat, the entertainment industry is promoting new *"digital rights management"* (DRM) schemes that permit a degree of control over what users can do that goes far beyond the traditional legal bounds of copyright.

Indeed, the acronym is more aptly expanded as "digital restrictions management" because it is concerned solely with content owners rights and not at all with user's rights. It is, in effect, a "private governance system in which computer systems regulate which acts users are and are not authorized to perform".

Anticircumvention rules are sanctioned by the *Digital Millennium Copyright Act* (DMCA) in the US. The DMCA has been used, for example, to prosecute a Norwegian teenager for writing software to play a DVD that he had purchased on a computer for which no commercial playback systems exist. Can DRM be applied to books? The motion picture industry can compel manufacturers to incorporate encryption into their products because it holds key patents on DVD players. Commercial book publishers are promoting e-book readers that, if adopted on a wide scale, would allow the same kind of control to be exerted over reading material.

Basic rights that we take for granted—such as the ability to lend a book to a friend, resell it on the second-hand market, keep it indefinitely, continue to use it when your e-book reader breaks down, donate it to charity, preserve it for your grandchildren, copy excerpts without resorting to a handwritten transcription—are in jeopardy.

DRM allows such rights to be controlled, monitored, and withdrawn instantly, and DMCA legislation makes it illegal for users to seek redress by taking matters into their own hands. Fortunately, perhaps, lack of standardization and compatibility issues are delaying consumer adoption of e-books.

In the realm of scholarly publishing, digital rights management is more advanced. Academic libraries license access to content in electronic form, often in tandem with purchase of print versions too. They have been able to negotiate reasonable conditions with publishers—probably because they represent the lion's share of the scholarly market.

However, the extent of libraries' power in the consumer book market is moot. One can envisage a scenario where publishers establish a system of commercial, pay-per-view, libraries for e-books and refuse public libraries access to books in a form that can be circulated. These new directions present our society with puzzling challenges, and it would be rash to predict what society's response will be. But one thing is certain: they will surely increase the degree of disenfranchisement of those who do not have access to the technology.

Public Information

In parallel with publishers' moves to reposition books as technological artifacts with refined and flexible control over how they can be used, an opposing trend has emerged: the ready availability of free information on the Internet. Of course, the world-wide web is an unreliable source of enlightenment, and undiscriminating use is dangerous—and widespread.

As early as 1996 complaints arose that the Web's contents are largely unattributed, undated, unannotated, unreliable; information about author and publisher is unavailable or incomplete; far too many resource catalogues are chasing far too few original or non-trivial documents—complaints that are very familiar today. But one thing has changed: search engines and other portals have enormously increased our ability to locate information that is at least ostensibly relevant to any given question.

Teachers complain bitterly that students view the Web as a replacement for the library, harvesting information indiscriminately to provide answers to assignments that are at best shallow and at worst incoherent and incorrect. One consolation is that the very same search facilities can be used to detect plagiarism.

Nevertheless, the Web abounds with accessible, high-quality information. Many social groups, non-profit societies and charities make it their business to create sites and collect and organize information there. To take a single example at random, a Google search for *diabetes* returns three national diabetes associations in the top ten hits, and of course many more exist.

Each of these sites offers a cornucopia of valuable information on the disease, which is not commercial and provided for the public good. Widespread use is strongly encouraged, and it seems likely that arrangements could be made for re-distribution of the material presented there, particularly it was intended as a not-for-profit service and appropriate acknowledgement was made.

One of the key problems with information distribution via the Web is that it disenfranchises developing countries. Although the Web does not extend into the homes of the socially disadvantaged in developed countries either, various national programmes are working to provide access.

But network access varies enormously across the world. Whereas in 1998 more than a quarter of the US population were surfing the Internet, the figures for Latin America and the Caribbean was 0.8 per cent, for Sub-Saharan Africa 0.1 per cent, and for South Asia 0.04 per cent. Schools and hospitals in developing countries are poorly connected. Even in South Africa, the bestconnected African country, many hospitals and 75 per cent of schools have no telephone line. Universities are better equipped, but even there up to 1,000 people can depend on just one terminal. The Internet "is failing the developing world".

Prompted by this inequity, the importance of information, and particularly public information, is today being highlighted by prominent international bodies. For example, UNESCO's "Information for all" programme was established in 2001 to foster debate on the political, ethical and societal challenges of the emerging global knowledge society and to carry out projects promoting equitable access to information.

It reflects a growing awareness that information is playing an increasing role in generating wealth and human capital, and that participation in the "global knowledge society" is essential for social and individual development.

Information literacy is described as "a new frontier" by the Director of UNESCO's Information Society Division. The Inter-national Telecommunications Union has established a World Summit on the Information Society, held in Geneva in December 2003 and Tunis in 2005, to promote a global discussion of the fundamental changes that are being brought about in our lives by the transformation from an industrial to an information society, and to confront the extreme disparities of access to information between the industrialized countries and the developing world.

Libraries and their Role

What is the librarian to make of all this? The mandate of today's public libraries, in sharp contrast to that of publishers, is to facilitate the open distribution of knowledge. Librarians strive to enable the free flow of information. Their traditions are liberal, founded on the belief that libraries should serve democracy.

To help fulfil their mission as resource centers for citizens, public libraries maintain collections of records, policy statements, government documents, and so on. A recent promotional video from the American Librarian's Association exults that "the library is democracy's place of worship".

Clearly, the impending redefinition of the book as a digital artifact that is licensed rather than sold, tied to a particular replay device, with restrictions that are clearly laid out and mechanically enforced, is an innovation that goes right to the heart of libraries.

The changing nature of the book may make it hard, or even impossible, for libraries to fulfill their mandate by providing quality information to readers. And on the other hand, the emergence of a vast storehouse of information on the Internet poses a different kind of conundrum. Librarians, the traditional gatekeepers of knowledge, are in danger of being bypassed, their skills ignored, their advice unsought. Search engines send users straight to the information they require—or so users think—without any need for an inter-mediary to classify, catalogue, cross-reference, advise on sources. The ready availability of information on the Internet, and its widespread use, really presents librarians with an opportunity, not a threat.

Savvy users realise they need help, which librarians can provide. A good example is Infomine, a cooperative project of the University of California and California State University. Infomine contains descriptions and links to a wealth of scholarly and educational Internet resources, each of which has been selected and described by a professional academic librarian who is a specialist in the subject and in resource description generally.

Participating librarians see this as an important expenditure of effort for their users, a natural evolution of their traditional task of collecting and organizing information in print. What kind of technical infrastructure is needed to support and promote this kind of work?

Open source software is a powerful ally for librarians who wish to extend liberal traditions of information access. These systems make the source code freely available for others to view, modify, and adapt; and the very nature of the licensing agreement prevents the software from being appropriated by proprietary vendors. But the open-source movement is more than just a vehicle for librarians to use: its link with library traditions goes much deeper.

Public libraries and open source software both enshrine the same philosophy: to promote learning and understanding through the dissemination of knowledge. Both are pervaded by a sense of community, on the one hand the kind of inter-institutional cooperation exemplified by interlibrary loan and on the other teams of designers and programmers that frequently cross national boundaries.

New trends in information access present librarians in developed countries with difficult and conflicting challenges. Meanwhile, however, the situation in the developing world is dire. Here, traditional publishing and distribution mechanisms have failed tragically.

For example, whereas a US medical library subscribes to about 5,000 journals, the Nairobi University Medical School Library, long regarded as a flagship center in East Africa, last year received just 20 journals. In Brazzaville, Congo, the university has only 40 medical books and a dozen journals, all from before 1993, and the library in a large district hospital consisted of a single bookshelf filled mostly with novels.

Digital Libraries and the Challenge for HCI

Traditional libraries are substantial institutions that occupy physical space, present a physical appearance, and exhibit tangible physical organization. When standing on the threshold of a large bricks-and-mortar library you gain a sense of presence and permanence that reflects the care taken in building and maintaining the collection inside. Digital libraries, in contrast, are lightweight.

But they provide potentially far greater accessibility, which means that they will have even greater social effects.

Once created, they can, without significant institutional support, continue to serve users. They can be distributed throughout most of the developed world over the Internet. In developing countries and remote corners of the developed world they can be circulated on removable media—CD-ROM, DVD, or 100 Gb disk units the size of videocassettes—and updated over radio. Issues of copyright pose difficult problems, but they are manageable.

For example, there is plenty of non-copyright material, or material whose owners are prepared to donate copyright for socially useful purposes, and trends towards more open access to academic and humanitarian information are visible. Not everyone sees digital rights management and the DMCA as the way forward, and in the longer term publishers, to remain viable, will have to investigate alternative revenue models for the information they own.

No wonder international organizations such as the United Nations, along with many smaller *non-government organizations* (NGOs), are keenly interested in digital library technology. Advances in digital library technology are radically lowering the bar for the design and production of richly-organized, coherent, focused collections of information.

Now, anyone with access to sufficient source material can use public-domain software to build large, fullysearchable, collections the size of traditional personal or institutional libraries—in minutes. Let the minutes stretch to hours and the collection can be polished, organized, branded, distributed. It can include fully-illustrated text, images, video, music.

It can present attractively-designed pages with consistent use of icons. Keywords, key phrases, even acronyms and their definitions, can be extracted—automatically—and used to underpin novel means of access. Let the hours stretch to days and metadata can be manually added that permits further levels of organization. Given access to programming skills, creative new facilities that stretch the imagination can be rapidly integrated into the system. All this, one might say, can be done with ordinary Web sites: there is no need for digital library technology.

However, bitter experience has shown that all but the most rudimentary sites do require significant institutional support—for organization and maintenance. The Web is littered with incomplete, unfinished, unmaintained, out-dated, inconsistently-organized, useless information collections.

Just as traditional library cataloging procedures integrate new works into existing collections with minimal overhead so that they immediately become first-class members of the collection, so digital libraries allow new documents to be added completely automatically.

In the case of traditional libraries this is done through the small but non-negligible overhead of generating a new catalog entry. With ordinary Web sites it requires inserting links manually into index pages and the like, and may involve adding links not only into the new document but also into existing ones that ought to reference it—it's like rewriting the book, and maybe revising all other books in the library too!

In contrast, digital libraries bring access structures instantly and effortlessly up to date whenever new documents are added. The challenge for HCI is to design and build digital library systems that fulfill the potential of digital libraries as a "killer app" for computers in developing countries, which will bring concomitant benefits in almost every other sphere of application.

For the information consumer we need access to information that is guaranteed across space, time, and culture. We need flexible distribution mechanisms for documents, and for information objects of all types, that can be accessed on all computer platforms—including the lowliest. We need a choice of distribution over the Web or on removable media such as CD-ROM or DVD.

Digital libraries can incorporate flexible presentation that caters to individual differences, such as large-font displays or spoken output for the visually impaired. Libraries are places where information is preserved, not rendered obsolete, and digital libraries must instill confidence that information prepared today can be accessed next week, next decade, next century—regardless of technological changes.

An important aspect of digital libraries is their ability to work in local languages, promoting pluralism and reducing the risks of homogeneity. Because language is the vehicle of thought, communication, and cultural identity, this will encourage diversity and strengthen individual cultures. But there is a long way to go: even Unicode is woefully incomplete in certain areas, such as African languages. Naturally, today's digital library systems focus principally on the reader: the consumer of the material stored in the library's treasure-house. But digital libraries make a more radical, and perhaps ultimately more important, contribution by empowering ordinary users to conceive, assemble, build, and disseminate new information collections themselves.

In principle, modest computing resources are quite sufficient to enable users to build new collections by gathering together material in local files or on the Web; augmenting it with appropriate metadata that supports convenient search and browsing operations; incorporating advanced features like keyphrase extraction, document summarization, and metadata extraction; designing an attractive and functional interface; and publishing the collection on a variety of different media that are suitable for the intended readership.

The HCI challenge is to realise this potential for users—such as most librarians—who have a strong understanding of information and its organization, but no more interest in computers than they have in papermaking technology, last millennium's vehicle for information dissemination.

5

e-Books and their Successors

Publishing is going through several huge, related changes. Bestselling books are critical to the success of local bookstores but many bestselling novels are more popular as ebooks than they are as printed books. This trend, combined with the fact that so many people buy their books on-line, means that some bookstores have disappeared and more will follow. Publishers are losing physical places where printed books can be sold.

A Canadian reality makes this situation even more critical. Since most on-line bookstores are not housed in Canada, Canadian publishers receive even less revenue from the titles they distribute. If we want a strong Canadian publishing industry, libraries and publishers need to work more closely together. This may include finding ways to allow customers to buy printed books through library web sites and for local bookstores, where they exist, to fill these orders. We need to become more active partners with the industry which is critical to our existence.

E-BOOKS USERS

Many people who currently express distain for electronic books will soon be reading them.

Amongst those who migrate towards some use of electronic books will be:

- *Avid readers who love works of fiction and have wide ranging tastes in books and authors*: This is an easy prediction. Backlist titles, literary fiction and books by new authors often lose money for publishing houses. The president of one large publishing house has said on many occasions that publishing such material only in ebook formats might allow publishers to develop new writers and re-print books that ordinarily would be unavailable to readers. Serious readers will have to move to ebooks or accept that they may lose access to writers they love. Readers who discover a good author and want to read past titles may discover that these books are only available in ebook formats. The good news for writers and for readers is that books will remain more accessible than at any time in the history of publishing.

The bad news for writers is that their books will face even more competition for reader attention.

- *Readers of large print material and those who use spoken books*: E-books offer the opportunity for any book to become a large print book. Technically, any electronic book can also become a spoken book, although some publishers are currently blocking this capability. Rights management should and will address this issue. The arrival of accessibility capabilities in ebooks is happening at the same time as record numbers of tech savvy seniors are beginning to retire. ebook readers are the first digital technology where an older demographic is proving to be early adopters.

A US report on the future of academic libraries states that the world of ebooks has reached a *tipping point* and that ebooks will become more dominant than print in an academic setting. If we accept this fact, then it is critical for schools to provide access to ebooks, preparing students for college and university. It will also become important for public libraries to provide material in formats that students will be learning to use.

WHAT COMES AFTER E-BOOKS

It is possible that ebooks have the same relationship to books that horseless carriages once had with horse-drawn buggies; ebooks are the first form of a new product that takes its name identification from the immediate past. This product will soon begin to morph into something far different from the printed book, just as the horseless carriage developed into something far different from the horse-drawn buggy. To glimpse the next stages of this new product and the opportunities that electronic learning and creative media represent, we should look more closely at graphic novels and at "apps" and at the rise of visual forms of information portrayal.

Graphic novels and apps are well-known. Visualisation of information is not. Visualisation attempts to convey complex ideas and thoughts through interactive graphics. Visualisations may help to teach complex ideas to students that think more visually than previous generations. In fact, one of top tech trends is listed as "The Visual Web". The fact that the younger generation both thinks visually and learns through play is well documented by the scholars.

The image to the below is an example of information presented through Visualisation. The bubbles are arranged to convey, with few words, a visual image of the scientific evidence that supports or criticizes various natural remedies and cures.

The higher the bubble on the chart, the more evidence exists to support claims that the holistic medicine inside the bubble can at least ease problems with the targeted ailment. The interactive version of this chart allows readers to explore the research behind each bubble and to set personal parameters about gender or unique circumstances. Bubbles sink or climb with each unique qualifier. To an extent, this image is one prototype of a new Table of Contents, one that can be customised to fit the reader.

PRIVATE PUBLISHING

We will also see a rise in the acceptance and the popularity of personally produced and published books. The qualitative difference between books produced by private sector publishing houses and by individuals will begin to blur. Book equivalents of YouTube videos will challenge traditional publishing for reader attention, just as YouTube is challenging traditional television. School and public libraries will face an opportunity to "publish" outstanding creative material to the web and to help these works find an audience. Although library print circulation remains strong, books will soon constitute less than half of the circulation figures for many library branches. This is already happening in some cities, particularly in more economically challenged, urban neighbourhoods.

It is important that libraries embrace the fact that their mission is not connected to a type of container (print) but to the ability of residents and students to access the best of the world's intellectual property, no matter the format in which it is presented. There are plenty of cautionary tales around us. For example, when downloaded music became popular, music industry did not establish its own digital network; they were too focused on trying to sell physical material through stores. The music industry forgot to focus on the customer instead of their own infrastructure and allowed a computer company, Apple, to create iTunes Clayton Christensen's book *The Innovator's Dilemma*, written before the music industry's radical changes, provides a cautionary tale for libraries and librarians who assume our business is immune to change or that the public will always protect us.

APPLICATION IN INFORMATION SYSTEM

Internet is a global information system, consisting of billions of web pages from which we can get information. The major activity on the Internet, that is electronic publishing and information uploading, are being done in quiet an unorganized way. The lack of proper organizing huge quantities of information has not retrieve from the Internet. In any information system, we have followed certain tools and techniques to tell us which document contains what information. These tools and techniques can be classification, cataloguing, indexing, etc., in the case of traditional information systems. As Internet is a distributed information system with disjoint information sources spread across the globe, we cannot bring the related documents together in the retrieval process. Hence the tools and techniques meant for pinpointing information on the Internet need to be more accurate.

XML is significant because it makes it much easier to share and search resources that are in different formats. Until fairly recently, this wasn't much of an issue for libraries. Historically, libraries have served as centralized repositories of information. They purchased books, journals, films, and other information resources on physical media, and patrons found what the library owned by consulting a catalogue that listed holdings. Most catalogs are designed with the assumption that once a library records some descriptive information about each resource it has purchased, this information won't have to be radically altered. For physical resources, this works pretty well, since the authors, titles, subjects, and physical characteristics of a book don't change. Once access to the Internet became widespread, it became clear that providing access to remote electronic resources could be very problematic. Catalogs are designed to provide access to physical resources that are under direct control of the library. However, people want to read journal articles, books, and useful Web pages stored in dynamically updated databases that are maintained and owned by other organizations that might be thousands of miles away. Online library catalogs are poorly suited for providing access to these works; so many libraries do not include these types of resources in the catalogue. As a result, it is often very difficult for patrons to know what electronic resources they can get t1hrough their libraries.

This is where XML comes into the picture. It is impossible to search or display information unless it is structured in a meaningful way. In plain English, this means that information providers need to agree on standards for encoding electronic documents so they can be retrieved in a uniform way. Libraries have encoded bibliographic records in MARC for many years, and that has allowed them to easily share catalogue records, which reduces costs while improving services. For a variety of reasons, it is not feasible to encode the new types of resources patrons want access to in MARC. However, when the information is stored in XML, it is possible to share and combine that data in ways that would not otherwise be possible.

INTERNET AND ITS' SEARCH ENGINES, SEARCH DIRECTORY AND META SEARCH ENGINES

There are many 'search engines'; 'meta search engines' and 'search directory' are available in the Internet. This is obvious from the two following important observations:

- The result of aparticular search is so high in recall and low in precision.
- The output of the search result has no standard of 2any kind.

The search tools on the Internet use robots to collect information about the documents to generate keyword indexes. Generally, these tools use different algorithms to assign keywords to the document. Some of the robots collect keywords from the title whereas some collect from the first few lines of the document. But the very pre-assumption of the search robots, that the titles are expressive and the beginning few lines of a document focuses the content, do not hold good for maximum documents.

To give an example, if we search the Internet for term 'data', we should be sure to get results at least regarding 'database', 'data center', 'data warehouse', etc. Certainly the recall will be very high. The retrieval of irrelevant result can be reduced by subject gateway approach, but cannot be eliminated. The main cause of the problem in *Hyper Text Markup Language* (HTML), the standard for web publication is system-defined tag. This *'tag set'* is mainly for display of the content and HTML provides no tag to address the content precisely. *eXtensible Markup Language* (XML) designed by *World Wide Web Consortium* (W3C) promises a possible solution to this problem. The major advantage of XML over HTML is its extensibility, *i.e.*, provision of user defined tags and attributes to identify the structural elements of a document. XML also provides structural complexity to define document structure that can be nested at any level of complexity.

WHAT IS XML?

XML is a extensible markup language for documents containing structured information. Structured information contains both content and some indication of what role that content plays. Almost all documents have some structure. A markup language is a mechanism to identify structures in a document. The XML specification defines a standard way to add markup to documents.

XML IS JUST LIKE HTML

No. In HTML, both the tag semantics and the tag set are fixed. An <h1> is always a first level heading and the tag <ati.product.code> is meaningless. The W3C, in conjunction with browser vendors and the WWW community, is constantly working to extend the definition of HTML to allow new tags to keep pace with changing technology and to bring variations in presentation to the Web. However, these changes are always rigidly confined by what the browser vendors have implemented and by the fact that backward compatibility is paramount. And for people who want to disseminate information widely, features supported by only the latest releases of Netscape and Internet Explorer are not useful.

XML IS JUST LIKE SGML

No. Well, yes, sort of. XML is defined as an application profile of SGML. SGML is the Standard Generalized Markup Language defined by ISO 8879. SGML has been the standard, vendor-independent way to maintain repositories of structured documentation for more than a decade, but it is not well suited to serving documents over the web. Defining XML as an application profile of SGML means that any fully conformant SGML system will be able to read XML documents. However, using and understanding XML documents *does not* require a system that is capable of understanding the full generality of SGML. XML is, roughly speaking, a restricted form of SGML.

WHY XML

It is important to understand why it was created. XML was created so that richly structured documents could be used over the web. The only viable alternatives, HTML and SGML, are not practical for this purpose. HTML comes bound with a set of semantics and does not provide arbitrary structure. SGML provides arbitrary structure, but is too difficult to implement just for a web browser.

Full SGML systems solve large, complex problems that justify their expense. Viewing structured documents sent over the web rarely carries such justification. This is not to say that XML can be expected to completely replace SGML. While XML is being designed to deliver structured content over the web, some of the very features it lacks to make this practical, make SGML a more satisfactory solution for the creation and long-time storage of complex documents. In many organizations, filtering SGML to XML will be the standard procedure for web delivery.

ORIGIN AND GOALS

XML was developed by an XML Working Group formed under the auspices of the *World Wide Web Consortium* (W3C) in 1996. It was chaired by Jon Bosak of Sun Microsystems with the active participation of an XML Special Interest Group also organized by the W3C. Dan Connolly served as the Working Group's contact with the W3C. The design goals for XML are:

- XML shall be straightforwardly usable over the Internet.
- XML shall support a wide variety of applications.
- XML shall be compatible with SGML.
- It shall be easy to write programmes which process XML documents.
- The number of optional features in XML is to be kept to the absolute minimum, ideally zero.
- XML documents should be human-legible and reasonably clear.
- The XML design should be prepared quickly.
- The design of XML shall be formal and concise.
- XML documents shall be easy to create.
- Terseness in XML markup is of minimal importance.

HOW XML WORKS

In XML, *Document Type Definitions* (DTDs) may accompany a document, essentially defining the rules of the document, such as which elements are present and the structural relationship between the elements. DTDs help to validate the data when the receiving application does not have a built-in description of the incoming data. With XML, however, DTDs are optional. Data sent along with a DTD is known as 'valid' XML. In this case, an XML parser could check incoming data against the rules defined in the DTD to make sure data was structured correctly.

Data sent without a DTD is known as 'well-formed ' XML. With both valid and well-formed XML, XML encoded data is self-describing. The open and flexible format used by XML allows it to be employed anywhere a need exists for the exchange and transfer of information. This makes it powerful. For instance, XML can be used to describe information about HTML pages, or it can be used to describe data contained in business rules or objects in an electronic - commerce transaction, such as invoices, purchase orders and order forms.

XML is separate from HTML, but XML could also be added inside HTML documents. By embedding XML data inside an HTML page, multiple views could be generated from the delivered data, using the semantic information contained in the XML. Moreover, XML can be used for such compelling applications as distributed printing, database searches, and others. When most people think of the things that can be done with XML, they are actually thinking about a family of related technologies rather than a single markup language. On a related note, it is better to think of XML as a grammar than as a language. XML establishes rules for defining new formats. In regular markup languages such as the *HyperText Markup Language* (HTML), authors must use certain tags that make the text bold, create clickable links, draw tables, apply style sheets, etc. With XML, authors are free to make up their own tags and attributes if they don't feel that those that have been created by others meet their needs.

XML AND LIBRARIES

For years, libraries have been quietly using XML to perform functions such as improving access to archival materials, simplifying interlibrary loan processing, and enhancing digital collections, but increased reliance on the Internet for delivering information resources has brought XML into the mainstream, where its impact is starting to be felt by libraries of all sizes. As early as 1993, the library at the University of California- Berkeley started developing a method for encoding archival materials in XML.

The outcome of this project was the development of the *Encoded Archival Description* (EAD) standard, which is now maintained by the Library of Congress. Use of EAD has been increasing steadily over the years as a growing number of archival finding aids have been moved to the Web. For the past several years, individual libraries have been improving their services and saving money by developing their own XML applications. Since 1998, Oregon State University has been using an application called *InterLibrary Loan Automated Search And Print* (ILL ASAP) to automatically search interlibrary loan requests and print request forms sorted by location and call number, complete with availability information, scannable Ariel addresses, shipping labels and billing data customized to the borrowing library or consortium involved.

This free application has been adopted by dozens of libraries around the country. More-ambitious XML projects have also been successfully implemented. The Washington Research Library Consortium uses XML to provide access to subscription databases, digital collections, materials requested via interlibrary loan, and library catalogs that run on a combination of commercial, open source, and locally developed platforms. This system, known as *Access to Library And Database Information Network* (ALADIN) not only delivers content to seven academic research libraries, but also performs critical related tasks such as patron authentication using XML messages transmitted between applications over the Web. In the spring of 2002, the Library of Congress announced an official specification for representing MARC data in an XML environment, MARC XML.

Even though sharing data between catalogs is relatively easy because of widespread support for the MARC format, the ability to express MARC data in XML is useful for any library trying to develop tools or access mechanisms that combine MARC data with non-MARC resources. Now that a standard has emerged for representing MARC, it is reasonable to assume that vendors and others will develop tools that take advantage of the huge amount of data already stored in MARC format.

As a matter of fact, within a few weeks of the announcement of LC's specification, well-known tools used for manipulating MARC records such as *Java MARC Events* (JAMES) and MarcEdit already contained support for the new standard. As more libraries use XML, they are finding more uses for it. The eScholarship initiative at the California Digital Library not only uses XML to store books in a standardized format, but it also uses XML technologies to allow users to define their own displays. The *Open Archives Initiative* (OAI), an effort supported by OCLC, has developed a protocol that makes it easy to send a query to a database over the Web and receive the results in XML. OAI effectively makes it possible to perform searches of multiple databases simultaneously without the need for proprietary hooks into local databases. While this functionality is very similar to what was promised with Z39.50, OAI is much easier to implement, so the hope is that it will be widely used for many kinds of databases.

ENVIRONMENTAL IMPACTS OF E-BOOKS

With the growth in the number of e-readers and sales of Ebooks, many have begun to question the environmental impacts of e-readers and e-Books. Currently e-Books make up a relatively small portion of the overall book market and about 9 per cent of the trade book market. However, sales of e-Books are rapidly increasing, as are the number of devices capable or displaying e-Books. With the rapid adoption of e-Books many have questioned what effects e-readers will have on the environmental impacts of the book industry.

At the time of this was written, none of the major manufacturers of dedicated e-readers have published information about the environmental impacts of their devices, however Apple has released an environmental report on its iPad, a tablet computer with a built in e-Book application, and the ability to download applications to read e-Books from other suppliers. Additionally others have estimated the environmental impacts of Amazon's Kindle, and other e-reader devices and attempted to compare them to the environmental impacts of paper books.

This report will summarise some of the information found in these reports and compare the environmental impacts of e-Books to those of paper books. While e-Books can be read on personal computers and smart phones this report will focus primarily on dedicated e-readers and tablet computers.

e-BOOK SALES

Since, Amazon launched its e-reader the Kindle in November of 2007, sales of e-Books have grown rapidly and more companies have released devices capable reading e-Books. The Amazon Kindle still leads the e-reader market, though a recent study indicates that the Kindle is rapidly losing market share to Apple's iPad. Together the Kindle and the iPad make up the vast majority of the e-reader market. A recent survey of e-reader owners showed that 47 per cent owned a Kindle and 32 per cent owned iPads. The Sony Reader and the Barnes and Noble Nook respectively accounted for 5 per cent and 4 per cent of the respondents e-readers.

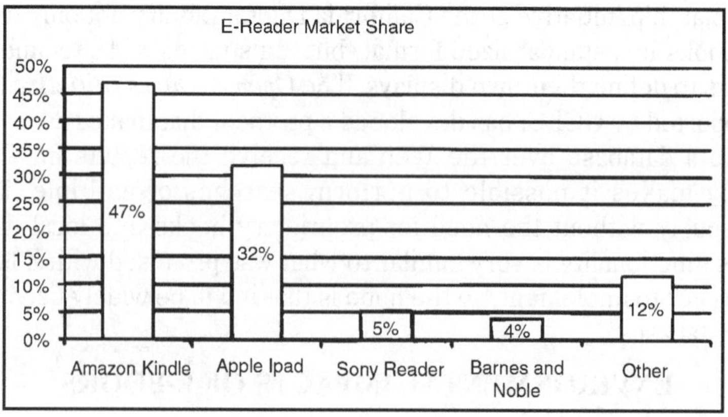

Fig. Market Share of E-readers

The rate at which e-Book sales have increased in recent years is impressive. In 2009 sales of e-Books totaled over $169.5 million and e-Books accounted for about 9 per cent of all trade book sales from January through August of 2010. It appears that the shift towards e-Books is only picking up steam. In January to August of 2010 e-Book sales were 193 per cent greater than they were for that same period in 2009.

The Book Industry Study Group's 'Survey of Consumer Attitudes Towards e-Book Reading' suggests that we may just be seeing the beginning of the shift in how people choose to read books. According to the study, which was released in January of 2010, 37 per cent of e-Book buyers had purchased their first e-Book in the past 6 months. Furthermore, the data from the BISG survey suggests that consumers of e-Books will purchase fewer printed books. 25 per cent of e-Book owners surveyed said they would buy fewer printed books, 15 per cent said they buy no printed books and 9 per cent said they would not buy a printed book even if the book they wanted was not available as an e-Book.

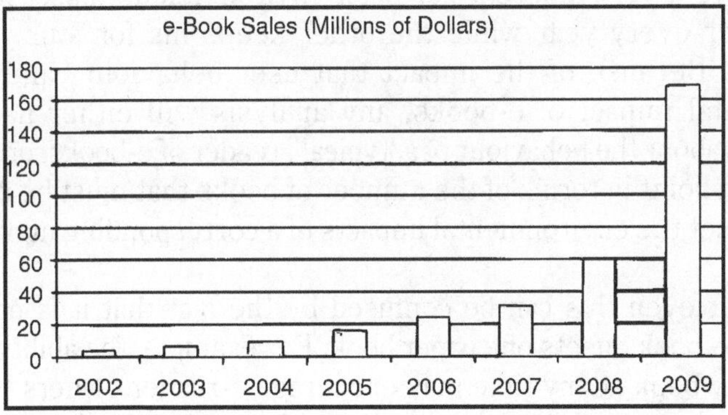

Fig. E-book Sales by Year

E-READER LIFECYCLE

Since, the data suggests that sales of e-Books are likely to increase while sales of printed books are likely to decrease, it is logical to question the environmental implications of this transition. In 2008 Green Press Initiative and the Book Industry Study Group commissioned a report on the environmental impacts of the U.S., book industry which included a lifecycle analysis of printed books. That report concluded that in 2006 the U.S., book industry consumed approximately 30 million trees and had a carbon footprint equivalent to 12.4 million metric tons of carbon dioxide, or 8.85 pounds per book sold.

Determining the environmental impacts of an e-Book presents a challenge that does not exist in estimating the impacts of a paper book. That challenge is the fact that user behaviour will significantly influence the impact of an e-book. This is due to the fact that the manufacturing of the e-reader device accounts for the vast majority of an e-books environmental impact. Because of this, on a per book basis, a reader who reads 100 books on an e-reader will have almost 1/100th of the impact of someone who reads only one book on the same device.

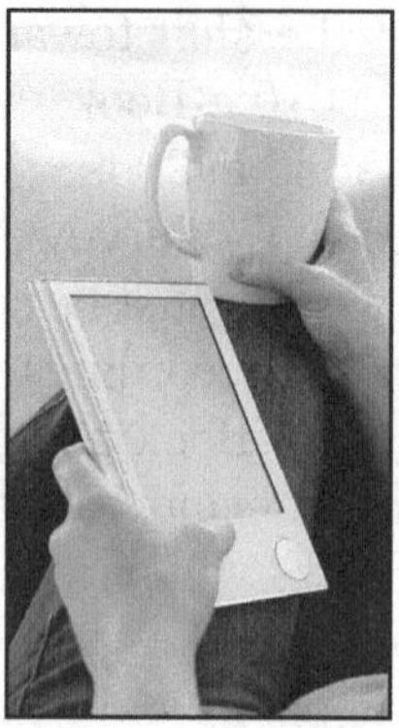

Additionally, two readers who each read the same number of books per year, can have a very different per-book environmental impact if one buys a new e-reader every year while the other keeps his for four years before replacing it. Because of the impact that user behaviour can have on the environmental impact of e-books, any analysis will either have to make assumptions about the behaviour of a 'typical" reader of e-books, or else identify a break-even point in terms of the number of books that must be read on an e-reader to offset the environmental impacts of a corresponding number of paper books.

However even this can be confused by the fact that it is not clear that reading one e-book offsets one paper book. For example, the ability to instantly download any book at any time may encourage e-reader owners to read more books in which case each e-book read would not necessarily correspond to a printed book that would have been read. Additionally someone who buys a printed book and later lends it to a friend to read would in effect halve the environmental impact of reading that book.

As such any analysis should strive to account for this and determine a break-even point in terms of 'printed books offset' rather than e-books read. Additional complexity is added by the fact that most e-readers can be used for a variety of tasks other than reading books. For example, most can read newspapers and magazines in addition to books and some e-readers can also read blogs and surf the internet. Tablet computers can allow a user to check e-mail, play games, view photos and videos, listen to music and surf the Internet in addition to other things.

Thus for the owner of a Tablet computer, who only spends 10 per cent of his time using the tablet to read books, it would seem reasonable to assume that only 10 per cent of the manufacturing impact of the tablet should be counted towards the impact of that users e-books.

APPLE iPAD

Apple is the only manufacturer that has completed an environmental report for its e-reader device. According to Apple's report, over its lifecycle, the iPad will be responsible for 130 kg of carbon equivalent greenhouse gas emissions. 130 kg is equal to about 287 pounds.

Using the carbon footprint of the book industry in the Environmental Trends Report, the average printed book is responsible 8.85 pounds of greenhouse gas emissions.

This means an iPad owner would need to offset 32.4 printed books during the iPad's lifetime to break even in terms of the carbon footprint of reading those books.

If you are also offsetting printed magazines and printed newspapers with the iPad then the number of books you would need to offset to break even could be much lower.

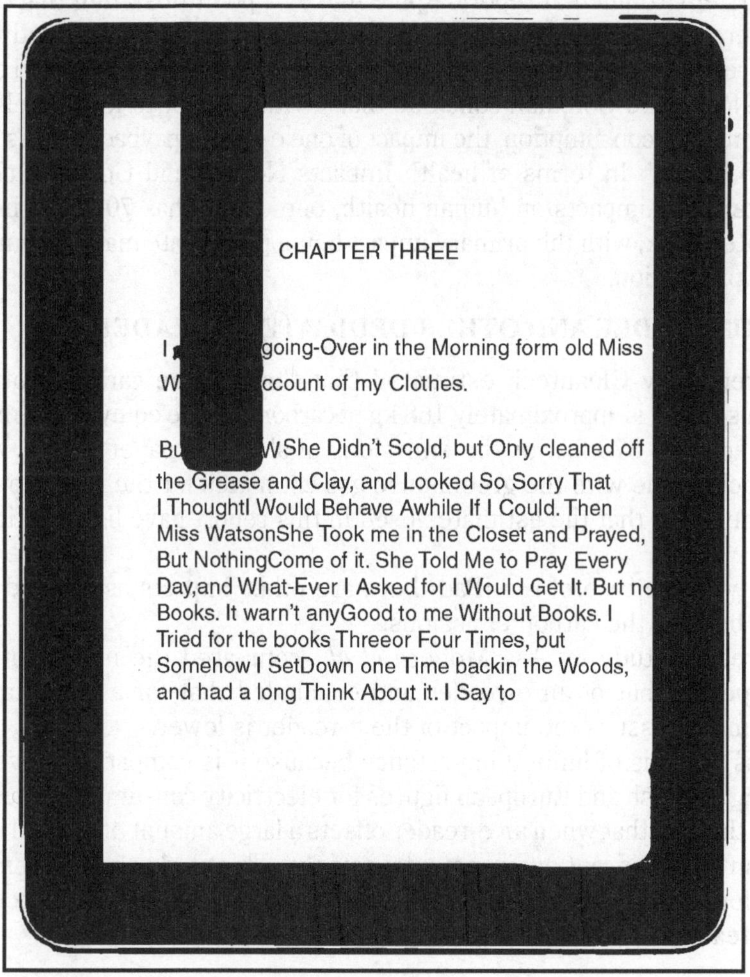

Daniel Goleman and Gregory Norris conducted their own lifecycle comparison of the iPad with printed books in an article printed in the New York Times titled 'How Green is My iPad' Their analysis concluded that it would be necessary to offset 100 printed books to make up for the carbon footprint of the iPad, however it is not clear if their analysis included the books impacts on forest carbon loss or not.

Of course greenhouse gas emissions are not the only environmental impacts of producing e-readers or printed books. Printed books require wood fibre which needs to be harvested from forests while e-readers require plastic metal and glass as well as other mineral resources to make up the various electronic components and battery. Norris and Goleman mention that some materials that are in e-readers, such as columbite and tantalite, are often mined in wartorn regions of Africa and sourcing these minerals can have negative social impacts.

In its environmental report, Apple makes a point of stating that the iPad has a mercury free LED display, that the glass is free of arsenic and that the iPad is free from Brominated Flame Retardants (BFRs) and Polyvinyl chloride (PVC). Norris and Goleman conclude that "With respect to fossil fuels, water use and mineral consumption, the impact of one e-reader payback equals roughly 40 to 50 books". In terms of health Impacts Norriss and Goleman conclude that in terms of impacts on human health, one e-book has 70 times impact of one printed book, with the primary impact being particulate matter from energy use and production.

AMAZON KINDLE AND OTHER DEDICATED e-READERS

A report by Cleantech estimated that the lifetime carbon footprint of Amazon's kindle is approximately 168 kg of carbon dioxide equivalent emissions. This is equal to 370 lbs. or the emissions of about 42 paper books, which is very much in line with the greenhouse gas estimates for the iPad, however it should be noted that the estimates used in this report have been criticised by some.

As with the case of the iPad there are other impacts associated with e-readers besides the carbon emissions.

A recent study by Asa Moberg *et al.,* compared the impact of a daily newspaper to that of an e-reader and concluded that for a wide variety of environmental issues the impact of the e-reader is lower.

This study is of limited importance because it is comparing newspapers, and using Swedish and European figures for electricity consumption, but it does support the idea that when an e-reader offsets a large amount of printed material there can be significant environmental savings. This study also suggested that more information is needed with respect to toxic materials that could potentially be in e-readers.

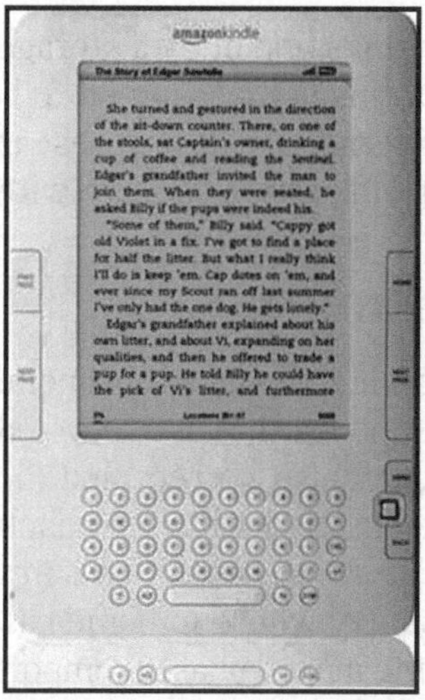

OTHER FACTORS TO CONSIDER AND ADDITIONAL RESEARCH NEEDS ENERGY CONSUMPTION

Unlike a printed book, an e-reader requires energy consumption during the 'use' stage of its lifecycle. In most of the estimates, this energy consumption used while the reader is reading is baked into the final estimates. Additionally, this number is likely to be relatively small compared to the energy used in manufacturing the device. For the iPad consumer energy use is equivalent to 30 per cent of the tablet's total carbon footprint.

This number is likely to be much lower for dedicated e-readers that use e-ink technology which only requires energy to change the words on the page and does use power while the user is actually reading. Even the iPad uses very little energy when someone is just reading on it. And Norris and Goleman point out that reading at night with a light on can use more electricity than charging an e-reader.

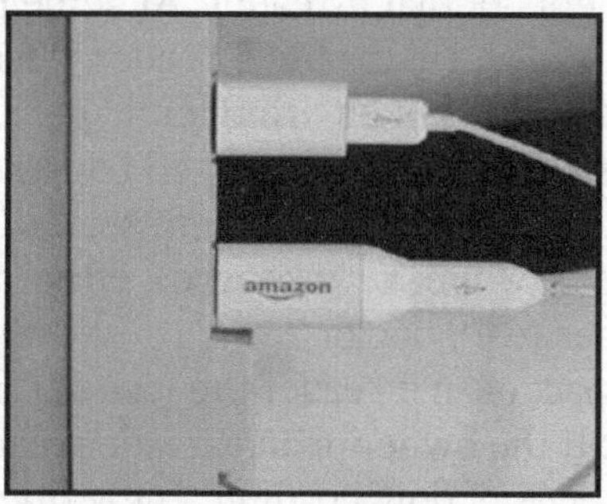

What is not clear is the degree to which the studies address the impact of the servers, modems and infrastructure that makes the delivery of e-books possible. To be certain energy demand for storing and transmitting data over the Internet is increasing rapidly and poses a very serious environmental challenge. However the total portion of data storage that is associated with e-books, while unknown, is at this point assumed to be quite minimal compared to the total content of the internet. Additional research should be conducted to determine the environmental impacts associated with data storage/transmission for e-books.

e-WASTE AND RECYCLING

Paper books can be recycled, though at this point not much data is available regarding the percentage of books that are recycled at the end of their useful life. Electronic equipment can also be recycled, however consumers should make sure they understand exactly what a manufacturer means when they say the will recycle a product. In some cases this simply means the item will be shipped to a developing country where in some cases children will dismantle the product removing only the most valuable components under unsafe working conditions. The rest of the 'recycled' product is then landfilled or incinerated sometimes exposing workers and the community to toxic materials. It should also be noted that not all e-book manufacturers have recycling programmes.

CALCULATING BOOKS OFFSET

The image to the right is a good way to visualise the environmental impacts of an e-reader. As the number of printed books that the e-reader offsets increases, so do the benefits of that e-reader. At some point these gains offset the impact of manufacturing and using the e-reader. This 'breakeven point' will be different for different metrics of environmental performance but for most it is likely somewhere between 30 and 70 printed books that are offset over the lifetime of the e-reader. For greenhouse gas emissions this number is probably between 20 and 35 books while for measures of human health impacts the number is probably closer to 70 books.

In assessing the impact of an e-reader the idea of printed books offset must be carefully considered. If the owner of an e-reader reads more books because of the ease and convenience of downloading a new title, then every book read on the device does not necessarily correspond to a printed book that is offset. Additionally the numbers in the figure are based on a very simple comparison that is not likely to be replicated in the real world. The assumption is that the reader would either purchase a new printed book once and not share it with anyone else or that the reader would read the books on an e-reader and only use the e-reader for reading books.

Fig. Environmental Benefits of an e-reader by Printed Books Offset

If a person would normally share a printed book with others, buy some used printed books, or borrow many of the printed books from the library then the numbers would need to be adjusted to account for that. Additionally, if the e-reader is used for other activities such as watching video, browsing the Internet, checking e-mail, or reading magazines and newspapers, it is unfair to assign the full impacts of producing the e-reader to e-books. More research is needed on typical user behaviour in terms of time spent reading e-books verses other activities on e-readers and Tablet computers in order to make a more accurate comparison.

If the trend of the iPad stealing market share from the Kindle continues, it seems likely that users will spend more time on the other activates that tablets like the iPad are optimised for. Additionally, if someone already owns a tablet computer or an e-reader, the marginal impact of downloading and reading an additional book is quite small. Thus for someone who already owns a device capable of reading e-books, the best choice from an environmental perspective would likely be to read a new book on that device.

THE E-BOOK REVOLUTION

SHOULD DEPOSIT LIBRARIES BE INTERESTED IN E-BOOK TECHNOLOGY

Essentially, this question can only be answered by another question. Will e-books have a major impact on publishing? Although the timing of consumer acceptance of the reading of books on portable electronic devices may remain uncertain, there appears very little doubt that the e-book is set to have a fundamental impact on the dissemination of what we might call 'book-like content'. Some publishers have already made major commitments to the conversion of part or all of their backlist to e-books; many of these are trade publishers, but the recent announcement from Taylor and Francis in the UK that they will digitise the whole of their backlist of 17,000 academic books cannot be ignored. However, despite much publicised initiatives from Stephen King and a few others, today the greater part of e-book activity is focussed on backlist titles. Several publishers have told us that this immediate emphasis on the conversion of backlist is not accidental.

There is so much uncertainty about the impact that e-books may have on frontlist sales that publishers are unwilling to add to the considerable uncertainty that already exists in their sales projections. Conversion of backlist provides the potential of revenue from an otherwise dormant asset, without creating significant risk. However, if ebooks become a significant medium for the consumption of backlist titles, it can only be a matter of time before market demand drives publishers in the direction of publishing their frontlist in e-book formats. 'e-book-only' publishing may currently be largely confined to what many dismiss as an enhanced form of vanity publishing in the US; this is unlikely to remain the case for long.

For this reason we believe that libraries cannot afford to ignore developments in e-book publishing, but should begin to think about the implications for deposit. While it may be several years before their impact becomes very significant, we believe that it is unlikely that e-books will not be having a major impact on publishing by the end of this decade.

ARE OUR RESPONDENTS INTERESTED IN E-BOOKS

Half of our twelve larger publisher respondents are either already publishing in e-book formats or expect to start doing so shortly. However, only one has already published anything solely in e-book format; and of the other five, three have no plans to publish only in e-book, and the other two say they regard it as premature to do so in 2001.

In terms of their commitment to e-book publishing, the five publishers already involved range from the very tentative and experimental to the fully committed—one of them is expecting to have their complete trade frontlist in e-book in 2001. The other publishers told us that they currently have no plans for publishing in e-book formats.

E-BOOK CONTENT DELIVERY FORMATS

The same 'content and form' division that we discussed in our introduction is also being played out in the e-book arena. ebook devices are divided between those which use content marked up for form and those which use page-based content. The following table sets out the formats used by each device and the current distribution channel for these formats in the United States.

One of our respondents referred to the OEB standard as "little more than HTML expressed as XML'. He went on to say that, as a result, the existing version of OEB, although theoretically extensible, is more suitable for novels than for more complex text. More complex ebooks can currently only be delivered using PDF-based formats. The OEB standard is also undergoing revision, and another of our respondents expressed concern about version control.

Primary Format channel (in the US)	Derivative Format	Current distribution
	Microsoft Reader	bn.com Lightning Source OEB Rocket
eBook	bn.com	
	(originally HTML)	Powell's, etc.
	SoftBook	SoftBook Press
	Peanut Press	Peanut Press
	Acrobat Reader	Adobe PDF Merchant
	Glassbook Reader	bn.com Glassbook, etc
PDF	Print-on-Demand	bn.com
		Lightning Source
		Replica Books
		Sprout
	SoftLock Systems	SoftLock Systems

It is also important to recognise that each of the different derivative formats are different file formats, to a greater or lesser extent. Although we expect to see the different devices becoming more conformant with standards as time passes, there are significant divergences today. Publishers who wish to provide content to multiple devices need to maintain multiple electronic versions of the same title. This is even the case with PDF-based formats, where the text layout for one device may not be suitable for another.

PRODUCING EBOOKS

For the time being at least, ebook production has not been embedded into publishers' standard production workflows. e-books today are typically being produced by scanning of printed products—we are told that this is often the case even for newly published titles. Publishers' workflows for books in the print on paper environment are typically much less standardised than they are for serial publications. Except in the case of major structured reference works, neutral coding of text is rare or non-existent. It is likely to take some time for ebook production to become a settled part of publisher's production workflows. Meanwhile, production workflows will remain somewhat *ad hoc*. It has also been suggested to us that vendors of tools for production of ebook formats may have a strong commercial interest in obstructing the adoption of stable, capable, neutral formats.

E-BOOKS AND OTHER CONTENT TYPES

For the time being, e-books are generally restricted to fairly straightforward text and still images. We would regard it as unlikely that this will remain the case for very long. The OEB standard allows for arbitrary external technology to manage other content types and it may be some time before there is any general agreement on the optimum file formats. In the meantime, in the same way as we have seen in online resources, there will almost certainly be many different proprietary approaches.

E-BOOKS AND METADATA

The OEB 'package' incorporates a simple Dublin Core (DC) metadata record in Version 1. We understand that is has been recognised that the DC set is not adequate for the purpose, and a significant revision of the metadata structure is expected in future releases.

E-BOOKS AND ENCRYPTION

An essential element in the marketing of all e-book devices is security, because of the 'distributed' model of distribution. The content on ebook devices is encrypted to prevent it being passed along to other users. There is an industry grouping, EBX, which is defining a standard approach to rights management and encryption. The different approaches used for encryption need not detain us here. However, the fact that the content is encrypted does create a particular problem for libraries, not least in managing long-term preservation. If e-books are to be deposited with libraries, it will clearly be advantageous if these are non-encrypted versions. However, publishers will be very reluctant to allow libraries to provide any public access to unencrypted versions.

MANAGING E-BOOK CONTENT

Only a small number of publishers are currently planning to manage their own ebook content in house. Most will be happy to see their ebook content managed by outside vendors. Since, this means that publishers will not be in direct control of their content, it is likely to complicate the process of deposit, particularly deposit of unencrypted versions of content.

SELECTION FOR PRESERVATION

"Preservation" refers to all the activities undertaken by an institution to ensure that its collections survive in usable condition for as long as they are needed. While this sounds relatively simple, the process of deciding what to preserve and how to preserve it can be complicated and challenging. Which materials will be important in the future? What items or collections should be preserved, and how?

Even with a national cooperative microfilming effort, cultural institutions with paper-based collections have increasingly realised that it is not possible to preserve every brittle item. As a result, various strategies have been developed for selecting collections for preservation.

This part will explore the various criteria that you should consider when selecting collections for preservation action. Once you have decided what materials merit preservation, the choice of preservation method will depend on the intellectual content, the physical characteristics, and the condition of the materials. We will learn more about evaluating the condition of your collections and choosing the appropriate preservation method(s).

The key to making effective selection decisions is to realise that:

- You cannot save everything (even with cooperative projects);
- Priorities must be set among collections (*e.g.,* you must define your collection's strengths and concentrate on them); and
- Every item may not need to be preserved (*e.g.,* will a representative sample of certain materials be acceptable?).

SELECTION FOR LIBRARY COLLECTIONS

The selection process for preservation has been discussed and analysed extensively within the library community because of the growing need to develop strategies for selecting collections for repair, replacement, and reformatting. Identification of damaged or deteriorated materials often occurs in the course of other library activities, although it may also happen as part of a special project. Consistent procedures for the identification of damaged items are necessary. When an item is identified for possible in-house or offsite preservation action, the librarian must indicate in the catalog record that the item has been temporarily removed from circulation and complete a form indicating what preservation action is needed. This form will accompany the item, which should be placed in a particular area and routed for further review or preservation action. Items must also be placed in a particular area and routed for further review or treatment. In her article "Selection for Preservation," Carolyn Harris summarizes the most common methods librarians use to identify collections whose importance and condition justify preservation action.

Some of these methods are appropriate in the archival context as well:

- *Condition and Use*: Deteriorated items in need of attention are identified as they are returned after circulation or pointed out to staff by users or stack maintenance staff.
- *Condition and Library Processing*: Items in need of attention are identified during acquisition, cataloging, or other processing activities.
- *Condition at the Shelf*: Special projects that require inspection of materials at the shelf (*e.g.,* bar coding, shelf reading) can also identify deteriorated collections. For historical or special collections, a conservator may be needed for further review.
- *Collection and Condition*: An entire collection is identified as important for preservation and individual items within that collection are reviewed to identify materials in need of preservation attention.
- *Scholarly Review*: Faculty, researchers, or scholars identify deteriorated items with particular research value. This may be on an individual basis or part of a special project.

- *Vulnerability to Loss or Deterioration*: Materials that are particularly subject to deterioration, such as newspapers or items to be exhibited, are identified for attention.
- *Value or Uniqueness*: Items that are particularly unique or valuable (in monetary or other senses) are identified for attention.

Decision-making on the Collection Level

While it is easy to identify materials already in special collections as important, a research library may hold other collections of importance as well. In many cases, libraries have chosen to preserve only those collections that are circulated and used. But the library community has also realised that research libraries have a responsibility to preserve collections that may be important for research in the future, even if they are not currently used. Thus, strategies have been developed to select collections for preservation according to their quality and importance.

The criteria used to identify important collections include size of the collection; subject strength (*e.g.,* the depth and extent of the collection as compared to other collections on that subject); past, current, or projected future use; quality and extent of bibliographic control of the materials; available funding for preservation of the collection; media contained in the collection; cooperative responsibilities of the institution; and scholarly interest in the collection.

Decision-making on the Item Level

Before any item is preserved, it must be reviewed to make sure that preservation is the proper action to be taken. How is the item related to others in the collection? Are there additional copies or other items by the same author? Does the item fit the collecting policy? Are there other copies that are easily accessible in a close geographic area? Has the item been preserved (*e.g.,* filmed or treated) elsewhere? Is a replacement (*e.g.,* reprint, facsimile, microfilm) commercially available?

If these questions do not establish that the item should be discarded or replaced, additional analysis will be needed to determine the item's priority for preservation action and how it should be preserved.

SELECTION FOR ARCHIVAL COLLECTIONS

As in libraries, selection for preservation in archives often happens as part of other activities, such as acquisition, appraisal, arrangement, and description. The process of selection for preservation is closely related to archival appraisal, since it involves identifying the value and importance of collections.

While many of the criteria libraries use to select printed collections for preservation can be used in the context of archival collections, identifying important historical and archival collections also requires consideration of types of value specific to those collections. Since archivists have no more time or resources than librarians, they cannot save everything. Thus, they have developed methods for deciding which records have long-term research value and which do not.

Types of Value for Archival/Historical Collections

Most archivists follow, at least in a general sense, the guidelines for value T.R. Schellenberg established at the National Archives in the mid-1950s. On the most basic level, Schellenberg distinguished between primary value and secondary value.

The primary value of records is their ongoing business value for the organization that created them, to assist in carrying out its administrative, financial, legal, and operating activities; this is referred to as administrative, fiscal, or legal value. Secondary value refers to the value records may have to external organizations and/or private researchers.

Schellenberg defined two types of secondary value: evidential value and informational value. Note that these two types of value are not mutually exclusive: a record may be valuable for both evidential and informational purposes.

Evidential value refers to the value of records in documenting the organizational structure and functions of the institution or the activities of the individual that created them. Who created the records? Do they accurately reflect the activities of the organization or person? Do the records provide evidence of the structure and policies of the organization or institution or evidence of the changing interests of the person? In the case of an organization, are these records also maintained elsewhere within the organization? Do the records reflect policymaking or implementation of functions?

Informational value refers to the subject content of the collection.

Types of informational value include:

- *Uniqueness*: The information in the records must be more complete and useful than that found on this topic in other existing sources, whether public or private. The records should also not be duplicated elsewhere, an occurrence that is fairly common in modern public records.
- *Form*: Records that provide concentrated information (*e.g.,* some information about many people, as in census records; or in-depth information about a few people, as in case files) are the best candidates for retention. The form of the record is also important: can it be accessed and understood easily by researchers?
- *Importance*: Value for long-term scholarly and public research is difficult to determine. Archivists generally try to document those subjects, people, and events that are considered important by the society within which the records were created.

Other types of value commonly encountered are:

- *Intrinsic Value*: This refers to records with characteristics that require them to be retained in their original form. They may be valuable because of their age (in general, older records have more significance, but this is not always the case), because the records have a unique physical form or aesthetic quality, because the records are directly associated with people or events of historical significance, because they might be useful for exhibition, etc.
- *Historical Value*: This term is used in many different ways; it might refer to materials that are valuable because of their age or association, or it might encompass both evidential and informational value.

Both value and condition must be considered in selecting archival and other historical collections for preservation. Additional considerations include whether the records are duplicated or maintained in another form elsewhere; whether they are complete (fragmentary materials can be frustrating for research); whether they need to be retained in their original form, or whether they can be reformatted (*e.g.,* onto microfilm); and whether there are donor or other restrictions on the use of the records.

6

Book Structure and Construction

The pages of a book, whether they are sewn or glued together, are called the text block. The covers of a book are called the case. The case is made of the front cover, the spine and the back cover.

TEXT BLOCKS IN SIGNATURES

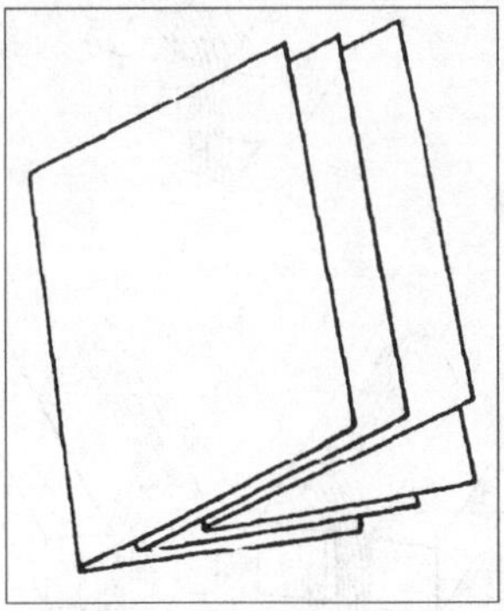

When the text block is sewn, the pages are gathered together in groups; then each group is folded in half.

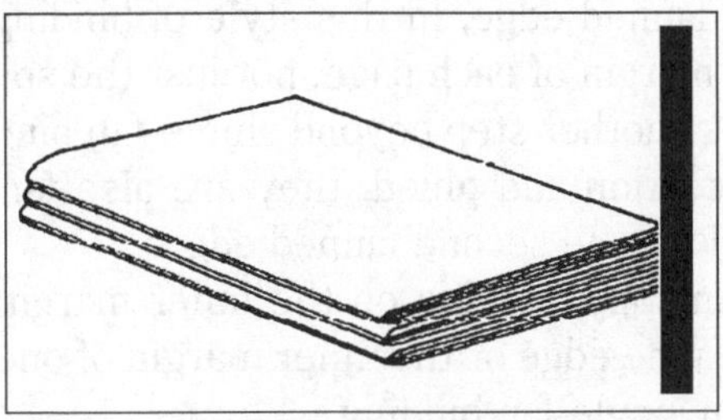

A group of folded pages is called a part or signature and is usually four to eight pieces of paper. Books that are constructed of sewn signatures tend to function best because the pages are securely attached to one another and they open flat. Modern manufacturing techniques enable book manufacturers to create a text block with signatures, cut small notches in the folded edge and insert glue to hold the pages together instead of sewing thread. These books look like they are sewn, but they are not. Open the text block to the centre of a signature and look for the thread, if it's not there, the book is glued.

Text Blocks in Loose Sheets

Text blocks can also be single sheets glued together in a process called adhesive, perfect, or fan binding. In this process, fast drying glue is applied to the spine of the text block. Adhesives that dry very quickly are often brittle and that is why the spine of a book cracks when the book is opened. Once the spine glue is cracked, the pages will begin to fall out. In addition to the problem of brittle glue, there is often very little glue attaching each page to the adjoining pages. When the glue is only in contact with the very thin edge of each sheet of paper, pages can easily separate over time.

Single and Double Fan Binding

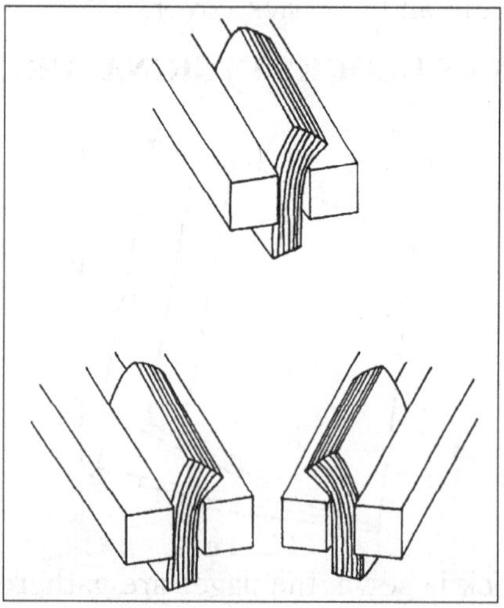

In single-fan binding, the pages of the text block are fanned in one direction and glued along that fanned edge. In this style of binding, a thin line of glue penetrates the inner margin of each page, not just the spine edge. Double-fan adhesive binding goes another step beyond single-fan binding. After the pages are fanned in one direction and glued, they are also fanned in the opposite direction and glued along the second fanned edge.

Double-fan binding applies glue on the inner margin of each side of the page, not just on the spine edge or the inner margin of one side of the paper. It is much stronger than single-fan binding.

When library binders bind a book using double fan binding, they use adhesives that dry slowly and flexible. In addition, they usually reinforce the spine edge of the adhesive bound text block with cloth and paper so it is stronger and the text block opens flat. A library binder can be a good source of information to understand the binding processes.

Keep in mind the bindery is selling a product and as the customer, you can question the binder until all the techniques are fully explained. The services offered must meet the specifications that a library has defined for its collections. In order to set minimum levels of excellence in library binding, the Library Binding Institute has published the Standard for Library Binding. This booklet explains the different types of bindings and what standards should be met in library bound books. The Guide to the Library Binding Institute Standard For Library Binding written by Jan Merril-Oldham is a plain English explanation of the Standard.

OVERSEWN TEXT BLOCKS

Before library binderies began to fan bind books, the most common form of library binding was oversewing. In the over-sewing process, the folds of the signatures are trimmed off and the pages of the text block are oversewn to one another with a diagonal whip stitch.

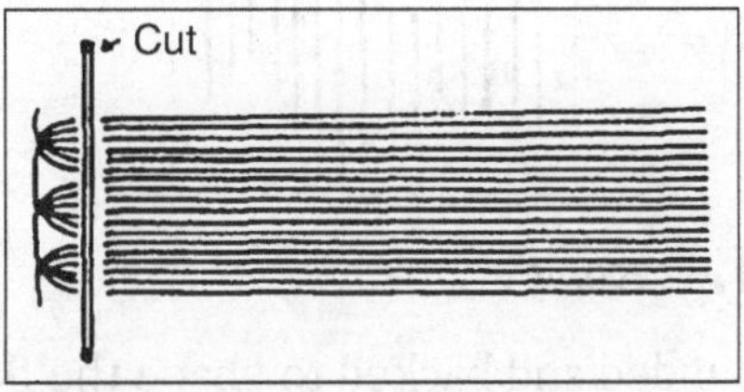

Since the sewing threads tend to pierce deep into the inner margin, the pages are restricted from turning easily.

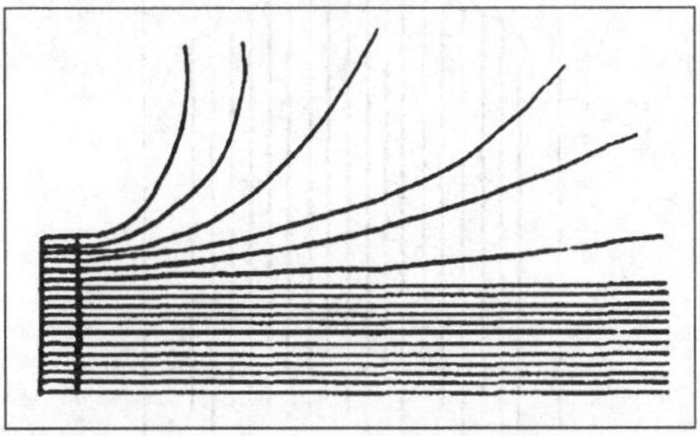

Oversewing is a strong form of binding, but it is often so strong that over time the pages can break out of the binding as they are forced to turn against the sewing threads. Oversewn books may not be candidates for rebinding since much of the inner margin was trimmed off or damaged by the oversewing threads. Books should not be oversewn unless they are very heavy and have wide gutter margins to accommodate the sewing threads. Many libraries stipulate their binders must have permission to oversew a volume.

Sewn Text Blocks: Flat Back and Rounded and Backed Text Blocks

The pages of a book attached together by sewing or gluing is called a text block. Before a text block is attached to a paper or book board case, it can be treated in several ways.

Flat Back Text Blocks

Flat back books are a type of binding which has a flat text block spine. The case spine of flat back books is usually a piece of book board covered with book cloth.

The spines of flat back text blocks have a tendency to become concave over time. To prevent this, the spine of the text block can be rounded and backed.

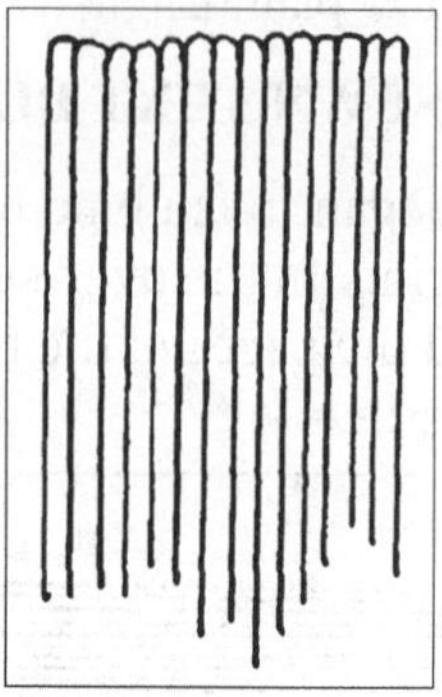

Rounded and Backed Text Blocks

Text blocks are rounded and backed to shape the flat spine of a text block into a curved spine with shoulders

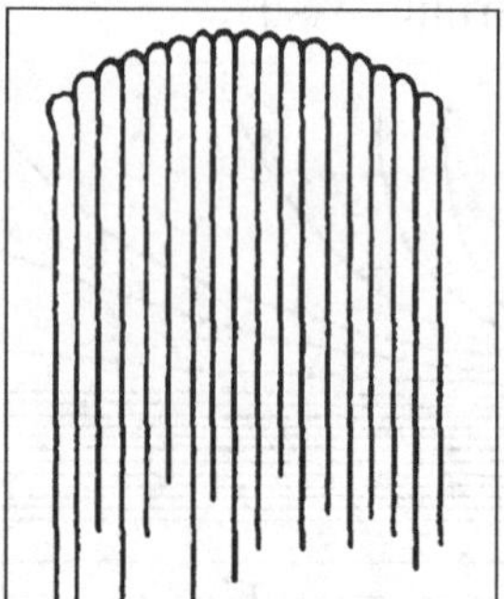

Reprinted from Bookbinding and the Conservation of Books

Rounding a text block is the process of molding the spine of a text block into an arc of approximately onethird of a circle. Rounding takes place after the pages of the text block are attached to one another by sewing or gluing. A light coat of adhesive is applied to the spine which is then worked into shape with light pressure, applied with your fingers or a special hammer called a backing hammer.

Backing is the process of shaping a ridge or shoulder on each side of the spine of a text block prior to attaching the spine lining material.

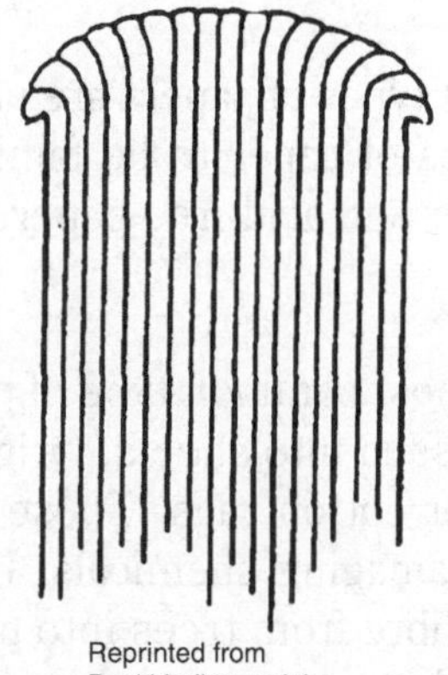

Reprinted from
Bookbinding and the
Conservation of Books

Using a backing hammer, the folds of each signature or glued pages are bent over from the centre to the left and right until shoulders are formed against which the boards will fit. The width of the shoulders is determined by the thickness of the cover boards. In addition to providing space for the cover boards, backing also distributes the swell caused by the sewing threads or adhesive and helps maintain the round of the text block over time.

BOOK CASE CONSTRUCTION

Regardless of how the text block is assembled, modern books are usually manufactured in two stages.

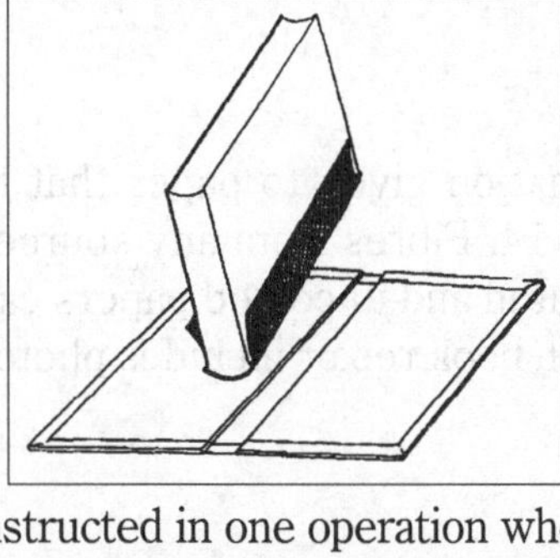

The text block is constructed in one operation where the pages are attached to one another, the spine covered with a cloth liner, called crash, and a paper spine liner is added over that. The book case, consisting of a front cover, a spine and a back cover, is constructed separately in a second operation and the two parts of the book are attached by gluing the crash and end papers to the case covers. The crash holds the text block into the case while the end papers cover up the crash.

PAPER AND BOOK CLOTH

Many types of paper or book cloth can be used in manufacturing, binding and repairing a book.

Paper

Although many different types of papers are used to print and manufacture books, three important types of paper to be familiar with in book repair are uncoated paper, coated paper and acid-free paper.

Uncoated Paper

Uncoated paper is the most common type of paper and is made from plant or tree fibres that are processed into sheets. Originally, most uncoated paper was handmade from linen or cotton rags. These older papers age very well because they contain few damaging chemicals. In the 1860s, a process was developed to turn cellulose fibre from trees into paper. This type of paper can be made in large quantities but contains some very damaging chemicals that cause paper to become brittle more quickly than paper made from cotton or linen.

Coated Paper

A sheet of paper can be impregnated with very fine clay to produce a very fine printing surface. Introduced at the end of the 19th century, coated papers is ideal for printing halftone illustrations. Unfortunately it is not very strong and is highly susceptible to water damage. Often the text pages of a book are printed on uncoated paper while the pages that contain illustrations are printed on coated paper.

The coated paper may be part of the signature or tipped onto a page uncoated page.

Acid-free Paper

Acid-free is a designation given to paper that has a pH value of 7.0 or greater on a scale of 1 to 14. Fibres from any source can be made into paper that is acid-free. Both coated and uncoated papers can be acid-free. Acid-free paper used in conservation book repair includes photocopy paper and Japanese repair tissue.

Book Cloth

Book cloth is a specially woven cloth backed with thin paper. The paper backing gives the cloth support, minimizes stretching and allows the material to maintain a crease.

There are three main categories of book cloth:

- Starch-filled book cloth in which the weave of the cloth is filled with starch. This type of cloth is sometimes called sized book cloth;
- Acrylic-, pryoxylin-, or vinyl-impregnated book cloth;
- Plastic coated book cloth.

Heavier book cloth is sometimes called buckram.

Paper and Book Cloth Grain

Paper and book cloth have a grain just as fabric does and it is important to understand how that grain affects repairs.

Reprinted from Library Materials Preservation Manual

When the grain of the paper and book cloth runs parallel to the spine of the book, the cover and pages open freely and stay open without much effort. This is called 'with the grain'. Paper that is bound into a book with the grain running perpendicular to the spine of the book is called 'against the grain'. Modern publishers often print the pages of a book against the grain to get more pages on a large sheet of paper.

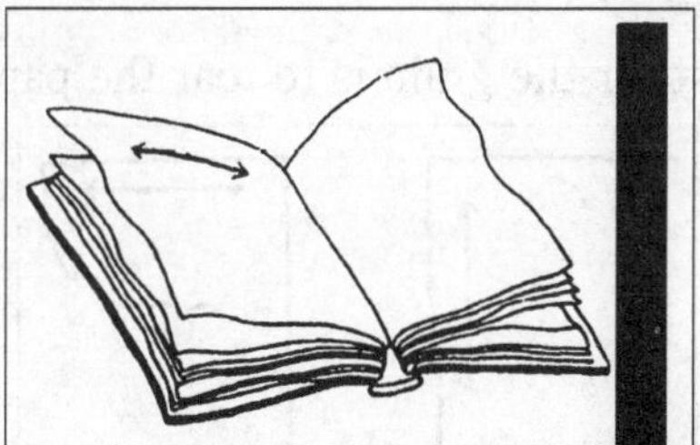

Reprinted from Library Materials Preservation Manual

When the grain runs perpendicular to the spine of a book, the book can be difficult to open and it will not remain open without a great deal of pressure. Books printed against the grain are easily damaged since patrons must force the book open to read or photocopy it. When pages or the case of a book are repaired, the grain of the repair materials should always run parallel to the spine of the book.

Determining the Grain of Paper or Book Cloth

All paper and book cloth has a dominate grain. Paper can be tested for grain using the bend test, the tear test or the water test. The grain of book cloth usually runs parallel to the selvage or bound edge of the fabric. If the selvage of the book cloth has been cut off or if there is any doubt about the grain of book cloth, the bend test or the tear test can be used to determine the grain.

Bend Test

The quickest way to test the grain is to bend the paper or cloth slightly in each direction.

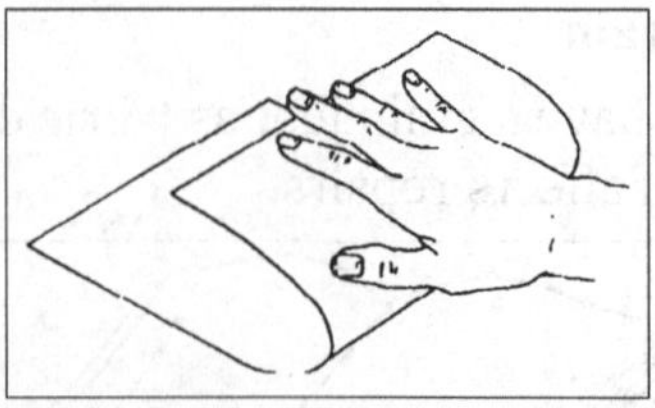

Bring two opposite edges of a piece of paper or cloth together but do not crease. Instead, gently press down on the bend with minimal pressure. Feel any resistance Now bring the other two opposite sides of the paper or cloth together and repeat the process. In one direction there is more resistance than the other. The greater resistance means the paper or cloth does not want to bend in that direction because it is bending against the grain. When the paper or cloth is bent in the opposite direction, there is much less resistance. The bend that offers the least resistance is the bend that goes with the grain of the paper or book cloth. Mark the direction of grain on the paper for future reference.

Tear Test

Another way to test for the grain is to tear the paper or cloth.

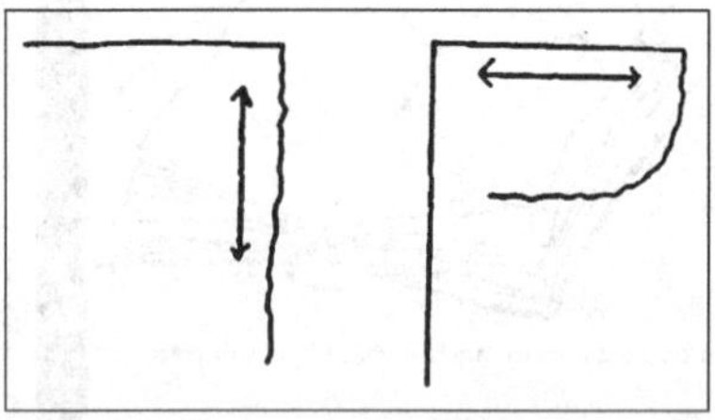

Paper or cloth will tear easily and straight along the direction of the grain. When forced to tear against the grain, the paper or cloth will be difficult to tear and the tear will tend to curve until it meets the grain. Tear the cloth or paper close to a comer and then pencil a small straight line in that comer indicating the direction of the grain so it won't need to be determined every time it is used.

Water Test

When grain is particularly difficult to find, a water test can be used. Use this test only to test paper being used to repair a volume, not on pages bound in a book.

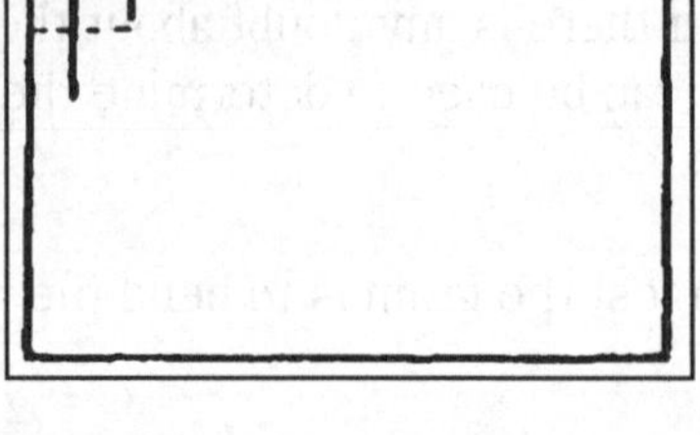

Draw a 4" straight line along one comer of a large sheet of paper. This line will not necessarily be the grain line, it is simply an orientation line. Cut a square out of the comer, including 1/2 of the line.

Moisten the small square of paper and lay it on a work surface. As the water is absorbed into the paper fibres, the square will begin to curl. The two edges that curl towards one another are parallel with the grain. Mark the correct grain on the square.

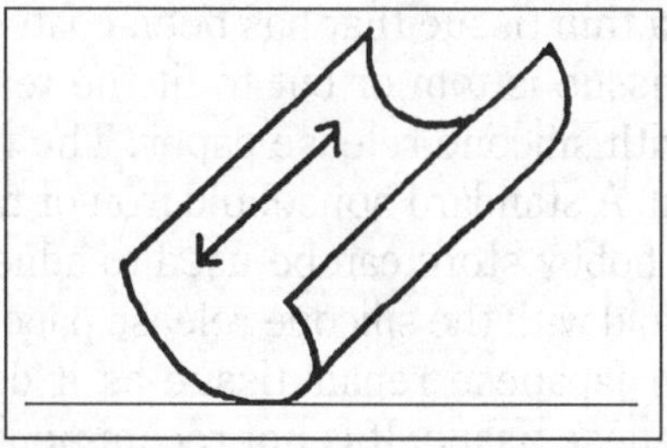

Replace the curled square in position on the large sheet of paper and mark the correct grain on the large sheet. Remember, the first pencil line is not necessarily the grain line.

PAPER REPAIR MATERIALS

Conservation book repair generally usesJ apaneser epair tissue, wheat paste, and heat-set tissue or archival repair tape to repair paper tears.

JAPANESE REPAIR TISSUE

Japanese repair tissue is sometimes called 'rice' paper, but this thin paper is made from the fibres of the mulberry tree, not from rice as the nickname implies. The strength of Japanese repair tissue comes from its long fibres which make the paper very strong, even though it is very thin. Hand made Japanese repair tissues are made on a mold and have mold or 'chain' lines which can be seen in the paper. These lines generally run the same direction as the paper grain. The lines are visible when the paper held up to a light or held down to let the light shine from above.

The grain can also be determined by using the tear, bend or water test discussed previously. In general, Japanese repair tissue is torn rather than cut. A piece of torn Japanese tissue has a delicate feather that blends into the repaired paper, so there is no sharp edge for the repaired page to turn against. Different methods of tearing Japanese tissue are discussed later in the Book Repair Tools and Techniques part. Japanese repair tissue can be purchased in different weights and colours. Generally, three weights will cover most repair needs.

Since most paper is not truly white, buy the 'natural' or 'toned' colours:

- TENGUJO light weight for working over type or illustrations

- KIZUKISHI medium weight for most repairs
- S~KISHU heavy weight for heavier paper

Although Japanese repair tissue may seem very expensive, only a small amount is used on any one tear. One sheet of Japanese repair tissue will last a long time.

Heat-set Tissue

Heat-set tissue is a thin tissue that has been coated with a heat activated, acrylic adhesive. The tissue is tom or cut to fit the tear or paper loss, laid in position and covered with silicone release paper. The tissue is adhered to the paper with a heated iron. A standard household iron or tacking iron from a book repair supply house or hobby store can be used to adhere heat-set tissue.

Heat-set tissue is sold with the silicone release paper. Heat-set tissue tends to be more brittle than Japanese repair tissue as it does not have the long, strong fibres of the Japanese tissue. It is not recommended for use on the folds in paper or areas that need to flex and bend. Since heat-set tissue is not applied with moisture, it works quite well on shiny, coated paper that can buckle when wet.

Document Repair Tape

Document repair tapes differ from common clear plastic in several ways. The carrier is thin, acid-free paper, not plastic. It is not as stiff as plastic tape so a page can turn and bend more easily. The adhesive used is a neutral acrylic adhesive that should not dry up, yellow over time or seep out the edges of the document repair tape. Because this adhesive is neutral, it should not react chemically with the paper.

The manufacturers of these tapes have tested the materials using artificial aging tests and they believe these tapes will remain stable over time and can be removed easily. Actual experience is not always so positive. Some libraries are finding that these tapes dry hard and crack or that the adhesive dries up and the paper carrier falls off leaving the paper discoloured.

In addition, some tapes are not reversible over time. Because of these problems, document repair tapes should not be used on valuable books or books that are a part of a long-term permanent collection. Document repair tape has become accepted for use in some circulating collections and is definitely better than clear plastic tape.

Some libraries choose to use document repair tape on materials that will not remain in the collection for a long time, such as reference books or children's books. Document repair tape can be a quick way to repair paper tears, and staff can use it easily after very little training. Document tape is sold under several brand names. Some of these are Fihnoplast P, Filmoplast P-90, and Document Repair Tape.

Clear Plastic Tape

Many library books are repaired with clear plastic tape. What appears to be a quick solution can become a long term headache in a library repair programme. Before using plastic tape, it is important to understand how it works and how it affects books. Plastic tape is dangerous to use in books because it is unstable and causes a great deal of damage. Often two or three layers of tape will cover a single repair. The first repair did not work and additional layers of tape were added to correct the problem.

Unfortunately, adding more layers of tape only creates a thick pile of tape; it does not repair the book.. Plastic tape has two main parts: a clear plastic carrier and an adhesive that sticks to the paper. As the tape ages on a piece of paper, the adhesive penetrates the paper fibres of the page and causes a chemical reaction that stains the paper and makes it brittle. Once the adhesive has dried, the plastic carrier falls away and the stain remains. The adhesive on the tape seeps out the edge of the plastic carrier, attracting dirt or adhering one page to another.

Once tape is in a book it is very difficult, if not impossible to remove. Simply lifting the tape off the page will damage the paper because the top layer of paper is removed with the tape. If the tape covers the text, it cannot be removed without damaging the print. Removing plastic tape is difficult even for trained conser-vators who work with chemicals and special tools. Using tape to reattach a loose page restricts the page from turning freely. The tape has a sharp edge and makes the original paper heavier than before so the paper tends to turn against the edge of the tape and not at the hinge.

Soon the paper breaks against the edge of the tape and falls out of the book. Now a second repair is needed and if the page is repaired a second time with plastic tape, the same problem occurs. Wide, clear plastic tape is also used to repair the cover spine or corners of a book and special 'repair wings' are sold to repair comers as well. While tape covers up the problem but it does not repair it.

Often the tape slides out of position or detaches entirely while the adhesive remains on the book cover attracting dirt or sticking books to one another on the shelf. Some libraries that practice conservation book repair may use plastic tape in very specific instances.

Plastic tape might be used when a book will not remain in the collection for a long tune, such as children's books, reference books that are updated regularly, or books that need 'one more circulation' before they are discarded. Decisions regarding when and how to use clear plastic tape should be made ahead of time.

Be certain a book is not important in a long term collection policy before repairing it with plastic tape. Keep in mind that once the tape is in the book, it cannot usually be removed without damaging the book.

REPAIR ADHESIVES

There are two main kinds of adhesives used in conservation book repair: paste and glue. Each has special properties and should be used in specific instances.

Paste

Paste is generally a cooked mixture of water and vegetable starch, such as wheat or rice. Repairing paper with paste will give a stronger bond than repairing it with glue because the paste soaks into the paper fibres and bonds them together. Since paste contains water, it can stretch and cockle paper. It dries slowly and can usually be reversed with water.

Wheat Paste

Wheat paste is used to mend tom paper, attach Japanese tissue or soften old paste and glue. It is not usually used on book cloth or the case of a book. Wheat paste can be purchased uncooked, instant or pie-made. Wheat paste prepared from scratch will last for 3-4 days before it begins to mold. Prepare a small amount of paste and keep it refrigerated. Instant commercial or prepared pastes can be convenient in some situations.

Thick Wheat Paste:

- 6 TBS wheat starch
- 2 Cups cold water
- Place the wheat starch in the top of a double boiler.
- Mix the water into the starch stirring constantly.
- Bring the mixture to a boil.
- Lower the heat and stir constantly as the mixture simmers.
- Cook until mixture thickens.
- Remove from heat and cool.
- Put through a sieve and store refrigerated for 3-4 days.

Thin Wheat Paste:

- 3 1/2 TBS wheat starch
- 2 Cups cold water
- Follow the instructions for Thick Wheat Paste above.

Microwave Wheat Paste:

- One tablespoon wheat starch
- Five tablespoons distilled water
- Place the wheat starch in a deep container, add distilled water and place in microwave. Microwave on high setting 20-30 seconds, remove paste and stir. Return to microwave and cook another 20-30 seconds. Remove and stir again. Continue this process for 3-4 minutes depending on the power of your microwave. Paste should stand a few minutes before using.

Glue

Several types of glue have been used in bookbinding over the years, the most common being animal hide glue. In recent years, animal-based glues have been replaced with synthetic vinyl resin glues, the most common of which is polyvinyl acetate emulsion.

Polyvinyl Acetate (PVA)

PVA is a good all-around adhesive. It has a low moisture content and dries quickly. It dries flexible, so it can be used to tighten hinges, repair book cover comers and reattach loose book cloth to book board. PVA is not affected by mold or fungi. However, it is damaged by freezing, so most book repair supply houses will not sell PVA by mail from October to March. If PVA freezes, it separates and loses its adhesive properties.

PVA can be thinned with water or thin wheat paste for different consistencies and effects. Thinning PVA with water adds moisture and does not add any additional adhesive properties while thinning with wheat paste adds the adhesive qualities of the paste to the glue. Many book binders or repair technicians use a 50/50 mixture of PVA and wheat paste strained through a sieve.

Other books may describe different adhesives or mixtures of adhesives. PVA glues cover a wide range of brand names and not all are used to repair books. For instance Elmer's glue is technically a PVA but is not flexible when dry so it has limited use for repairing books. Two common brand names for PVA glues used in book repair are AT-l 100 from Colophon Book Arts Supply and Jade 403 available from Talas. These companies are listed in the Supply Sources.

Working with Adhesives

Most people learning to repair books use too much adhesive. The belief seems to be that if a little is good, a lot is better. In book repair, that just isn't true. A thin, even coat of adhesive makes the best bond. Too much adhesive will ooze out of the edges of a repair and bond to the pages. Also, too much adhesive causes the paper to wrinkle and takes longer to dry. Watch each repair carefully. If there is excess glue or paste, wipe it away. Next time, try to use less paste or glue. When applying adhesive, choose a brush that matches the size of the surface. When pasting or gluing a small area, use a small brush. When the area is larger, use a bigger brush.

LINEN THREAD

Books are traditionally sewn with linen thread which is very strong and can be purchased in several sizes. Choosing the right thread is important for a successful repair. Using thread that is too thick can damage a book because the text block may not fit back in the original case. Thread that is too thin can tear through the folded signature paper. In general, it's best to use as thin a thread as possible, but choosing the right thread depends on the kind of paper and how many signatures are being resewn.

Thread Sizes

Common sizes of linen thread are 12/4,18/3,25/3,35/3 and 60/3. The first number is the thickness of the strand or ply and the second number is the number of strands or ply per thread. So 12/4 is composed of 4 strands that are 12 thick.

The 12 refers to an industry designation that relates to the weight of the wholesale quantities of thread. In this sizing system, the smaller the number, the thicker the thread so 12 thread is thicker than 60 thread. 35/3,30/5, and 18/3 are a good assortment of thread to have on hand.

It can be hard to recognize a particular thread size so it's a good idea to mark the size of thread on the inner cardboard spool before discarding the paper wrapper.

Waxing and Threading Linen Thread

Like all thread, linen thread has a tendency to tangle. Waxing sewing thread with beeswax keeps the thread from tangling and helps the thread 'grip' the paper. Run the thread through a cake of beeswax two or three times to coat it with wax, then run the thread through your fingers. The heat generated from the friction will melt the wax into the thread.

Measuring Thread Length

The length of thread needed depends on the height of the book and how many signatures need to be resewn. Save time by measuring the thread directly on the book.

For instance, a book with one unattached signature will need a piece of thread that is at least three text block heights long plus one text block height for tying knots.

Adding Additional Lengths of Thread

It's not a good idea to try to work with more than 4-5 book heights of thread at one time. There are two ways to add additional lengths of thread discussed in Tying Knots In Thread, which follows.

Locking the Thread onto the Needle

It can be very frustrating to have a needle fall off the sewing thread in the middle of a repair. Lock the needle onto the thread before beginning a repair to assure the needle will not fall off during the repair. Thread the needle as usual. Grasp the leading end of thread and wrap it around your thumb:

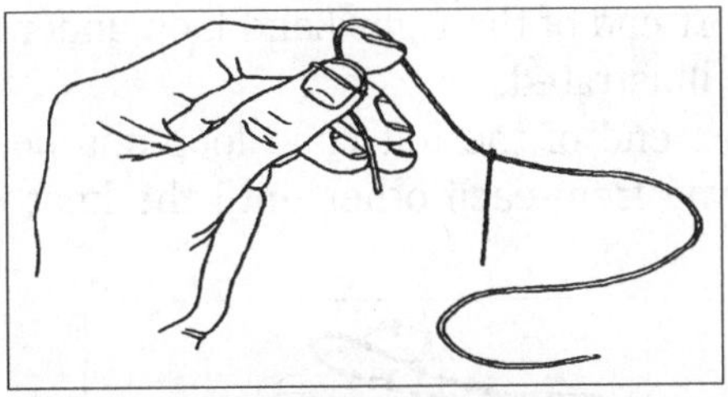

Carefully pierce the thread with the needle against your thumbnail:

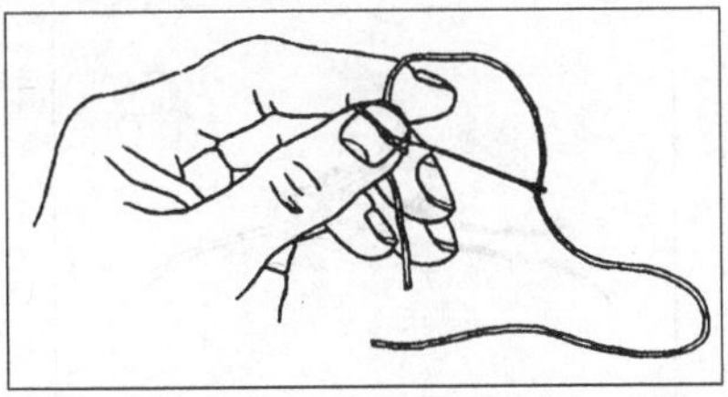

Pull the needle through the pierced thread:

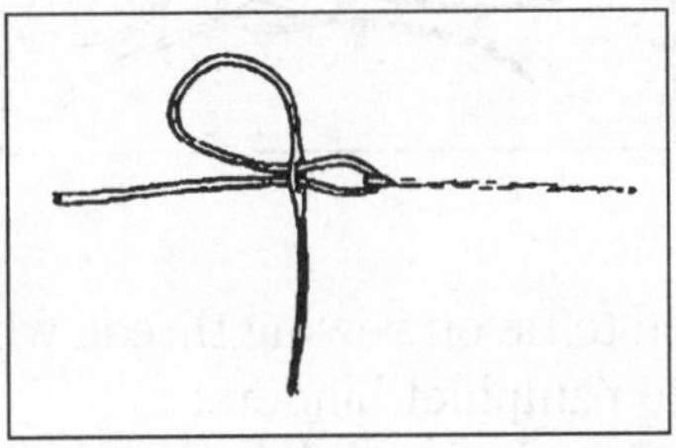

Hold onto the sewing thread and pull until the pierced thread is tight against the sewing needle.

Tying Knots in Thread

There are two basic knots used in book repair, the weaver's knot and the square knot.

The Weaver's Knot

Since sewing with a very long piece of linen thread can be difficult, the weaver's knot is used to tie on additional lengths of thread so shorter lengths can be used. Tie on additional thread when there is about 6" of thread left on the needle. Tie the knot inside the signature, as close to the last sewing station as possible.

A knot cannot easily pass through a sewing station hole so it should lie between the sewing station holes on the inside of the signature:

- Make a loop of the remaining thread and hold it in your left hand, with the short end of the loop on the bottom.
- With a new thread, make a loop with the short end on the bottom and hold it in your right hand.
- Insert the left-hand loop underneath and into the right-hand loop and hold both in place with your left thumb.

- Take the short end of the right-hand loop under and through the left-hand loop as illustrated.
- Pull the short end of the left-hand loop and both ends of the right-hand loop away from each other until the knot is secure. Trim both ends.

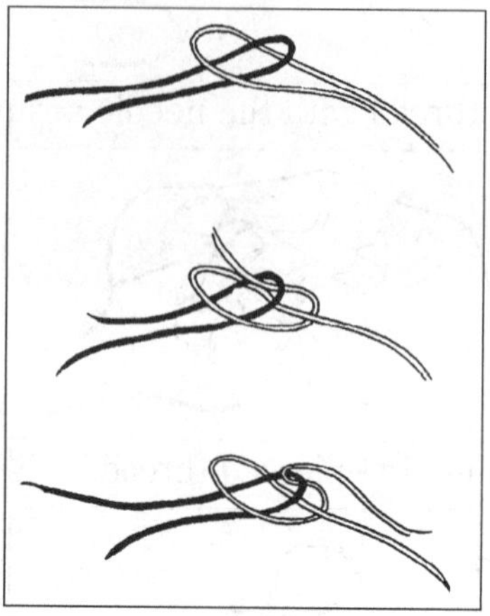

The Square Knot

Square knots are used to tie off sewing thread when resewing a text block or attaching materials into pamphlet binders:

- Take one end of thread in each hand.
- Pass the right-hand thread over the lefthand thread and through the loop. Pull tight.
- The original right-hand thread is now on the left side. Place it over the right-hand thread and bring it through the loop. Pulltight. Trim the end of the original thread. Do not cut the added thread..

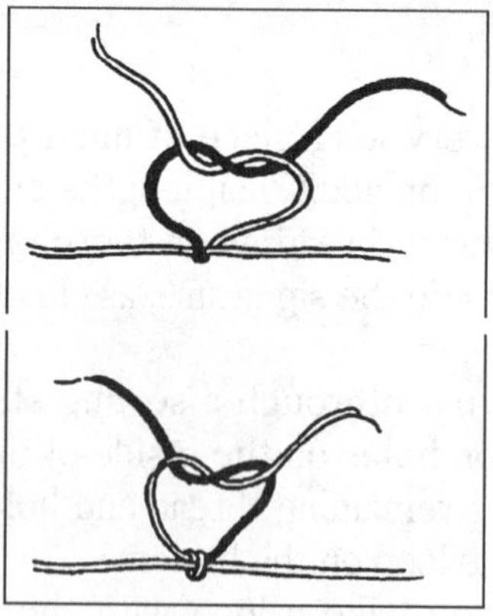

SEWING NEEDLES?

Using the right needle will make sewing easy and more successful. Needles should be as small in diametre as possible, have a blunt point, and have an eye no larger than the shaft of the needle. If the sewing needle is much bigger than the thread used, it will make a hole that the sewing thread cannot fill up. Many book suppliers advertise needles that are very large, sometimes much larger than the sewing thread. Leather harness called Egg Eye needles work very well with most thread and are available in leather shops. Sources are listed in the Supply Sources list.

REBACKING A CASE BOUND BOOK

Books with worn cloth joints or loose, flapping spines can be repaired by replacing the original book cloth spine. Before rebacking a book, check the condition of the original crash in the hinge area. If more than 1/4 of the crash's total height is broken, replace it before rebacking the book. That procedure is covered in Recasing A Case Bound Book. Two methods of rebacking are illustrated in this part.

The first method, Rebacking With Book Cloth On The Outside Of The Original Book Cloth, puts the new book cloth on the outside of the old book cloth with the turn-ins glued on top of the original endpapers. This method can sometimes be faster but the new spine can be difficult to position well since it is constructed off the book.

From a cosmetic point of view, more of the repair shows because the book cloth is on the outside of the original book cloth. This method is also described in Books Their Care and Repair by Jane Greenfield, These instructions and Ms. Greenfield's drawings are reprinted with her permission. In the second method, Rebacking With The New Book Cloth Under The Original Book Cloth And The Turn-ins Under The End Papers, the new spine is constructed on the book with the tumins glued under the end papers. When the original spine is replaced, the new book cloth shows in only a small portion of the joint area. Often different methods work for different books so practice each method, then decide which to use on a particular book.

PREPARING A BOOK TO BE REBACKED

Remove the Original Book Cloth Spine

If the print or decoration on the spine is legible, save the spine to glue to the new book cloth spine. If the print or decoration is not legible, discard the spine after it is removed. Carefully remove the original spine if it is still attached to the book. If the cloth in the joint is broken or terribly frayed, gently pull it loose. If the original spine is more firmly attached to the case, lay a straight edge 1/16-1/8" from the spine edge of the front board and use a knife to cut through the cover cloth. Be careful not to cut through the crash or the end paper and try not to trim away any print or decoration on the cover.

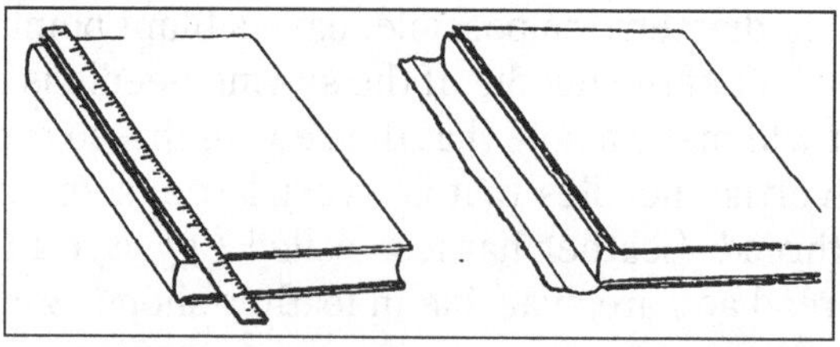

Turn the book over and repeat on the other side.

Check the Original Crash

If more than 1/4 of the total height of the original crash is tom or broken, it should be replaced before the book is rebacked.

Lining the Text Block Spine

When the book cloth spine is removed, examine the paper spine liner attached to the text block. This paper spine liner consolidates the signatures of the text block and helps evenly distribute the stress of opening the book. Many modem book manufacturers do use enough paper liners or a good quality of paper to line the spine. In many instances, the paper spine liner is not even completely glued down. Many libraries do not replace the paper spine liner when rebacking books. Taking the time to replace the spine liner ensures the book will function better and last longer.

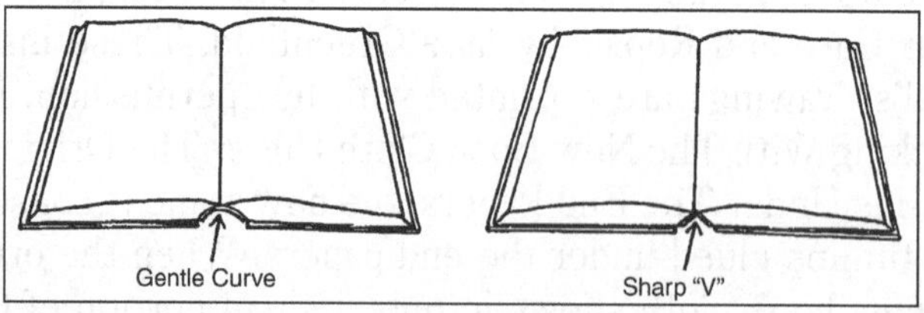

Open the text block to the centre of the book and see how the spine arches. Does it form a gentle curve or a sharp 'V'? When a book opens with a sharp 'V', all the stress of opening the book is concentrated in one place. A gentle curve evens out the stress of opening the book. If the original paper liner is not adhered to the spine of the text block, remove it by gently pulling it away or scraping it away with a dull knife.

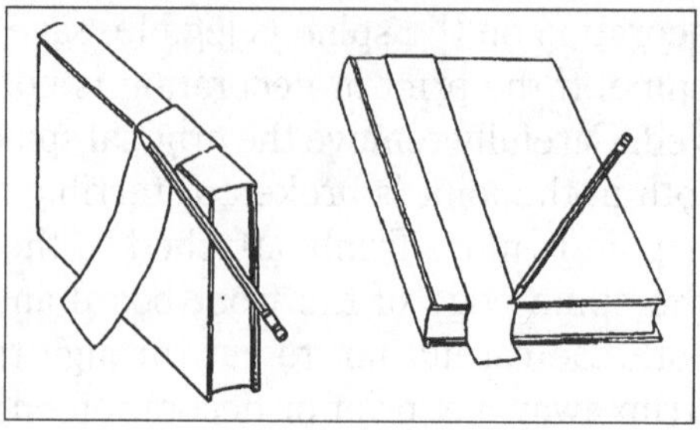

Be careful not to damage the crash or the sewing threads. It is not essential that all the paper be removed. If the original paper spine liner is well adhered but not heavy enough to form a gentle curve when the book opens, add additional paper liners to create the gentle curve. Measure the thickness of the text block from shoulder to shoulder with a strip of paper. Save this measurements until the repair is completed.

Transfer measurement A to the spine liner paper and cut a strip of spine liner paper.

The cut strip should be longer than the height of the book boards. Remember the grain of the spine liner should run up and down the spine of the book.

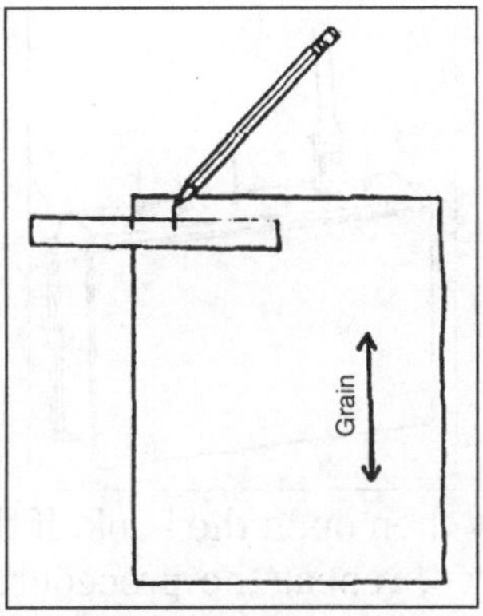

It is best to use a medium weight paper to line the text block spine; two or three layers of thin paper is better than one thick layer. Acid-free papers such as Permalife, Mohawk Superfine or Japanese repair tissue can be used. The paper spine liner must have the grain running from the head to the tail of the book and should be the exact height and width of the text block spine. Lay the spine liner against the spine of the text block, mark the height and then trim the spine liner to the exact height of the text block.

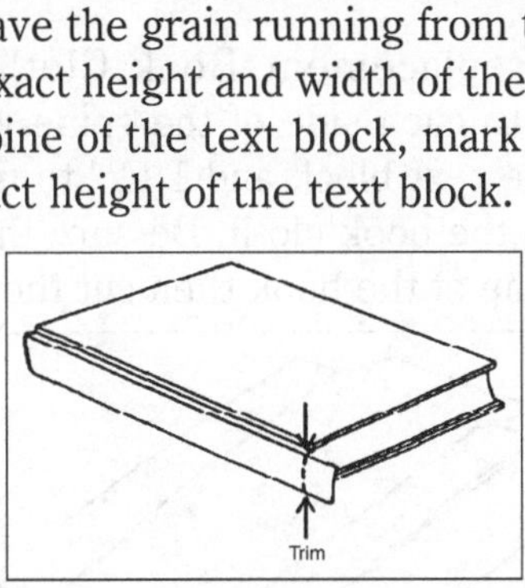

Apply adhesive to the spine liner paper in a star burst pattern and position on the text block spine. Firmly attach the paper spine liner to the text block spine using one or both of the methods below.

Use a folder to rub the paper spine liner to the text block spine. Make sure the paper liner is well adhered to the text block; pay special attention that the edges are firmly attached.

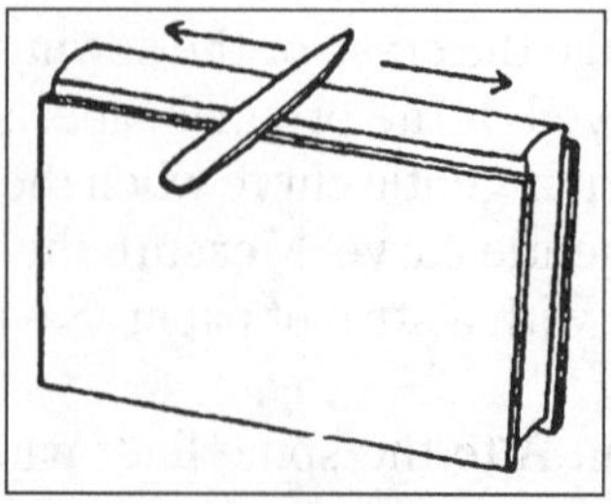

OR,

A 1" stencil brush makes a good tool to firmly attach the spine liner to the text block. Use an up and down tapping motion to work the spine liner into the text block. Pay special attention that the edges are firmly attached.

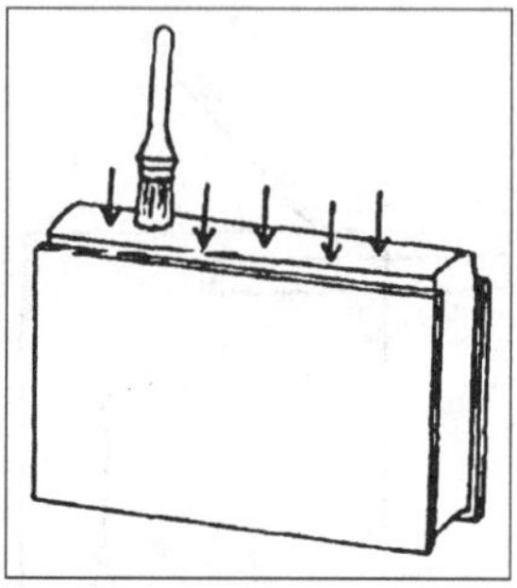

Let the paper liner dry then open the book. If the open text block forms a 'V' instead of a gentle curve, repeat the procedure. Many books need more than one layer of paper liner, especially if they are large or heavy.

Method One: Rebacking with Book Cloth on the Outside of the Original Book Cloth

Constructing the Replacement Book Cloth Spine Make or reuse Measurement A. Add 1" to each side of the spine width in measurement A. Measure the height of the text block and 1 1/2" to measurement B. Transfer measurement A and B to the book cloth. Be sure the-grain of the book cloth runs up and down the spine of the book then cut the book cloth.

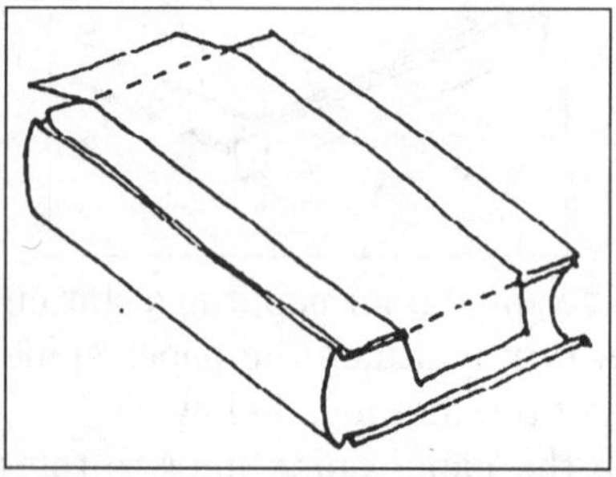

The new book cloth should be as close to the original colour and texture as possible. If it is not possible to match the colour, select a colour that has the least amount of contrast, *i.e.*, new black book cloth on a dark blue book. Centre the new book cloth on the front book board so the same amount hangs over the top and bottom. Crease the top and bottom of the book cloth to mark the height of the finished spine.

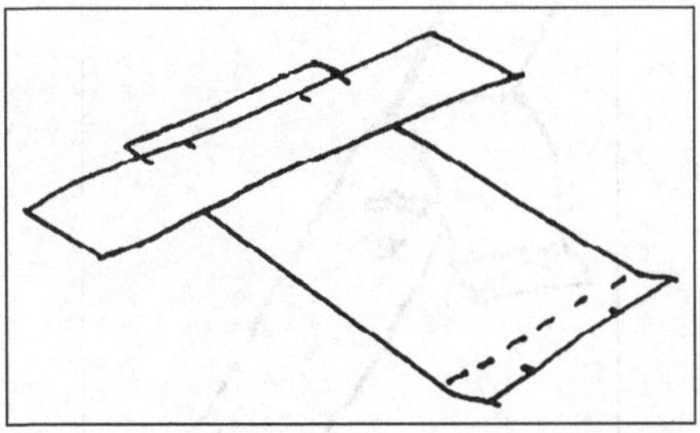

Centre measurement A on each crease and mark.

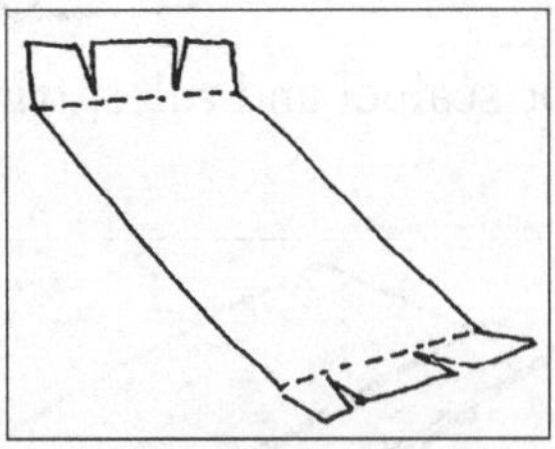

Cut V-slits at the crease line marks that correspond to the text block spine Measurements Cut a piece of acid-free paper to line and stiffen the book cloth spine. This liner is called the spine inlay. Sometimes two or more layers of acid-free bond are used for the spine liner. Mohawk Superfine or Daniel Smith Archival Paper has also been used with good results.

The Book Binding Supply Sources lists sources for purchasing acid-free paper. Always make sure the grain of the spine inlay runs in the same direction as the spine of the text block. If it does not, the book will not open easily. Place the spine inlay on a sheet of waste paper. Apply glue to the wrong side in the star burst pattern. Using the text block measurement marks and top and bottom creases, centre the spine inlay on the wrong side of the new spine cloth. Apply glue to the centre part of the spine turn-in at the top and bottom of the spine cloth; fold them over, and rub them down with a folder.

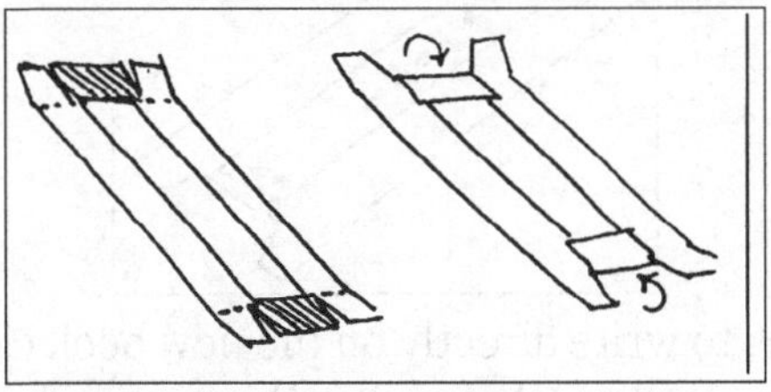

Protect the spine cloth with a piece of wax paper and place under weight to dry. If the original spine can be reused, lift up the turn-ins and peel the paper inlay away from the book cloth spine. If the paper is well attached to the spine, use a microspatula or dull knife to scrape it off. Dampening the inlay can release the adhesive. It is not essential to remove every bit of the paper inlay if it doesn't come off easily. The spine can be easily distorted or damaged so handle it carefully.

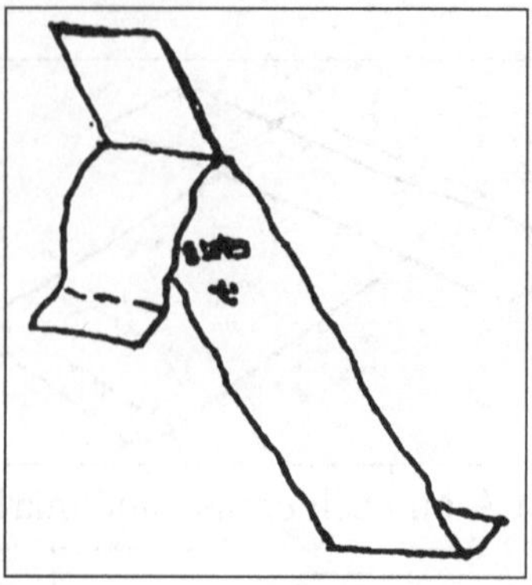

Using an X-acto knife or scalpel and ruler, trim away the ragged edges of the original spine.

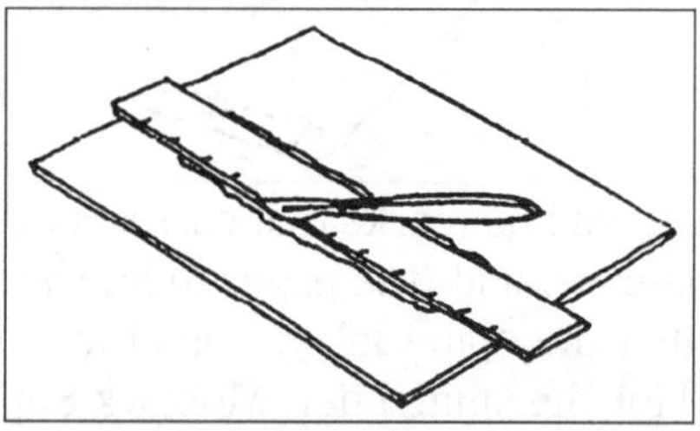

The original spine should be slightly narrower than the text block spine, so the original cloth won't interfere with the joint cloth of the replacement spine when the book opens and closes. Do not trim away any lettering or decoration. If the original spine is being re-used, save it. If the original spine is too damaged or worn to use, there are other ways to label the spine of the book. A paper label can be hand written, typed or typeset on a computer, then glued to the new spine cloth.

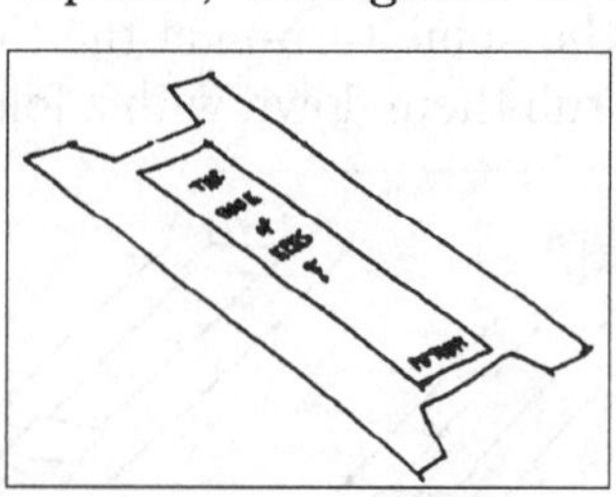

Another option is to write directly on the new book cloth with a permanent marker, such as those used to label quilts. Practice on a scrap of book cloth to make sure the label will be legible and attractive. If the option is an unsightly label, consider leaving the title off the spine. Lay the original spine or new label on a piece of waste paper wrong side up. Apply glue in a star burst pattern working from the centre towards the edges. Centre the original spine or new label on the right side-of the replacement spine. Cover it with a piece of waste paper, and rub it down with a folder. All the edges should be well adhered. Protect the spine cloth with a piece of wax paper, and place under weight to dry.

Attaching the New Spine Cloth to the Text Block

Position the spine so the glued-down part of the turn-ins are centred on the text block spine, even with the top and bottom of the book boards. Mark the edges of the replacement spine cloth on the cover board.

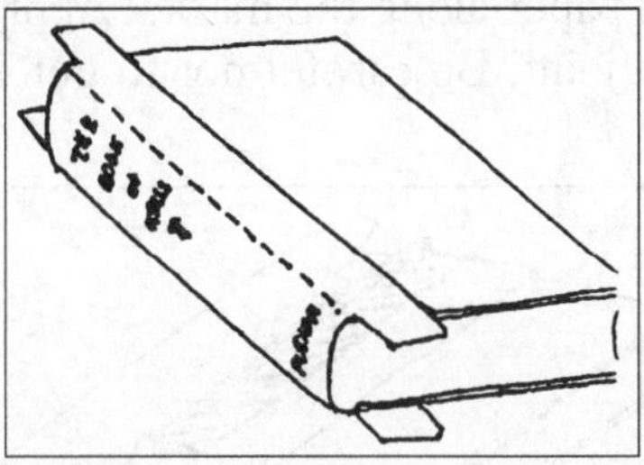

Put a strip of waste paper on the cover, lined up with the marks and glue from the waste paper towards the spine of the text block. Be careful not to get glue on the spine of the text block.

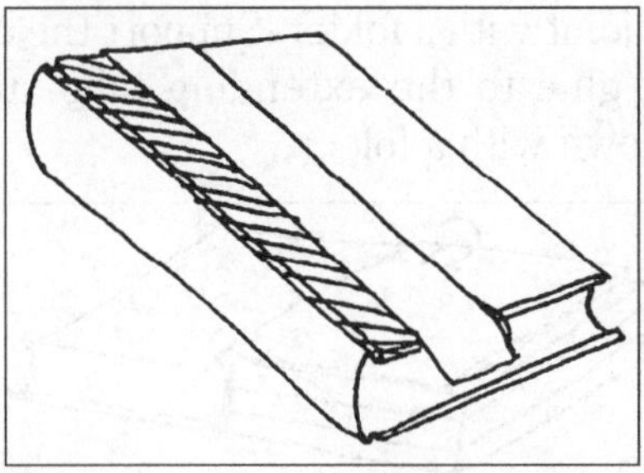

Before proceeding further, make sure the spine is right-side up on the text block. Position the replacement spine on the book. Centre the head and tail; then lay the edge of the replacement spine against the line of glue on the cover. Press the replacement spine onto the book board. Work the book cloth into the joint with a folder. Insert rods into the joint. Dry under weight for a few minutes.

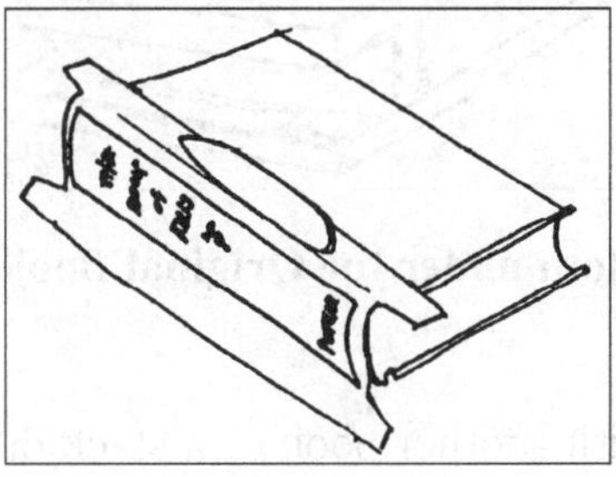

Turn the book. Wrap the replacement spine tightly around the book. Mark the position of the replacement spine on the book cover.

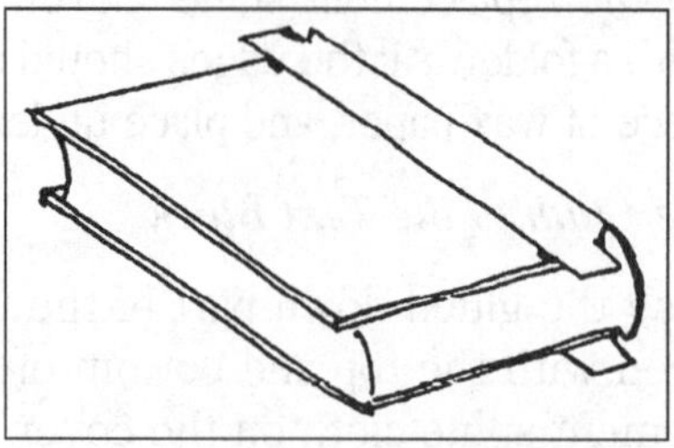

Lay a piece of waste paper along the marks. Apply glue working from the waste paper towards the joint. Be careful not to get glue on the spine of the text block.

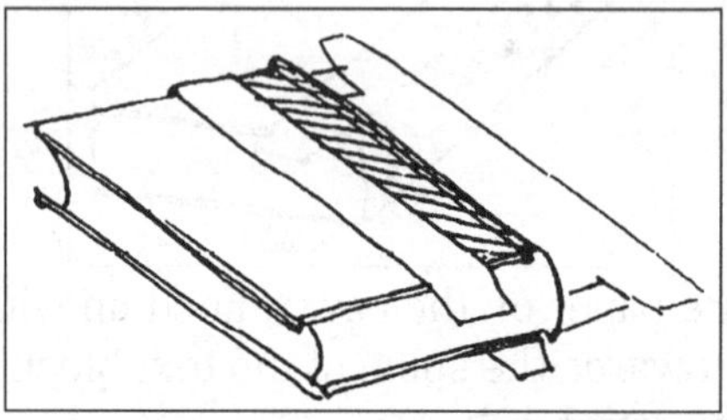

The replacement spine should fit tight around the spine of the text block. Work the cloth into the joint with a folder. Support the cover with book boards or other books. Apply glue to the extending tabs and fold them onto the endpapers. Rub them down with a folder.

Put rods in the joints. Dry the book overnight in a press or under weight.

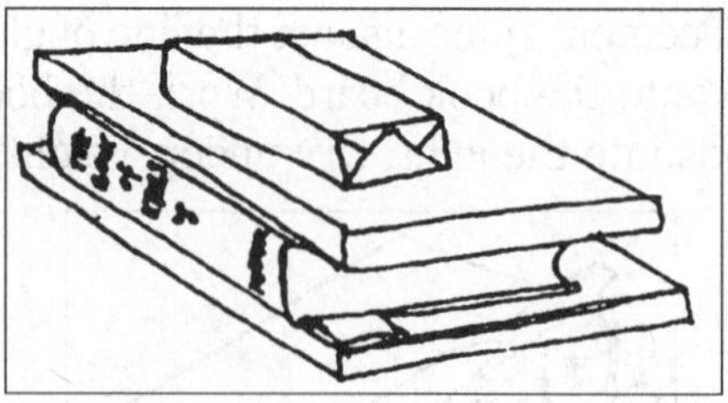

Rebacking with Book Cloth under the Original Book Cloth

Lifting the Endpapers

Support the book with another book or a stack of boards.

Use an X-acto knife or scalpel and ruler to cut through the book cloth along the edge of the endpapers at the head and tail. The cut should be about 1-2" long. At the outer edge of the first cut make a second, go-degree cut across the book cloth from the edge of the endpaper to the top of the book board.

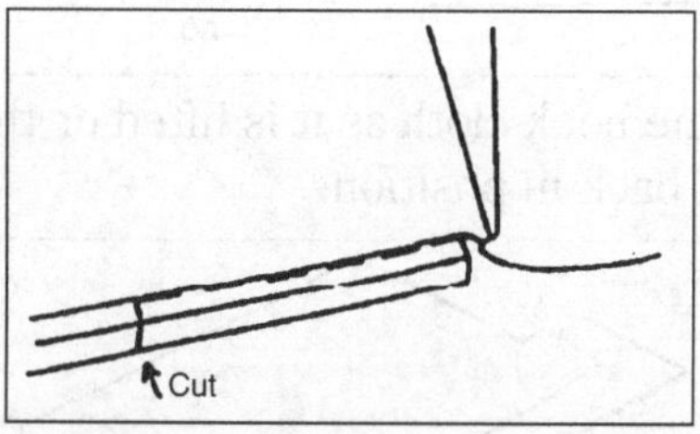

Use a knife or microspatula to lift the book cloth away from the book board. If necessary, clip through the original book cloth turn-in at the hinge to allow the cloth to lift up.

DO NOT clip through the endpaper or the crash. Repeat this cut at the other end of the cover and on the opposite book board. If the turn-in in the spine area is completely loose, remove it. Insert a microspatula or dull knife between the original turn-in under the endpapers. The original book cloth turn-in will support the endpaper as it is lifted. Loosen only a small amount of the endpaper as more can be separated later if needed.

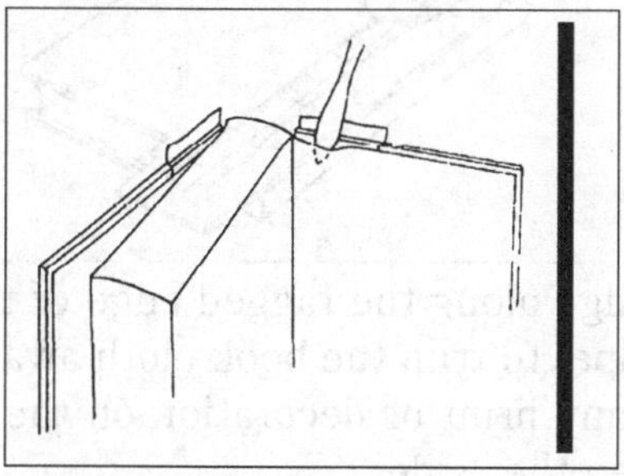

Lifting and Trimming the Original Book Cloth

Gently lift the book cloth away from the board by sliding a folder or dull knife under the book cloth on the outer cover.

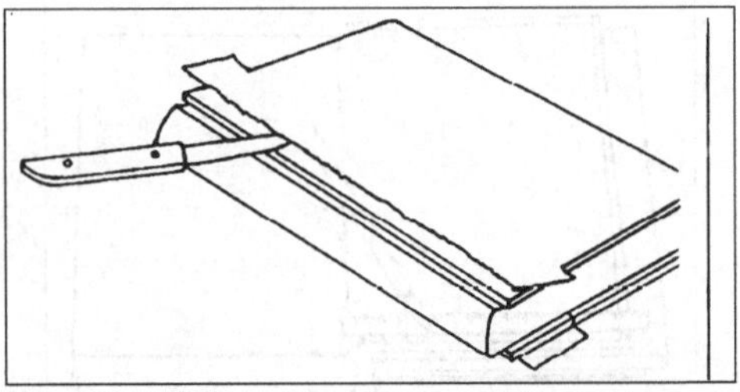

Lift the book cloth only as far as the cut at the top of the endpaper will allow, lifting a thin layer of book board with the cloth if necessary

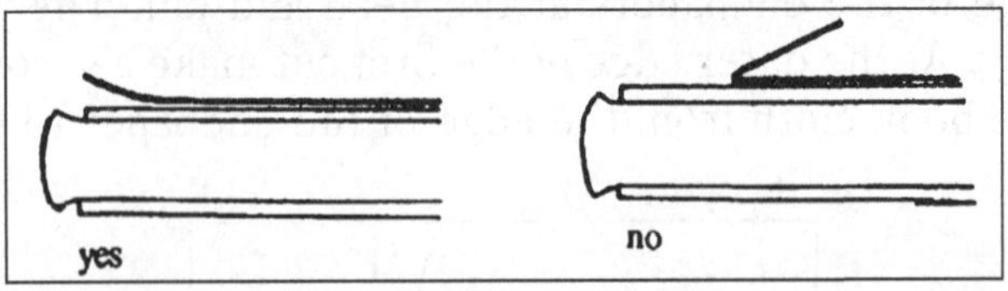

Try not to crease the book cloth as it is lifted or the crease line will show when the cloth is glued back in position.

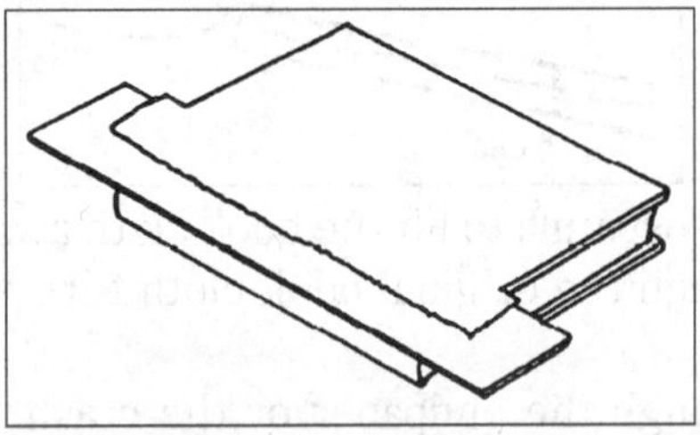

Insert a piece of thin cardboard between the original book cloth and the book board to use as a cutting surface.

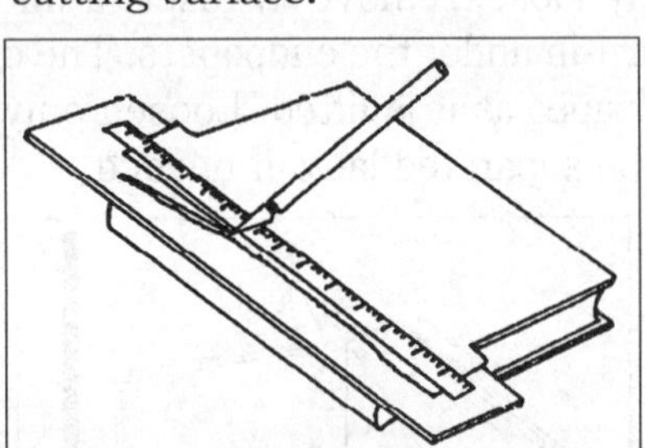

Place a straight edge along the ragged edge of the book cloth and use an X-acto knife or scalpel to trim the book cloth away from the hinge area. Try not to trim away any print or decoration on the cover. Turn the book over and repeat on the other side.

Measuring the Text Block Spine

Use a strip of paper to measure the width of the text block spine, then add 1-2" to each side of the spine measurement marks.

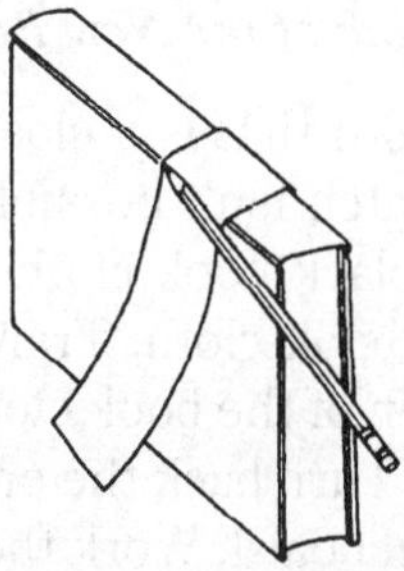

The exact amount added to measurement A depends on how much of the original book cloth is trimmed away from the cover board. It's better to have this measurement too wide as any excess can be trimmed away later. Use the same technique to measure the height of the book boards then add 1" to measurement B.

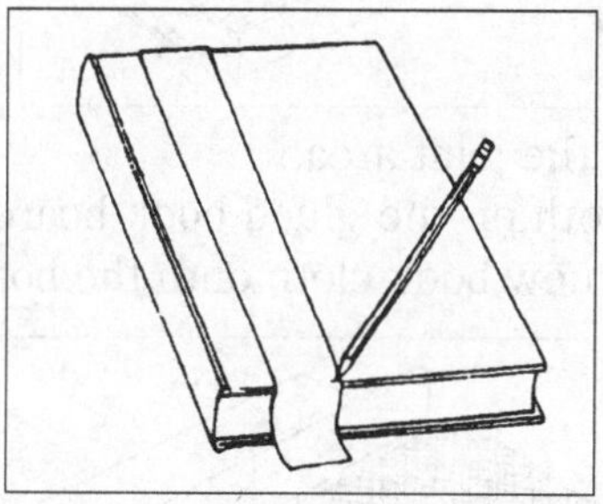

Reinforcing the Spine of the New Book Cloth

The spine area of the new spine cloth should be reinforced with an acid-free paper such as Bristol, Mohawk Superfine paper, or several layers of acidfree bond paper. The spine inlay should be the same width as the text block spine and the height of the book boards, not the text block. It is a common mistake to cut the spine inlay the same height as the text block, which is shorter than the book boards. Cut a spine inlay the width of the text block spine and longer than the height of the book boards. It will be trimmed later. The grain of the spine liner must be parallel to the spine of the text block.

Double check the width of the spine inlay paper by laying it against the text block spine. It should fit the spine from shoulder to shoulder without curving into the joint area. Trim the spine inlay to the correct height. Remember it should be the height of the cover boards, not the text block.

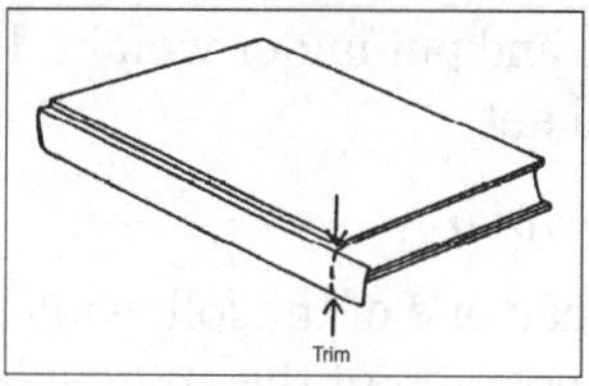

Choosing and Attaching One Side of the New Book Cloth Spine

Choose a piece of book cloth that is a close colour match to the original book cloth. If a close colour match isn't possible, select a colour that has the least amount of contrast, *i.e.*, black book cloth on a dark blue book would be less noticeable than light blue book cloth. Transfer measurement A and B to the book cloth. Be sure the grain of the book cloth is parallel to the spine of the book. Cut the new spine piece. Turn back the original book cloth on one cover. Brush PVA glue on the exposed board. Work the glue all the way back into the area where the original book cloth and book board are still attached.

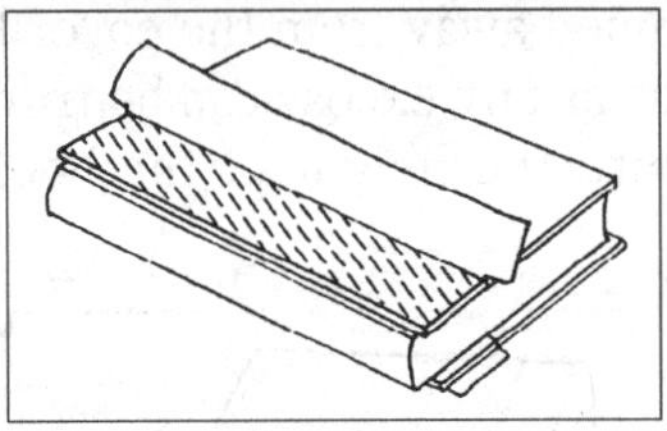

DO NOT put glue in the joint area.

Lay the new book cloth on the glued book board, with the right side up. Use a folder to press the new book cloth onto the board.

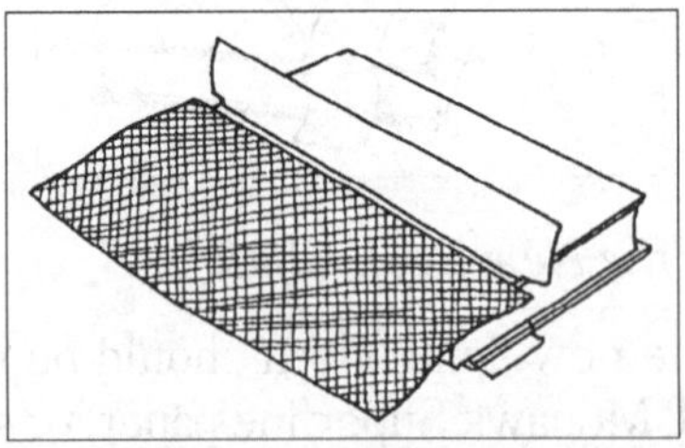

DO NOT glue down the original book cloth. Work the cloth into the joint with the long edge of a folder. Protect the new book cloth with a piece of Hollytex or wax paper if necessary.

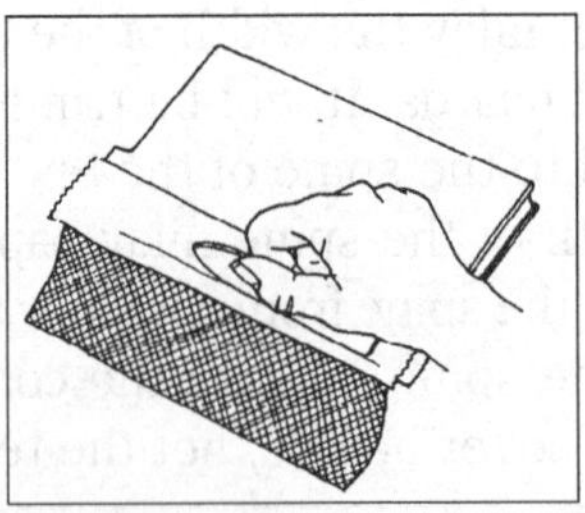

Insert rods in the joints and put under weight. Let the book dry for at least 10 minutes, so the glue will set.

Measuring the Width of the Joint

After the glue has set, use one of the following methods to mark the width of the joint. This gives the position of the spine inlay on the new spine cloth.

Method 1

Lay the book on the work surface-with the new spine cloth against the table, wrong side up.

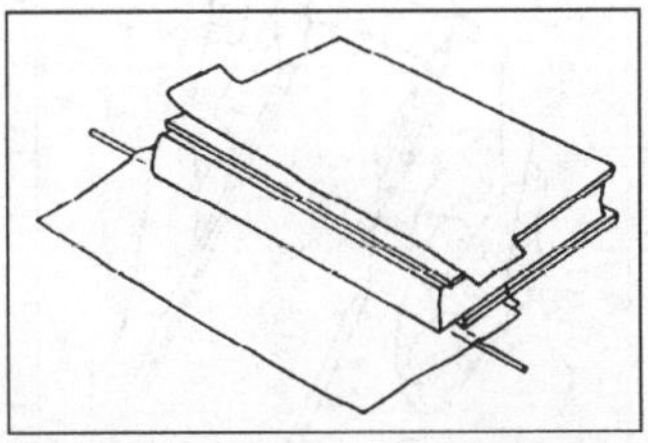

Slip a rod into the joint against the table, press down gently on the joint area. Mark the position where the shoulder of the text block spine meets the new book cloth.

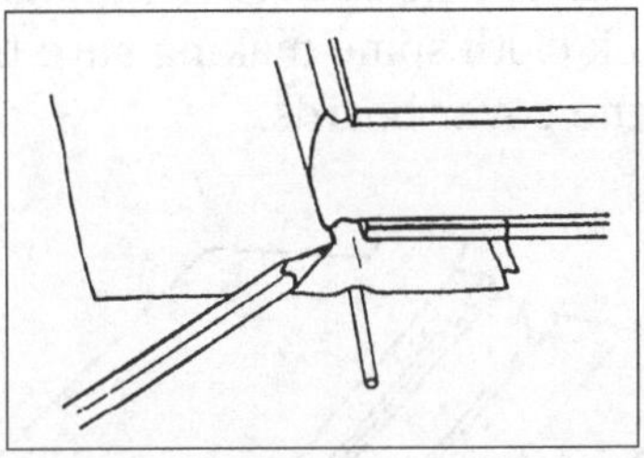

Repeat this measurement on the other end of the book.

Method 2

The joint width can also be measured with the book upright. Protect the new book cloth by supporting the text block on the edge of the work table or a pile of books.

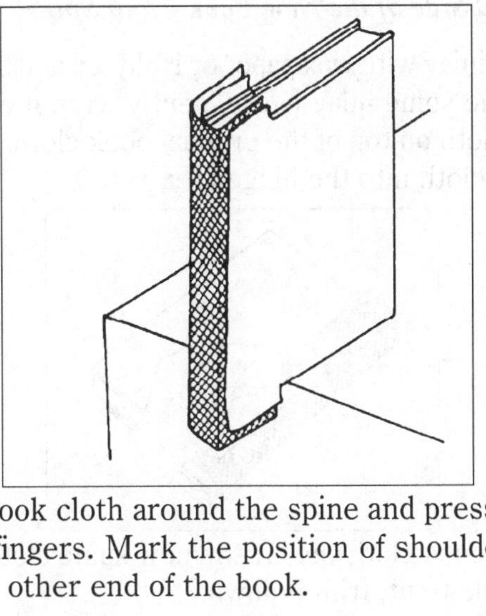

Wrap the new book cloth around the spine and press the new cloth into the joint with your fingers. Mark the position of shoulder on the new book cloth. Repeat on the other end of the book.

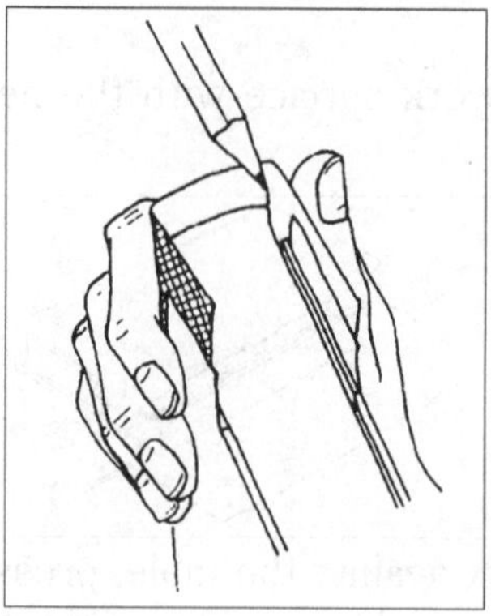

Lay the paper spine inlay on a piece of waste paper and apply glue in a star burst pattern. Use the pencil marks to position the glued spine inlay onto the wrong side of the new book cloth spine making sure the inlay is even with the top and bottom edges of the cover boards.

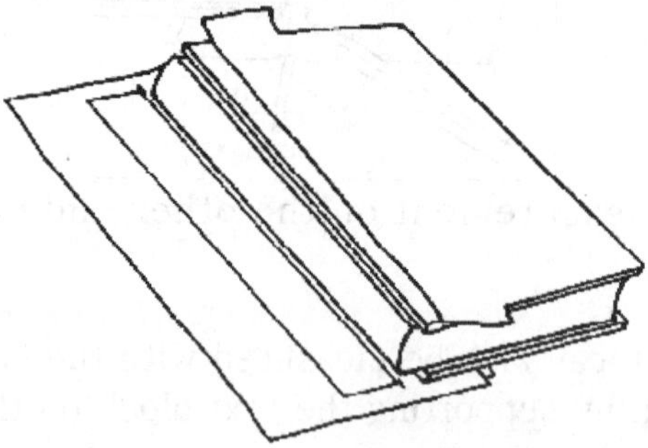

Attaching the Second Side of the New Book Cloth Spine

Cover the spine inlay with wax paper or Hollytex and blotters. Apply weight and let dry. When the spine inlay is dry, gently wrap it around the text block with the new book cloth on top of the original book cloth. Use the long edge of a folder to work the cloth into the hinge area.

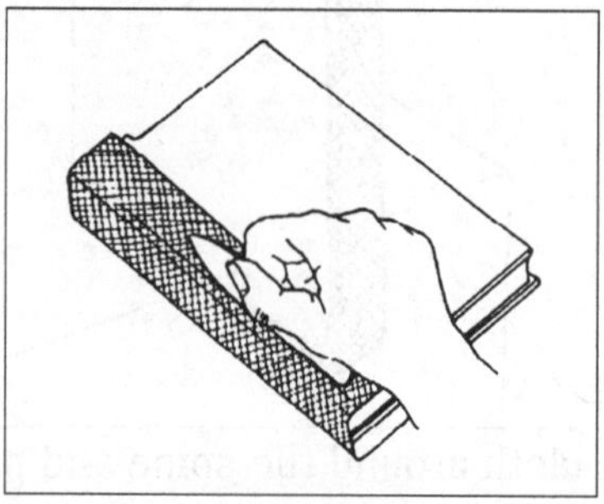

Lift the original book cloth and lay the new spine cloth in place. If the new spine cloth is too wide to fit, trim it down.

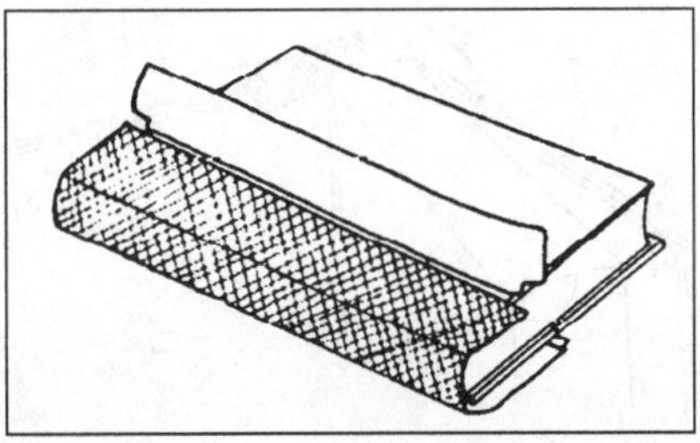

Lift up the new book cloth and apply PVA glue to the book board. Work the glue all the way back into the area where the original book cloth and book board are still attached. DO NOT put glue in the joint area or glue down the original book cloth.

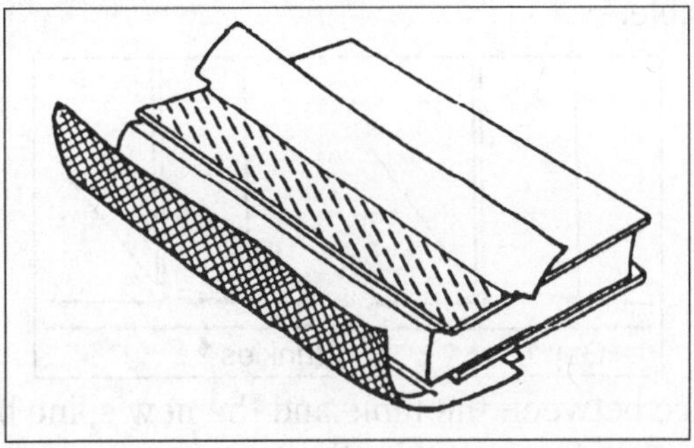

Lay the new book cloth back in place. Work the cloth into the hinge area with the long edge of a folder. Protect the cloth with wax paper or Hollytex if necessary.

Put the book under weight to dry for at least 10 minutes so the glue will set. If the new spine cloth extends past the top or bottom of the book more than 5/8", trim it down. Clip the points off the comers for ease in turning-in.

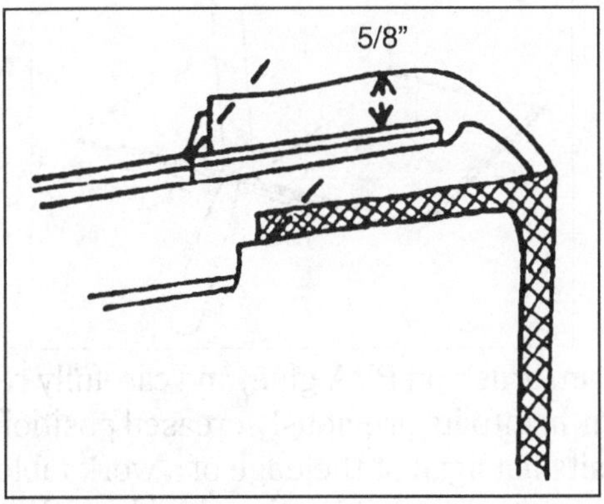

Protect the bottom extension of spine book cloth by placing the book on another stack of boards or another book. Carefully tuck in the right side of the turn-in, then the spine area, and finally the left side of the turn-in.

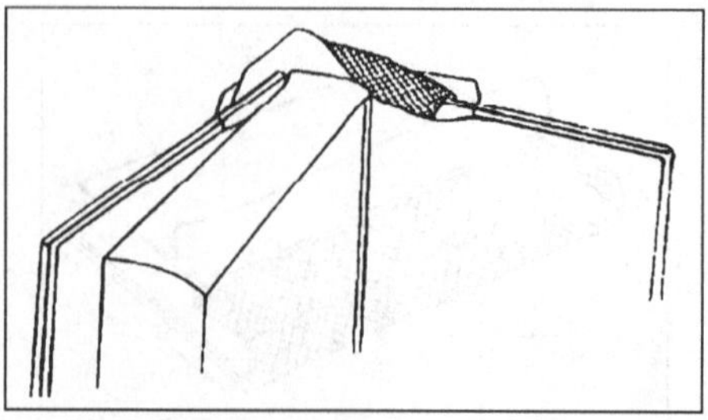

With the entire patch tucked in place, gently crease the top edge of the patch along the boards and in the spine area with your fingers. Set the book on the work table to check the position of the turn-in area. The edge of the new spine book cloth should be level with the original boards so it rests flat and even against the table.

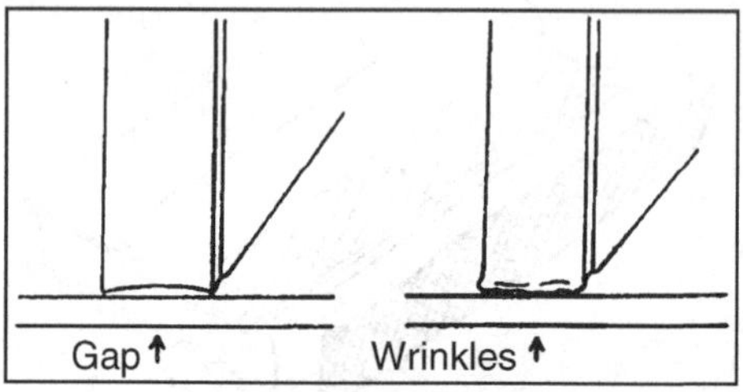

If there is space between the table and the new spine book cloth or if the book cloth wrinkles against the table, the turn-in is not correct. Readjust the turn in. Check it again. When the turn-in is positioned correctly, lay the book on its spine. Use a folder to crease the turn-in in position. This crease sets the turn-in position and makes it easy to reposition it once the glue is applied.

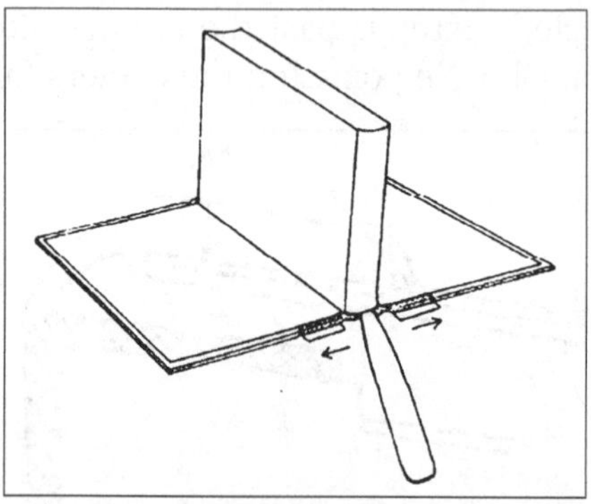

Unfold the turn-in, brush on PVA glue, and carefully refold. Use a folder to crease the glued turn-in into its previously creased position. Re-check to make sure the spine area sits flat against the edge of a work table. If there is a gap or wrinkles, reposition the turn-in before the glue dries. Wipe away any excess glue. Work the new book cloth into the hinge area with a folder. Put wax paper or Hollytex inside the book hinge area to protect the end sheet from excess glue. Insert rods or knitting needles in the joint and dry under weight. Let dry for at least ten minutes and repeat the procedure on the other end of the book. Apply glue to the raised flaps, and lay them into position, pressing them onto the new book cloth. There may be a slight gap between the flap and the edge of the endpaper

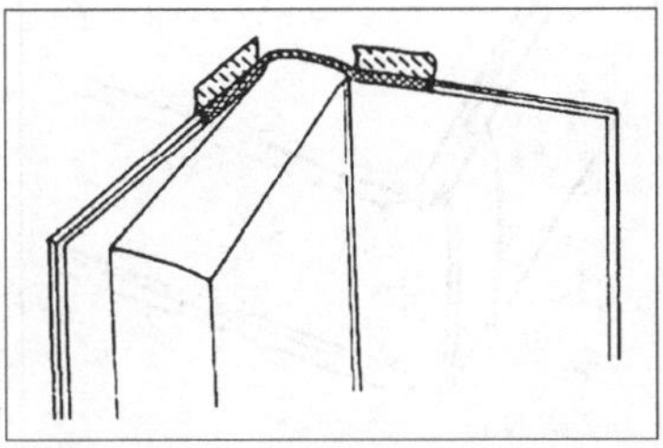

Lay a strip of wax paper in the joint areas, insert rods or knitting needles and dry overnight under weight.

Mounting the Original Spine onto the New Book Cloth Spine

Peel as much of the original paper spine inlay from the original spine cloth as possible. If the paper is well adhered to the cloth, don't force it off the spine cloth.

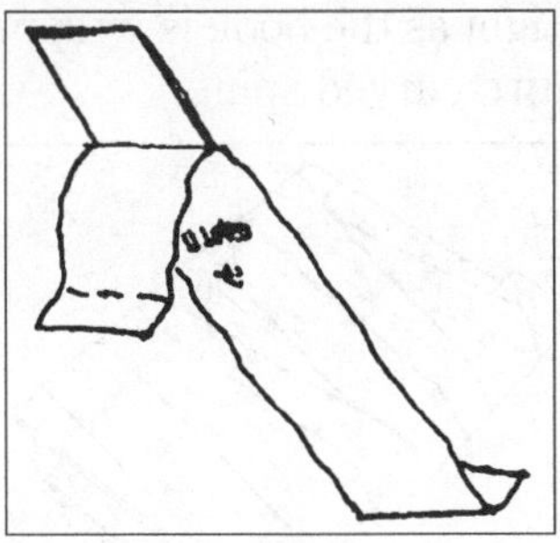

Trim the frayed edges with a straight edge and X-acto knife, taking care not to remove any of the letters or design.

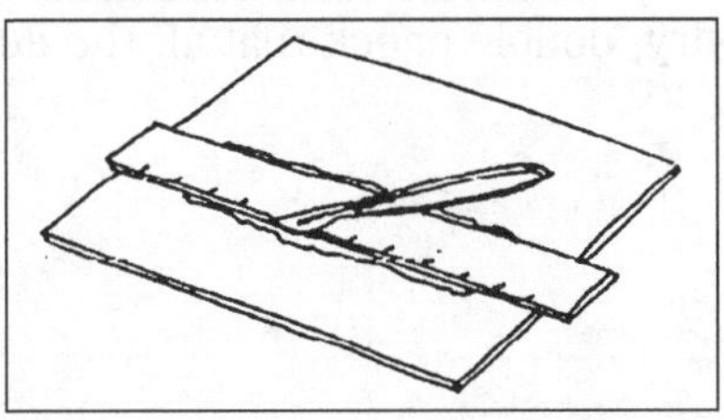

Lay the original spine against the new book cloth spine to check for a proper fit.

The original spine should not extend into the hinge area as it will add bulk that will inhibit the cover from opening freely. Trim the original if it is too wide.

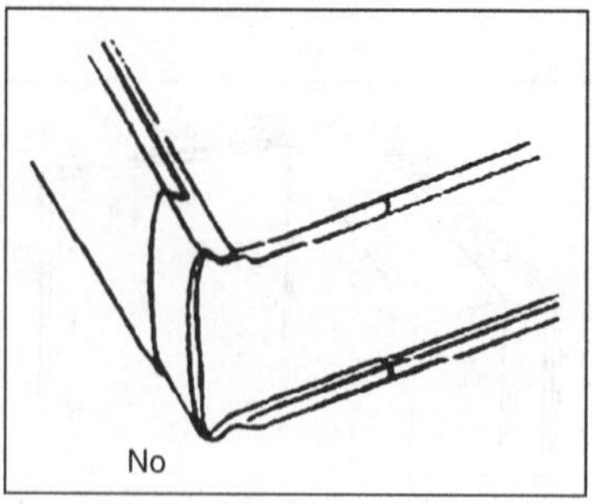

Lay the original spine wrong side up on a piece of waste paper and apply PVA glue in a star burst pattern. Position the original spine over the new book cloth spine.

Make Sure the Spine is Right Side up to the Text Block

Cover the original spine with a piece of wax with a folder. With the wax paper or Hollytex still covering the spine, wrap the book snugly in an elastic bandage. Pull the bandage tight as the book is wrapped. The bandage will apply even pressure over the entire curved spine.

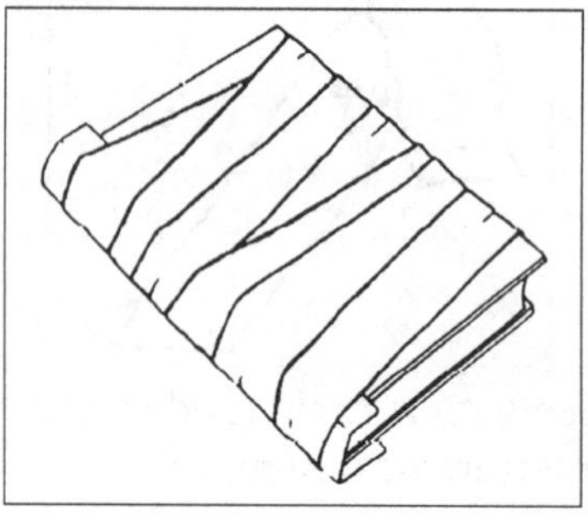

When the spine is dry, double check that all the edges are adhered.

7

Book Repair Tools and Techniques

The repairs explained in this book will be easier to accomplish using the right tools and a few specific techniques. If you already have tools and techniques that seem to work, practice each repair using the tools and techniques given in the instructions, then decide which is better. If a tool or technique does the same job and doesn't harm the book, feel free to use it.

BOOK REPAIR TOOLS

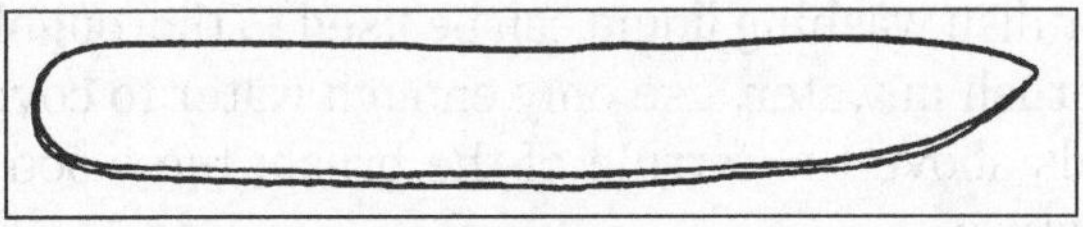

A folder is a tool approximately 6-8" long and about 1-1 1/2" wide. A typical folder is approximately 1/8" thick, smooth with one pointed end and one rounded end made from animal bone or plastic. Folders are used for many things such as creasing paper, smoothing down repair tissues and working cloth into a joint area. Some plastic folders are available with two round ends. When purchasing a folder, try to buy one made of bone with one rounded end and one pointed end. That tool will be much more versatile. Bone folders can also be filed to a desired shape and size while plastic folders cannot.

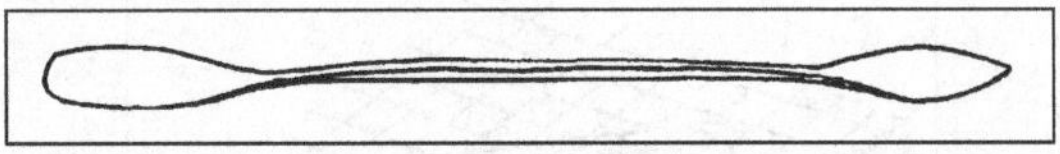

A microspatula is a metal tool, approximately 6-8" long with one rounded end and one pointed end. Use a microspatula to pick up pasted strips of Japanese repair tissue, lift book cloth or end papers away from the book board, or apply glue or paste in a very tight area. Microspatulas are manufactured very thin and many book binders file or sand them even thinner.

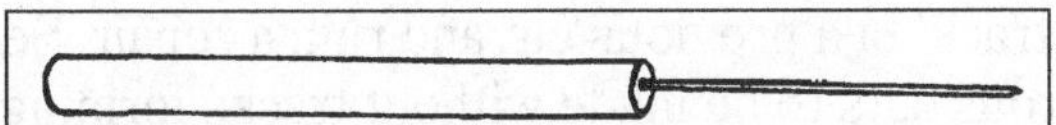

A needle-in-a-stick can be used to apply glue to small, tight areas, mark cutting lines or score tear lines on Japanese repair tissue. This kind of tool can be purchased from a pottery material supply house or botany material supplier. It can also be constructed by drilling a very small hole in the end of a wooden dowel and inserting the needle into the hole. The needle should fit tightly into the hole in the dowel. A small drop of glue on the end of the needle will help it hold better.

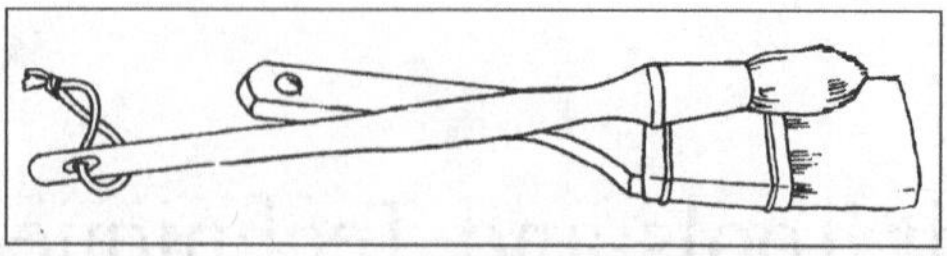

A good assortment of brushes makes repairing books much easier. The size of the surface to be pasted or glued determines the size of the brush used, so keep a variety on hand.

Round or flat bristle brushes be used. While natural bristle brushes are usually best for performing repairs, some libraries recommend using a synthetic bristle brush for PVA glue as it can be difficult to wash all the glue out of a natural bristle brush. A buildup of PVA glue can ruin a brush. Some people like to use separate brushes for paste and glue.

A brush should never be allowed to dry with the adhesive on it. Keep the brush in the adhesive or water and always wash a brush out when finished. Mild hand soap or dish washing liquid can be used to thoroughly clean brushes. When storing a brush in water, use only enough water to cover the bristles. If the water extends above the ferrule of the brush, the wood of the shaft can expand with moisture.

As the wood dries and contracts, the ferrule and the brush's bristles can loosen. Shake out all the water from a brush before putting it in paste or glue. A self-healing cutting mat and sharp Xacto knife, scalpel or breakaway utility knife such as Olfa Silver makes precise cutting easy and fast. It is important to always work with a sharp blade when cutting or trimming repair materials. Attempting to cut with a dull blade will usually result in a torn edge that needs even more repair.

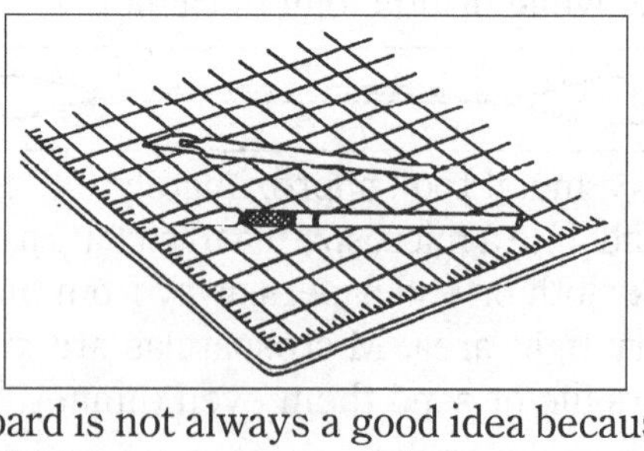

Cutting on cardboard is not always a good idea because the knife blade can be caught in the 'track' of a previous cut and ruin a repair. Self-healing cutting mats allow numerous cuts to be made without tracks forming. These mats can be purchased in various sizes from book supply sources, art stores or fabric stores.

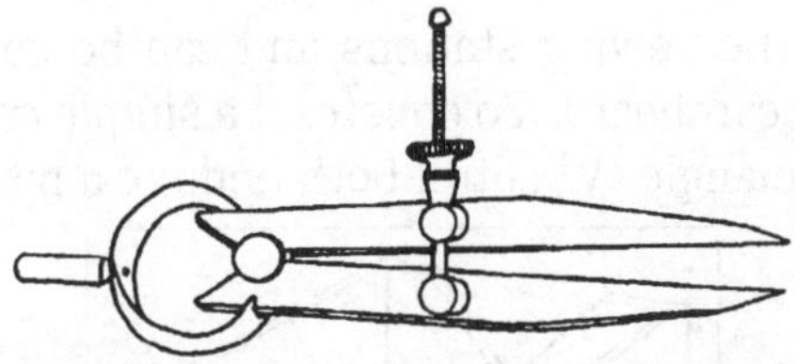

Dividers can be used to transfer and mark measurements from one place to another. Other basic tools include sharp scissors and a rigid, metal straightedge. Punching sewing holes in folded signatures can be tricky. Using a punching jig and a signature punching cradle will make the job much easier. To construct a punching jig, simply fold a piece of paper in half lengthwise and clip one end diagonally. This diagonal cut marks the top of the printed page.

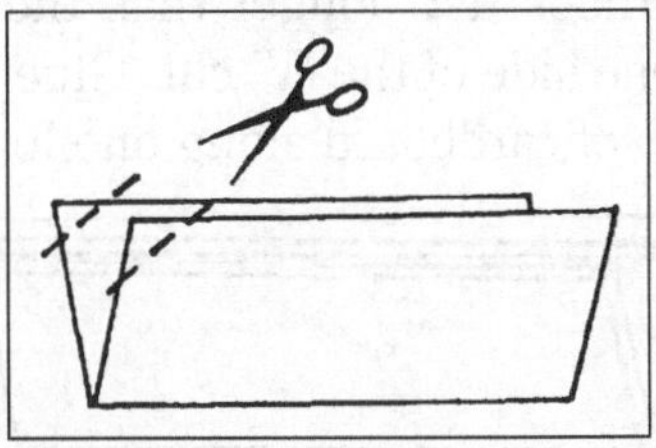

Mark the desired sewing hole stations on the outside of the fold in pencil.

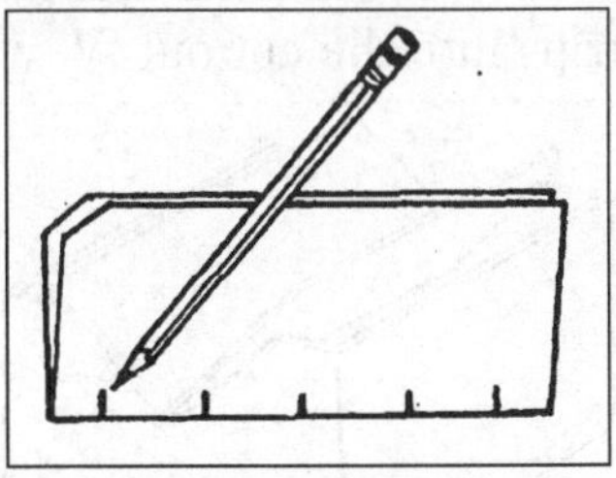

Turn the jig inside out so the pencil marks are on the inside of the fold. Place the punching jig inside the pamphlet or folded signature. The jig should be seated all the way down into the fold and lined up with the top edge of the book.

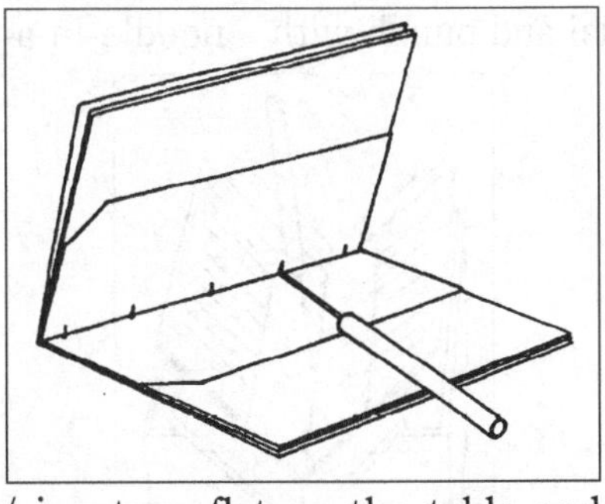

Lay the pamphlet/signature flat on the table and carefully punch holes through the fold with the needle-in-a-stick. A signature punching cradle helps control placement of the sewing stations and can be constructed out of thin plywood, mat board or cardboard. To construct a simple cradle from a cardboard box, make a 45 degree angle 'V' cut in both ends of a box.

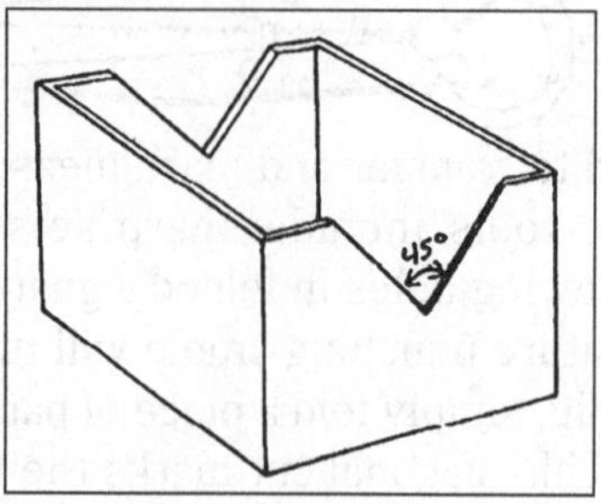

Cut two pieces of cardboard 2" longer than the length of the box and 1" wider than the length of one side of the 'V' cut. Glue a 1 1/2" strip of book cloth connecting the two pieces of cardboard along one long edge.

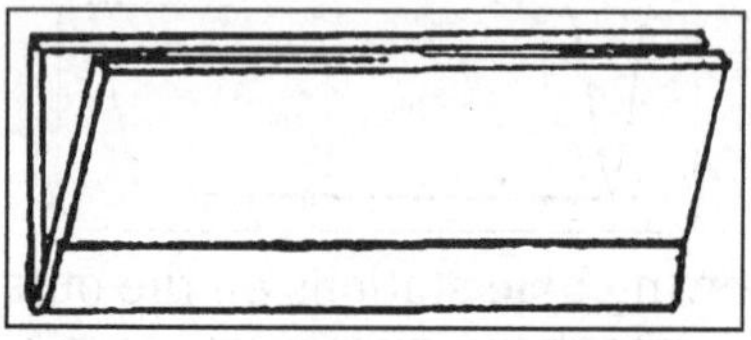

Glue the cardboard strips into the cut out 'V' with PVA.

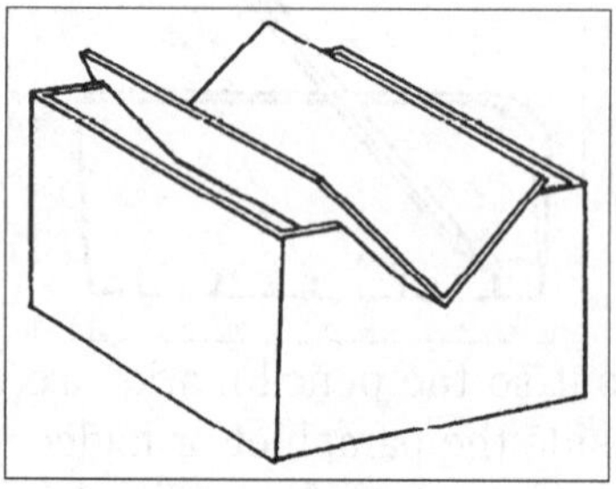

Open the material to the centre of the signature and lay it in the cradle. Make sure the material is seated all the way down into the cradle. Lay a punching jig on top of the material and punch with a needle-in-a-stick.

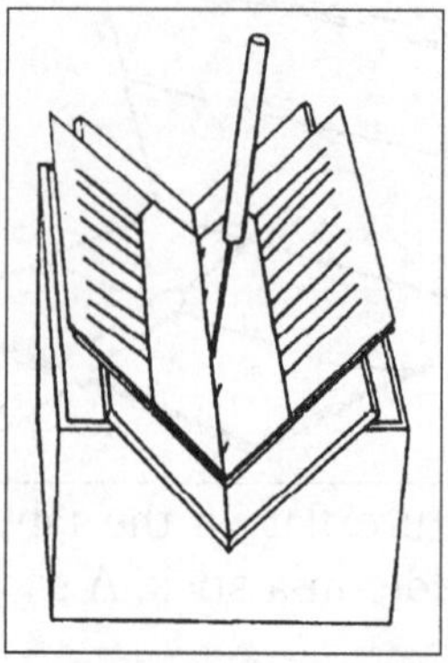

Paper wrapped bricks or jars filled with coins or buckshot can be used as weights while a repair is drying.

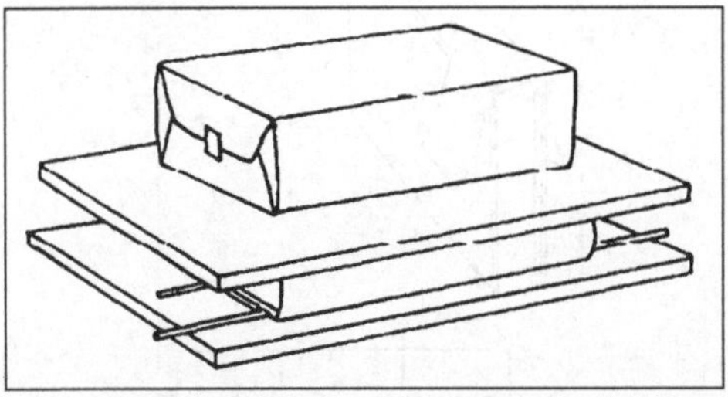

1/4" glass with ground edges makes a perfectly flat work or drying surface. The glass should not be larger than 18" x 18" or it can be difficult to move from one place to another. Thin pieces of plywood or Formica can also be used.

Caring for Tools

It is very important to keep book repair tools clean, especially tools that are used to apply paste or glue. Wash folders, knives, needle-in-a-stick and brushes with warm soap and water. If adhesive is left to dry on a tool, it can build up over time and damage the tool. This is especially true for brushes.

ADVANCED REPAIRS OF BOOK

Serious repair problems take more time and skill to accomplish than any other level of repair. Often, books that need advanced repairs were poorly repaired in the past so a library beginning a conservation book repair programme may have a great many volumes in need of advanced repairs. As the repair programme progresses, there will be fewer and fewer books needing this level of treatment.

REPAIRING THE SPINE HEAD OR TAIL

Often the head or tail area of a book cover spine wears out while the rest of the book is still in good condition. Damage at the head of the spine is often caused by improper handling and shelving techniques, especially pulling a book off the shelf incorrectly.

While these problems can be easily repaired, staff and patrons should be educated on safe book handling.

Measuring and Cutting the Repair Patch

Cut a strip of paper 2" wide and 6-10" long. Wrap the paper snugly around the book spine and mark the edges of the spine. Place the marks at the edge of the paper. Add 1-2" to both sides of the book spine marks depending on the amount of damage. This measurement is the width of the book cloth patch needed to repair the tom header.

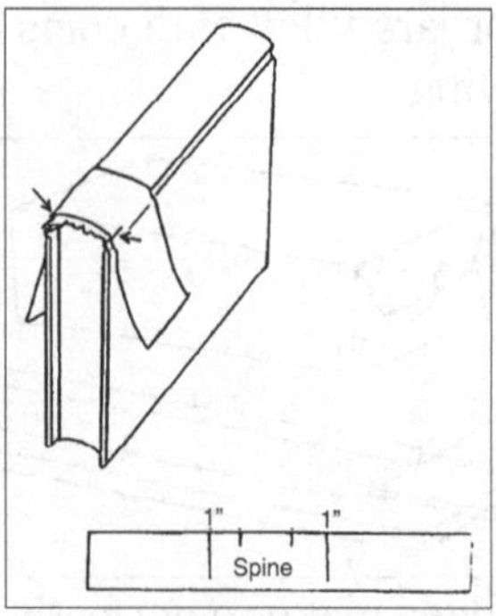

Cut a piece of book cloth the width of the total measurement and the length of the spine damage plus 1 1/2". The comers of the repair patch tend to curl when the patch is inserted, so trim them off diagonally. Cut only the very tip of the comer.

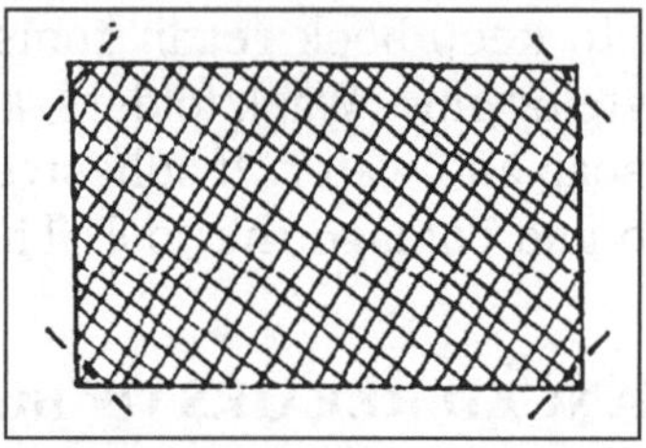

Fit the repair patch on the outside of the book and check to see that the fit is correct. The patch should extend at least 5/8" above the book board and 1/2" below the bottom of the spine damage.

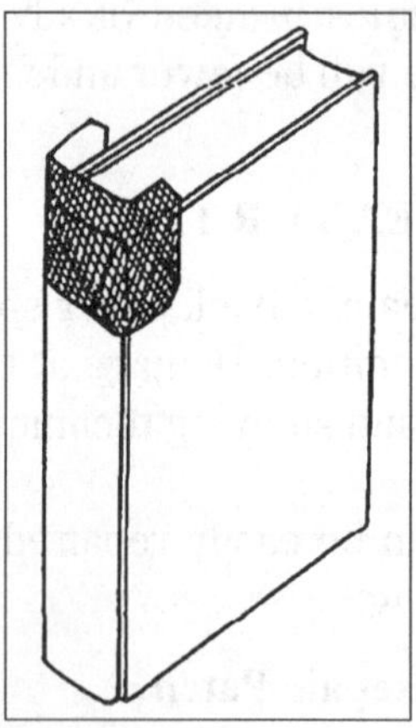

Fitting the Repair Patch to the Book

Slip the repair patch in place between the original book cloth and the book board. Make sure the patch is long enough and wide enough to cover the damaged area.

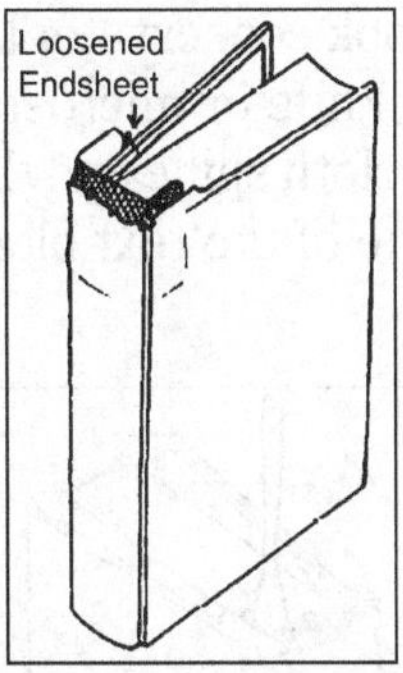

Use the long edge of a folder to work the patch into both cover joints.

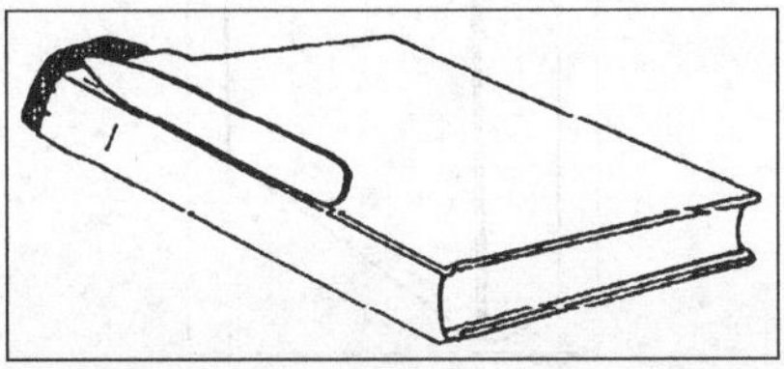

Take a moment to check the position of the patch. The new book cloth patch should lie flat against the book boards and spine of the text block. There should not be any wrinkles or buckles in the patch or the book cloth shine.

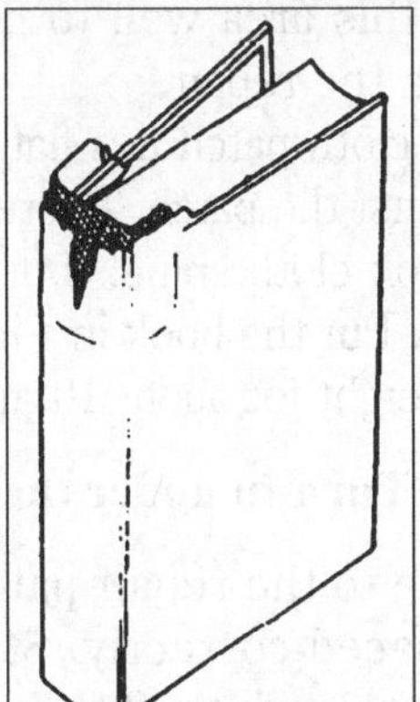

The patch should extend about 5/8" above the top of the book board and should extend at least l/2" below the bottom of the spine damage. It should also extend past both hinges towards the fore edge of the book. If the repair patch does not fit correctly, trim it down or cut a new one.

Gluing the Repair Patch in Place

In modem book case construction, the spine of the book cloth and the spine of the text block must move independently of one another in order for the book to open properly. DO NOT glue the repair patch to the spine of the text block. There are many older book structures that function differently from a case bound book. If a book looks or operates in an unusual way, carefully research the book structure or consult a trained book conservator before attempting a repair. With the repair patch in place, use a knife or microspatula to feed glue between the wrong side of the original book cloth spine and the right side of the repair patch. Do not put any glue on the spine of the text block or on the cut and lifted flaps of book cloth.

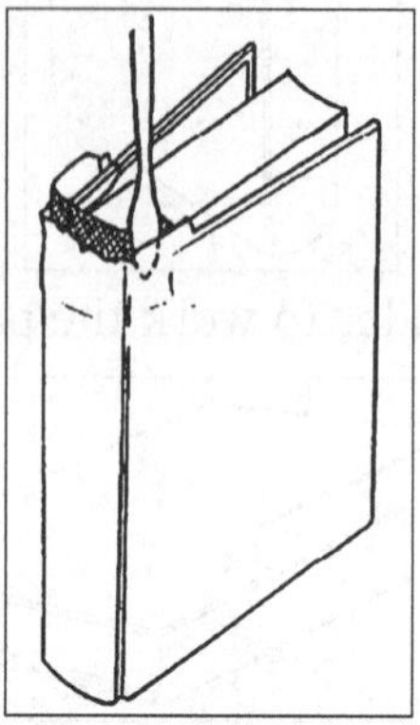

Use a folder to gently press the original book cloth against the repair patch. Work on both covers and the spine. Wipe away any excess glue that is pushed out the top of the repair patch. Use the long edge of a folder to work the patch into both cover joints. work this area well to make sure the patch is in the proper position. Double check the repair.

Make sure the new book cloth patch lies flat against the text block and the original book cloth lies flat against the patch. There should not be any wrinkles or buckles in the patch or the book cloth spine. If it is not a good fit, readjust it or replace it before the glue dries. Put the book in a book press or insert rods in the hinge areas and press under weight for about 10 minutes to allow the glue to set.

Tucking-in the Repair Patch Turn-in under the End Paper

Before applying any glue to the repair patch turn-in, fold it in position to make sure the patch is placed correctly. Starting on either edge of the repair patch, carefully begin to tuck the tumin into the space between the end paper and the board. As one side is tucked in, the rest of the turn-in will follow.

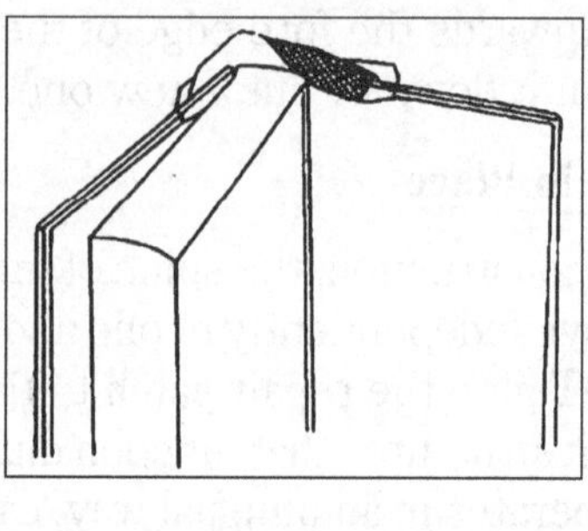

With the entire patch tucked in place, gently crease the top edge of the patch along the boards and in the spine area with your fingers. Set the book on the work table with the repaired end of the spine resting on the table. The edge of the new spine book cloth should be level with the original boards so it rests flat and even against the table.

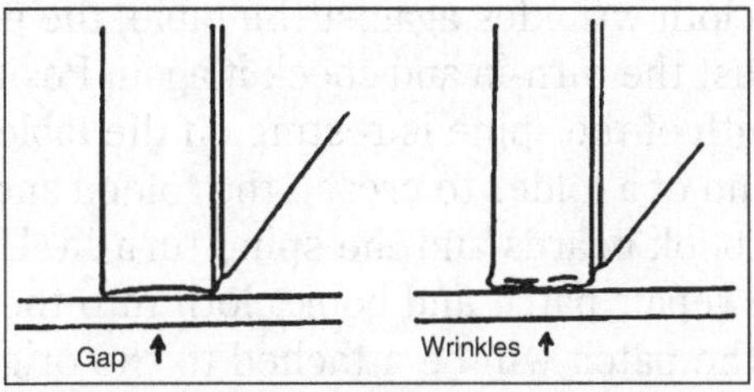

If there is space between the table and repair patch or if the book cloth wrinkles against the table, the position of the turn-in is not correct. Readjust the turn-in and check it again. When the turn-in is positioned correctly, lay the book on the table so that the spine is flat against the table: Use the pointed end of a folder to crease the folded repair patch along the top of the book boards and the spine turn-in.

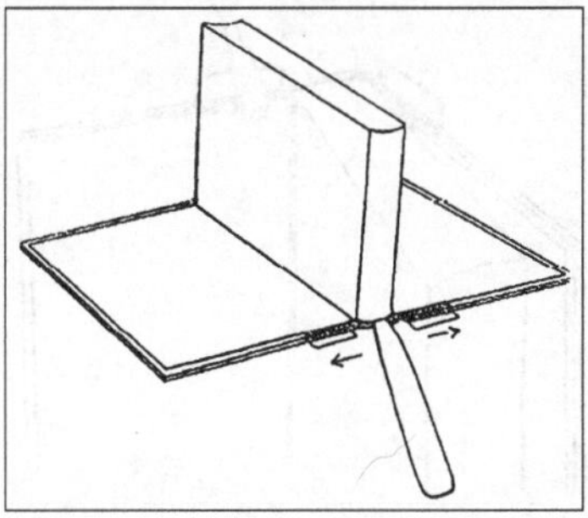

This crease will help correctly position the turn-in after the glue is applied. Folding and creasing the turn-in before it is glued assures the finished tumin will be in the correct position. Unfold the turn-in and apply glue to the inside of the patch turn-in.

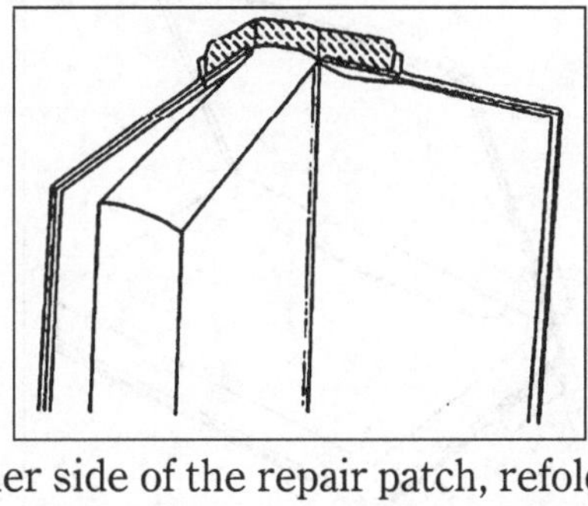

Working from either side of the repair patch, refold the glued repair patch turn-in under the end paper. Continue until the entire patch is tucked in place then crease the edge of the patch with your fingers. Set the book on the work table with the repaired end of the spine resting on the table. Check that the spine edge of the new spine book cloth is level with the original boards and rests even against the table.

Remember, if there is any space visible between the table and the repair patch or if the book cloth wrinkles against the table, the position of the tumin is not correct. Readjust the turn-in and check it again Position the book on the table so that the length of the spine is resting on the table.

Use a pointed end of a folder to crease the folded and glued repair patch along the top of the book boards and the spine turn-in. Use the long edge of a folder to work the repair patch and book cloth into the hinge joints of the book. At this point the patch will be attached to the original book cloth and the book boards.

Gluing Down the Endpapers and Tightening the Hinges

Use the rounded end of a microspatula to feed glue between the lifted endpapers and the cover boards. Feed the glue all the way down to the point where the end papers are still attached to the board and into the hinge area.

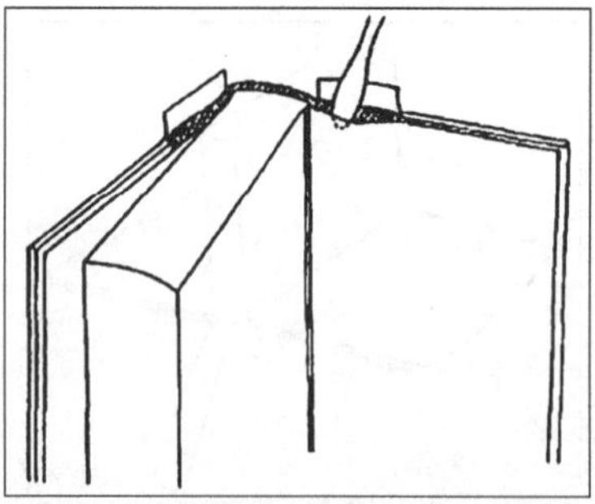

Use a folder to work the end papers into position, working from the centre of the end paper towards the edge of the book board. Wipe away any excess glue that is worked out.

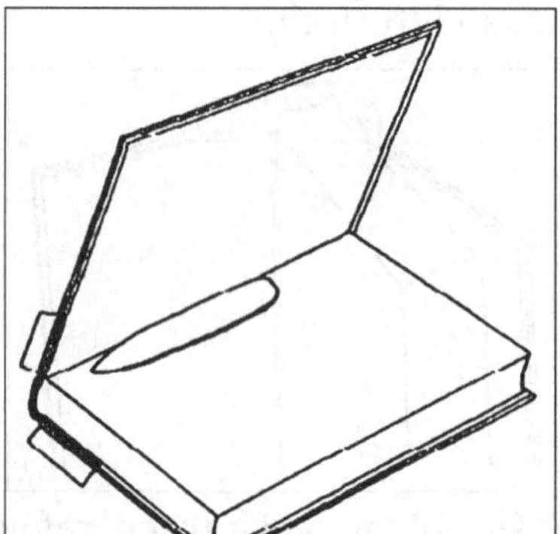

Apply glue to the cut flaps and press them into position. There may be a thin gap between the flap and the edge of the endpaper.

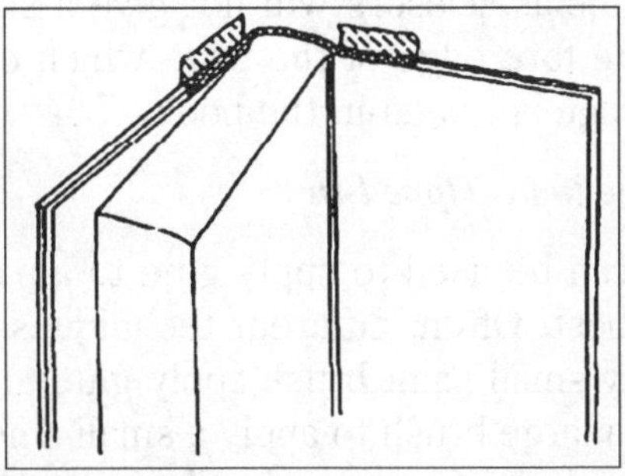

Lay a strip of wax paper in the joint areas. Put the book in a book press or insert rods in the hinges and press under weight for 10 minutes. Open the book carefully and test the front and back hinges.

TOOLS OF INTERMEDIATE BOOK REPAIRS

Intermediate repairs can be handled easily in a library and will keep books circulating and available to patrons. Read through the directions for each repair before starting and be sure to have all the materials needed on hand.

TIPPING-IN DETACHED PAGES

Tipping-in is one way to reattach a detached page or plate, errata sheet or replacement page. Tipping-in is not used to put a entire book back together. If too many pages are loose from the binding, the book should be re-sewn, sent to the bindery, or replaced.

'Too many pages' can vary from book to book, but generally more than 3-5 pages is too many. Tipping-in is generally used on text blocks that are adhesive bound with tightly glued spines. The tight spine keeps the book from opening flat and will help to hold the tipped-in page in place. While the general rule is to use paste when repairing paper, glue is used when tipping in a page. Paste can be a better bond between paper, but it is not as flexible as glue. Since the tipped-in pages need to flex and bend, flexible adhesive is very important.

Tipping-in a Single Text Page

Each book will accept a repaired or replaced page in a different way. Some pages will sit easily into the hinge area, others will slide in from the top or bottom of the text block. Practice putting the page into the book before gluing to see how the page goes in the best.

Often a repaired page cannot be replaced as far back into the spine as when the book was new. If the edges of the repaired or replacement page extend beyond the text block, the page can tear and need future repair. If the page does not fit correctly in the text block, especially in the case of replacement pages, trim the height of the page so that the top and bottom edges will be flush with the edges of the text block. Use a sharp X-acto knife and straight edge to trim the margins as scissors will not give a straight edge. Leave an oversized margin at the fore edge of the page which can be trimmed to the correct size after the page is tipped-in the book.

Applying Glue to a Page to be Tipped-in

Several methods can be used to apply glue to a page; practice each one and see which works best. Often, different techniques will work in different situations. Using a very small paint brush apply glue to the edge of the page. Do not attempt to use a large brush to apply a small amount of glue. It is very difficult to control a large brush in such a small area and the glue could wind up in all the wrong places.

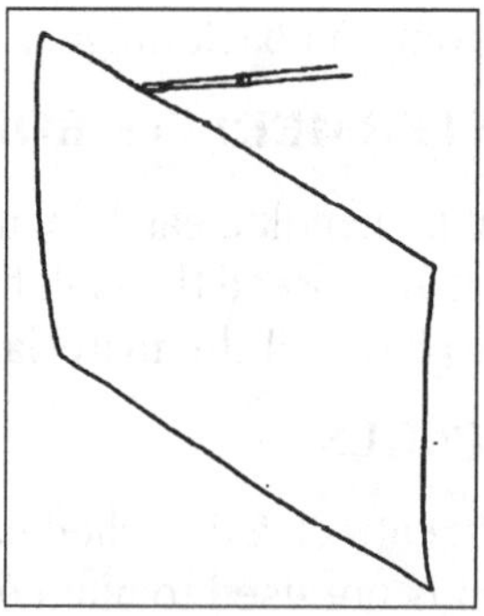

Use a piece of waste paper to mask the inner margin of the page. Leave approximately 1/16" exposed of the page exposed. Apply glue across the waste paper towards the edge of the page. Remove the waste paper before placing the page in the book.

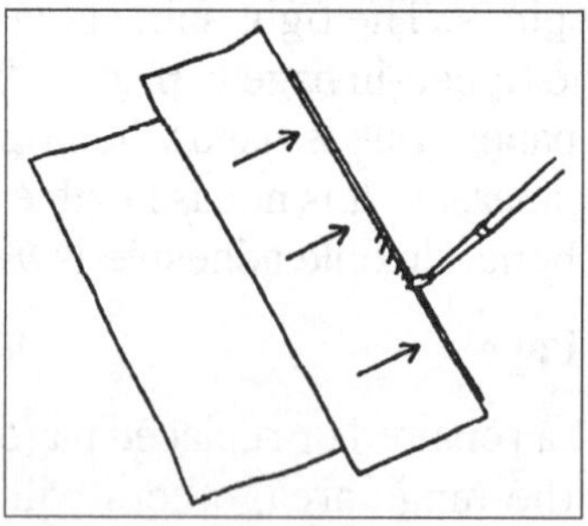

Apply a 1/8" line of glue on a discarded shelf list card or a piece of stiff card stock. Draw the inner edge of the paper along the line of glue making sure the paper edge is covered in a thin, even bead of glue. If the page needs more glue, draw it through the glue again. If there are some areas that have too much glue and others that are not covered, draw the page over a dry piece of card stock to even out the adhesive.

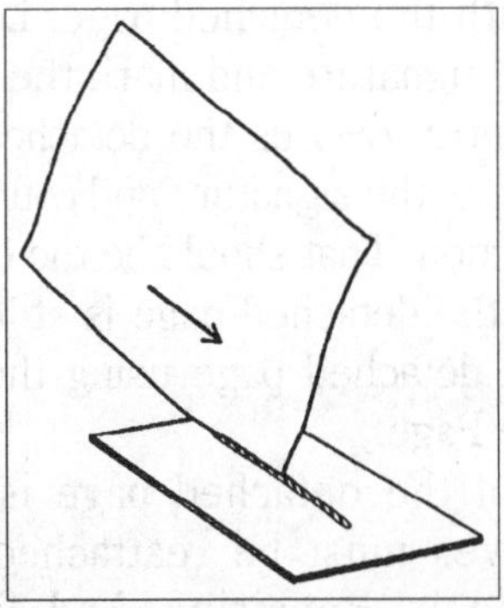

Once the glue is applied to the page, carefully maneuver the page into the book. Use the technique that worked best when the page was positioned in the book before the glue was applied. Put wax paper directly in front and behind the tipped-m page. Besides keeping moisture from traveling throughout the book it also protects the pages from excess glue that can adhere the pages to each other. Put the repaired book under weight and let dry overnight. When the repair is dry, carefully remove the wax paper and make sure the page is securely attached in the book, then return it to the shelf.

Tipping-in Plates

Plates are illustrations that are printed separately from the text of a book. Many plates are smaller than the text block page and are attached to a page of a text block by tipping them in along one edge. This is common even in books with sewn text blocks because plates are often printed on coated paper that is heavier than the paper used to print the text block. When the original glue dries up, the plate separates from the text and falls out of the book.

HINGING-IN DETACHED PAGES

Hinging-in is generally used when the text block is sewn and the pages open flat, or when reattaching a plate that was originally tipped onto a page in the text block. A detached page can be hinged to the page in front or in back of it. While each mend should be evaluated individually, the strongest mend is usually accomplished by hinging from the back of the detached page to the front of the page irnrnediately behind it. That way, the Japanese repair tissue will support the page underneath as it is turned.

Checking the Attachment of Both Halves of a Folio

Each signature of paper is made of folios and each folio is made of 2 leaves. When one leaf is detached, always check that its other half is still well attached to the text block.

The other half might still held in place by the original glue, or it might also be loose:

- Check the attachment of the second half of a folio by finding the centre of the signature with the detached page. Look for the sewing threads at the centre of the signature and mark the centre with a slip of paper.

- Count from that centre towards the detached page, then go back to the marker at the centre of the signature and count the same number of pages in the opposite direction. That should be the other half of the folio.
- If the other half of the detached page is still firmly attached to the text block, hinge in the detached page using the technique outlined in the Hinging In A Single Page.
- If the other half of the detached page is also detached or loosely attached, both halves must be reattached. Options to reattach the pages are covered in Repairing And Reattaching Damaged Or Separated Leaves, Folios Or Signatures.
- If the spine of the text block is accessible, use the instructions in reattaching a separated signature page to reattach both pages.

Hinging-in A Single Text Page

Tear a strip of Japanese repair tissue approximately l/2" wide and as long as the height of the page. Japanese tissue tends to stretch a little lengthwise when wet so it can be trimmed a little shorter than the page. Lay the page to be hinged on a piece of wax paper or non-stick material. Lay a strip of Japanese repair tissue on a piece of waste paper and mask one half of the width of the tissue. Brush wheat paste on to the exposed side, remembering to brush across the waste paper towards the edge of the Japanese tissue.

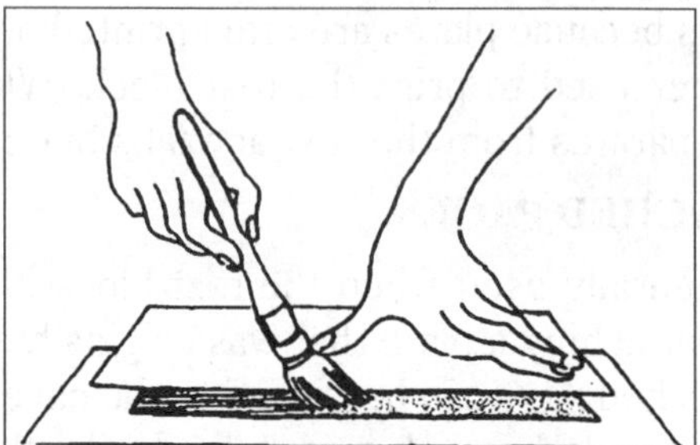

Remove the waste paper from the Japanese repair tissue and carefully lay the repair tissue on the inner margin of the page to be hinged. The pasted half of the Japanese tissue strip should be laid on the page while the half that is not pasted hangs off the page.

Use a folder to gently smooth the feathered edge of the repair tissue into the repaired page working from the middle of the Japanese tissue strip towards the edge. Take note of any excess paste. Try to use just enough paste to adhere the tissue to the paper and not so much that it is forced out the edge of the repair.

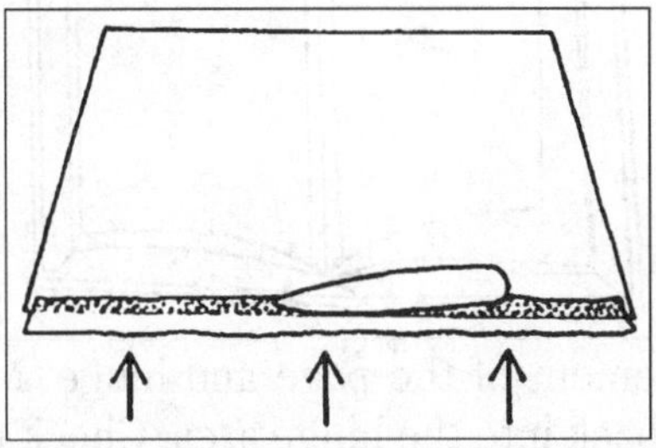

Cover the repair with wax paper or non-stick material and blotter paper then dry under weight. If blotter paper is used, changing it every 10-15 minutes will speed the drying time. When the first half of the repair is dry, trim the top and bottom edges of the Japanese tissue if they extend past the edge of the paper.

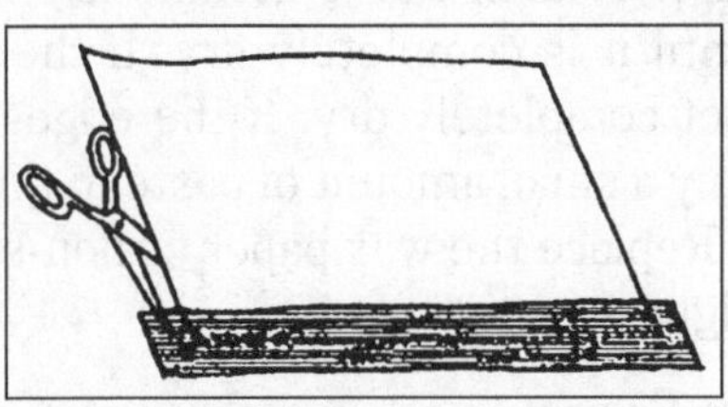

Fold the Japanese tissue back towards itself to form the hinge. Place wax paper and waste paper under the folded hinge, with the waste paper closest to the pasted Japanese tissue.

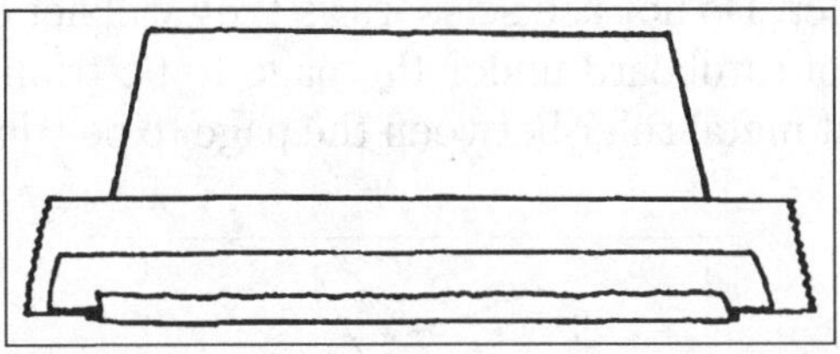

Lay the page, wax paper and waste paper on a sheet of waste paper and carefully paste the exposed Japanese tissue. Be careful not to get paste under the Japanese repair tissue or beneath the printed page.

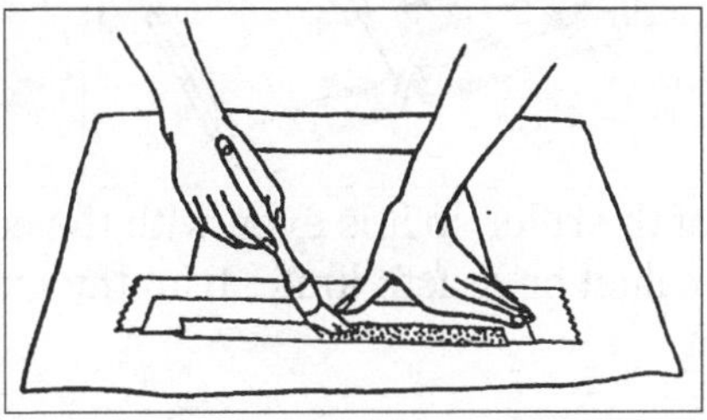

Remove the waste paper and carefully position the hinged page in the book. Use a folder to work the page and repair hinge into the inner hinge.

Double check placement of the page and hinge. Make sure the hinge is smooth and all the way back into the hinge area. Check to see that the edges of the hinged page match the edges of the top and bottom of the text block. Make Sure The Page Is Right Side Up! Place a piece of wax paper on either side of the Japanese tissue repair so the moisture will not travel into the text block. Put the book in a press or rods in the joints and dry under weight Keep the book under pressure until it is completely dry. If the Japanese hinge or the paper feels cool, it is not completely dry. If the edges of the hinge have not adhered to the page, apply a small amount of paste to the edge and gently work it in place with a folder. Replace the wax paper or non-stick material, close the book and dry under weight.

Trimming the Hinged-in Page

The edges of the hinged-in page may not be even with the rest of the text block. If the paper extends beyond the edges of the text block, trim it with an X-acto knife and ruler. Do not use scissors as they will not cut a straight edge. Place a thin piece of cardboard under the page to be trimmed-to protect the text block. Slip a flat metal ruler between the page to be trimmed and the page before it.

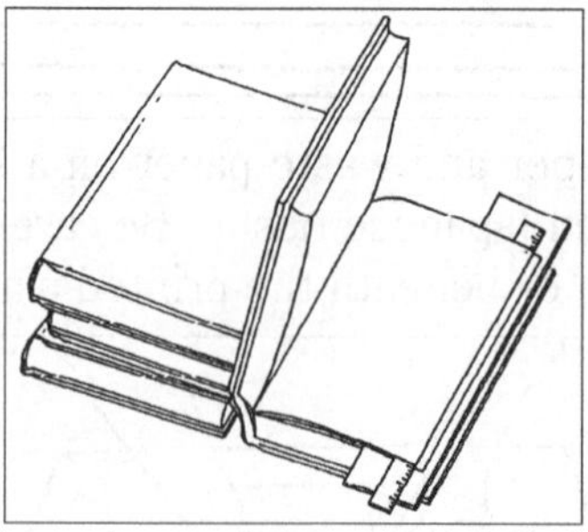

Line up the edge of the ruler so it is even with the edge of the page before it. With a very sharp scalpel or X-acto knife, trim the excess margin from the page beneath the ruler.

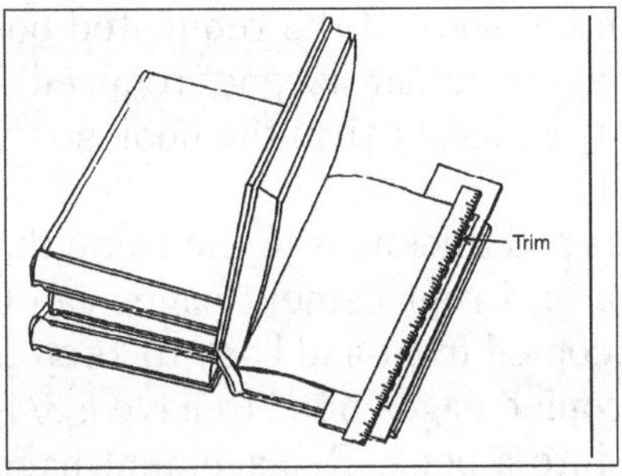

Hinging-in Several Pages

The exact number of pages that can be successfully hinged-in will vary from book to book. Remember, when pages are hinged-in, additional thickness are being added. Do not attempt to replace more pages than the width of the book spine will allow. There are several options to use when hinging in multiple pages.

One choice is to hinge the loose pages to one another as a unit and then hinge the unit into the text block. In another case it is best to hinge each page into the text block one page at a time, especially if only 1 or 2 pages are being hinged-in. The method used will be determined by the individual book.

Hinging-in Plates

Plates can be attached to a text block in several ways. Some plates are printed on folded sheets that are sewn into the text block as part of a signature. Other plates are printed on shiny, stiff paper, then tipped onto the page with glue. As the original glue dries up, the plate can separate from the text and fall out of the book. Plates can be replaced by re-tipping them to the page or reattached by creating a Japanese tissue hinge between the plate and the text block page. Use the Hinging-in A Single Text Page technique to hinge a plate into a book. Check the original placement of the plate on the page as some plates are smaller than the pages of the book and are often centred on the page. If the plate was originally tipped in along the side it can be reattached along that edge or along the top edge of the plate. Hinging from the top edge of the plate gives more support to a heavy plate.

REPLACING DAMAGED OR MISSING PAGES

When a page is damaged beyond repair or has been previously mended with clear plastic tape, it may have to be replaced to keep the book usable. If a page is missing entirely, the only option is to replace the page. Check to see if the library has a second copy of the damaged book to use to photocopy a replacement page. If there is not a second copy, request one through interlibrary loan, noting that the book is being used to photocopy replacement pages to repair a library book. Whenever possible, ask to receive the book, not photocopied pages from the book. If the requested book does not circulate, ask for photo-copies that are actual size, not reduced. The 8 1/2" x 11" photo-copy paper will probably be larger than the book so the page will need to be trimmed to fit the book.

Replacement pages add thickness to the spine that can cause it to swell or split. Usually only 3 or 4 replacement pages can be safely inserted. All pages should be photocopied front and back to keep the added thickness to a minimum. All photocopied pages need to have a 3/4-1" wide inner margin for tipping or hinging into a book. Replacement pages that fold out of the book, such as maps, should be copied in parts, hinged together, then trimmed to text block height.

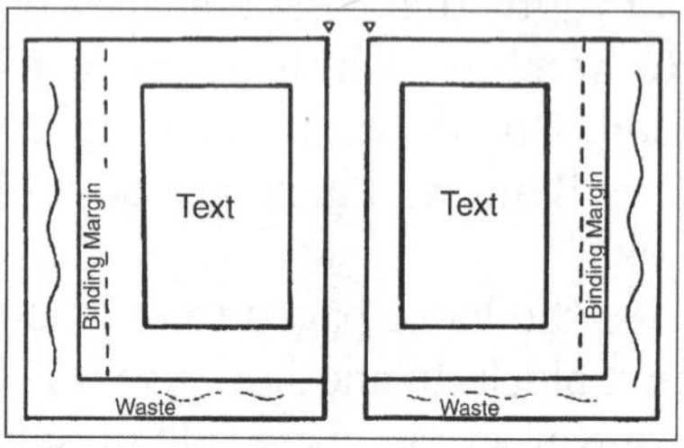

The margins of the copied page should be uniform. The text on both sides should be in alignment. Single-sided copies should be aligned with the upper right hand corner of the paper.

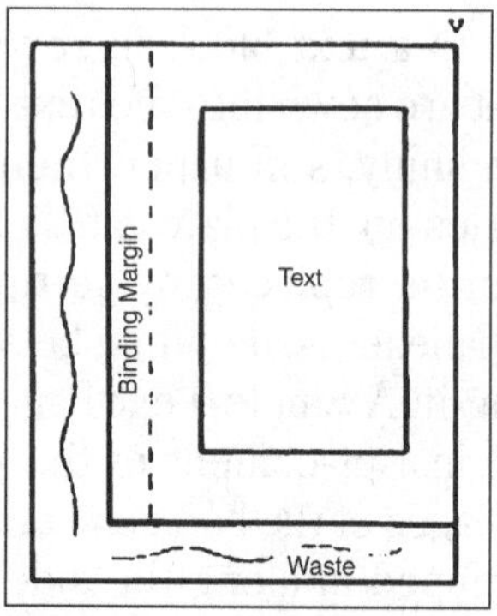

Since most books are not 8 1/2 x 1 1', it will be easiest to photocopy each page, cut and paste them into the correct position on a single sheet of paper, and then photocopy that page front and back. The edge margins can be trimmed to the correct size after the page is copied. Use a light table or work on an outside window to line up the print and margins on the two pages for the correct placement. If the cut and pasted photocopy came directly from the book, the finished replacement page will be a second generation copy. The more generations a copy is from the original, the less clear the print will be. If possible, use acid-free bond paper to make copies for replacement pages.

Regular bond paper is acidic and can cause future damage to the book. Acid-free bond can be more expensive than regular photocopy paper but one package of acid-free paper will last a long time if it is only used for photocopying replacement pages. Acid-free paper is also available in 11 x 14" and 11 x 17". These larger sizes can be useful when replacing end sheets printed with maps or printed information. Some photocopy machines have double-sided copy features, but it is not always best to use this feature. When a photocopy machine has a doublesided copy feature two separate paper trays are used, one outside the machine to load the paper and one inside the machine to store the paper between the first and second printing steps.

Using two different paper trays often means the margins on the two sides of paper do not line up correctly. Each machine is different so experiment to see how a particular machine works. If a photocopy machine does not have a double-sided copy feature or it does not make accurate double-sided copies, double-sided photocopies can still be made by copying the first page and then manually re-inserting the paper into the paper tray to print the second. For proper registration, It is important to use the same leading edge of paper in both procedures. There may still be a difference in the margins but it will be consistent each time and the cut and pasted copy can be readjusted to compensate for it. For instance, the second page of copy might need to be 3/8" lower than the first for the final copy to be even on both pages. Trim the finished copy to the correct height then tip-in or hinge-in the page. Trim the fore edge to the correct width using the instructions in this chapter.

REPLACING MISSING CORNERS ON CASE BOUND BOOKS

It is not uncommon for a corner of a hard cover book to be damaged or destroyed while the rest of the case is in reasonably good condition.

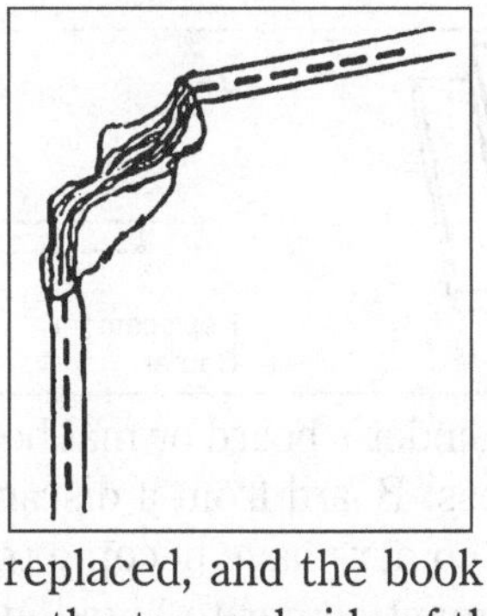

These corners can be replaced, and the book returned to the shelf. Cut through the book cloth along the top and side of the book board, cutting from the undamaged cloth towards the damaged corner. Make sure to cut far enough back so that the ragged edge of the book board is fully exposed.

Fold the book cloth out of the way and make a diagonal cut, trimming off the ragged edge of the damaged corner. Trim only as much board as necessary

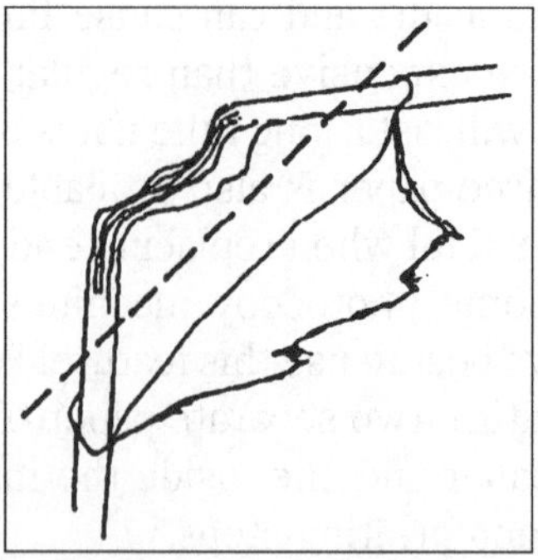

Make a second diagonal cut, about 3/8-1/2" inside the first cut. This cut should only go through half of the thickness of the book board. Use a knife or microspatula to remove half the thickness of the book board to create a step

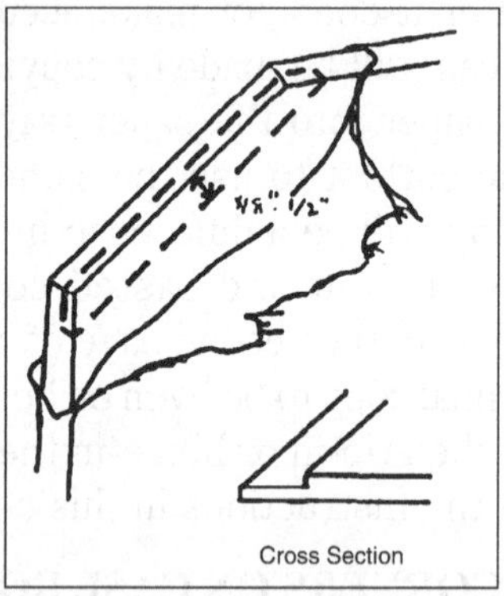

Cut a replacement comer out of binder's book board or mat board. This replacement comer should be the same thickness as the original board and should have a reverse step that will fit into the cut out step on the book cover.

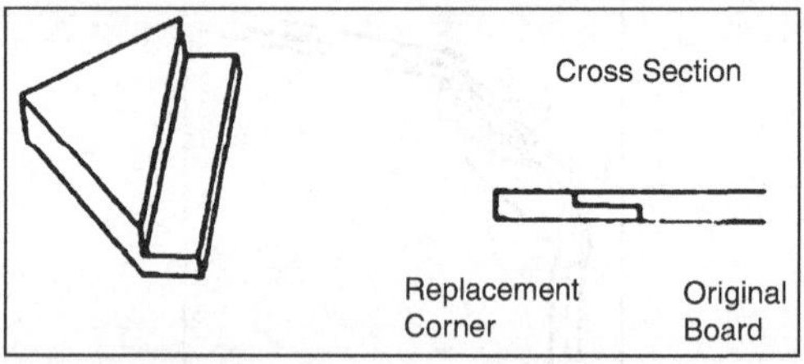

Two or more layers of binder's board or mat board can be glued together to achieve the desired thickness. Board from a discarded book can also be saved and used. If the undamaged comers have become rounded with use, it might be better to round the replacement comer to blend in with the other comers. Fit the replacement comer onto the book and make sure it is the proper fit. Apply glue to the 'step' in the book board and the replacement comer and fit in place. Dry the repair under weight using paper covered bricks. Cut a piece of new book cloth to fit the comer repair. Remember the grain of the comer cloth must run parallel with the spine of the book.

TECHNIQUES OF SIMPLE BOOK REPAIRS

Most book repairs begin as simple problems. If a simple problem is ignored or handled incorrectly, it becomes a complex repair. When a book is repaired early, there is much less work and the volume stays in circulation longer.

CLEANING PAGES

When attempting to clean paper, always start with the least abrasive cleaning method before trying others. Keep in mind that cleaning library materials be a time consuming task. Evaluate each book before attempting to dry clean it. Make sure that cleaning a particular volume is a good use of time.

Dry Cleaning

Dry cleaning is any kind of cleaning that does not use water or liquid cleaners. Done correctly, dry cleaning will not damage library materials. Some dirt can be swept off the page using a soft, natural bristle brush. Always brush from the centre of the page out towards the edges in a star burst pattern and up and down the hinge area to remove dirt or eraser crumbs.

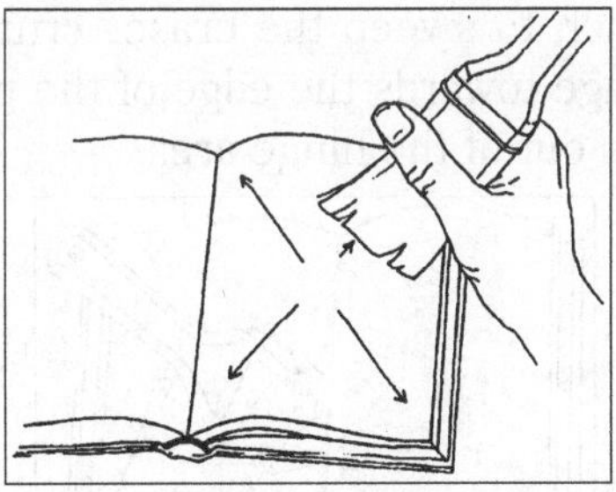

Brushes can be of any size but should have soft, natural bristles. Plastic or nylon bristles can scratch the paper. Brushes used for dry cleaning should not be used for water, paste or glue so it's best to designate a brush just for dry cleaning. Watch out for paper tears that can catch on the brush and NEVER brush from the edge of the paper towards the middle. The brush could 'grab' the edge of the page, pull it back on itself and cause a tear. This is especially important to remember when there are small tears on the edge of the page. After using a dry brush to sweep off the surface dirt, products such as Opaline or Skum-X can be used to remove more stubborn surface dirt. Opaline and andurn-X are both eraser products. Opaline comes in a bag and Skum-X in a shaker dispenser. Opaline is applied by kneading the bag above the paper until the paper is covered with a fine powder of tiny eraser crumbs. Skum-X is applied like salt from a salt shaker. Using clean fingers, rub the paper lightly in a circular pattern.

Do Not Rub The Paper With The Opaline Cloth Bag or the bag will become soiled quickly and transfer that dirt onto the page. It is possible to protect the page from skin oil by rubbing through a soft cloth or a piece of polyester film, such as Mylar.

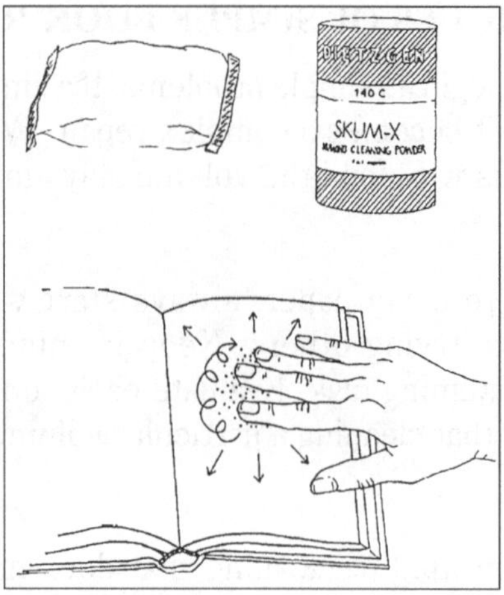

Always work in a circular motion from the centre of the page towards the outside edge. Be very careful of the edges of the page; they tear easily.

The eraser crumbs change colour as they pick up dirt. Once they seem to have picked up as much dirt as possible, brush the eraser crumbs off the page. Use a natural bristle brush to sweep the eraser crumbs off the page. Brush from the centre of the page towards the edge of the paper and don't forget to sweep the eraser crumbs out of the hinge area.

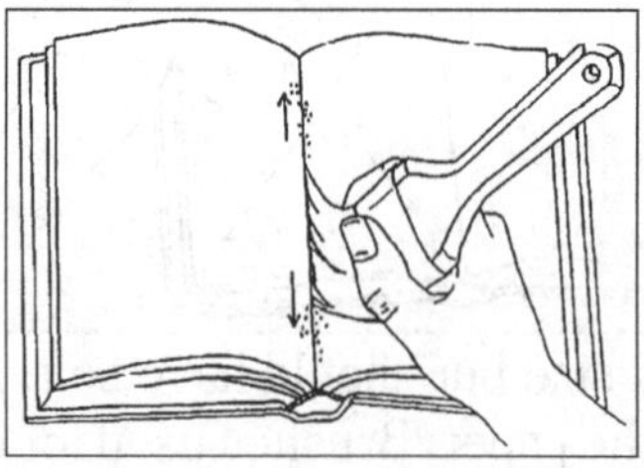

TIGHTENING OR REPAIRING CASE BINDING HINGES

Case binding is a general term for the process of constructing a hard cover book in two parts: the text block and the case or cover. As detailed in Book Case Construction, the major point of attachment between the text block and the cover is the crash cloth that covers the spine of the text block and is glued to the cover boards. The text block is usually attached to the case so that it sits approximately 1/8-3/16 above the shelf.

This means that gravity is constantly pulling the text block down. The adhesive in the hinge area can dry up over time and become weak while the spine and endpapers are still intact.

When the glue dries up, the crash separates from the book board and the hinge area becomes loose. Often the end paper will split along the hinge and the crash will be visible underneath. The common repair practice of applying plastic tape to the hinge area does nothing to reattach the crash to the case board, it only adds a layer of tape in the book.

Tightening Loose Hinges

When the hinge area is loose and the endpaper is not tom, use a wooden stick such as a bamboo skewer or thin knitting needle coated with PVA to feed a small amount of PVA into the joint area. Carefully insert the PVA-coated knitting needle or stick into the hinge area at the top of the book, rotating as the stick is pushed down.

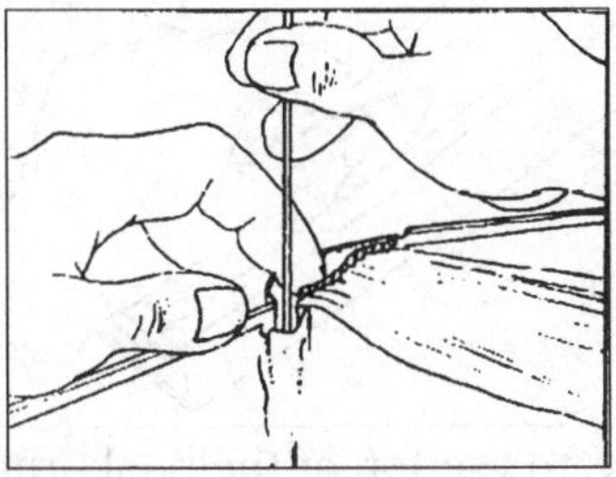

Librarians often find pencil or pen notations on the page of a book. While most pens are permanent, some pencil marks can be erased from paper. A white vinyl eraser, such as Faber Castelblr and Magic-Rub eraser, is recommended because it is less abrasive than most other erasers.

These vinyl erasers come in several sizes and can be shaped with a knife or purchased in a pencil form and sharpened to reach small areas or between lines of print. Erase in one direction, working from the centre of the paper towards the edges of the paper. DO NOT rub the eraser back and forth or erase from the edge of the paper towards the centre of the book. Use a natural bristle brush to sweep away the eraser crumbs, paying special attention to removing eraser crumbs from the inner margin of the page. Remember to brush from the centre of the page towards the edge.

Other Types of Cleaning

Dry cleaning will only remove surface dirt. More advanced cleaning techniques include taking the book apart and washing each page. That is a time consuming and costly process. If simple dry cleaning does not seem to be successful, it may not be feasible to clean the book.

If the book is still usable as is, return it to the shelf. If it is not usable, consider replacing the book. Keep in mind that staff time is valuable and many books need attention. Consider educating patrons with a 'Keep Our Books Clean' campaign. Pull the stick out, turn the book over and repeat on the opposite end. Be careful not to get any glue on the spine of the text block.

After both ends of the hinge are glued, put a piece of wax paper or non-stick material in the hinge area to protect the end paper from any excess glue that might seep through the tom hinge area or out the head or tail. Remember, glue in the wrong place could glue the book shut! Close the book and use the long thin edge of a folder on the outside of the cover to work the book cloth down into the case joint. Use the long edge of the folder as the ends, even the rounded one, can sometimes tear through the book cloth.

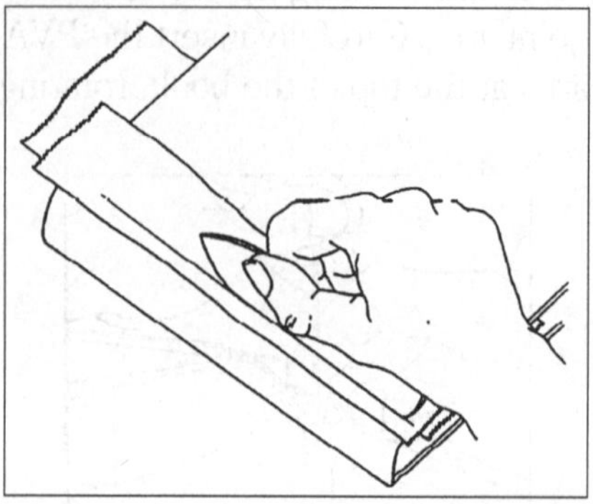

Work from the centre to the top of the book, then from the centre to the bottom of the book. This will adhere the crash, end paper and book board and move any excess glue out of the hinge area.

Open the book cover and use a folder to gently work the end paper back into the hinge. Again, use the long flat edge of the folder as the ends can tear through the paper. Replace the wax paper in the hinge, close the book and rub the folder in the outer joint once again.

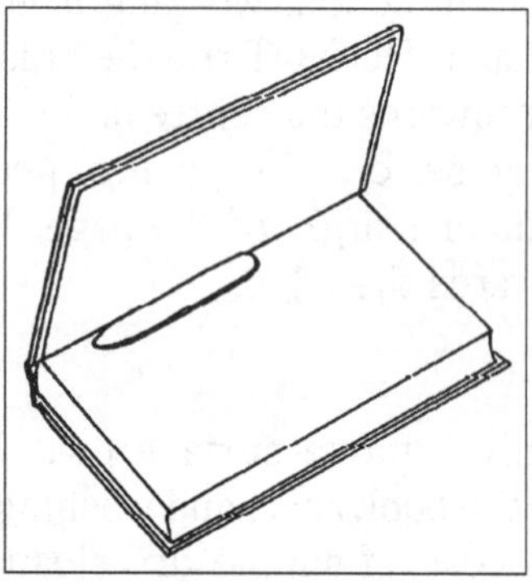

Place the book in a book press to dry. If a book press is not available, put knitting—needles or shelf list drawer rods in the hinge areas of the case and place weight on the book. Let dry overnight and return to the shelf.

Tightening/Repairing Damaged Hinges on a Case Bindings

A variation of the Tightening Loose Hinges technique can be used when an endpaper is split at the hinge.

Check the crash carefully, if more than 1/4 of the crash is torn, it should be replaced. Use a small paint brush or microspatula to apply glue to the split end papers and work them into position.

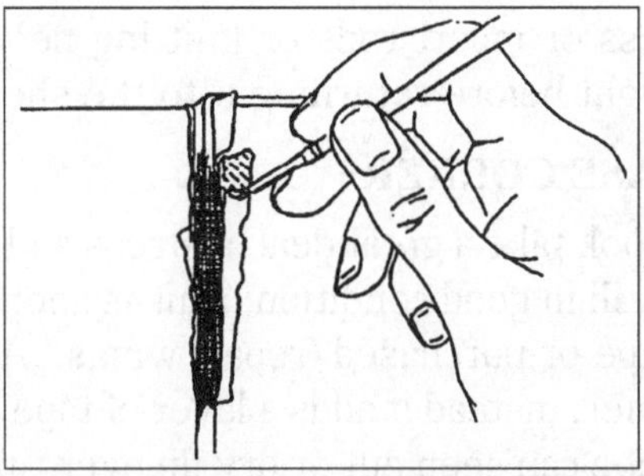

Put a piece of wax paper or non-stick material in the hinge area to protect the paper from any excess glue and close the book. Use the long thin edge of a folder on the outside of the cover to work the book cloth down into the case joint. Remember the rounded ends of the folder can sometimes tear through the book cloth. Work from the centre to the top of the book, then from the centre to the bottom of the book.

This will adhere the crash, end paper and book board and move any excess glue out of the hinge area. Wipe away any excess glue and try to use less glue in the future, After setting the joint with the folder, carefully open the book cover and gently work the folder along the inside hinge, working the end paper back into the hinge. Again, use the long flat edge of the folder as the ends can tear through the paper.

Replace the wax paper. Place the book in a book press or put knitting needles or shelf list drawer rods in the hinges and weight with paper covered bricks.

Let dry for at least one hour, then check the repair. Sometimes the repaired end papers will not quite meet. This space will not affect the strength of the repair but it can be covered with a strip of Japanese tissue and wheat paste for a cosmetic touch. Tear a piece of Japanese tissue the height of the text block and wide enough to cover the hinge repair.

Apply paste to the Japanese tissue and gently lay the tissue on the hinge. Use a folder to carefully work the tissue back into the hinge.

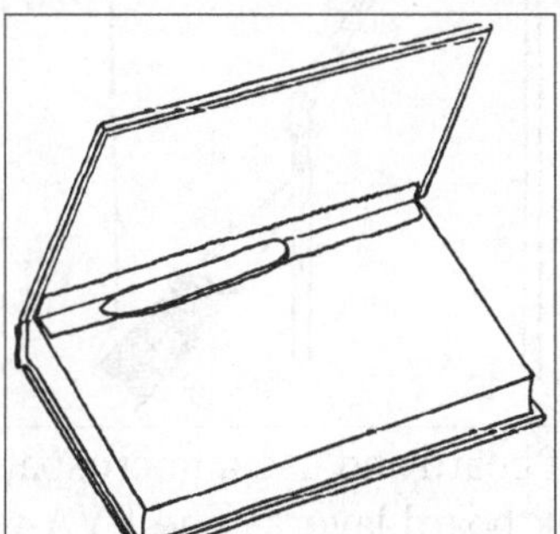

Insert a piece of wax paper or non-stick material, close the book and use the long edge of the folder to work the cloth into the cover joint. Place the repaired book in a press or insert rods or knitting needles in the joints, add weight, and dry overnight before returning it to the shelf.

MENDING BOOK CASE CORNERS

The corners of a book take a great deal of stress and can be damaged while the rest of the case is still in good condition. This is another repair that is often handled with plastic tape or purchased 'repair wings.' Applying tape or wings does not repair the comer; instead it adds a layer of tape on top of the problem. The adhesive on the tape can seep out or dry up over time, causing the plastic carrier to fall off. That can leave behind a sticky residue that is often impossible to clean up.

Repairing Book Boards Corners

The book board used in book case construction consists of many layers of board. If the book cloth is damaged or tom open at a corner, the different layers of board are often visible.

When damaged comers are repaired with plastic tape, the book board is not repaired, it is only covered up. To truly repair the book corner, the various layers of book board must be glued to one another and the book cloth repaired or replaced.

In some cases the corners are damaged while the book cloth is still intact. Other times the book cloth will be tom or missing. In either case, cut through the book cloth on the top and fore edge of the board. Cut well past the damaged board into sound board and cloth.

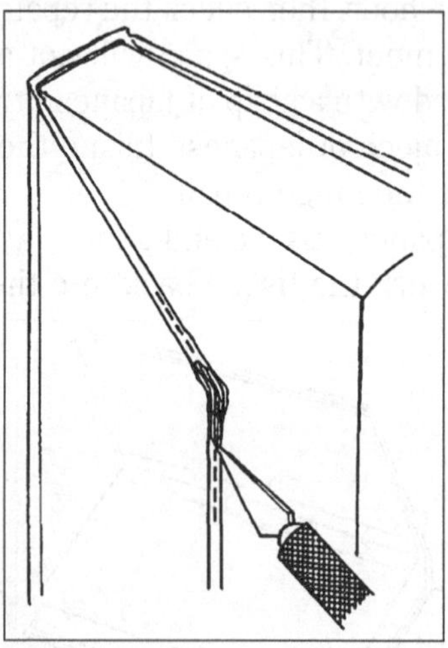

Separate the layers of board and use a microspatula or knife to apply PVA glue to several of the book board layers. The PVA will seep through the thin layers of board so every layer does not need to be glued. The number of glued layers depends on the condition of the book board.

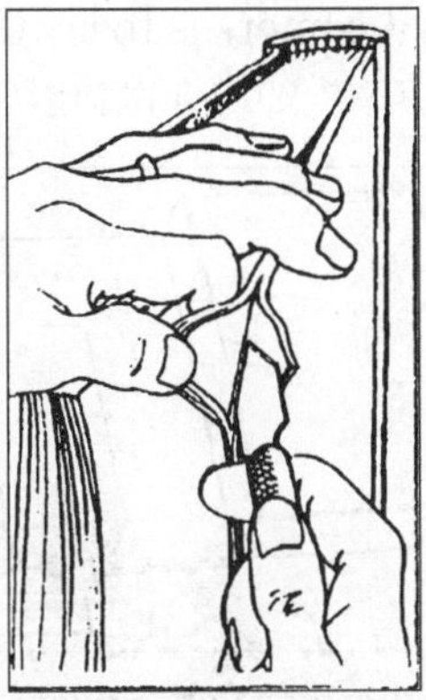

If the original book cloth covers the comer, paint a small amount of glue on the wrong side of the book cloth and smooth it over the comer. If the book cloth needs to be replaced, follow the instructions for Attaching New Corner Book Cloth. With fingers or a folder, press the book cloth onto the board, moving from the base of the repair up towards the comer edge. Wipe away any excess glue with a cloth or paper towel.

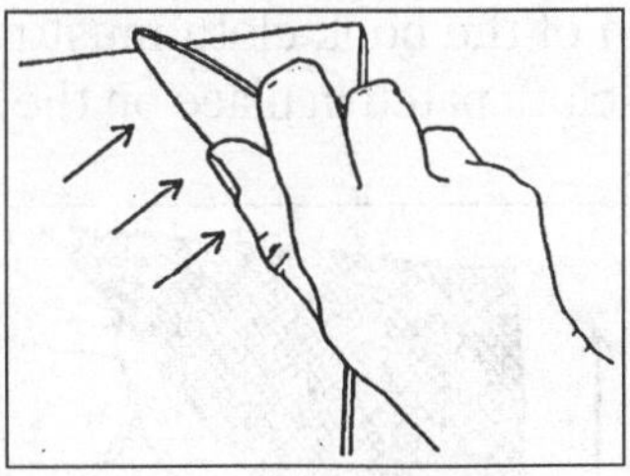

Note how much excess glue came out of the corner and use that as a gauge to decrease or increase the amount of glue used. A small amount seeping out is good because it means that the glue has reached all the layers of cardboard. Too much adhesive seeping out is wasteful and makes a mess to clean up. For sharp flat comers, cover each side of the comer with wax paper or non-stick material and clamp between two pieces of book board using Binders or Bulldog clips. Use dense mat board or book board, not corrugated cardboard that will compress under the pressure of the clips.

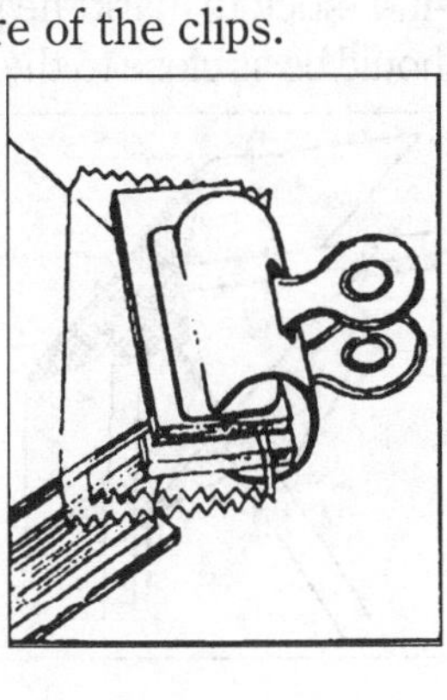

Another way to achieve flat comers is to lay the repaired comer flat against the work table and weight it down with a paper covered brick.

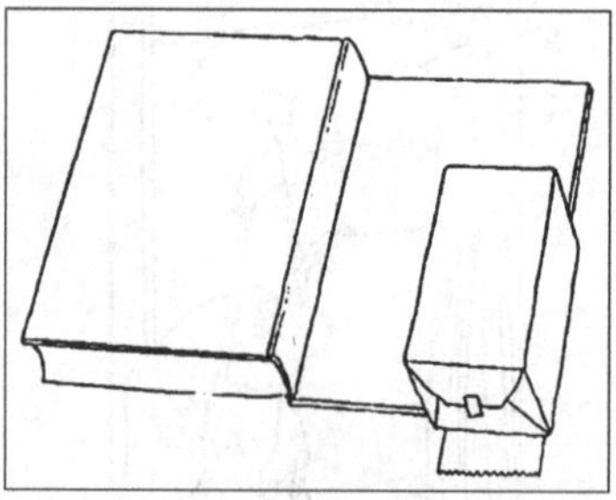

Comers do not have to be sharp or flat to protect the book. Some older books may look more 'natural' with rounded corners, especially when only one or two corners are repaired. If rounded comers would look better, mold the comers into position while the glue is wet and let the repair dry without weight or pressure.

Attaching New Corner Book Cloth to a Repaired Corner

After the corner book board is repaired, cut a piece of new book cloth to cover the repair. The grain of the book cloth must run parallel with the spine of the book. Glue the book cloth patch in place on the outside of the book cover. Dry under weight.

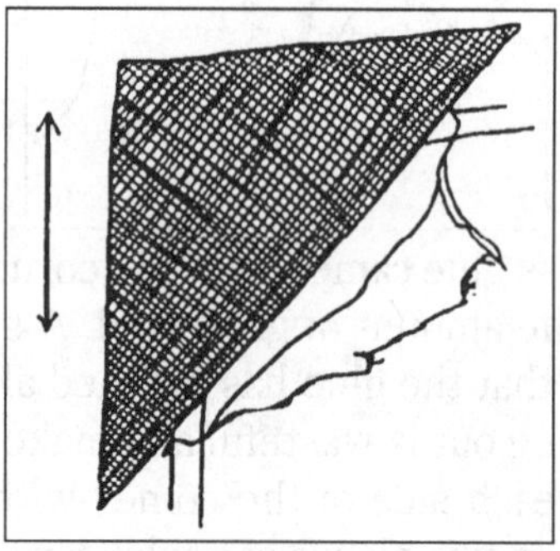

Fold the point of the new book cloth comer over the book board so it forms a 45 degree angle. Use a needle-in-a-stick to mark the position where the book cloth covers the comer. This mark should be as close to the edge of the comer as possible

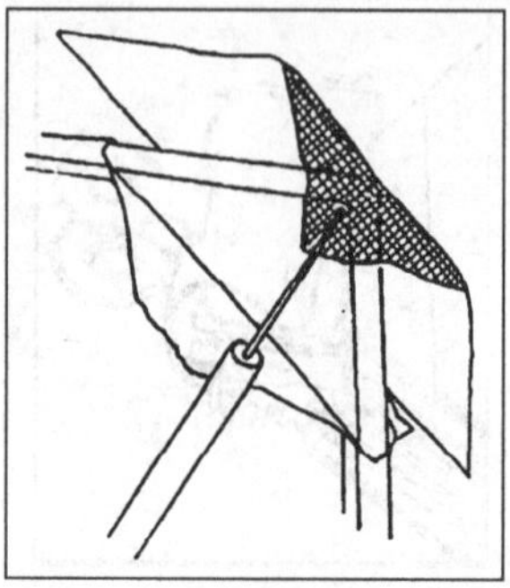

Unfold the new book cloth comer and draw a line through the needle point, along the 45 degree fold. Cut the book cloth along this line.

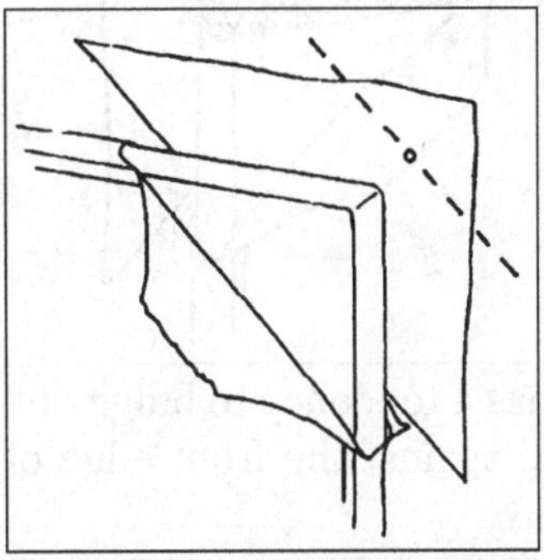

The new book cloth patch has two edges. Regardless of which corner is being repaired, the top or bottom edge of the book will be designated as the top.

The other edge will be the fore edge of new book cloth patch.

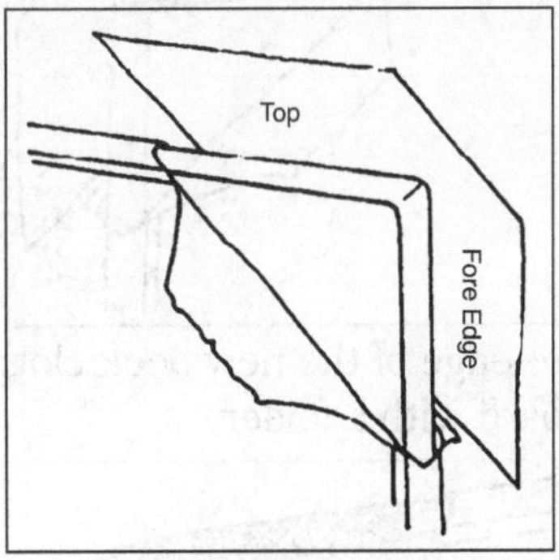

Apply PVA along the top edge of the new book cloth then fold the edge over the book board.

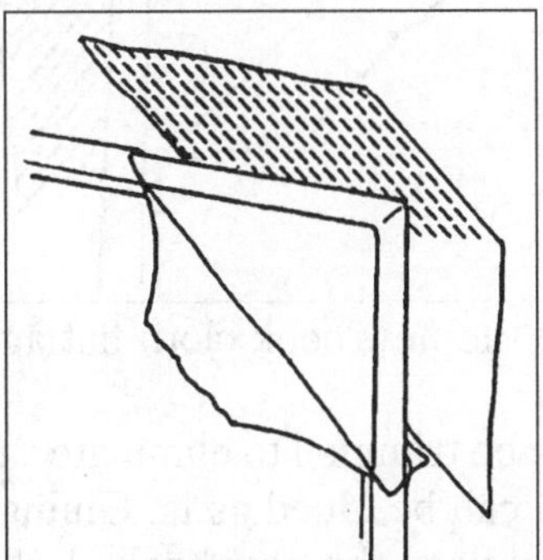

Use a folder to press the book cloth flush against the thickness of the book board. The book cloth should be glued completely flat to all sides of the book board.

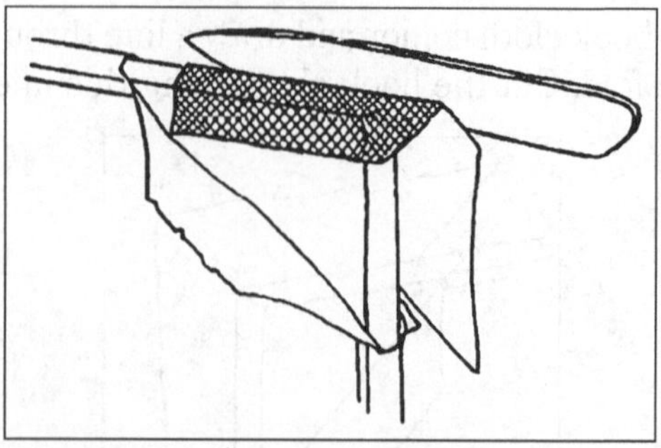

The new book cloth has a tendency to bulge out at the corner so push the new book cloth downward against the front edge of the book board with the point of a folder.

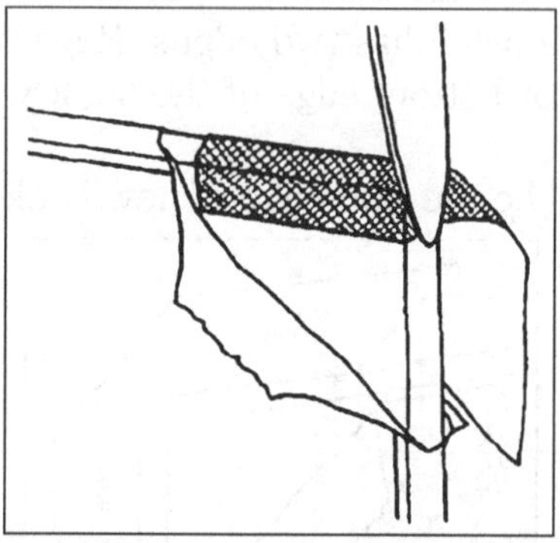

Apply glue to the fore edge of the new book cloth and work the cloth into position over the book board with a folder.

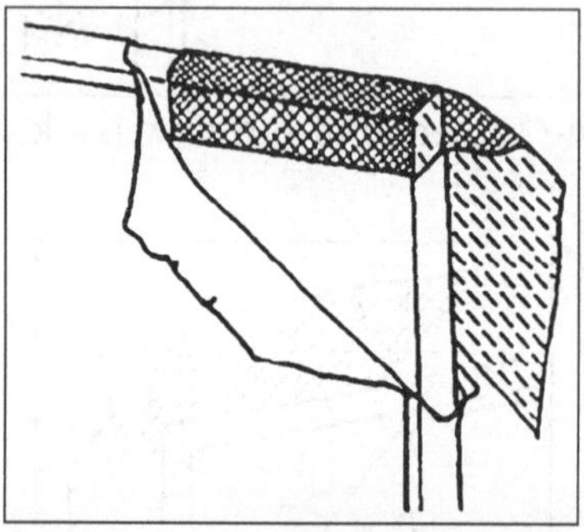

Use a folder to work the new book cloth flat against the book board and slightly round the corner.

The original cloth can be trimmed to eliminate the ragged edges and glued down or the ragged edge can be glued as is. Gluing the loose threads down can sometimes help camouflage the new book cloth if it is not a good colour match.

Dry the repair under weight using paper covered bricks or between pieces of book board with Bulldog clips.

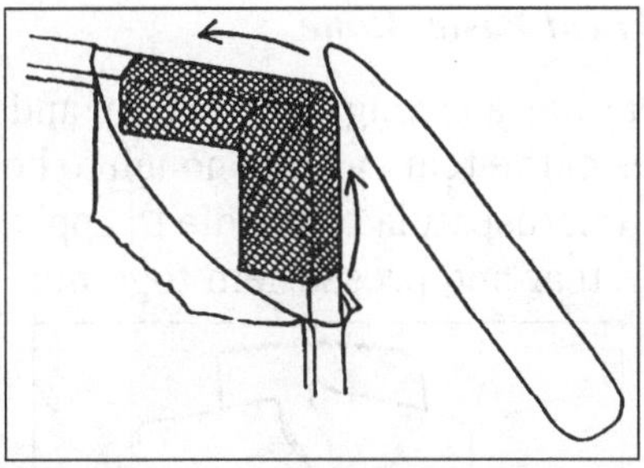

Some older books may look more 'natural' with rounded corners, especially if only one comer is being repaired. For rounded comers, mold the corners into position while the glue is wet; dry without weight or pressure.

PAPER TEARS, CUTS AND LOSSES

Illustrations in this part show each repair completed in a bound book. The same techniques are used for a single sheet of paper not bound in a book.. Paper tears are a simple repair often handled incorrectly with clear plastic tape. Clear plastic tape covers up the problem but it does not repair it and it can cause additional damage to the paper over time.

Repairing Simple or Complex Tear

Paper tends to tear at an angle so most tears will have a top and a bottom. If the tear passes through the text or an illustration, it is easy to see which is the top or bottom because the bottom of the tear will show the white paper fibres. If the tear does not pass through text, look at the tear very carefully before pasting it together.

Some tears will go with the grain of the paper while others go against the grain. Tears that go with the grain of the paper will usually be smooth and straight while tears that go against the grain will tend to have more feathered edges and will curve as they try to align themselves with the paper grain. In simple paper tears the page has been torn one time and the tear has an obvious top and bottom.

This is easy to see when the tear passes through the text or illustrations. Complex tears are really more than one tear. When a tom page is not repaired, the page can easily tear again and the second tear can have a different top and bottom. Always look at the tear and lay the edges in position before applying adhesive to make sure the tear is in the correct position. If the edges are not in the correct position, the repair will not lie flat and the text or illustration may be obscured.

There are three ways to repair paper tears in conservation book repair:

- using wheat paste alone
- wheat paste with Japanese repair tissue
- document repair tape.

Repairing Tears with Wheat Paste Alone

When the paper tear has a strong, obvious top and bottom edge, applying wheat paste to the edges of the tear can be enough to bond them together. Use a very fine paint brush, microspatula or needle to apply wheat paste to the top and bottom edges of the tear and press them together.

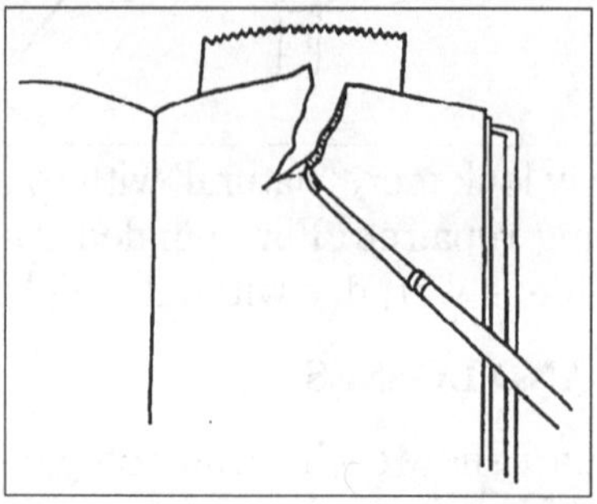

Cover the repair with wax paper or Hollytex and press the edges of the tear together with a folder. Remember to always best to work form the base of the repair towards the edge of the page.

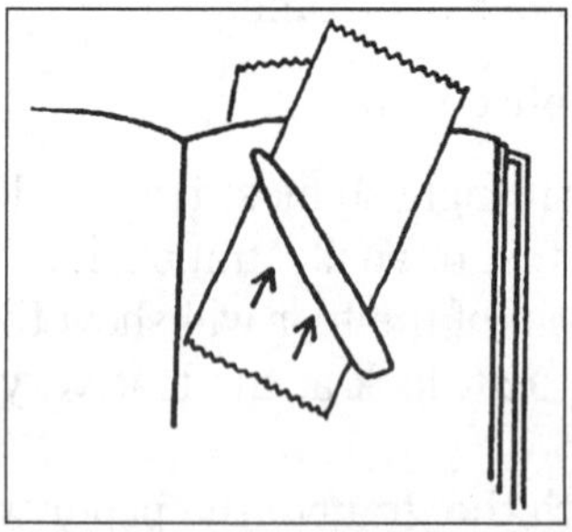

Wipe away any excess paste that is forced out of the edge of the tear. Note how much excess paste was used and try to use less for the next repair. Always aim for enough paste; not too little, not too much.

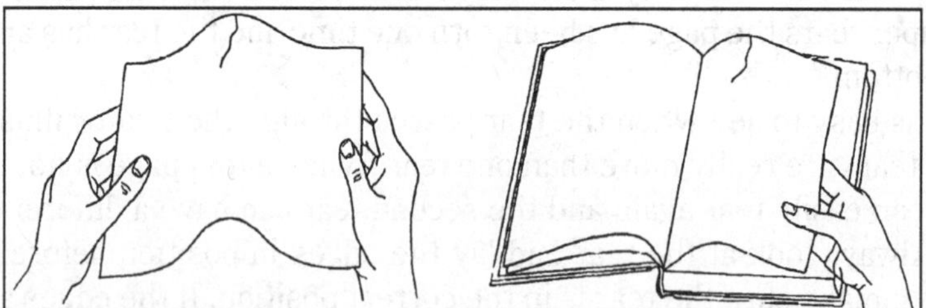

When the repair is dry, curl the paper around all the edges are well adhered. the repaired tear and make sure If there are loose edges, repaste and dry under weight.

If the page creases at the repair, consider applying a Japanese repair tissue patch over the repair. If the tear is not properly aligned, moisten the area with water to release the repair and redo it.

Repairing Tears with Japanese Repair Tissue Patch and Wheat Paste

Japanese repair tissue adds strength to a repair. It is used when the tear does not have wide, overlapping edges and needs reinforcement. Read book repair tools and techniques for instructions on tearing and applying paste to Japanese repair tissue. Choose the best method for tearing and applying paste before beginning the repair. Apply paste on the Japanese repair tissue, then pick up the tissue using a needle, micro spatula or fine tweezers.

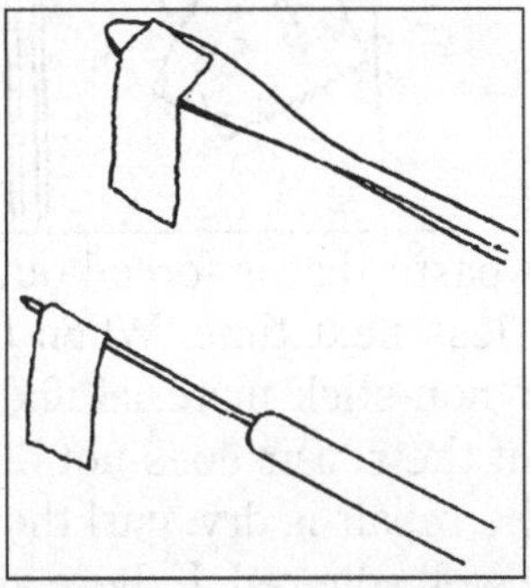

Carefully lay the tissue on the tear. If the tear is at the edge of the page, extend the Japanese tissue 3/8" past the edge of the paper. This extension can be turned under now or trimmed when the repair is dry.

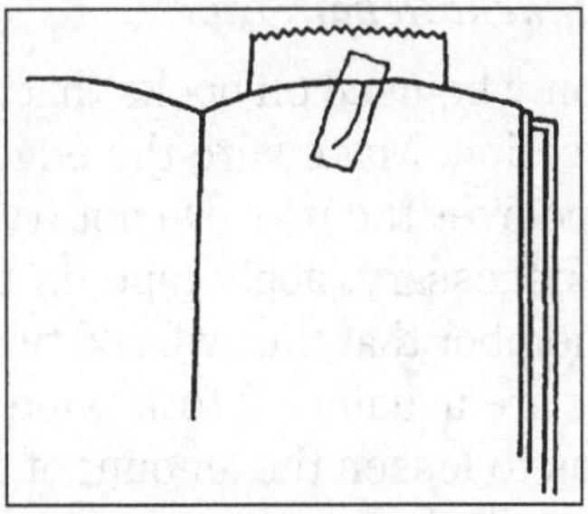

It can be difficult to work with a piece of Japanese repair tissue over 3" so try repairing long tears with several short, overlapping pieces of Japanese tissue. While it may seem inviting to use one long piece of tissue, it is much harder to control, and the finished repair can look clumsy.

Once the pasted Japanese tissue is laid over the tear, cover it with a strip of wax paper and use a folder to gently press the edges of the tear together. Remember to always work from the base of the repair towards the edge of the page.

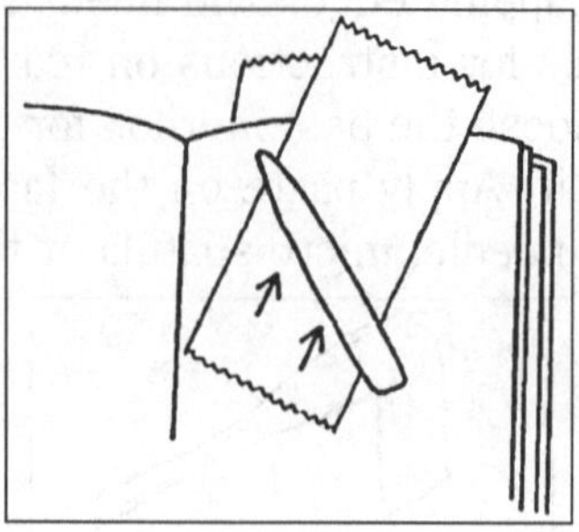

Wipe away any excess paste that is forced out of the edge of the tear. If there is much excess, use less next time. When the entire tear is repaired, cover it with wax paper or non-stick material and blotter paper, then put it under weight. Remember, if the repair does not dry under weight, the paper can buckle and curl After the repair is dry, curl the paper around the tear and make sure all the edges are well adhered. If there are loose edges, repaste and dry under weight. If the page creases at the repair, consider applying a second Japanese repair tissue patch on the opposite side of the original repair.

Repairing Tears with Document Repair Tape

In general, it should only be used on books that are not valuable or part of a library's permanent collection. Make sure the edges of the tear are lined up correctly and apply the tape over the tear. Do not try to repair a long tear with only one piece of tape. If necessary, apply tape on both sides of the paper to attach loose edges but remember that this will add two extra layers of thickness to the book. Archival tapes are usually 5/8 to 1" wide. Tape that wide can often be cut in half or thirds so as to lessen the amount of tape used in each book. In addition to saving money, it will also be better for the book. When tape is applied to both sides of a repair, cut the second piece a little wider than the first so the edges are offset.

Repairing Paper Cuts

Paper cuts slice completely through the paper fibres so they do not have a top or bottom feathered edge. Paper cuts must be repaired with a Japanese repair tissue patch or document repair tape. Since the cut is unsupported, it might be better to put repair tissue on both sides of the cut or wrap a short amount of the Japanese repair tissue or document repair tape around to-the back side of the repair to reinforce the repair. Follow the instructions for applying Japanese Repair Tissue Patch and Wheat Paste or Applying Document Repair Tape.

Repairing Paper Losses

It is not too common to find holes in the middle of the page, but it can happen. While the print can not be restored, the page should be mended to prevent further damage. Choose two layers of Japanese tissue that will be close in thickness to the repaired page. Tear two pieces of Japanese tissue to cover the hole using the techniques covered in Tear A Japanese Tissue Patch Over The Damaged Area. Protect the text block with wax paper on either side of the damaged page. Paste up one piece of Japanese tissue, position it on the page and work the edges into place. Paste up the second piece of repair tissue and lay it in place, working edges down with a folder. Cover with wax paper or non-stick material and blotter. dry under weight. After the repair is dry, curl the paper around the tear to ensure all the edges are well adhered. If the edges are loose, re-paste and dry under weight, then test again.

Repairing Missing Page Corners

Choose two layers of Japanese tissue that together will be close in thickness to the repaired page. Protect the pages behind the repair with wax paper. Use a piece of black mat board to highlight the edge of the repair. Fold a piece of Japanese tissue in half and place over the missing comer. The edges of the patch should extend past the edges of the page.

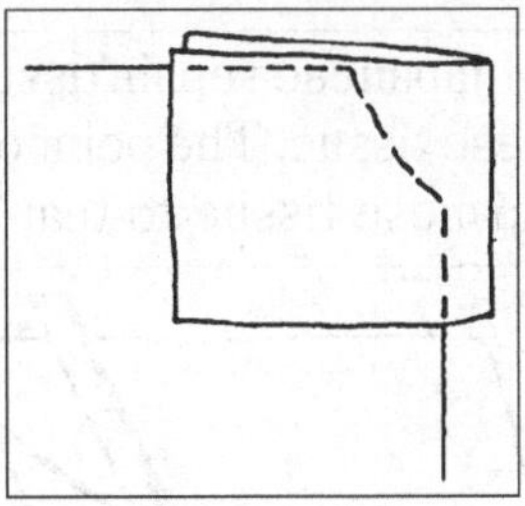

Needle or water tear the two layers of tissue. The patch should be about l/ 16" wider than the loss.

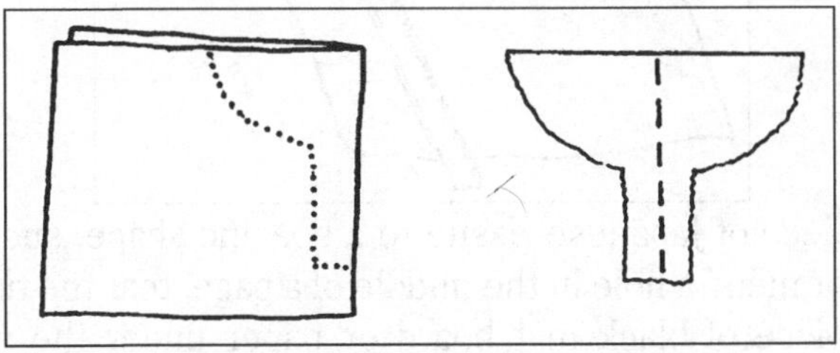

Apply paste to the repair patch and position the repair patch on one side of the missing comer. Work the edge of the patch into place. Fold the patch over and work the edges of the patch into the page. Dry under weight and trim any excess margin. After the repair is dry, curl the paper around the tear to ensure all the edges are well adhered. If the edges are loose, repaste and dry under weight, then test again.

BOOK REPAIR TECHNIQUES

TEARING JAPANESE REPAIR TISSUE

Japanese repair tissue is usually tom so that the edges are feathered, not cut sharp as they would be with a knife or scissors. The feathered edge allows the repair tissue to 'blend' onto the text paper. Repair tissue can be tom with a water tear or needle tear. A needle tear gives a slightly less feathered edge than a water tear. To water-tear a piece of Japanese repair tissue, use a small, pointed natural bristle paint brush to draw a wet line or shape on the Japanese tissue. For a straight line, wet a piece of repair tissue against the edge of a ruler or straight edge. The water weakens the fibres of the tissue and allows it to tear along the wet line.

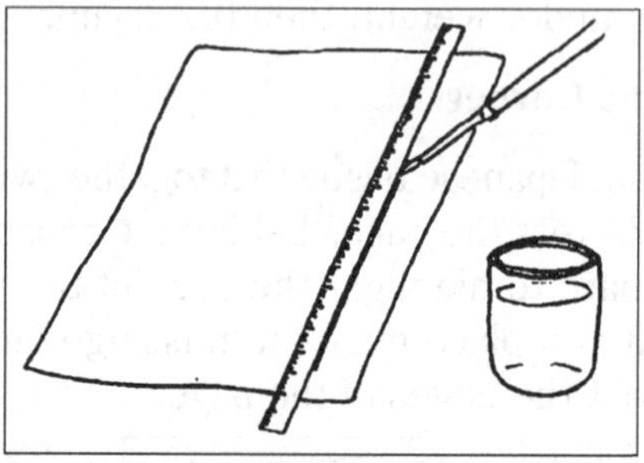

To needle-tear a piece of Japanese repair tissue, use a needle-in-a-stick to score the surface of the Japanese tissue. The point of the needle creates a 'dotted line' on the surface of the Japanese tissue to tear along.

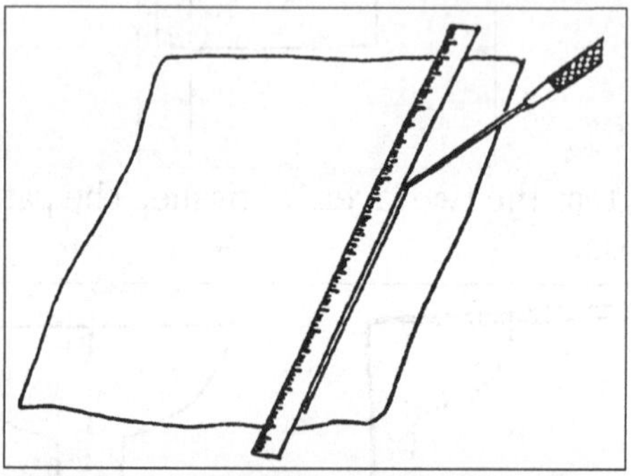

To tear a piece of Japanese tissue to a specific shape, such as to repair a missing comer or mend a hole in the middle of a page, tear the tissue as follows:

- Lay a piece of black mat board or paper under the missing area to make the outline of the loss more visible.
- Put a piece of Mylar polyester film over the loss to protect the page from the water and needle; then lay two layers of Japanese repair tissue over the Mylar and water tear or needle tear the patches to fit the loss. One patch will go on each side of the loss.

If the damaged page is not attached to the text block, it is possible to use a light table or the light from a window to see the area that needs to be patched. Put the text page on a light table or window, cover with Mylar and repair tissue.

With the Mylar film protecting the page, needle or water tear the Japanese repair tissue to the desired shape.

Applying Adhesive to Japanese Tissue

When applying adhesive, choose a brush that matches the size of the surface. If the area is small, use a small brush; a bigger area needs a bigger brush.

A thin, even coat of adhesive makes the best bond. Too much adhesive will ooze out the edges of a repair and can stain other surfaces. Apply paste or glue to paper or cloth by brushing from the centre of the materials being glued towards the outer edges in a star burst pattern.

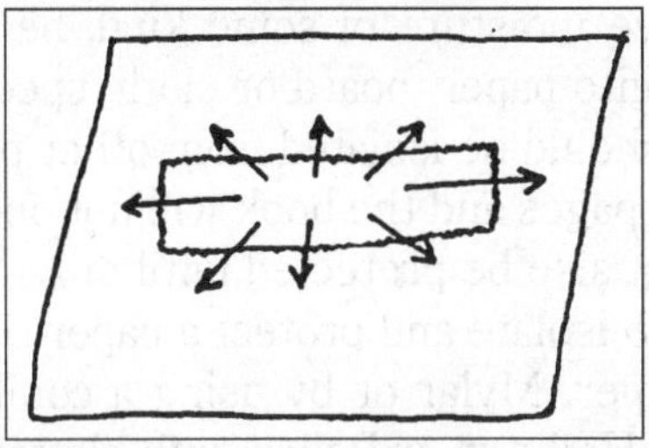

Brushing from the centre out in a starburst pattern protects the edge of the paper or cloth. There might be small tears at the outer edges of a piece of paper or cloth that the brush could catch and tear or the brush might 'grab' the edge of the paper and turn it back on itself, sticking the two surfaces together. In addition to applying adhesive directly to a piece of paper, it can also be applied indirectly.

This method is especially useful when working with very small pieces of paper or cloth. Brush the adhesive onto a piece of glass or plastic then lay the paper or cloth on top of it. The paper or cloth acts as a sponge and absorbs the adhesive from below. Use the bristles of a brush or fingers to work the paste into the Japanese tissue. When Japanese repair tissue is transparent, it has soaked up all the paste it can.

Masking is another technique used to apply adhesive to paper. By using a strip of waste paper to protect most of a sheet of paper, you can apply adhesive to a very specific area in a controlled way. This is especially helpful in operations such as TIPPING-IN A PAGE.

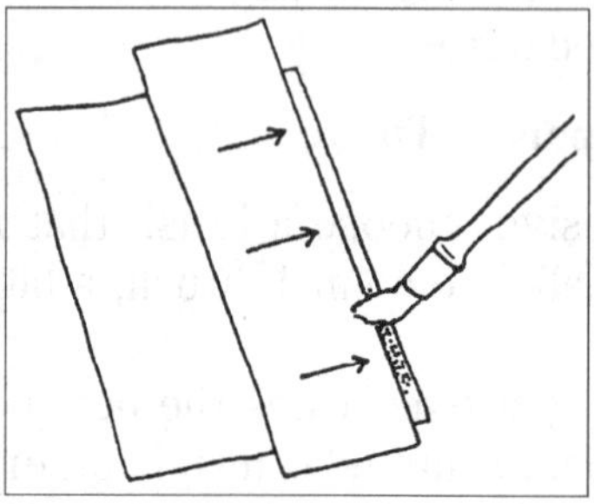

Drying Repairs

Most repairs involve moisture of some kind, be it paste or glue. When moisture is introduced into paper, board or cloth, special precautions need to be taken. A wet repair should be isolated from other pages in a book or it can adhere itself to adjacent pages and the book will not open correctly. Repairs to the cover of a book must also be protected until dry.

The simplest way to isolate and protect a paper repair is with a moisture barrier, such as wax paper, Mylar or by using a combination of a non-stick, porous material such as Hollytex or Pellon with blotter paper. Since moisture cannot pass through a barrier such as wax paper the repair can take longer to dry. Non-stick, porous material, such as Hollytex and Pellon, a woven polyester material can also be used to protect a repair. Both these materials allow moisture to pass through so repairs dry faster, but keep in mind the moisture has to go somewhere.

When using porous materials, be sure to use blotter paper to absorb the moisture so it does not travel to the pages of the book. Blotter paper is a thick unsized paper made from rag or cotton Enters. Because it does not contain size, it can absorb moisture easily.

When blotters are used to absorb moisture in a book repair, they should be replaced with dry blotters periodically so the moisture of the blotter will not remain in the book.

Repairs must always dry on a smooth surface under weight so that they do not buckle and curl. 1/4" glass with ground edges or pieces of plywood covered with Formica can be used to create a smooth surface anywhere.

Glass or plywood can be stacked so that several repairs take up very little space. Paper wrapped bricks, jars filled with coins or buckshot can be used on top of the glass for weight.

Measuring Books

Measuring books accurately can be a challenge since books are not always square or flat. It's standard practice in book repair to take most repair measurements with a piece of scratch paper rather than a ruler.

Measuring the Height of a Book

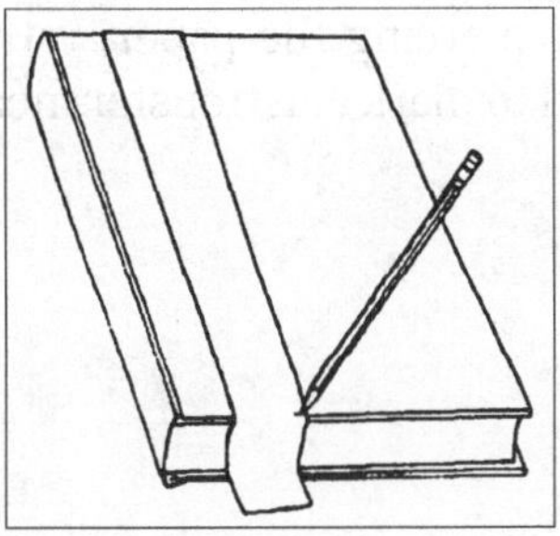

Lay the scratch paper in position and mark one or both ends of the measurement. Add direction arrows to indicate where the measurement starts and stops.

Measuring the Spine Width

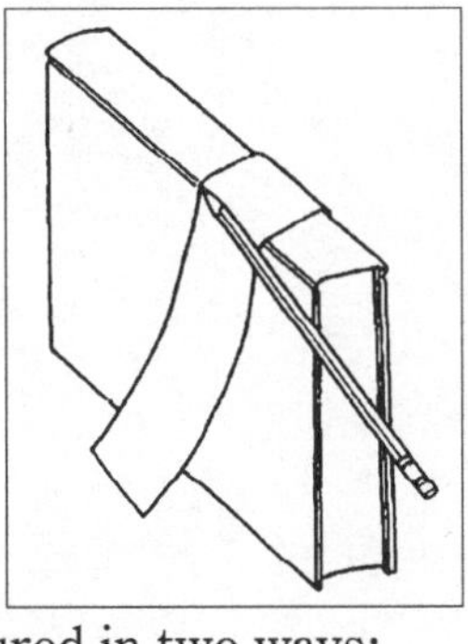

The spine can be measured in two ways:

- Measure actual distance across the spine from shoulder to shoulder;
- Measure the actual thickness of the spine by laying the book flat on the table and measuring vertically across the spine.

Be sure to measure the thickest part of the book. It might be the spine, the fore edge or part way in between.

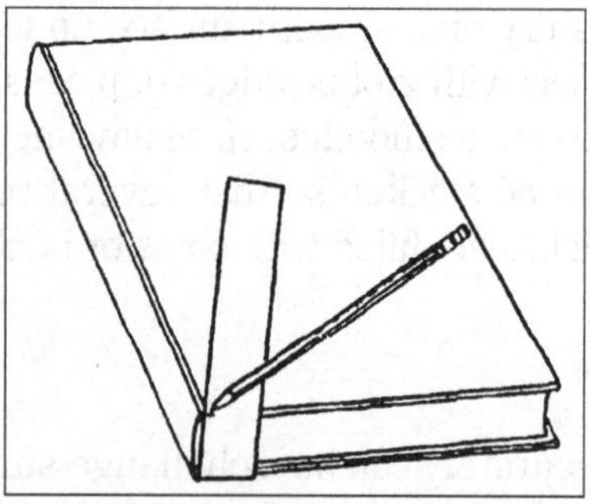

With the measurements on paper, the exact measurement can be transferred to paper or cloth as often as necessary. Label each measurement so as not be confused later. Sometimes it is easier and faster to mark a cutting line with a needle point instead of a pencil. Use the needle-on-a-stick to mark a measurement by slightly piercing the paper, rather than marking it with a pencil. Dividers can be used to mark and transfer measurements from one place to another.

8

Modes of Formation of Subjects Selection in Library

UNIVERSE OF SUBJECTS

Library service is, in essence, the retrieval and dissemination of embodied knowledge to individual members and groups in a community.

Hence, the two essential parameters which affect the value of library services are:

- Universe of Readers; and
- Universe of Subjects.

In order to achieve efficiency of services to readers, it has become imperative to adopt and develop such tools and techniques which would facilitate the classification of subjects embodied in documents and thus help in retrieval and service to the satisfaction of the laws of library science.

But, for this to happen, it is essential that the discipline of library science must keep developing itself to meet changes in the value of each of the parameters. In the succeeding parts, we shall consider the concern of library science with one of the parameters, namely, the Universe of Subjects (UoS).

Laws of Library Science vis-$\bar{\alpha}$-vis Universe of Subjects

The study of the structure and development of the UoS by the information professional can be shown to be a necessary implication of the five laws of library science.

Law 1 and Its Implications

The first law is "Books are for use". Here, the term "book" is a generic term to denote all kinds of documents, including books themselves, periodicals, technical reports, patents, specifications, non-conventional and meta-documents.

The document, in its turn, is a trinity of:

- Soul - embodied knowledge;
- Subtle body - language and expression of the knowledge; and
- Gross body - physical body of the document.

The term "use", on the other hand, implies essentially the use of organised, expressed and embodied knowledge - that is, the subject dealt with in documents - by the readers, although the subtle body is indispensable for the acquisition of knowledge and as a vehicle `for its communication, and the physical body is a convenient means of transport of the embodied knowledge across space and through time. A document retrieval system is, therefore, essentially concerned with the classification, search, retrieval, and service of the "subject".

A subject, in. its turn, is an organised or systematised body of ideas, whose extension and intension are likely to fall coherently within the field of interest and comfortably within the intellectual competence of and the field of inevitable specialisation of a normal person.

Implication

To satisfy law 1, the arrangement of documents and the main entries should primarily be based on the characteristics of the subjects embodied in the documents. The study of these characteristics is, therefore, essential for the efficient classification, search, and retrieval of subjects and service to readers.

Further, the criterion for "use" assumes significance. Therefore, it may be helpful to examine the differences, if any in the respective purposes of the reader. Certain affinities and dissimilarities among the subjects will then be recognised.

Law 2 and Its Implication

The second law "Every reader his book" implies that the classification and arrangement of documents and/or the main entries for them should bring together at every point of approach just those documents relevant to the interest of the reader at the moment, and also arrange them on either side in the decreasing degree of affinity. In other words, an APUPA (Alien, Penumbral, Umbral, Penumbral, Alien) pattern everywhere of documents and/or main entries is desirable.

Law 3 and Its Implication

The third law "Every book its reader" implies that at the time of retrieval no document relevant to the interest of the reader at the moment should be missed, irrespective of his approach. Again, a study of the structure and development of the UoS indicates that no single tool of library science can fully satisfy this law. Several of its tools and methods have to be used concurrently or in succession according to need to meet the interest of the majority as well as the minority.

Law 4 and Its Implication

The fourth law "Save the time of the reader and of the staff" implies that:

- The intellectual and mental potential of the reader should be conserved by pinpointed and expeditious retrieval; and

- The retrieval and service should be done in the most economic manner.

To Satisfy Law 4 One Requires

An analysis of the UoS to recognise each of its constituents and their relevant characteristics; and formulation of a methodology for the design and development of a document retrieval system which can implement, the findings. The work done and to be done in this context pertains to the constituents/ characteristics of the Uos.

Lawn 5 and Its Implication

The fifth law "Library is a growing organism" implies that the UoS is ever growing and, therefore, library science is ever growing. Hence, a historical study of the pattern of development and the structure at different stages of growth will help to recognise the modes of formation of subjects and thereby it would be possible to develop and refine techniques tools for efficient information retrieval and dissemination. From the foregoing account, it becomes clear that the study of the structure and development of the UoS by the librarian is a necessary implication of the five laws of library science.

MODES OF FORMATION OF SUBJECTS

In order to give unique co-extensive representation to each subject in the UoS, the classificationist has to ascertain the various attributes - infinite, turbulently dynamic, continuum, manifold multidimensional quality, different modes of formation of subjects, etc., in the UoS that affect library classification. While many of the attributes are self-explanatory, the attribute "modes of formation of subjects" is complex.

The modes of formation of subjects that have been recognised are.

- Lamination
- Loose Assemblage
- Fission
- Fusion
- Distillation
- Clustering
- Agglomeration.

Lamination

Lamination is construction by an over layering facet, just as one makes a sandwich by layering a vegetable over a layer of bread. According. to Ranganathan "when the basic layer is a basic subject and the other layers are isolate ideas, a compound subject is formed". Lamination is of two types:

Lamination 1

In this mode, one or more isolate facets are laminated over a basic facet. This results in compound subjects.

Example:				
1) Anatomy of the human body				
Basic facet		Medicine		
Isolate facets	=	Human body (P)		Anatomy (MP)
2) Treatment of diseases of plant				
Basic facets	=	Botany		
Isolate facets	=	Plants, *(P)*	Diseases, *(MP)*	Treatment *(E)*

Lamination 2

In this mode two or more sub-facets of a compound facet are laminated over one another. Such subjects were called earlier as non-main basic subjects, the components of which were host main subject. The latter had the canonical/ special/ environment/system component.

For example, the ayurvedic system of medicine is a non-main basic subjects. In this example medicine is the host-main subject and the ayurvedic system is the system component.

The following table gives the revised terminology:

Original Terminology	Revised Terminology
Non-Main Basic Subjects or Basic Subjects (BS)	Non-Primary Basic Subjects (BS)
Canonical BS	Secondary BS
Compound BS	Compound BS

Other Examples:

- Medicine = Host-main subject
- Child = Special component
- Mathematics = Host-main subject
- Geometry = Canonical component

The sequence among the non-main components is System Environment - Special

Loose Assemblage

Loose assemblage is assembling together of two or more of:

- Subjects (basic or compound)
- Isolate ideas (in one and the same facet, or isolate ideas in one and the same array)

Assembling is done to express one or the other of possible relations, between the components of the assembly. The result is a complex subject, or a complex isolate idea, or a complex array isolate idea, as the case may be. Loose assemblage may be of three kinds. They are: Loose Assemblage of Kind-1, Kind-2 and Kind-3.

Loose Assemblage of Kind-1

Two or more subjects - simple or compound - are studied in their mutual relationship. It is called "inter subject phase relation" and can be one of the following five types:

- General;
- Bias;
- Comparison;
- Difference and
- Influencing.

Loose assemblage results in complex subjects.

Here are examples of complex subjects:

- General relation between political science and economics
- Statistics for librarians
- Influence of geography on history

Loose Assemblage of Kind-2

Two or more isolates taken from one and the same schedule are brought into a mutual relationship. This is called an "intro facet phase relation" and results in a complex isolate.

Examples:

- Influence of Buddhism on Christianity
- Difference between Lemuroidea and Anthropoidea

Loose Assemblage of Kind-3

Two or more isolates taken from one and the same array of an order higher than I in one and the same schedule are brought into mutual relation. This is called an "intra array phase relation" and results in a complex array isolate.

Canonical Basic Subject

This denotes a traditional division of a main subject. The traditional division is denoted by the term "canonical constituent".

Examples:

- C3 : Sound
- C4 : Heat
- C5 : Radiation

Special Basic Subject

This denotes a division of a main subject (MS), in which the subject of the study is restricted in some special manner, not amounting to any of the anteriorising common isolates or any other isolate ideas. This special division is denoted by the term "special constituent" of the MS. Generally, the class number for a special BS is got by the enumeration device.

Examples:

- L-9C : Child medicine

- L-917 : Geriatrics
- L-9H : Female medicine

Environmental Basic Subject

This denotes a division of a MS, in which the entity of the study of the MS is within an extra normal environment, such as those enumerated in the schedule of environment divisions.

Examples:

- D-9Uk2 : Desert engineering
- D-9Um7 : Mountain engineering
- D-9V4 : War engineering

System Basic Subject

This denotes a division of a MS or a non-main BS expounded according to a specific system, or School of Thought, other than what is currently popular.

Examples:

- B2-N : Boolean algebra
- L-B : Ayurvedic system of medicine
- S-N : Gestalt psychology

When all non-main constituents occur in a compound basic subject, the sequence among them should be system constituent, environment constituent, special constituent, and canonical constituent.

Example:

- Medicine ayurvedic system—tropical environment —child

Fission

The initial set of primary basic subjects (PBS) included in a scheme for library classification results from a division/fission of the UoS in a manner similar to the division of the UoS by scholars among themselves as convenient fields of specialisation. It may not be possible to discern a specific characteristic used in this initial division.

Fission is the process of division or splitting or breaking up into parts. This process has, until recently, been denoted by the term "dissection". However, dissection usually implies the splitting, breaking up, etc., of an entity into parts by an outside agency. On the other hand, fission is an internal process of division without the involvement of an outside agency.

Example:

In CC, the initial schedule of traditional Primary Basic Subject (PBS) was derived by a direct' fission of the UoS and the following broad groups may be noted:

- Primary BS covering natural sciences
- Primary BS covering useful arts
- Primary BS covering humanities
- Primary BS covering social sciences

The term "dissection" is used to denote fission when we consider an array of divisions of an isolate or of a basic subject, resulting from fission.

On the other hand, the term 'denudation' is used to denote fission when we consider one and only one of the subdivisions of an isolate or of a BS, resulting from fission. Prolegomena defines as "Denudation is the progressive decrease of the extension and the increase of the intension (or the depth) of a BS or an isolate idea, even as we scoop out the flesh of a soft-fruit from deeper and deeper layers or as we excavate the well". In the words of J.H. Shera, denudation is "the exposure of a new area of knowledge by erosion or divestment through research or enquiry"..

Example:
Philosophy
Logic
Deductive Logic

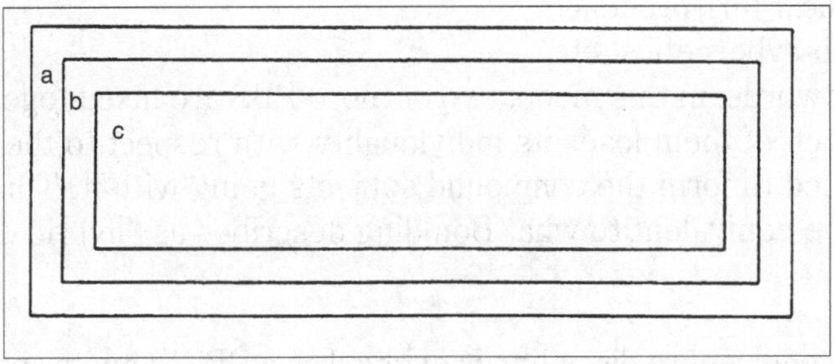

Fusion

One result of interdisciplinary research, which is characteristic of present day organisation and conduct of research programmes, is the emergence of new ideas and new subjects of an interdisciplinary character. Often, an interdisciplinary subject may be deemed to go with more than one of the existing primary basic subjects (PBS).

The subjects going with this PBS will usually contain the core entity whose attributes are examined by the research team. Let us call.this host PBS 1. The subjects going with another PBS - that is, host PBS 2 may be related to the subjects going with the host PBS1 in a variety of ways, *e.g.*, phase relation (*i.e.*, application of statistics to biology).

In due course, as the field develops, there may be a number of new ideas arising out of the interdisciplinary research, such that:

- The classificationist may find that they cannot be conveniently and helpfully deemed to go with the host PBSI selected earlier;
- These new ideas attract for themselves a group of specialists; and
- A new field of specialisation concretises with normative principles/ theory of its own, in addition to using the normative principles/ theory of the subjects going with the host PBS 1 and 2.

At this stage, the classificationist may find it helpful to deem the new field of specialisation to go' with a new PBS - which is not already enumerated in the schedule of PBS in the scheme of classification concerned. Subjects going with this new PBS may contain isolate ideas drawn from the schedules of the host PBS 1 and 2 as well as ideas special to the new discipline. The new PBS may be considered, for convenience, as a combination of the host PB S 1 and 2.

This mode of formation is called fusion.

Examples of fused PBS included in CC edition are given below:

- Astrophysics
- Biolinguists
- Astrochemistry
- Sociolinguists
- Bio-physics
- Educametry
- Medical Jurisprudence
- Socio-cybernetics, etc.

In other words, in this mode, two or more PBS are fused together in such a way that each of them loses its individuality with respect to the schedule of isolates needed to form the compound subjects going with it. This mode may be taken to be equivalent to what Boulding describes as "hybrid discipline".

Distillation

In this mode, a pure discipline is evolved as a PBS from its appearance-in-action in diverse compound subjects going with either different BS or one and the same BS. It gives rise to PBS by distillation. This mode may be taken to be equivalent to what Boulding describes as "Multi-hybrid with common methodology". Thus, distillation may be of 2 kinds (Kind 1 and Kind 2. In Kind 1, the new PBS essentially accommodates the theory of discipline emerging 'or distilled out of an idea(s) occurring as a practice - in-action in subjects going with diverse BS. However, it should be remembered that, even after the formulation of a new pure discipline, the appearance of the idea as a practice-in-action will continue and should be treated as such - that is, it should be placed as an isolate idea in the subject concerned.

On the other hand, in distillation of Kind-2, the idea occurs in subjects going with a particular BS only and there may be a trend towards the formulation of a new discipline with recognisable literary warrant, and, perhaps, some principles and postulates for guiding its development.

Examples: Statistical calculus, Microbiology, Anesthesio-logy, International relations, Ergonomics, Forestry.

Clustering

In the past, in the Universe of Documents, the general trend has been to narrow the extension of a subject embodied in a document taken as a whole. Therefore, there has been a general tendency not to bring into one and the same document, compound subjects going with the different basic subjects, except in the case of complex subjects involving phase relation and the subjects involving the use of subject device in forming or sharpening isolate facets. In recent years, however, interdisciplinary team research has often, for practical convenience, necessitated bringing together in one and the same document two or more compound subjects going with different BS.

For example, for the convenience of organising research, the preliminary results and data obtained in work falling in different subject fields involved in the study of one phenomenon or entity may be brought together in one and the same document and treated disjunctively that is, without any substantial integral treatment. Subsequent elaboration of the work falling in different subject fields may be by specialists in the respective subjects and the results may be published separately. The document in which the preliminary results are brought together just as in a collection, taken as a whole, presents a subject field in which there is a core entity of study with inputs or viewpoints or work on it coming from specialists in subjects going with diverse BS. This feature is something like clustering around a nodal idea - that is, forming a group of similar entities, because of their relationship with each other, or their simultaneity of occurrence or for convenience in treatment or discussion.

Examples:

- Area study, in which geographical area forms the focus of the cluster, like Sinology (Chinese studies), Nippinology (Japanese studies).
- Generalia person study, in which a multi-faceted personality forms the focus of a cluster Gandhiana.
- Study of entity or phenomena forming the focus of a cluster Soil science, Surface science.

Agglomeration

Agglomeration (earlier called partial comprehension) is the process of collecting together of entities into larger masses without cohesion among the components. An agglomerate can be a BS, or it can also be an isolate idea. Agglomeration may be made up of consecutive constituents or even non-consecutive constituents with respect to a classification scheme.

Examples in CC:

- Natural sciences,
- Humanities,
- Social sciences

METHODOLOGY FOR THE STUDY OF SUBJECTS

Until recently, information consolidation products (ICP) were prepared by subject specialists themselves on the basis of the documents furnished by libraries and information centers. But with advances made in the held of library and information science, especially in the techniques of organising and displaying information, the library and information science (LIS) personnel have started playing a dominant role in the preparation of ICPs.

But, for them to play an useful role, the following prerequisites become necessary:

- Familiarity with the different aspects of the subject;
- Familiarity with reader's requirements on the subject of his pursuit; and
- Knowledge of the helpful methods of presentation of ideas in an ICP.

UNDERSTANDING THE HIGHWAYS AND BYWAYS OF SUBJECTS

The majority of the queries/questions that LIS personnel will have to deal with are about subjects. An answer to such a query, in whatever form it may finally be presented to suit the requirements of the reader, will be derived from the subjects embodied in documents. Therefore, the LIS personnel should become familiar with the subjects they have to deal with predominantly. The more intensive the knowledge they have of the subjects, the more helpful it will be in making the information services productive.

Obviously, such a knowledge of all the subjects cannot be acquired by one person. A person with a basic background in a subject - say, at the graduate or post-graduate level - can build upon it through experience, - such as doing research and/or teaching the subject, But the LIS personnel's work does not admit of doing research simultaneously (other than in library and information science).

Further, it is not the intensive specialisation in a narrow region of a subject that will be useful in the work of the LIS personnel. What they require is a broad perspective that is, the highways and byways of the different subjects with which their clientele are concerned.

Specific Implication

In general, the kind of knowledge that the LIS personnel should gain about the subjects may be specified as follows:

- Scope of the subject as a whole;
- Its main branches and subdivisions within each branch and the scope of each of them;
- The ideas generally falling in relation to the subject and their grouping in relation to the branches and subdivisions within each branch of the subject;
- The interrelation between the component ideas and the relevant characteristics on the basis of which they can be grouped;

- The landmarks in the evolution of the subject: the important contributors and their respective contributions;
- The state-of-the art and trend in each of the different branches of the subject;
- The interrelation of a subject with other subjects; and
- The technical terminology of each of the different subjects.

SYSTEMATIC STUDY OF SUBJECTS THROUGH DOCUMENTS

READING ABOUT MAJOR SUBJECT FIELDS

LIS personnel should recognize the major subject fields related to the work of the institution concerned. Further, it would be helpful to group the subjects as of umbral and penumbral interest. This implies that the person should develop the ability to read through the documents in such a way that the ideas relevant to his purpose are picked up without his plodding through each and every sentence in the document.

Kinds of Documents for Study

The following varieties of documents may be helpful in the systematic study of a subject to acquire the kind of knowledge mentioned under the heading Specific Implication.

- Standard general dictionaries and technical glossaries for definitions and synonyms of terms,
- Articles in general encyclopaedia for getting an overview of the scope and major divisions of the subject.
- Specialised encyclopaedias, if any, mainly" devoted to the subject for getting a deeper knowledge of the subject than that from the general encyclopaedias.
- An orientation book, specially written with a flair and/or with a bias to the requirements of the LIS personnel.
- Books on the history of the subjects for sensing the landmarks in the evolution of the subject.
- Treatises for getting ‘a deeper knowledge of the ideas falling in the different divisions ‘of the subject, their interrelations, and also to get a proper perspective of the subject as a whole.
- Good review articles and trend reports for sensing the current developments and trends in the subject.

Proforma for Collection and Organisation of Information

In the course of reading about a subject, it is helpful to make a record of the information selected in a systematic way.

A systematic proforma may be used for this purpose.

- *Introduction*: Statement of the purpose and the plan of the project on

"Study of Subjects", indicating also the need and method of keeping the results of study up-to-date.

- *Definition*: The definition of a term denotes the subject concerned given in different authoritative sources. A comparative study of the collected definitions showing their similarity and differences is called for.
- *Terminological Development*: Terminological development of the term used to denote the subject, if any; the current synonyms, and different views on them. This generally applies to a subject which has been denoted by different terms at different points of time. For example, this applies to the term "library science". It started as "library economy"; passed through' librarianship' and, now it is denoted by the term' library science'.
- *Scope*: General scope of the subject as a whole. The general scope of the subject is to be taken note of under the following subheadings:
- *Divisions and Subdivisions*: This includes all topics studied under the subject concerned - that is, primarily its divisions and subdivisions. For the purpose of this part, the terms (including synonyms) denoting the different broad divisions and their respective immediate subdivisions along with the definition and scope of each are to be given. It would be convenient to take note of the divisions and subdivisions from a selection of representative textbooks and advanced treatises on the subject concerned by analysing their contents. This would amount to taking note of the classificatory treatment of the subject concerned by specialists for the purpose of study, teaching, learning, etc. Definitions are to be collected from different authoritative sources.
- *Application*: Topics to which the subject concerned may be applied for their development. For example, when physics is the subject of study, engineering sciences, chemical sciences and biological sciences are the areas of its application.
- *Tool-Subjects*: These are subjects applicable to the subject concerned for its development. For example, when chemistry is the subject of study,mathematics, statistics, physics, etc., are applicable to it as tool-subjects, for its development.,
- *Classification*: This part, is intended to take note of how the subject concerned, and its divisions and subdivisions, are treated by the different schemes for classification - general and special. The first point of interest would be to find out the rank of the subject concerned in the whole Universe of Subjects, as recognized by different classificationists. *For example, the rank of the subject "chemistry" in the Universe of Subjects is commonly recognized as follows*:

- Universe of Subjects
  - Sciences
    - Natural Sciences
      - Physical Sciences
        - Chemistry

The use of the indention in the example is to show the superordinate-subordinate relationships.

Treatment of the subject concerned in different schemes for classification is to be noted under the following subheadings:

- *Special Classification*: This subsection is intended to take note if there is any special subject classification designed by specialists for the purpose of a deeper understanding of the entities falling within the purview of the subject as a whole, or of any division or subdivision of it; for example, the taxonomical classification in geology, botany, and zoology, and the periodic table in chemistry. For the purpose of this subsection, generally a summary table of comparatively broader classes, with introductory remarks and a short description of the scheme, is to be given.
- *Document Classification*: This subsection is to take note of the treatment of the subject in classification systems, including thesauri and lists of subject headings. Such a scheme may be general in scope; for example, the Dewey Decimal Classification, Colon Classification, Thesaurus of Engineering and Scientific Terms, Thesaurofacet, etc. Such a scheme may be special in scope; for example, the Classification Schedule and Alphabetical Index for Packaging Documentation, the London Education Classification, the INIS: Thesaurus, the Thesaurus of Federal Aviation Agency Descriptors (USA), the Medical Subject Headings (MeSH), Subject Headings for Engineering (SHE), etc. Besides, if there is an indexing or abstracting periodical on the subject concerned, it would normally be expected to follow a special document classification scheme. Taking note of the treatment would consist of extracting a summary table from each of such schemes. When the scheme consists of a systematic part and an alphabetical part,it would be necessary to look for the subject concerned in both the parts to extract relevant portions from them.
- *Development of the Subject*: The development of the subject concerned is to be noted down under the following subheadings:
- *Landmarks*: The landmarks in the development of the subject - that is, the contributions - are to be noted down, as far as applicable, under its broad divisions and subdivisions. Under each divisions or subdivisions as the case may be, the part will consist of entries

arranged chronologically. *Each entry, as far as ascertainable, will consist of the following items of information*:

- The year or period of contribution as far as determinable;
- The name of the contributor;
- A short biographical note of the contributor;
- Each of his significant contributions;
- The title and the year of publication of the original document, giving wherever applicable, its host and locus

- *Trend of Research*: The trend of research in the subject concerned., This can be collected from review documents, indexing and abstracting periodicals, etc. The idea is to mark out the broad areas in the subject concerned in which research is in progress. Additionally, attempts are to be made to ascertain in general the growth of literature (documents) on the subject concerned; and the degree of documentary seepage, and the scatter of information on research results in the subject concerned.
- *Trend of Education*: The trend of education in the subject concerned. This part is intended to take note of the development of education in the subject concerned and of its different levels - such as, undergraduate, graduate, postgraduate, research, etc.
- *Sources of Information*: This includes the information on the subject concerned. Three varieties of sources of information are readily recognisable. They are:
  - Documentary sources;
  - Institutional sources; and
  - Human sources.

  This part is intended to take note of the various sources of information on the subject concerned. As such, information about the various sources is to be collected under the subheadings. For this purpose, different standard proforma are to be used. The specification of these proforma will be provided separately. Each entry pertaining to the sources of information is to be classified according to a standard scheme for classification. The entries under each subsection are to be arranged systematically according to the scheme used. The sources may not always be directly turned on the specific subject concerned. For the purpose of the subsections of this part, it would be required to take note of the sources on the:
  - Specific subject;
  - The subjects of extension greater than that of the specific subject; and
  - The subjects of extension smaller than that of the specific subject.

  For example, when the specific subject of study is "chemistry", the subjects "science", "physical sciences", "chemical sciences", etc., are subjects of greater extension; while the subjects "inorganic chemistry", organic chemistry", "physical chemistry", etc., are subjects of smaller extension.

- *Documentary Sources*: This subsection is intended to take note of the various documentary sources of information on the subject concerned. *Such sources fall in two distinct categories*:
  - Primary, and
  - Secondary.

  The sources in each of these two categories are many. To start with, it would be necessary to take note of a selection of the outstanding documentary sources - both primary and secondary. In the primary category will fall:
  - Outstanding textbooks;
  - Advanced treatises; and
  - Primary periodical 'publications.

  In' the secondary category will fall:
  - Conventional refe-rence books - that is, encyclopaedias, handbooks, directories, dictionaries, glossaries, etc.;
  - Adhoc bibliographies;'
  - Indexing and abstracting periodi-cals; and
  - Review documents (annual reviews, advances in, year's work, etc).

  As a part of this subsection, it would be helpful to add a list, of the organisations (with addresses) specialising in' the publication of documents in the subject concerned.
- *Institutional Sources*: This subsection is intended to take note of the various institutional sources of information on the subject concerned. For the purpose of 'this part, the conferences and projects turned on the subject concerned are to be taken note of. The idea is to identify the institutions, including conferences and projects, specialising in the subject by way of research, education, or organisation. As such, they are in a position to provide information on many aspects of the subject which is not readily available from other sources. Selection should include, as far as practicable, the institutions in the following three categories:
  - International;
  - National; and
  - local.
- *Human Resources*: This subsection is intended to take note of the human sources of information on the subject concerned. The idea is to identify the living persons recognized as specialists in the subject concerned because of their educational achievements and experience. Such a specialist, when consulted, may be in a position to provide

specific information on the subject concerned which is not readily available from any other source. The selection should include, as far as practicable, living persons of repute at the international, national and local levels.

- *Information Transfer Processes*: This part is intended to take note of:
  - The information transfer process among the users of information on the subject;
  - The information seeking Behaviour of persons specialising in the subject; and
  - Typical informa-tion queries on the subject. Information about these aspects of the subject is to be collected primarily from documents dealing with these aspects as a whole, or some portion of it, or some broader subject comprehending-the subject concerned.

When no such specific treatment is available, general information on information transfer processes and information seeking behaviours is to be taken note of. Typical information queries on the subject may have to be formulated on the analogy of such queries in other subjects; for, in the majority of cases, they may not be readily available.

- *Conclusion*: The conclusion may focus attention on any one of the following aspects relating to the subjects concerned;
  - The impact of research on the growth of the primary documents;
  - Adequacy or otherwise of the secondary documentary sources of information;
  - Problems of physical access to the sources of information;
  - Problems of organising information; and
  - Remarks and suggestions relating to any aspect of the subject falling within the purview of the study.
- *References*: This part is intended to list the documents actually used to compile the handbook. For the purpose of this part, a short entry is to be prepared for each document. The entry is to be prepared according to the prescription of a standard code for cataloguing practice. In the majority of cases, an entry for a macro document is to be prepared in the following style:
- ATKINS (Kenneth R). Physics – once over – lightly 1972. If a particular portion of a macrodocument is referred to, its exact location is to be incorporated as the last item in the following style; Part 2; or Chap 3; or Sec. 52; or Page 20-28; etc., depending upon what the document admits as appropriate. Normally an entry for a microdocument is to be prepared in the following style:
- ROBERTSON (Andrew). Behaviour pattern of scientists and engineers in information seeking for problem-solving.

- *Entries prepared in the styles are to be arranged alphabetically and serially numbered*: The serial number of the document is to be used in the appropriate part of the text to indicate the sources from which the information has been collected. On the other side, the part number is to be used as a part of the appropriate entry. As a result, an entry in the Reference Part will appear in the style analogous to the following.

SUBJECT ANALYSIS

This review updates the 1986 *ARIST* chapter on subject analysis by SCHWARTZ and EISENMANN. The aim is a global approach. Thus, efforts were made to locate and include studies beyond those performed or published in the United States. Although the items reviewed come mainly from the period 1986-1988, earlier works not covered by the previous *ARIST* chapter have occasionally been included. Some much earlier items are referred to when necessary for purposes of comparison or context.

Subject analysis here means the presence, identification, and expression of subject matter in document texts, databases, controlled and natural languages, information requests, and search strategies. From the user's viewpoint, subject analysis is tightly bound to subject access. Therefore, the means by which information on a subject can be retrieved from various sources is also pertinent.

The literature reviewed is grouped into six broad categories:

- Indexing theory and practice;
- Controlled vocabularies;
- Search strategies and searching methods;
- Natural-language searching;
- Automatic indexing and related procedures; and
- The use of citation relationships in information retrieval.

Clearly these categories are not mutually exclusive, and some of the items reviewed could legitimately belong to more than one category.

INDEXING THEORY AND PRACTICE

General Discussions

Much has been written on various aspects of indexing over the years, but no really comprehensive book on the subject seems to have been produced, and those texts that do exist are now somewhat out of date. WEINBERG has compiled a volume of papers that, she claims, covers the 'state of our knowledge and the state of our ignorance' on the subject of indexing. Because her book is based solely on papers presented at a 1988 conference of the American Society of Indexers, the individual chapters vary in quality.

Topics covered include book indexing, automatic indexing, indexing software, database design, and the literature of indexing. Ironically, the outstanding chapter is about searching rather than indexing and is authored by SARACEVIC, who summarises the results of the comprehensive study described elsewhere in this review. He correctly points out that 'people who do research on searching rarely, if ever, cite literature on indexing research and *vice versa*. Yet there is an obvious connection, and perhaps more bridges need to be built between the research and practice of indexing and that of searching."

This observation coincides closely with one of the conclusions made by LANCASTER 20 years ago as a result of the evaluation of MEDLARS—namely, it is highly desirable that the indexers also be the searchers. Elsewhere, WEINBERG hypothesises that indexing fails the researcher because it deals only in a general way with what a document is 'about' and does not focus on what the document offers that is 'new' concerning a topic. She suggests that this distinction is reflected in the difference between 'aboutness' and 'aspect,' between 'topic' and 'comment,' or between 'theme' and 'rheme' but she fails to convince that these distinctions are really useful in the context of indexing or that it might be possible for indexers to maintain them.

A related study is the doctoral dissertation by CROWE, who discusses the feasibility of indexing the 'subjective viewpoint' of an author. She suggests that the indexer focus on the "problem situation' addressed by the author, including the questions addressed in the author's work. Aboutness is a slippery concept. The subject content of a document is sometimes referred to as intrinsic aboutness. What the document may be used for, why it was acquired, and other variable external' considerations are referred' to as extrinsic aboutness.

GORDON looks at indexing not in the context of aboutness as used by BEGHTOL and KHANZHIN but in relation to the interdependencies of the document descriptions, queries, and matching algorithms of the information retrieval system in use. He argues that a change in any of the three parts of the system mandates alterations in the other two if the system is to operate effectively. COCHRANE also reflects this holistic point of view. GRUNBERGER tested the assumptions that the frequency of a term on a page and the location of that term within a paragraph are good indicators that such a term would be selected in indexing. Neither of the hypotheses was supported.

AZUBUIKE and UMOH advocate maximum indexing, a concept that calls for exhaustively indexing a document using a variety of indexing strategies. While some would maintain that exhaustively indexing a document from both general and specific aspects leads to low precision in retrieval, the authors argue against this view. CHANG refers to the limitations associated with permuted title indexing and citation indexing and concludes that intellectual effort in indexing is still necessary. Based on the idea that knowledge is symbolic, VICKERY provides a review of methods whereby knowledge can be represented.

The review includes discussion of the use of symbols and symbol structures, semantics, and roles, categories, and relations present in subject statements. The arrangement and representation of knowledge as reflected in classification schemes and thesauri are also touched on. In addition, work in the area of 'semantic primitives' or 'semantic factoring' is reviewed and leads to a brief discussion of several means of representing knowledge for reasoning, including symbolic equations, frames, and semantic nets.

The review closes with a short description of a prototype reference and referral expert system developed by the author and his colleagues that uses many of the knowledge representation techniques reviewed. The continual problem of the interaction of the subjective and objective in the organisation and retrieval of information is addressed by NEILL through a review of the works of Brenda Dervin and Karl Popper as well as other writers whose works were influenced by or amplify Dervin and/or Popper.

The effect of the subjective in classificati6h and in indexing is discussed along with its impact on information retrieval, leading to a description of an information system called Projekt INSTRAT, which utilises some of Popper's concepts. The review concludes that although subjective and objective viewpoints follow different paths, their final solutions are similar. BLAIR looks at indeterminacy in indexing — *i.e.,* the probability that a term the user chooses will be in the set of potential terms available to the indexer *and* in the set of terms used by the indexer.

Increasing the number of terms assigned to a document increases the chances of a hit, but success is not guaranteed. Blair suggests that the user should always identify a highly relevant document as a model for further searching. CROFT outlines some areas of research in artificial intelligence, such as the development of expert systems, that should be fruitful in solving the problems of indeterminacy in both indexing and term selection for retrieval. Expert systems are designed to assist the user in query formulation and selection of relevant documents.

Predominantly non-verbal fields of knowledge present special difficulties in indexing. Geographical and geological mapping are two primarily visual fields that are not served well by verbal systems. GRANDE explores the ideograph as a model for database design, indexing, and retrieval of geological information, while MARKEY discusses consistency aspects in the indexing of visual materials.

The requirements for indexing in videotex and related systems are addressed by YEATES, with special reference to the British Prestel system. Prestel's indexing approaches include: menu-controlled reference frames, alphabetical name and subject indexes, keyword indexes, gateway indexing to other systems, online and print indexes, user-controlled indexes, mnemonic page numbers, and Pagemarker—a 'bookmark' feature that allows users to tag specific pages for later rapid recall. ASRIBEKOV deals with the broad subject of textual compression in information systems. Conversion of primary text to alternative forms and to secondary represen-tations are both covered.

Precoordinate Indexes

It is a curious anomaly that in an age in which the online searching of databases is commonplace, greater interest exists than ever before in the characteristics of precoordinate indexes in printed form. Moreover, literature on this subject continues to pour out. The reason, of course, is that computer processing provides an efficient means for generating multiple entries systematically from a single input supplied by an indexer. A book by CRAVEN gives a useful overview of the subject, although its value is reduced by the fact that some of the approaches included are not described clearly or illustrated with sufficient examples.

Elsewhere CRAVEN describes a coding scheme for expressing relationships among terms within a string used as input to index-generation programmes. He also examines the possibility of extending the concept of string indexing from index display to the provision of descriptor phrases for proximity searching. One of the most sophisticated approaches to precoordinate indexing was developed by Jason Farradane more than 30 years ago. Termed 'relational indexing,' the method involves the use of role indicators to express precise relationships among terms.

Farradane's work is described by BROOKES. SCHNELLING points out the limitations of alphabetical subject catalogues based on a controlled vocabulary of subject headings. He proposes a method combining standardised and free terms. For each broad area covered by a catalogue it is necessary to derive a 'pattern'—a set of categories into which the literature seems to fall naturally. These categories can then be adapted as standardised subject headings or subheadings.

However, within the general framework provided by this pattern, it will be necessary to index in more detail by the use of free terms. He illustrates the approach advocated by a discussion of indexing requirements in the field of literary scholarship in general and Shakespeare in particular. The somewhat grandiose title applied to this approach—'pattern indexing'—suggests something quite new.

In fact, the only thing claimed is that while a broad terminological structure can be pre-established for any field, the fine details of indexing will always require the use of free terms. While this is eminently sensible, it is hardly original. This fact is recognised by HARRIS, who refers to the process of indexing with a combination of controlled and uncontrolled terms as use of a 'part-controlled vocabulary.' He suggests that this technique is "probably widely used in various kinds of information service, but has not been formally recognised as a design option for librarians". The string indexing system that has generated the most literature, of course, is PRECIS and it continues to do so. DYKSTRA contributes a primer on the subject.

MAHAPATRA and BISWAS study the interrelationships of the role operators used in PRECIS indexing, and DYKSTRA suggests that PRECIS'S clear rules lend themselves to use in automatic indexing. Somewhat related to PRECIS is POPSI. BISWAS and SMITH describe a variation of POPSI that they refer to as a computerised deep structure indexing system. One of the oldest and most respected of the printed indexes is that produced by Chemical Abstracts Service (CAS). The indexing policies of CAS are discussed by ROWLETT, and the history of subject indexing at CAS is covered by ZAYE *ET AL.* On the international front, BIELICKA and SCIBOR review indexing trends in Poland and compare them with international trends. GHANI explores the potentialities and problems of using uniterm indexing in the Arabic language. Many of the problems outlined center around problems of standardisation in the language itself.

Quality of Indexing

It is difficult to look at the quality of indexing in isolation—*i.e.,* without evaluating some information retrieval 'system' in which the indexing is only one of several factors affecting overall performance. Indeed, more work may have been done on consistency of indexing than on quality. Recently, however, some interesting approaches to the evaluation of indexing have been introduced. WHITE and GRIFFITH use methods external to the indexing system being studied to establish a set of documents judged to be 'similar in content.'

Using sets of this kind as the basis for evaluation, they look at three characteristics of the index terms assigned to items in the set within a particular database:

- The extent to which terms link related items. The obvious measure of this is the number of terms that have been applied to all or most items in the set. The items can be considered closely linked if several subject terms apply to all of them.
- The extent to which terms discriminate among these sets within the database. The most obvious measure of this is the frequency with which terms that apply to most documents in the set occur in the database as a whole. Very common terms are not good discriminators. For example, in MEDLINE the term 'human' may apply to every item in a set but is of little value in separating this set from others since, it applies to so many items in the database. On the other hand, terms that occur rarely in the database will be useful in highly specific searches but of little use in identifying somewhat larger sets.
- The extent to which terms discriminate finely among individual documents. Rarity is an applicable measure here also. So is the

exhaustivity of the indexing: a term may apply to all items in a set, but cannot discriminate among its members; the more additional terms that are assigned to each member, the more individual differences can be identified.

To look at quality in this way, one must first establish the test sets, retrieve records from a database for the members of each set, and study the characteristics of the terms assigned. White and Griffith used the technique to compare the indexing of their test sets in different databases: MEDLINE was compared with PsycINFO, BIOSIS Previews, and Excerpta Medica. A comparison of databases in this way is a check on the assumption that test-set items are in fact similar in content. White and Griffith used co-citation as the basis for establishing their test sets, although other methods, including bibliographic coupling, could be used.

The value of this work is limited by the fact that only very small clusters were used. Moreover, the validity of the method as a test of human indexing depends entirely on one's willingness to accept a co-citation cluster as being a legitimate standard. One could make a persuasive argument that it makes more sense to use expert indexers as a standard for judging the legitimacy of the co-citation cluster. WHITE and GRIFFITH claim that the method is useful to a database producer as a check on the quality of indexing, and they present examples of terms that should perhaps have been used by MEDLINE indexers or added to the controlled vocabulary. However, such 'quality' checks can be done more simply. Sets of items defined by a particular term or terms can be retrieved from several databases and their indexing compared without the use of co-citation as a standard. In fact, this type of study has also been done by the same group of investigators. For 11 requests posed by specialists in the medical behavioural sciences, comparative searches were performed in MEDLINE, Excerpta Medica, PsycINFO, SciSearch, and Social SciSearch.

In the first three databases the searches were performed on:

- Controlled terms; and
- Natural language.

In the citation databases, searches were performed:

- Using the natural language of titles; and
- Using citations to known relevant items as entry points.

While the purpose of the investigation was to study the quality of MEDLINE indexing, little was discovered that could be posed as recommendations to the National Library of Medicine (NLM) on indexing practice, although some recommendations on indexing coverage could be made.

The most important findings of the study were that:

- The incorporation of natural-language approaches into search strategies resulted in significant improvements in recall compared with the use of controlled terms only;

- Citation retrieval should be considered an important adjunct to term-based retrieval because additional relevant items can be found using the citation approach; and
- No single database is likely to provide complete coverage of a complex multidisciplinary literature.

The work reported by White and Griffith and by McCain *et al.* forms part of a series of investigations done at the College of Information Studies, Drexel University, to evaluate various aspects of NLM's coverage and handling of the literature of the medical behavioural sciences. GRIFFITH *ET AL.* present an overview of all the studies, including the coverage of the databases, the quality of the indexing, and the results of searches in the medical behavioural sciences.

AJIFERUKE and CHU are critical of the 'discriminating index' for terms used by White and Griffith, which takes into account how many times a term is used within a database but not the size of the database. They propose a new measure that does. HRAŠOVA and JANÁKOVÁ conclude that consistency in keyword indexing is greatest when very few or very many keywords are chosen. This makes sense. It is relatively easy to agree on the two or three most important terms. Consistency will begin to decline after this but is likely to increase again when virtually all terms that could possibly be assigned to a document have been assigned.

One factor that might have some influence on the quality of indexing is the availability to the indexer of appropriate reference tools. BAKEWELL gives details on almost 200 books of possible value to indexers. To improve indexing and classification procedures, to make them more responsive to user needs, it is necessary to understand the bases on which people categorise or group documents in everyday life. KWASNIK, for example, is looking at the categories into which people sort their mail. She presents some preliminary results based on her observations of eight members of a university faculty.

The average number of terms assigned to a document in indexing tends to have a significant effect on the performance of a retrieval system. CLEVELAND and CLEVELAND studied the effect of indexing depth on retrieval performance for conventional Boolean searching methods and for the 'indirect method' of retrieval devised by GOFFMAN. They concluded that the latter, unlike the former, is relatively insensitive to indexing depth.

The indirect method involves the matching of a query against document clusters, which are established on the basis of term co-occurrence, the identification of the cluster that best matches the query, and the identification of the cluster member closest to the query. This document can then be used to locate other related items. CLEVELAND *ET AL.* also tested the hypothesis that when the indirect method is used for searching, indexing from full text is not essential to optimum retrieval. They conclude that optimum retrieval results can be achieved with less than full text when the indirect method is used.

CONTROLLED VOCABULARIES

General Discussions

The term 'index language devices,' which can be traced back more than 20 years, is somewhat misleading in that some of the 'devices' referred to are legitimate components of index languages while others, such as term weighting, are outside the index language *per se* and are more correctly referred to as 'indexing devices.' A detailed analysis of two important devices—weighting and relational indicators—is provided by KÖRNER. Role and relational indicators, various approaches to the linking of terms, facets, human and automatic weighting are all included in his review. KRISTALÑYI *et al.* suggest the use of the universal facets of time and space as a way to increase compatibility in various automated systems in the Soviet Union.

CHANDRASEKHARAN *et al.* apply graph-theoretic techniques to solve the 'minimum vocabulary problem' for a dictionary—*i.e.,* to identify the smallest set of words needed to define all the words in the dictionary. They claim that the minimum vocabulary principle can be applied to reduce the size of a controlled index language but fail to elaborate on this application. EASTMAN reports on a preliminary study of the extent to which overlap in postings occurs among hierarchically related terms in a controlled vocabulary, using data from MEDLINE and Medical Subject Headings, and she considers the implications of the overlap phenomenon for searches involving negations.

NELSON and TAGUE discuss the distribution of index terms over a collection of documents. They point out that a rank-frequency distribution well describes the distribution of terms of high frequency, while a frequency-size distribution provides a better picture of the distribution pattern for low frequency terms. They describe a 'split model,' using a rank function for the high frequency terms and a size function for the low frequency terms, the point of transition between the two being determined empirically or by rule.

On a more practical level, NELSON found that users of an online public access catalogue (OPAC) at the University of Western Ontario tend to employ terms that occur very frequently in the catalogue. The construction of controlled vocabularies involves the establishment of relationships among 'subjects.' JOHANSEN makes a distinction between relationships established on 'linguistic' and 'non-linguistic' levels and attempts to present a 'method of disclosing the structure of a subject by examining its constituent elements and their mutual relationships.'

SUOMINEN deals with the subject of syntactic relations in index languages. STIEG and ATKINSON compare indexing and indexing languages in the ERIC, LISA, and Library Literature databases as one aspect of a broader comparison of these three sources. Bibliographic classification schemes, lists of subject headings, and thesauri are all examples of index languages—*i.e.,* vocabularies that can be used to represent the subject matter of documents and of information needs. BIELICKA *et al.* and JABRZEMSKA and SCIBOR review the types of index languages in use in Poland, and STANCIKOVA presents a similar review for Czechoslovakia.

Information retrieval in the humanities is generally considered to be more difficult than it is in the sciences because the terminology used by humanists is less precise. WIBERLEY explores this situation by studying the entry terms used in leading encyclopaedias and dictionaries in the humanities. He concludes that although some of the terms are imprecise, most of them are quite precise and consist of names of individuals or of creative works; this finding suggests that subject access in the humanities may be less of a problem than previously supposed.

SANTAVICCA points out the crucial role that a knowledge of languages plays in the selection of terms for indexing, thesaurus control, cross-references, and access points. He suggests that the manipulation of text in international databases requires a kind of trilingualism: a knowledge of the user's native language, a knowledge of the foreign language in question, and a knowledge of the system's operating language. An inability to exploit any of these will result in diminished system performance. He concludes that the importance of studying foreign languages must be recognised if users are to be well served.

Classification Schemes

In a brief overview, ROMAN provides an introduction to classification, which is seen as the adaptation of prevalent philosophical views to library materials. She examines recent changes in thinking that have influenced current views of classification. BEGHTOL discusses classification in terms of the underlying justification of the system.

In the past, classification systems have been based on literary, scientific, philosophical, or educational warrant. She suggests that more investigations will occur in the future in the area of 'enquiry warrant' systems built as direct responses to user demands. While she seems to trace the idea back only to 1984, it was discussed as 'user warrant' by LANCASTER in 1972. In a comparison of five classification schemes for physics and chemistry, SNOER considers the impact of online catalogues on classification systems.

The schemes examined are the Library of Congress Classification system (LCC), the Dewey Decimal Classification system (DDC), the Universal Decimal Classification system (UDC), and the former and present systems of the University of Copenhagen.

The author stresses the value of using UDC's Common Auxiliary for Place in existing call numbers to enhance retrieval. She concludes that radical revision of classification to suit the online environment is not necessary but that improvements can be made to existing schemes.

In a more global view than is often encountered, HOLLEY examines the impact of electronic technology on classification and subject cataloging and speculates on how this might affect third world countries. He fears that changes occurring in approaches to subject access and subject analysis in the developed countries will not take the needs of the third world into consideration. The International Federation of Library Associations (IFLA) is encouraged to provide a forum for the third world to cope with this situation.

The value to users of an index to a classification scheme is observed by NAKAMURA, who points out that even though such indexes are often rejected on the grounds of inflexibility, the very nature of such a fixed system is helpful for the user who is unfamiliar with a particular scheme. However helpful an index may be, it cannot fully compensate for the difficulty in using classification as a search tool. The author suggests a number of approaches to concept classification as possible remedies.

Since, its controversial entrance into American public libraries over a century ago, fiction has remained something of a stepchild in terms of access. BAKER, BAKER and SHEPHERD, and SHEPHERD and BAKER examine the application of classification to fiction in American public libraries. Their survey of the literature indicates that patrons find classification a useful tool in locating the types of books they want. Suggestions for further study are included. On the same topic, SAPP describes four classification schemes for fiction: LCC system, DDC system, Frank Haigh's fiction classification scheme of 1933 (HAIGH), and L. A. Burgess's scheme of 1936 (BURGESS). These are evaluated along with discussions of shelving schemes, subject headings, and topical access to fiction through standard print indexes.

Mention is also made of experiments by the Danish librarian Annelise Mark Pejtersen in online subject indexing for fiction. SAPP recognises the difficulties in classifying fiction and recommends further study to determine if the need for classification here justifies the effort. New systems, and modifications to older ones, are evolving in response to demands for more effective subject retrieval. LIU-LENGYEL describes the development of the Chinese Classification System over 2,000 years and notes the problems that lack of standardisation has caused in Chinese libraries. This may have been somewhat remedied by the adoption of the new Chinese Book Classification system as a standard in 1981.

SUKIASYAN examines trends in classification in the Soviet Union. Several projects have explored the value of classification schemes for retrieval in OPACs. Some researchers are looking at the LCC system and the DDC system for this purpose. Using OCLC MARC records as a research base, MARKEY and MARKEY and DEMEYER have tested the potential of the DDC system for retrieval. They demonstrate that, used in combination with Library of Congress Subject Headings (LCSH) and keywords in title, DDC can increase recall and retrieve relevant items not retrievable by any of the other fields on the record. CHAN has examined theoretical issues related to whether or not the LCC can be used to enhance subject retrieval in an online catalogue, while WILLIAMSON is also working on a project to test the potential of using LCC for subject retrieval. HUESTIS reviews strategies for overcoming the major problems involved in the use of LCC in OPACs. KHOSH-KHUI has looked at the relationship between length of class numbers in LCC and DDC and subject specificity.

Although the length of number in both schemes does increase with specificity, it is not in itself a good indicator of specificity of subject headings assigned to items or of the number of headings assigned. GOPINATH discusses the use of classification schemes and thesauri in a symbiotic relationship that can improve information retrieval. The concept of a 'thesaurofacet' or 'classaurus'—a device that incorporates features of a faceted hierarchical scheme with those of a thesaurus—is a practical application of this symbiotic relationship.

AITCHISON looks at two thesauri that have used the H. E. Bliss classification as a source for construction and considers the merits of using the second edition of Bliss for this purpose. O'NEILL *et al.* look at the problems involved in mapping from one classification scheme to another, with particular reference to the LCC and the DDC systems. They introduce the notion of 'class dispersion' as a measure of the ease with which a class in one scheme can be mapped to another scheme. DUNAYEV and POLYAKOV describe the problems involved in deriving a mathematical description of classification schemes.

Subject Headings

The emergence of OPACs has also caused a revival of interest in subject headings, as they are traditionally used in libraries, and the limitations of these vocabularies for effective subject access in the online environment. WYKOFF provides a brief overview of the history of the use of subject headings in online access. MASSICOTTE describes how displays of subject headings in OPACs can be made more browsable, while MARKEY discusses the integration of Library of Congress Subject Headings (LCSH) in machine-readable form into online catalogues. Over the years LCSH has been the subject of much criticism.

COCHRANE groups the criticisms into four categories of needs:

- The need to improve the form of headings and to add more scope notes;
- The need to improve the cross-reference structure;
- The need to improve subdivision access; and
- The need to improve the syndetic structure of the system by use of classification.

She examines suggestions for improvements and discusses how these fit into the online environment. In an article that begins by reiterating the criticisms of Anglo/Western bias in LCSH and the inability of the Library of Congress (LC) to keep the vocabulary up to date, HENIGE presents a further concern that headings are not being changed to reflect current scholarly consensus. To be effective in reference work, he says that headings must be accurate and in step with current scholarly thought. LC, however, has always taken the position that LCSH should reflect the content of published literature rather than the cutting edge of scholarly research.

DYKSTRA points out that the 11th edition of LCSH adopts the very precisely defined terminology of thesaurus construction, but she argues that its use of 'broader term,' 'narrower term,' and 'related term' is misleading because LCSH does not maintain the precise logical relationships implied by these terms in a carefully constructed thesaurus. LCSH can only be considered as a list of accepted subject terms used in LC; it is not a true thesaurus. It has always been difficult to determine the policies and practices that LC adopts *vis- à-vis* LCSH.

With the exception of Haykin's guide published in 1951, there has been very little explanation available. The revised edition of LC's *Subject Headings Manual* and the second edition of *Library of Congress Subject Headings: Principles and Application* provide two excellent sources to guide the librarian in using the subject headings for items in a collection. Knowing how headings are interpreted and used by LC will help promote consistency among libraries in their application. FROST and DEDE have studied the compatibility between LCSH and the use of subject headings by one large research library.

Methods by which a controlled vocabulary is updated are another matter of general interest. A study by BACKUS *et al.* tested two hypotheses concerning the annual revision of the National Library of Medicine's (NLM) MeSH vocabulary. It was hypothesised that new terms are added to the vocabulary when their broader terms have increased in number of postings and that the distribution of terms in the hierarchical 'trees' of the vocabulary would reflect the distribution of terms in search requests made to the system.

Neither hypothesis was supported. MCCARTHY discusses the extent to which consistency occurs in the assignment of headings in order to bring like works together. She concludes that consistency is not as high as it should be and proposes an increase in the number both of headings assigned to an item, as well as cross-references, as possible remedies. She also recommends that cataloguers examine the literature on the subject in question to see what headings have been applied in the past. She believes that the use of online catalogues increases the importance of consistency in assigning subject headings and also simplifies its achievement.

MILLER presents a very brief outline of the application of automation to the production of LCSH and points out the advantages and disadvantages of the programme. Many libraries have made it a standard policy to review and revise the subject headings assigned to catalogue records by member libraries of OCLC, Inc. SALAS-TULL and HALVERSON evaluate this practice in light of the time and expense involved in comparison with the number of changes libraries actually make to the OCLC records.

They examined revisions made by research, academic, and public libraries and found that there was little difference in the number of revisions among the three types of libraries and that the total number of revisions was lower than expected. They conclude with several suggestions for cataloging departments that use subject heading review policies. Since, the 1940s there has been interest in a uniform code for subject headings. With the general adoption of the *Anglo-American Cataloguing Rules,* 2nd edition *(AACR2),* interest in a similarly uniform guide for subject access has been renewed.

STUDWELL and ROLLAND-THOMAS suggest a form for such a code and urge an international effort to develop a standard code. In the same spirit, STREBI offers examples of revision and retrospective conversion of subject headings performed by the Austrian National Library as models for other libraries to consider. The use and effectiveness of subject headings for biomedical materials have also been the subject of recent research.

MASARIE and MILLER compare terms used by health professionals with the standardised vocabulary found in MeSH. Fifty hospital charts were randomly selected and subjected to a computer analysis that matched terms with two MeSH-based vocabularies; the first consisted of MeSH terms, and the second consisted of MeSH terms plus cross-references. Approximately 50 per cent of the words used in the charts matched the MeSH-related vocabularies, with about 40 per cent of these proving to be exact MeSH terms or entry terms. Also working with MeSH, RADA *et al.* evaluated entry terms and tested a method for producing new entry terms.

Documents indexed by MeSH terms were compared with documents indexed automatically to see if the automatic indexer could map from title words to controlled terms through the use of entry terms better than it could without using entry terms. Some entry terms were found to be ambiguous. In a method for producing new entry terms, the authors present an algorithm to map terms from the *Systematised Nomenclature of Medicine* to MeSH. While the new *SNOMED* terms were not helpful in indexing, they did suggest how MeSH might be improved. A new algorithm was formulated to join the two sets of terms, and the combined *SNOMED*/MeSH vocabulary was judged to permit improved indexing over the MeSH terms alone.

Thesauri

WEINBERG and CUNNINGHAM provide a brief comparison of online thesauri with print versions. The interfaces for a number of different vendor systems are evaluated, and the article includes recommendations for improving online thesauri. CHAN and POLLARD provide an annotated directory of thesauri used in online databases. The linking and evaluation of thesauri are necessary tasks in improving retrieval systems. RADA presents a number of considerations in connecting and evaluating thesauri. Experimental linkings of MeSH with the *SNOMED,* CMIT (Current Medical Information and Terminology), and PDQ thesauri are discussed.

In these experiments, similarities are identified and differences are exploited to generate better thesauri. MILI and RADA also report on efforts to merge thesauri to create more powerful vocabularies, and MANDEL reviews the problems involved in integrating thesauri and other forms of controlled vocabulary within an online bibliographic network. SCHONDORF presents a study utilising the Thesaurus Database developed by the Gesellschaft fur Information und Dokumentation in Frankfurt, which examines unconventional relationships among thesaurus terms.

The study presents examples of how these relationships provide orientation support within the thesaurus's vocabulary for indexing and retrieval. ROSTEK and FISCHER describe the computer 'modelling' of a thesaurus within a frame system with a graphical interface. BELLAMY and BICKHAM deal with the development of a thesaurus for the subject cataloging of books in a special library in biomedicine.

SEARCH STRATEGIES AND SEARCHING METHODS

General Discussions

An enormous study of factors affecting the performance of online searches was undertaken over a period of several years at the now defunct Matthew A. Baxter School of Library and Information Science at Case Western Reserve University. The methodology and results for the final phase of this project are presented by SARACEVIC *et al.* The study involved 40 users, each providing one question, and 39 searchers. Interviews with the users were tape recorded. For each question, nine searches were performed, four by project staff and five by outside searchers, for a total of 360 different searches.

A related experiment was also undertaken, involving the classification of user questions by 21 judges. The results of the searches were evaluated by the users in terms of relevance and utility. The bewildering variety of data collected during the project makes effective summarisation virtually impossible. Perhaps the most significant finding was that different searchers were likely to have quite different interpretations of a question and, thus, used different search approaches and retrieved different items.

Moreover, each searcher tended to find some relevant items not found by the others, although the chance that an item would be judged relevant increased with the number of searchers retrieving it. The investigators suggest that these results argue the need for multiple searches for the same question by different searchers, but an alternative conclusion might be that a team approach to the analysis of a question and a consensus approach to an initial search strategy might be the preferred mode of operation.

Earlier FIDEL had also discovered that experienced searchers show little agreement in the selection of terms, and even earlier studies consistently revealed that users of card catalogues also tend not to agree much on what terms to use in searching for items on a particular topic. HARTER looks at problem-solving attitudes and abilities of searchers as factors affecting search success. FAIRHALL categorises the various skills associated with searching performance, while SCHIFFMANN reminds us of the value of 'hedges' in the handling of repeated search requests.

VIGIL contributes a major monograph on the searching of online databases, including psychological factors in searching. Over the past 25 years a number of attempts have been made to measure unobtrusively the quality of reference services offered by libraries. Such studies have focussed on the ability of libraries to answer factual questions. MCCUE has now pioneered the unobtrusive evaluation of online searching in libraries.

Twenty-one public libraries throughout the United States were each asked to perform the same search in two different databases; the searchers did not know that they were being tested. Two 'outside expert database searchers' evaluated the results. Using a point system, each search was scored on strategy, general techniques, and results. General techniques covered such aspects as searcher mistakes in entering terms or use of incorrect procedures. Results were also given numerical scores; a worthless citation earned no points, an excellent one earned.

The library scores ranged from 419 to 155. McCue concludes from her statistical analysis that the only variable that correlated positively with high search scores was the number of items retrieved. This is hardly surprising. In effect the scoring method takes recall into account since, it gives positive scores to 'useful' items but not precision. The entire method of scoring, however, is of dubious quality. In the long run it is the results that matter, so it seems pointless to devise a scoring method that takes not only results but search strategy and search technique as well into account.

HANSEN compares the results of a group of inexperienced subjects who performed manual searches followed by online searches with the results achieved by a matched group of subjects who performed online searches followed by manual ones.

The differences in the results were not statistically significant. Nevertheless, she concludes that inexperienced searchers may get the best results when performing a manual search after an online search, at least in the case of 'a large and complex topic with an expanding literature," a conclusion that receives very weak support from her data.

In a doctoral dissertation, DALRYMPLE compares the searching of card catalogues with the searching of online catalogues, looking at the activity as essentially a problem-solving task. Within her experimental setting, users found more relevant items and were more satisfied with their results from the card catalogue. Users spent more time and reformulated their strategies more often when using the online catalogue. The search patterns of users of the CATLINE database of NLM are analysed by TOLLE and HAH and compared with the search patterns of MEDLINE users.

FIDEL discusses how analysis of the search behaviour of human intermediaries can be used to identify rules by which such experts select 'search keys'—descriptors from a controlled vocabulary or free-text terms. She claims that when more research has been performed on expert search behaviour, it should be possible to build a knowledge base for use in an intermediary expert system for online searching. By observing 47 searchers in action, FIDEL concludes that free-text terms and descriptors are selected with about the same frequency.

However, those who prefer the free-text approach and avoid controlled vocabularies are more likely to be searchers on science topics who search several databases for each request. The evaluation of the results of a search involves some criterion for judging the relevance of retrieved items. EISENBERG and SCHAMBER review various approaches to the definition of 'relevance' used by earlier writers and propose a 'user-centric-cognitive model' that views the user as the 'central and active determinant of the dimensions of relevance.'

In a related paper, HALPERN and NILAN discuss the subject of relevance in terms of 'source evaluation,' the weight that a person places on a source of information beyond its substantive content—authority or expertise represented, uniqueness, and so on. After using judges to rate documents on both relevance and utility, REGAZZI claims that no operational difference exists between relevance-theoretic and utility-theoretic models of evaluation.

WAGNER examines the cause of 'false drops' in online searching. They are less prevalent in searches that use only controlled vocabulary terms, but in any case they account for only a small percentage of errors, and that retrieval error is, to some degree, unavoidable, especially in searches seeking high recall. The author stresses awareness of the causes of false drops and advises that the professional be able to explain their occurrence to the user.

BLACKSHAW and FISCHHOFF view online searching as a decision-making process. Volunteer searchers were observed while performing author, title, or subject searches in an online catalogue in a public library. The authors report that searcher performance resembles that revealed in studies of decision making in other contexts. BELLARDO looked at variables that might affect the performance of online searchers, using two test searches with students from six different library schools. Findings suggest that differences in performance can be attributed to general verbal and quantitative aptitude, artistic creativity, and an inclination towards critical and analytical creative thinking, but the associations are all very weak. High intelligence and other factors often cited as important attributes may not be *necessary* for high performance.

Bellardo claims that searching performance may not be predictable on the basis of cognitive and personality traits. End-user searching has become increasingly common with the growth of home computers, favourable searching rates for the home user and, most particularly, the emergence of more and more databases on CD-ROM. OJALA looks at who end users are, where they are, and why they are searching and makes some projections for the future. SEWELL and TEITELBAUM report the results of investigations of end-user searching of NLM databases over 11 years through transaction logs, interviews, and questionnaires.

SULLIVAN *et al.* compared end-user searching with delegated searching and discovered that the end users were no less satisfied with their results, retrieved fewer items, and achieved a high precision. All aspects of end-user searching are reviewed in a compilation by KESSELMAN and WATSTEIN. End-user searching, in some environments at least, may require a user-friendly interface to make the search process as simple as possible.

POLLITT describes one approach, based on use of a menu, that has been developed at NLM. Called Men USE, it is an improved version of an earlier prototype, CANSEARCH. Pollitt claims that it "provides inexpensive, high-quality, subject-specific browsing and searching of the MEDLINE database for users who have no training or experience in information retrieval". The interface described by BATES is intended to help users develop their own search strategies rather than to be an automatic 'transparent' aid to the user.

WILLIAMS discusses the wider issues involved in the design of transparent systems and describes a number of approaches, which she categorises as gateways, front ends, intermediaries, and interfaces. However, her article is tangential to this chapter because it deals more with interface technology than with interface content. INGWERSEN emphasises the importance of browsing facilities in solving search problems.

Information retrieval studies have increasingly taken the viewpoint that computer-human interfaces can be better designed if they are based on the concept of an adaptive, cognitive model. A review of cognitive models in information retrieval by DANIELS examines recent literature in this area, mainly from the standpoint of the user. A number of natural-language and controlled-vocabulary information retrieval systems that use cognitive models are discussed. The review concludes that cognitive models in the various systems work reasonably well because they function in constrained environments.

Suggestions for further incorporation of cognitive models in future systems designs are offered. VECCIA describes nine online systems that can be used to search the *Washington Post.* She compares the various types of searches the systems permit and notes items excluded from indexing. The downloading of bibliographic records from online searches has become increasingly common. LARGE discusses the subject, including downloading from CD-ROM databases, and looks at the reuse of downloaded records in local databases. JAMESON treats downloading and uploading in greater detail, including legal aspects.

Searching in Online Library Catalogues

Traditionally library catalogues have provided somewhat limited capabilities for searching by subject. The replacement of the card catalogue by online public access catalogues has brought about a great resurgence of interest throughout the library profession in all aspects of subject access. For one thing, it has been found that the proportion of catalogue searches that are subject searches has tended to increase considerably as OPACs fall into place. LIPETZ and PAULSON confirm this trend in a 'before and after' study at the New York State Library.

FROST studied catalogue users at the University of Houston and concluded that students search more often by subject than do faculty. However, on the basis of a study at the City University prior to the automating of their catalogue, HANCOCK suggests that subject searching of manual catalogues may have been more prevalent than previously thought. KASKE has found great variability in the proportion of OPAC searches that are subject searches—by hour of day, day of week, and week of semester. In discussions of online catalogue development in libraries two approaches are particularly evident.

One is to improve the interface between user and system, and the other is to enhance or augment the system itself. An analysis of online subject searches led one group of librarians and information specialists to conclude that an online catalogue must compensate for a user's inability to match his or her subject headings exactly with those of LCSH, must provide more than one searching option, and should permit users to refine large retrieval sets. HILDRETH also argues for a more interactive interface between the user and the system.

One essential feature is to provide the user with information concerning the status of the search as it progresses. The Subject Access Project performed at Syracuse University in the late 1970s determined that augmenting subject headings of traditional bibliographic records with terms from tables of contents and back-of-the-book indexes may be an efficient and relatively inexpensive way to improve subject access in the catalogue. BYRNE and MICCO describe a study in which an average of 21 multiword terms, drawn from indexes or tables of contents, were added to MARC records for 6,000 books.

Results of their studies indicate that searches of these augmented records achieved much improved recall compared with searches on titles or subject headings. DIODATO considers the same issue from a slightly different point of view when he studies readers' descriptions of books to determine if the descriptions match terms from the tables of contents and indexes. He concludes that tables of contents and indexes are two sources of terms that are likely to reflect terms that the user would use in searching for the books.

JAMIESON *et al.* have compared the searching of uncontrolled keywords occurring in bibliographic records with the searching of controlled terms in the records. In recognition of the millions of bibliographic records presently in MARC format in libraries and information centers, CHITTY argues that the issue is not how to improve the information on the record but how best to use the information already present. In actuality, the approaches to improving online catalogues are not a choice between whether the content is enhanced or the interface is improved. The content, the system/user interface, and the user are all integral parts of the system.

DWYER points out that many developments in the bibliographic organisation of libraries over the years have resulted in split files; he proposes that a total retrospective conversion be implemented as one means towards building better catalogues. Quality cataloging is a necessity because the accuracy of a system's content ultimately determines the success of retrieval. Because any transition to an online catalogue involves choices and trade-offs, Dwyer stresses the importance of understanding the true costs involved and of understanding the users' requirements in order to make intelligent choices in questions of design.

LAWRY raises the question, 'Can online catalogues be too easy'? The question indicates a concern that a system that appears to 'think' for the user, by assisting the user in query formulation, search strategy selection, and evaluation of retrieved titles, is unintentionally misleading the user. Lawry stresses the importance of user education to make effective use of all the tools available in the library.

BATES presents a model of subject access in online catalogues based on three design principles:

- Uncertainty;
- Variety; and
- Complexity.

Bates argues that because indexing is characterised by variety, searching should no longer be based on the exact matching of terms but, instead, should help the searcher by displaying and 'making it easier to explore' a variety of terms. Two tools proposed for improving search performance are an end-user thesaurus and a 'front-end system mind'; the former is basically a vast entry vocabulary, and the latter is a semantic network, incorporating the entry terms, that allows a searcher to select from a variety of methods for generating semantic associations. The design approach proposed is intended to be implemented in existing catalogues based on LCSH without the need for any reindexing. Bates seems optimistic about the future of subject access in online catalogues. Not so BORGMAN, her colleague at UCLA. Based on studies of user behaviour in subject searching—whether in library catalogues or in broader bibliographic databases—she concludes that "we do not yet have sufficient knowledge of user behaviour to make improvements in system design".

Using the OKAPI (Online Keyword Access to Public Information) system, WALKER and WALKER and JONES investigated possible methods for improving subject searches. Automatic word stemming, synonym and cross-reference tables, and techniques for the approximate matching of words were all studied. They concluded that weak stemming is beneficial but that strong stemming is of doubtful utility, that semiautomatic spelling correction should be used in online catalogues, and that cross-reference lists to allow automatic cross-referencing should be compiled using input from cooperating libraries.

The cross-reference lists investigated were extremely simple, incorporating abbreviations, noun-adjective pairs, alternative terminology, alternative spellings, irregular plurals, related terms, numbers, and phrases. The phrases category is a little different from the others in that it consists of word combinations that should not be split up by searching algorithms because the meaning of the individual words is quite different from that of their combination.

A much more comprehensive study was the doctoral research project of LESTER. Her objective was to determine what features would be needed in online catalogues to increase the success of users in matching their search terms with LCSH. Random samples of user subject terms, selected from the transaction logs associated with the NOTIS/LUIS online catalogue at Northwestern University were compared with LCSH. For user terms that failed to match the headings, 22 different strategies for achieving a match were investigated.

Strategies that did *not* improve matching significantly were: use of a spelling checker, singular/plural conflation, phonetic spelling, exact matching in either subject or personal name authority files, and any process involving geographic name authority files. The strategies of right truncation, string searching with adjacency, and searching of keywords with Boolean operators significantly improved the matching whether or not the database were augmented by the inclusion of subject and name authority files and/or the ability to search all fields of a bibliographic record. It is interesting to compare Lester's finding on authority files—that they would have little effect on subject retrieval—with the finding of VAN PULIS and LUDY—that subject authority files are little used even when made available online.

MICCO *et al.* report on a project at Chatham College to develop an expert system capable of searching for and providing access to knowledge at the same level as a skilled reference librarian. The project proposes a system that will develop a user profile and diagnose information need, then connect the user to the information through a network interface that will include the use of CD-ROM technologies. The system is envisioned as using a Macintosh-style interface with windows and a mouse. It would have a three-tiered structure: the first level providing access tools, the second providing access to monographs, and the third providing access to periodicals.

As currently projected, the system will use the same types of heuristics employed by expert human searchers rather than the textual keyword searching approach frequently used in computer-based systems. Several projects that have dealt with the use of classification schemes in OPACs were reviewed in the earlier section on classification schemes.

Information Requests

The effectiveness of a delegated search, of course, very much depends on how well a request made by a user actually reflects the user's information need. Much work has been done on user-intermediary interaction in information retrieval. AUSTER and LAWTON look at various characteristics of the pre-search interview as factors affecting the success of a search. ALLEN claims that the way users understand and express their needs will be affected by the cognitive structures by which they have organised their knowledge of the topic and by the schemata introduced in the questions that intermediaries ask. Differences in personal schemata may mean that the same problem could result in completely different questions as filtered through the minds of different individuals.

One major problem in user-intermediary interaction is that the personal schemata of the user and that of the information specialist may be quite far apart. Moreover, various 'external schemata' may also exert strong influence on the interactions between user and intermediary. Somewhat related to Allen's work is that of DERR, who identifies five types of expressions used by individuals in making demands on information services; he discusses the implications of the differences for practices in information retrieval. PETRUS points out that the imperfect nature of requests makes information retrieval an operation based on probability. The retrieval situation can be described by the theory of statistical solutions.

NATURAL-LANGUAGE SEARCHING

The searching of text by computer can be traced back to the late 1950s, but interest has continued to increase as more and more text becomes accessible online. Based on studies performed with the full text of popular magazines, TENOPIR presents a useful but brief discussion of the relative effectiveness of various types of strategies for full-text searching. COVE and WALSH look at the feasibility of a browsing approach to searching text online. They describe a system that will display text extracts to prompt the user to select words. These can then lead to 'associated words'—*i.e.,* words occurring as the 'nearest neighbours' of the words originally selected—which can generate further displays of text, from which additional 'browse words' can be selected, and so on.

The type of text that is generally accessible online consists of relatively brief items such as journal articles, abstracts, or patents. Because of rapidly declining costs, it is now becoming increasingly feasible to store and exploit the text of much longer items, but how useful would it be to be able to search the complete text of, say, monographs? Based on studies of how library patrons use non-fiction books, PRABHA and RICE conclude that systems that permit the searching of the full text of non-fiction books would be of value to the users of at least the academic libraries. Over the years a number of studies have compared the results of searches in humanly indexed bibliographic databases with results of searches in full-text databases.

The common finding is that full-text databases give greater recall but reduced precision. SIEVERT *et al.* confirm this by comparing results achieved in searching MEDLINE with those achieved through searching two full-text databases in medicine; RO comes to the same conclusion in a different environment.

Unfortunately, this type of result is frequently mis-interpreted. The fact that a full-text database gives better recall than a database of humanly indexed bibliographic records has nothing to do with the properties of text *per se*; it is simply due to the fact that text records tend to be longer and thus provide more access points.

A database of records indexed with an average of, say, 50 descriptors may well give better recall than a database of brief abstracts, but one could change these results dramatically by greatly increasing the length of the abstracts or drastically reducing the number of descriptors assigned. It is the length of the record that is the major determinant of what is and is not retrieved, but this fact is sometimes overlooked.

AUSTIN examines some of the implications of natural-language searching, illustrating cases in which natural-language searches have failed. These failures are analysed for possible solutions, leading the author to conclude that computers exacerbate rather than alleviate the need for vocabulary control. HOOD reaches a similar conclusion. Full-text searching tends to uncover details, whereas controlled-vocabulary searching tends to uncover broad concepts. He concludes that a comprehensive search would require more than one method.

Investigators at Syracuse University have undertaken several related studies on what is assumed to be one of the problems of text searching—the implicit reference to topics through anaphora. For example, AIDS can be variously represented by 'the disease,' 'it,' and so on, in a text. In one study the anaphors occurring in abstracts were replaced by their referents. It was then determined what effect this replacement would have on term weighting, based on word frequency counts, and subsequently on retrieval.

The results were inconclusive: in some searches the replacement improved the ranking of documents in search outputs, while in others it actually caused a deterioration of the ranking. It was hypothesised that this anomaly might be caused by the fact that anaphors sometimes refer to topics that are integral to a text, while at other times they refer to topics that are peripheral. This hypothesis was tested. Using abstracts from the PsycINFO database, words or phrases serving as anaphors were judged as being integral in 52 per cent of the cases studied; the comparable value for abstracts from the INSPEC database was 68 per cent.

The authors concluded that the resolution of anaphora may indeed be important if the effectiveness of text searching is to be improved. This is an example of a conclusion that is based on the processing of abstracts but that may not apply to the full-text situation. Presumably, the redundancy of full text will create a situation wherein the frequency with which a topic occurs *explicitly* will generally reflect its importance in the text regardless of how many implicit references may be missed. DOSZKOCS gives a useful general overview of natural-language processing in information retrieval.

The relative merits of natural-language *vs.* controlled-vocabulary approaches to information retrieval are still debated. DUBOIS compares the two approaches, and SVENONIUS looks at the history of the issue and suggests areas for research that "would clarify it in such a way as to contribute to a rational basis for the design of retrieval tools such as thesauri".

BAER and JOHNSON, considering in particular the OP AC situation, conclude that vocabulary control is even more important in the online environment than it is in manual systems. As full-text databases become the norm, there looms a danger that the mere presence of the complete text may be viewed as a labour-saving substitute for subject indexing.

YANCEY points out that the growth of information through full-text services will place even more importance on relevance and warns of the loss of retrieval capability through lack of subject indexing. A combination of full-text and subject-searching techniques to link past and present knowledge is presented as the preferable alternative. TEUFEL describes an approach to text retrieval that he refers to as '*n*-gram indexing.' The texts of abstracts are reduced to significant words through use of a stop list, then reduced further to word stems.

The stems are converted into trigrams; 'high noise' trigrams are replaced by tetragrams or even pentagrams. Natural-language queries are processed in the same way. Retrieval consists of looking for the best matches between *n*-

gram representations of documents and of requests. Teufel presents some results of tests using abstracts from the INSPEC database. Problems in the portability of natural-language queries from one database to another are addressed by DAMERAU.

AUTOMATIC INDEXING AND RELATED ACTIVITIES

For more than 30 years investigators have sought ways to replace human intellectual processing by computer processing of text. Methods investigated include automatic indexing by extraction or assignment, automatic extracting, the automatic organisation of terms or documents into classes, automatic approaches to thesaurus construction or the development of networks of semantic relations among terms, and methods for matching natural-language requests against the text of documents or their indexed representations. SGALL and VRBOVA have described work in automatic indexing, automatic extracting, machine translation, and related aspects of text processing under way at Charles University in Prague.

VON KEITZ presents a brief overview of the three types of automatic indexing currently available:

- Inverted-file full-text indexing;
- Dictionary-based indexing; and
- Dictionary/rule-based indexing.

The author asks what roles in automatic indexing should be played by humans and what roles should be played by machines. Although only full-text indexing is fully automatic and is the most frequently encountered, the dictionary and dictionary/rule systems provide higher precision; thus, better dictionaries and rules will yield better indexing. The author concludes that the human role should be one of continuing to develop better dictionaries and rules.

SUZUKI and TOCHINAI compare the keyword density method with a 'mean order' method for extracting sentences in automatic abstracting, and DAS-GUPTA compares the Two-Poisson model of automatic indexing with inverse document frequency and discrimination value models. While the automatic extraction of 'significant' words, phrases, or sentences from documents, based on frequency and/or positional criteria, has been successful for many years, automatic assignment indexing, involving even very small controlled vocabularies, has met with much less success.

However, natural-language processing has progressed to the point at which assignment indexing by computer should now be possible. At least, machine-aided assignment indexing should be practicable. VLEDUTS-STOKOLOV, for example, describes experiments performed at BIOSIS in which terms from a limited vocabulary of 600 biological concept headings are assigned automatically to journal articles. The assignment is achieved by matching article titles against a semantic vocabulary containing about 15,000 biological terms, which, in turn, are mapped to the concept headings. The automatic aid to indexing developed at BIOSIS is described in detail, and the disambiguation techniques used are illustrated.

While, overassignment and underassignment of terms still occur, automatic assignment indexing has certainly made some progress since, the 1960s. Machine-aided assignment indexing is also in place at the National Aeronautics and Space Administration (NASA). This work is described by BUCHAN but in insufficient detail. As might be expected, considerable interest now exists in the possibility of devising 'expert systems' to aid the indexing process. One example is the MedlndEx System being developed at NLM.

Referred to as a 'prototype interactive knowledge-based system,' it uses an experimental frame language and is designed to interact with trained MEDLINE indexers by prompting them to enter MeSH terms as 'slot fillers' in completing document-specific indexing frames derived from the knowledge-base frames. MARTINEZ *et al2.* describe another rule-based system. The American Petroleum Institute's (API) Central Abstracting and Indexing Service (CAIS) incorporates a rule-based, expert system founded on the API Thesaurus, which has been in operation since, 1985.

Terms automatically generated by the system and by API's human indexers are reviewed by a human editor, and the edited terms are added to print indexes and the online index. At present the base contains about 14,000 text rules. SALTON presents suggestions for the automatic indexing of monographs. The method proposed performs a syntactic analysis of the text, selects nominal constructs, weights the terms, and selects terms to act as index terms. Approaches to the machine-aided indexing of patents are discussed by SCHRAMM and BIELA.

ALADESULU studies methods of improving automatic indexing operations to make them more closely approach the intellectual level of human indexing. The approach used involves the recognition of phrases that are semantically equivalent but syntactically different. DYKSTRA observes that the clear rules of the PRECIS system lend themselves to the process of content analysis and automatic indexing. CONGREVE describes a project designed to evaluate the automatic production of PRECIS-based indexes. Among other methods used for automatic indexing are user manipulation of index commands imbedded in the document and system manipulation of keywords in and out of context.

LAMEIN examines the advantages and disadvantages of keyword-out-of-title indexing and describes its use in the law library of the Free University of Amsterdam. The processing of the text of a request against the text of a document collection can be considered as essentially a pattern-matching operation. The objective is to retrieve items in a ranked order, with those that best match the request at the top of the ranking. One way of achieving such a ranking is by weighting the search terms by the frequency with which they are associated with items already known to be relevant, their rate of occurrence in the database as a whole, or other statistical properties.

ROBERTSON describes one weighting formula that he considers an improvement over those previously used. SALTON and BUCKLEY summarise findings of research on automatic term weighting and present models for comparison with more complex techniques of content analysis. CHOROS and DANILOWICZ describe an approach to 'relative indexing,' in which the weights assigned to descriptors associated with documents are modified on the basis of user relevance feedback.

BUELL discusses problems associated with the fuzzy-set approach to weighted retrieval. The calculation of term discrimination values is discussed by WILLETT, EL-HAMDOUCHI and WILLETT, and CROUCH, while BARTSCHI presents a general mathematical framework for looking at retrieval approaches involving term weighting and the ranking of output, and MURTAGH describes hierarchic clustering methods applicable to information retrieval. CAN and OZKARAHAN also deal with term discrimination values. They introduce a 'cover coefficient' and describe how this can be used in computing the discrimination value for a term.

FAGAN compares two methods for automatically extracting phrases from texts to serve as content indicators. Non-syntactic methods are based on simple text characteristics, such as word frequency and word proximity, while syntactic methods selectively extract phrases from parse trees generated by an automatic syntactic analyser. Retrieval tests were inconsistent but tended to indicate that the non-syntactic methods produced better results. Nevertheless, Fagan suggests that the syntactic approach does have certain advantages and has a greater potential for improvement than does the non-syntactic method. The ranking of documents in 'automatic' information systems is usually based on probabilistic, vector, or fuzzy-logic criteria.

LOSEE building on the work of BOOKSTEIN, presents a probabilistic sequential learning model for ranking. The proposed system will retrieve documents, accept feedback on the retrieved items, and 'learn' from the feedback to enhance future performance, the relevance feedback being an intrinsic element in the sequential learning model itself. An earlier article describes how coordination-level matching can be used for ranking outputs from retrieval systems incorporating sequential learning.

CROFT describes a method for integrating Boolean approaches with probabilistic retrieval methods. He claims that term dependencies derived from queries, when incorporated into a probabilistic retrieval model, can improve performance. The term dependencies can be derived automatically from Boolean queries or from user selection of important phrases from their natural-language queries. RADECKI, MARON, LOSEE and BOOKSTEIN, FOX and KOLL, S ALTON, and COOPER all deal with the limitations of conventional Boolean searching methods and propose ways in which such approaches can be improved. Relevance feedback is usually considered an essential element in any probabilistic retrieval method, and this implies the ability of the searcher to locate 'a few relevant items' in a database.

One way of achieving this is to match the query against clusters of items rather than against individual items. PANYR considers the place of cluster analysis in information retrieval along with possible search strategies to exploit clusters. GRIFFITHS *et al.* have compared various clustering methods and found that the best retrieval results were achieved by procedures that divide a database into many small clusters. This led them to propose that the optimal cluster will consist of only two items, the ones that are most similar.

However, further tests showed that searches based on nearest-neighbour clusters did not perform any better than conventional 'best-match' searches, although they retrieved a different set of items. Consequently, these authors propose that a retrieval system incorporate both approaches. SALTON *et al.* discuss the use of automatic relevance feedback techniques with Boolean query statements. An extended or 'fuzzy' Boolean logic approach, which relaxes the normally strict interpretation of the Boolean operators, can improve search performance.

ENSER examines clustering techniques using terms from tables of contents, title, and back-of-the-book indexes, and concludes that this technique is viable in a book/text database. SHAW looks at the empirical significance of document clusters as a function of term weight and similarity thresholds. In related work SHAW also looks at the validity of partitions formed on the basis of co-citation. Approaches to the automatic indexing/classification of documents are generally based on data derived from a document/term matrix, showing which index terms or text words are associated with which documents.

Documents may be grouped according to such factors as the frequency with which a term occurs in a document and the frequency with which it occurs in the database as a whole. The relationships between documents and terms need not be considered 'absolute.' For example, words that do not occur in a document may nevertheless be judged 'close' to that document when they tend to co-occur in other contexts with the words that do occur frequently in the document. DEERWESTER *et al.* propose an approach to indexing based on the 'latent' relations among terms and documents, derivable from the document/term matrix. They refer to this as 'latent semantic indexing.'

The model uses a reduced set of about 100 'descriptive parameters' derived by the linear decomposition of a document/term matrix. Each term, document, and query can be represented by values on this small set of orthogonal dimensions, which may be considered as 'artificial concepts.' The investigators claim that results achieved in retrieval tests for the method ranged from considerably better to roughly comparable with performance based on weighted keyword searching. A more abstract, mathematical discussion of the analysis of weighted graphs in the clustering of items is given by GOETSCHEL, while CAN and OZKARAHAN compare two clustering algorithms in terms of stability and similarity factors.

YAKUBOVITZ refers to an associative retrieval system that can overcome some problems of text retrieval without the need for daily updating of a system thesaurus. This system links keyword-bearing documents with adjacent, associated documents having only one keyword in common to form an associative path. An algorithm for the construction of a path that changes keyword three times is presented as an example. THÖNSSEN reports on an interface that connects automatic indexing programmes with automatic thesaurus maintenance programmes. The interface can be used with a personal computer.

STREETER and LOCHBAUM present details on an expert/expert locator (EEL), which matches requests for information with technical organisations. The technical organisations in EEL are represented by their documents, and these documents provide the system with input. The automatic indexing places terms and organisations in a 100-dimension semantic space and determines similarities among organisations on the basis of their use of terms. When queried, the system computes the degree of similarity between the request and all objects in this structure, retrieving those that are most similar.

The approach is similar to the latent semantic indexing described by DEERWESTER *et al.* Another approach to 'automatic' retrieval consists of the development of natural-language interfaces that allow a user to enter queries as phrases or sentences without the need to deal with controlled vocabularies or to express logical relationships among terms. Various natural-language interfaces have been developed over the years.

BISWAS *et al.* introduce an approach that uses fuzzy-set techniques, and they describe it in considerable detail. CLEMENCIN describes a natural-language interface to the 'yellow pages' of France's online telephone directory, while SPIEGLER and ELATA propose a model for analysing a query at a local workstation to determine whether it is 'answerable' before submitting it to some accessible database. Rather than mapping natural-language expressions to a limited number of controlled terms, words occurring in text can be decomposed into smaller semantic units. This is the basis of 'semantic analysis' and the 'semantic code' that was applied to information retrieval at Western Reserve University more than 25 years ago.

SMETÁÈEK describes the SEMAN system that will decompose text words into 630 distinctive 'semantic features'. He mentions several possible information retrieval applications but does not elaborate on them. BELONOGOV *et al.* compare the performance of a retrieval system based on automatic indexing with the performance of a system based on text searching. They conclude that the system with automatic indexing has significantly better recall/precision characteristics and is faster than the other approach. Also, because low-performance terms can be eliminated, the database can be smaller.

BLAIR and MARON, using IBM's STAIRS for full-text legal retrieval, reported average precision values of around 75 per cent; but recall values of only about 20 per cent. SALTON comments on these results and suggests that they are typical of conventional retrieval operations. He presents results for studies that have compared conventional with automated approaches and emphasises that the future lies with the latter. BLAIR reviews the basic model of a relational document retrieval system and demonstrates how documents can be linked during a search in a relational system. He presents an extended model that includes weighted subjects, associative features such as thesaurus links, citation indexing, and co-occurring terms.

At a more general level, CANISIUS discusses potential uses of knowledge-based systems in information service applications and argues that the information profession could become redundant if it fails to exploit the capabilities of such systems, while WORMELL and BALDACCI deal with artificial intelligence and expert systems applied to information retrieval problems. SPARCK JONES, on the other hand, questions the need for artificial intelligence applications in information retrieval systems.

CITATION RELATIONSHIPS

Related documents can be grouped on the basis of direct citation, co-citation, or bibliographic coupling as well as through the more conventional methods of subject indexing. A number of recent studies deal with various aspects of these citation relationships in information retrieval. PAO and PAO and FU have compared results of searches based on citation relationships with results from conventional subject searches in MEDLINE. Not surprisingly, they find that the two methods are essentially complementary, each retrieving some relevant items not found by the other. One conclusion was that the conventional approach by descriptors could retrieve only about half of the 'quality' papers.

In reviewing their own bibliographic references, however, it is distressing to note that none of the items cited was published before 1979, giving the impression that studies of this kind are relatively new. In fact, comparisons of citation retrieval with conventional descriptor retrieval go back more than 20 years. Moreover, the complementarity of citation and traditional approaches was demonstrated long ago and is now taken pretty much for granted. We really don't need more studies to prove it.

MCCAIN reports a similar study. Results from co-citation searches in SciSearch were compared with results from conventional searches in BIOSIS Previews. The subject was the genetics of fruit flies. One of McCain's conclusions is that co-cited author searching "is capable of capturing a large percentage of relevant documents in a broad subject retrieval." TRIVISON compares items retrieved by subject indexes and citation indexes in the field of information science.

Unfortunately, neither conventional subject indexing nor citation links offer a foolproof way of linking documents or groups of documents that are 'logically' related. SWANSON points to two groups of logically related articles—one on the effects of dietary fish oils on changes in the blood and the other on the possible beneficial effects of similar blood changes for patients with Raynaud's disease—that are not closely related by co-citation, bibliographic coupling, or statistical associations among assigned descriptors. In a similar study SWANSON looks at the problems of linking the literature of magnesium to the literature of migraine.

SHAW raises doubts about the validity of some subject relationships supposedly demonstrated by co-citation. Classes formed by co-citation can be statistically invalid even at a high co-citation level. However, critical thresholds that define the limits of statistical validity can be identified. Within these limits there does exist "a narrow region of statistical validity where the associated structures are not an artifact of the clustering procedure and can be interpreted".

KWOK refers to the fact that reference/citation links can be used in information retrieval to form an 'augmented collection' of retrieved items. That is, when a search strategy is applied to a database in the normal way, using text words or controlled terms, the set of items thus retrieved can be augmented by those items linked to them through bibliographic citations. He suggests that the set of terms associated with the items originally retrieved might be augmented by the addition of terms drawn from the items that they cite.

These new terms could be index terms assigned to the cited items, or they could be text expressions drawn from abstracts or titles. He suggests that augmentation by drawing terms from the titles of cited items is most practicable. This is virtually what Mary Elizabeth Stevens was working on more than 20 years ago. SALTON and ZHANG have tested the value of augmenting the set of terms associated with retrieved items by adding title words drawn from 'bibliographically related' items.

Title words were drawn from:

- Items cited by the retrieved items;
- Items citing the retrieved items; and
- Co-cited items.

The authors conclude that while many 'useful' content words can be extracted in this way, many terms of doubtful value will also be extracted; further, the procedure is not sufficiently reliable to warrant inclusion in operating retrieval systems. KWOK, on the other hand, reinterprets their results and concludes that the enhancement may still be worth further investigation. REES-POTTER looks at the potential for using citation, co-citation analysis, and citation context analysis in the updating of thesauri or other controlled vocabularies. She concludes that the analysis of citation content may be used in the development of indexing vocabularies in specialty areas.

CONTENTS AND INDEX

Evidently, for the purpose of the project on the "Study of Subjects", necessary information is to be collected from the existing documentary sources of information - both primary and secondary. The techniques to be employed for this purpose in the majority of cases will be the technique of "abstracting" - that is, briefly, summarising the essential contents. When the collected information is systematised according to the prescriptions of the proforma, it will result in a handbook of information on some facets of the subject concerned, considered to be essential for professional information work and service.

In order to turn this handbook into an effective externalised memory, it has to be equipped with:

- A detailed list of contents; and
- A good alphabetical subject index

The preparation of the list of contents will be largely governed by the headings in the proforma. For the purpose of indexing, a suitable procedure of indexing is to be adopted. The.Indian Standard on this maybe used with advantage.

Use of Scheme for Classification

Among the tools and techniques used in a library, classification is concerned with the analysis' and structuring of subjects. embodied in documents. Here, classification essentially denotes the process of recognising the component ideas of a subject, determining the degree of interrelationship among these ideas and arranging the ideas in a sequence preferred by the majority of the specialists in that subject. Such an analysis and arrangement of components should preferably be guided by explicitly stated postulates and principles, such that a consistent pattern of structuring of subjects is secured. Thus, a study and use of a scheme for classification, based on a set of helpful postulates and principles, and examining the way in which it throws the components of each subject into a sequence preferred by specialists and also arranges the different subjects in a helpful pattern, would naturally aid the LIS personnel in understanding a subject in such a way that he can make use of the knowledge so gained in designing an information consolidation service to meet the specific needs of users. Of course, incidentally, he also becomes increasingly more familiar with the terminology of the subjects concerned.

Design and Development of a Scheme for Classification

In recent times, the dynamic development and rapid. pace of growth in the

Universe of Subjects have made it necessary for the, classifier to play the role of classificationist-in-little, from time to time for no scheme can anticipate and make provision for accommodating all the future developments in the Universe of Subjects.

Therefore, even as a classifier, he will find it necessary to extend and develop the capacity of the preferred scheme for classification for co-extensively structuring the newly emerging subjects and providing them with class or code numbers.

Hence, classifying present day documents requires not merely a knowledge to use a ready made scheme for classification but also a knowledge of the foundation and the methodology of the design and development of schemes for classification.

Steps in Designing

The major steps include a study of the appropriate documents on the subjects in a. graded sequence so as to recognise the component ideas, their interrelations, the modes of combination of the components and the sequence of the components preferred by the majority of specialists in the subject. Irrespective of the model on which the designing of the classification is based.

Inference

It is obvious that the design and development of a classification scheme provides an excellent opportunity to the LIS personnel to learn about subjects, keeping up with the development in each of them, and to some extent, envisage the likely development in the near future.

Other Methods

The following are the other varieties of opportunities and methods by which LIS personnel may learn about the highways and byways of subjects.

- Attending and participating in lectures and discussions by subject specialists oriented to the needs of LIS personnel;
- Consultation with subject specialists while designing a scheme for classification;
- Attending other lectures by and discussions among subject specialists; and
- Attending new-entrant-training schemes, which are in the form of a series of lectures by senior personnel in the organisation - and sometimes from outside the organisation - spread over a period of three to six months.

SUBJECT INDEXING LANGUAGES

Analogously with natural languages, artificial languages with which the mediation between a collection of documents and its potential users takes place are also made up, as Elaine Svenonius has often explained, of four necessary components:

- Vocabulary, that is, all the elementary expressions used to define individual entities, attributes and relationships semantics, that regards the meaning for which a determined expression is included in the vocabulary and used in the language, that is, the relationships which are derived a priori from that meaning and which define it syntax, that regards the composition, by means of the structure of individual elements taken from the vocabulary, of more complex expressions pragmatics, which concerns the conditions and modalities for language application.

Authority control, or with the term vocabulary control, which Elaine Svenonius considers to be equivalent, involves the first component, vocabulary, and comes about in the second, semantics. This analytical approach to linguistic systems of 'cataloguing' mediation provides the most correct theoretical reference for a series of considerations, from which the properties and functions of authority control should result easier to recognise and consequently once clarified the relationships between authority control and the different cataloguing languages, to mark the subject indexing languages.

- Authority control can not be identified, nor is it advisable that it be identified, with a particular cataloguing language, since, syntax and pragmatic components are extraneous to authority control, which vice versa more than the vocabulary and semantic components characterise and diversify the single languages. This independence in relation to single cataloguing languages, or to particular types of language, constitutes a fundamental property and strong element of authority control. Its efficiency must be preserved and widely extended, with the punctual exclusion of the procedures of vocabulary control of those elements and aspects which, being distinctive of single languages, result reciprocally incompatible and thus do not lead to a process of unitary control. The origins of authority control are easy to locate in the paragraphs of the rules for bibliographic cataloguing by author and title, but it is now time to completely abandon the idea that authority control is a phase in the application of a particular cataloguing language, in order to project and realise a system of an unique and general authority control, which satisfies not only the needs of systems of truly bibliographic mediation, but also of systems of, among others, archival and museum mediation. The more it is general and international, the more vocabulary control is efficient, since, it permits the reduction of the waste of resources produced by the repetition of the same operations of control in different places, times and contexts. That is something particularly appreciated in an epoch in which everything is aimed at economising even on intellectual work. Especially, however, the more it is unique and general, the more authority control is efficient, since, it furnishes the unifying element between different cataloguing systems, indispensable for the realisation of instruments, logicians and informatics, which facilitate, and make coherent to the utmost, the research for information in documentary spheres which are traditionally separated, as for example, that of collections in libraries, archives, museums and those in digital formats accessible only by telematic means.

- Cataloguing languages are different, first of all, because of diverse pragmatics, that is because they are destined for use in distinct circumstances with distinct functions and modalities. But, authority control does not concern pragmatics. This means that the conditions and relationships which depend upon the material, formal and substantial characteristics of the single objects to describe and index, the various contexts in which such objects are described and indexed, the particular purposes for their description and indexing, and which determine the use of specific cataloguing languages, at any rate do not determine a diversification of authority control, either regarding the process or the product of such a process, which will be an univocal normalised expression inserted in a web of relationships. Inserting this consideration into the specific theme of this paper, it is impossible not to observe that the conviction that authority control is distinguishable, and must be distinguished, without ulterior specifications is still widespread, and that it is commonly held regarding 'authors'. This conviction, which is certainly involuntary, and thus not justified, in the normative activity of the IFLA, which on this subject published two distinctive guidelines, one which was formally presented as relating to the 'authority records' and one which was formally presented as relating to the 'subject authority entries' Moreover it is also easy to establish that such a persistent conviction has determined, although with non-identical consequences, the same organisation of two of the most important national systems of vocabulary control, that of the Library of Congress and that of the Bibliothèque Nationale de France. In the search screens the Library of Congress authorities are divided into subject authority headings, name authority headings, title authority headings and name/title authority headings; nevertheless, searching for the same expression either as name, title or name/title or as subject the authority record is retrieved. This demonstrates that the authority file is unique, that the control operations relating to the same expression are carried out only once, and that it is simply considered necessary to adjust the appearance of the control system to the conviction held above, making the 'subjects' seem separate from the rest of the entries. The *Notices d'autorité* of the BNF are analogically presented separated into *personnes physiques*, *collectivités*, *titres uniformes* and RAMEAU effectively divided. This means that at the BNF all the management and control operations for the same expression are duplicated, with a waste of resources which does not correspond to an increase of visible efficiency in the system, and which would be sad if it were motivated only by the obligation to conserve some, slightly justifiable formal differences between expressions which are equivalent the most evident case is that of the dates of birth and death, not normally stated in the terms given in the *fichier d'autorité personnes physiques*—which proposes, for example, the preferred form Dante Alighieri—but are present in the RAMEAU *vedettes*—where the preferred form is Dante Alighieri. These solution differences and uncertainties in the authority control systems, from which can be derived only problems and waste, beginning with the error of considering the 'subjects' as semantically distinguishable entities, on the same level as persons, corporate bodies and works. It is therefore indispensable to clarify that it is impossible to identify an entity as a subject if not in relation to the to pragmatics, that is, to the concrete circumstances which have implied in such a case the use of a subject indexing language in the cataloguing record of a document. However since, authority control does not regard those circumstances, it is not theoretically correct, nor practically useful, to perceive and practice a subject authority control as a process in itself. In the FRBR model, which in reality is also reflected in the *Guidelines for authority records and references*, are the classes of entities *work, expression, manifestation, item, person, corporate body, concept, object, event* and *place*. These entities "represents the key objects of interest to users of bibliographic data", and each one having a formal expression as the primary necessary attribute which designates it can be subjected, and it is potentially opportune that they all be subjected, to the authority control procedures. The 'subject' is not an entity in the FRBR model, it is a relationship, which does not rigidly correspond to single classes of entities, but which can involve vice versa entities belonging to each of the classes proposed in the model. It was certainly not indispensable that FRBR remind cataloguers that the name of a person, the corporate body name or the title of a work can be inserted in a cataloguing record in order to realise different functions. However, FRBR goes further since, it suggests the possibility that even the terms which represent these entities for which only the subject function is indicated can be linked to a cataloguing record with a diverse function. If in fact "typically the user will formulate a search query using one or more attributes of the entity for which he or she is searching, and it is through the attribute that the user finds the entity sought", and if, for example, the second and most important attribute of the work, after the title, is the 'form', that is "the class to which the work belongs', how is it possible to allow an efficient search, using this attribute, of a work concretely expressed in a manifestation if not designating this attribute with a controlled term, which cannot but be the same used, in the context of other cataloguing records, for subject access? Putting it very simply, if Walter Scott's *Ivanhoe* is an historic novel, how is it possible to retrieve, by literary genre, the various manifestations of this novel if not directly or indirectly linking the relative cataloguing records to the term 'Historical novel', thus inserting into the search mechanisms of the editions of a work a term presumably also used in the subject indexes, but which in this case does not express the subject of the work? It is true that above all in our catalogues until now, we did not bother to activate retrieval requirements for 'genre' too much, but this has been only a convenient default, seeing as how Cutter already, over a century before the FRBR, had indicated the search by literary genre as one of the requisites of the catalogue. If we then move from the bibliographic context to other cataloguing contexts, the use of potentially expressive subject descriptors in order to indicate something else becomes quite prevalent. 'Etruscan Ceramics' for example, is a term for which the function of a subject is typical in a bibliography, but probably is to be excluded in the catalogue of a museum collection, in which 'Etruscan ceramics' will indicate what the indexed object is, not its theme. That of the 'form of the work' in FRBR is the most relevant, but not the only case of the potential use of an entity *concept, object, event or place* for the purpose of indicating not the subject, but another characteristic of the indexed and described document. Absolutely nothing in the form and the meaning of a term can predetermine the function that the term will play in the single cataloguing record and consequently in a particular index, above all if from the bibliographic context we widen the field to other cataloguing contexts. On the other hand however, to be efficient, unique and general, authority control must leave that function out of this consideration. This further confirms that there is no theoretical or practical justification for continuing to distinguish a subject authority control in the general activity of vocabulary control. It is not by chance that IFLA, having produced the two guidelines on authority records quoted, has nevertheless produced an inevitably unique guideline for the codification of authority records in a readable format for the machine, that is to say *Unimarc. Authorities* in which a specific field for all subject entries alone as such do not exist.

- Semantics is pertinent in authority control, in the three forms described by Elaine Svenonius: referential, relational, category. Referential semantics concerns the uniqueness of meaning of each of the elementary expressions included in the vocabulary: it is the task of authority control to guarantee this uniqueness, supplying each strictly indispensable and sufficient expression of all the formal elements to impede any misunderstanding in use and interpretation. The potential polysemy of an expression is a frequent phenomenon in natural languages, which has no effect on communication, since, normally pragmatic circumstances clarify the meaning for which the polysemic expression is effectively used. But a general authority control, although it is functional in most cataloguing contexts, cannot delegate the referential semantics to the clarifying properties of a single context, nor be conditioned by those properties, and must rather satisfy completely and alone the needs of unambiguousness of the expressions of the vocabulary in all the cataloguing contexts. In this regard, the case that immediately comes to mind is that of those proper names, often called 'geographic', which, in common use, can indicate both a territory and the population of that territory, as well as the corporate body that holds sovereignty over that territory. In some contexts these proper names do not result poysemic: in the context of the author cataloguing 'Italy' is not effectively polysemic, since, the meanings of the territory and of the population are not pertinent to the context; while, certainly but not alone in other contexts, of the subject indexing, those proper names are very polysemic, to the point of sometimes making syntactic relationships ambiguous and the compre-hensive meaning of the entries in which they are inserted doubtful, as well as often making the search and selection of the cataloguing information fastidiously heavy. To be efficient, general authority control must resolve the problems of real polysemy even when not common to all the cataloguing context, and must guarantee the unambiguousness of the expressions in any context in which they are used. The relational semantics concerns the relationship of meaning between all the expressions included in the vocabulary. Among these relationships one is unquestionably considered pertinent to any form of authority control, and that is the equivalence relationship: if in various cataloguing contexts two or more expressions can be used with the same meaning, that is if they indicate the same entity, these two or more expressions are correlated in the authority file, in such a way to guarantee the individualisation of that entity by means of any of these expressions. Traditionally the principle of uniformity was applied to the equivalence relationship, for which one of the expressions was designated as preferred, and became the only one effectively present in the cataloguing records. The informatics management of authority control can offer alternatives to this solution, which allow us to realise a unique and general authority control without imposing the use of the same expression in all contexts, but it must be kept in mind that uniformity has its value as an element of coherence and of predictability in catalogues, and that thus it is opportune to give it up only in the presence of real and fundamental cataloguing needs. The control of equivalence relationships, however, does not exhaust the needs of semantic correlation of any cataloguing language. Author and title bibliographic cataloguing imposes control of some cases of associative relationships in point and of hierarchical relationships. The opportunity of controlling this type of relationship can only increase with the application of the FRBR model. Extended to all categories of entities, the control of associative and hierarchical relationships represents a fundamental need for the subject indexing languages, but it is presumable that it is indispensable or useful for any other cataloguing language too, and certainly advantageous for the interconnection between different languages. It is thus appropriate carried out on the level of general authority control. Obviously on this level of control only hierarchical and associative relationships of universal validity may be expressed, that is those explainable by the typical and essential definition of the entity submitted to authority control, and which thus cannot be contradicted in any particular context. Any entity can then be involved in semantic relationships that are not universally valid, but inherent to the context of application of a determined language. Such relationships must not be expressed on the level of general authority control, but in specific and sectorial vocabulary and classification control instruments, for the elaboration of which the existence of a general semantic control instrument does not necessarily constitute an obstacle, rather a facilitation. Substantially a semantic relationship structure is a classification structure, and thus needs a primary general criteria of subdivision, upon which ulterior articulations can be based. General bibliographic classifications are based upon a primary articulation by subject, which implies the possibility that the same concept, if pertinent to more than one subject, belongs to several classes. This does not correspond to the needs of characteristic semantic structuring of authority control, since, as has been repeated several times in this paper, such a process must leave out of consideration the single context, even when disciplinary, in which the single entities are concretely quoted. With a view to authority control it is therefore necessary to adopt another general criterion of classification which is independent of single contexts, but is valid and useful in all of them and has a secure application. More than a century of studies and of practice in indexing has shown that the criterion of categorical analysis which consists, as regards semantics in the individuation of a limited number of general and universal semantic categories answers these requisites, so that each entity can belong to only one category and in the assigning of each entity, for the single attributes which constitute the typical definition, to one of the individuated categories. The individuation of semantic categories is necessary to avoid incongruities and contradictions in the identification and expression of semantic relationships, but it is also more generally necessary for the normalisation and the informatics management of authority control. It is certainly not a case that upon the citation of general semantic categories is based all of the mentioned *Guidelines for subject authority and reference entries*, nor is it a case that every field of *Unimarc. Authorities*, excluding those of the notes and equipment information, correspond to a semantic category. In the exercise of this general categorial semantics the authority control is however not alone. Even in the FRBR model, in order to control other types of cataloguing relationships, some general semantic categories have been individuated principally usable even in authority control. This shows a convergence of needs and solutions which induce one to hypothesise that the full actuation of the FRBR model make a unique and general authority control realisable, but that even a unique and general authority control is indispensable for the full actuation of the FRBR model.

- Authority control is applied to the single units of vocabulary regarding a priori their characteristics and relationships, those which are constantly valid and for which the single unit is admitted in the comprehensively understood linguistic system. That is, authority control concerns the paradigmatic, not the syntagmatic, side of linguistic communication, and does not thus a posteriori regard the relationships which depend upon connotations of objects to describe and index, and which exist between the unit of vocabulary only when and since, both are present together in a determined statement. Thus the syntax which is the representation of these relationships through the ordering in sequence of correlated units, and which is one of the most distinctive elements between diverse languages cannot be object of a real authority control, but can be object, when necessary, of only a correction verification and of substantial uniformity in the area of the application of a particular cataloguing language. Understanding the syntax of authority control involves a series of inconveniences, which do not appear to be compensated for by any particular advantage. It impedes the realisation of a unique and general vocabulary control which is a connecting factor between different cataloguing languages. This is because syntax is the element for which less compatibility is shown not only between typologically distinct languages, but also between kindred languages which could easily share the same vocabulary. The cases of subject indexing languages are seen as emblematic. The differences between various languages which express a theme in pre-coordinated form, and of those with post coordinated languages, are not so many differences in terminology, but are rather differences in the grade and form of expression of the syntactic relationships, which sometimes makes it impossible to establish the equivalencies not only between index entries expressed by languages which draw from different natural languages, as the MACS project has shown, but even between entries expressed by languages which draw from the same natural language. As an inevitably ulterior consequence, the authority control pretext of syntactic constructions adds a notable heaviness to the entire process to this contraction of its own area of efficiency, with a very useless increase. It does not determine a major expressive-ness, since, it is virtually uncontainable of the whole of the forms submitted to control, which contradicts the first requisite of controlled vocabulary which is to be such even regarding its growth. The constant expansion of the vocabulary is a need of cataloguing languages, but it has the condition that the gathering of new forms is always motivated by the need to express new unitary concepts as a general limit, not new concept correlations which can easily be expressed through the combination of pre-existing forms. To create a new authority record for the string Hospitals—Administration—Data processing—Evaluation—Computer programmes, when authority records already exist for each of the single terms that compose it, it is not in any way useful to the expressiveness of the language, but obliges us, at least in theory, to the fulfillment for this entry of all the procedures of control and of semantic correlation. Being in this case particularly articulated and heavy, such procedures were not in the least way effected, which confirms the complete uselessness of this authority record, the creation and measurement of which has nevertheless absorbed resources. And here is one of the motives, certainly the most concrete and practical, for which the authority control of syntactically constructed entries must be avoided. The creation of authority records for this type of entry determines a waste of resources, which are subtracted from the more qualifying aspects of authority control, making the realisation more difficult, if not impossible. Moreover, the problem is noticed even in the Library of Congress and the Bibliothèque Nationale de France since, both institutions, in order to avoid the collapse of their vocabulary control systems, are activating a review of the procedures aimed at limiting the application of authority control to only elementary expressions, at least to the extent that they are compatible with the use of indexing languages which remain substantially enumerative. Inverting the preceding procedure at the Library of Congress a new one has been established to avoid the creation of new phrase headings and the progressive transformation of many pre-existing phrase headings in entries with subdivisions is in course. At the same time the list of free-floating subdivisions has been notably amplified, with the attribution of the qualification of free-floating to many subdivisions which were not previously free-floating, which has offered the eventuality that for a new entry constructed combining pre-existing expressions it will be quite rare that a new authority record will be produced. Analogous interventions are also taking place in RAMEAU, although it is a more recent language conception and thus less enumerative that LCSH. When improperly extended to expressions constructed for syntax authority control results quite weakened and inefficient in its semantic component, which loses the necessary rigour both in individuali-sation of relationships and in categorial analysis. To give a simple example, what is the entry immediately above, the BT of Hospitals—Administration? Hospitals? Administration? Health facilities—Administration? Health facilities—Organisation? Hospitals—Organisation? And what is the category to which the entry belongs? Is it the category of Hospitals given in the entry in the first position or that of Administration, which is the focus of the corresponding syntax? But above all, can such uncertain semantics ever satisfy the general needs of authority control? Or again, to ask a final question, does it make sense to corrupt to such a point authority control only to extend partially and occasionally syntax to an aspect of cataloguing languages, which is not pertinent to it?

In the articulation of preceding considerations, the sense of the relation between authority control and subject indexing languages is given, but almost hidden behind the closer examination of the single problems. It is well to reassume them here. The existence of subject indexing languages certainly does not call for or imply the existence of a particular authority control exclusively dedicated to subjects. Authority control, being an interconnecting element between different cataloguing languages, must concern all the categories of entities, and in such a way satisfy even the lexical needs of subject indexing languages.

The use of subject indexing languages, as for other cataloguing languages, contributes to the individuation of new expressions to be submitted to authority control, expressions whose ordinary use can not predetermine their possible successive uses, and that thus, once completed the control procedures, can be used in any cataloguing context, either for indicating a subject or for indicating something else. Cataloguing languages, which include among others subject indexing languages, necessitate a verification of the expressions used which are not merely formal, but in addition more completely semantic. Such a verification, since, it sticks to meanings and relationships of universal validity, is appropriate that it be effected at the level of general authority control.

On the other hand, it is not opportune to extend authority control to syntactic constructions, because this reduces the rigour and efficiency of the control process, weighing it down until it becomes unfeasible, and impeding its function of unifying element between diverse cataloguing languages. Each cataloguing language, and thus each subject indexing language, possesses its own syntax and the verification of the correctness of its syntax can only be effected in the circum-scribed context of the application of each language. This conception of relationship between authority control and subject indexing languages is born from the meeting, already fertile, but which can become even more so, between technological progress and theoretic reflection.

Informatics has made telematic interconnection between different documentary contexts, virtually simultaneous access to several contexts and deriving of data from one context to another not only possible but technologically easy. However a common logical linguistic instrument is lacking, and this is evident to everyone, but it is not the duty of informatics to furnish it. As concerns subject indexing languages the theoretic reflection has already individuated the principles which are functional in the elaboration of that instrument. Principles which in Italy have already been adapted, diffused and often clearly defined by the Gruppo di ricerca sull'indicizzazione per soggetto, and which can now find application in the project for renewing the *Soggettario*, promoted by the Biblioteca Nazionale Centrale di Firenze.

Among the most important are: the principle of the subject as relationship property, a factor of coherence and pertinence in a text and no longer as a pre-existing entity supplied with a name; the principle of the separation between semantics and syntax, with the control of the first which can leave the proper formal structures out of consideration of the single languages, and thus be potentially unique and general, and the control of the second which is rather the actuation of those structures; the principle of the definable relationship, for which the semantic correlation of the vocabulary unity is exclusively founded on the essential definition of each unity which is universally valid. Authority control being unique and general, and thus adequate for the situation created by technological progress, must make use of the most advanced theoretic reflection on subject indexing languages, and at the same time must satisfy the needs of subject indexing languages much more than it has until now.

SUBJECT CLASSIFICATION SCHEDULE

The subject schedule has three main divisions: general works, earth sciences, and pure sciences. The collection consists chiefly of monographs but includes those periodicals that are narrow in scope, international in scope, or those issued by an international agency.

GENERAL OUTLINE OF THE SUBJECT CLASSIFICATION SCHEDULE

General works:

- 001-095: Science, computer science, information systems, bibliographies, directories, dictionaries, and biographies.

Earth sciences:

- 101-190:Mineralogy and petrology
- 201-298:General geology, geologic hazards, tectonics, geodynamics, structural geology, geophysics, and geochemistry.
- 301-371: Historical and stratigraphic geology.
- 401-471: Mineral resources, mineral industries, mines and mining, and groups of minerals.
- 501-590: Geography, geomorphology, meteorology, landforms, oceanography, and environmental sciences.
- 601-699:Paleontology, paleoecology paleogeography.

Pure sciences:

- 701-795: Mathematics, astronomy, engineering, geodesy, surveying, cartography, and hydrology.
- 801-895: Physics and chemistry.
- 901-999: Biology, ecology, evolution, botany, agriculture, forestry, and zoology.

Constructing Call Numbers

Call numbers consist of a classification number, shelf list number, title mark and date.

Classification Number

The classification number consists of numbers 001-999 taken from the subject schedule.

Geographic Notation

To add a region to a call number, consult the geographic schedule and choose the appropriate parenthetical number, (000)-(995), for the geographic locale represented in the study.

Example:

- *Title*: China's energy and mineral industries/ by J.P. Dorian, 1988.
- *Class no.*: 403
- *Geographic no.*: (610)
- *Complete class no.*: 403(610)

Shelf List Number

The shelf list number contains information about the main entry of the piece being classified and also provides the work with its singular location on the shelves or in the library online system. The first part of the number consists of an upper case letter and usually a three digit number representing either an author or a title main entry. The number for an author main entry is unique for each author. The shelf list number for an author main entry is completed by lower case letter representing the title of a work and is called a title mark. The title mark allows the various works of an author to be arranged in alphabetical order after the unique three digit number. The shelf list number for a title main entry is usually complete with an uppercase letter and a three digit number. If the shelf list number duplicates another number, add a title mark to make it unique. Titles beginning with numbers are treated as words when creating shelf list numbers. If the title consists of one word, construct the shelf list number from successive letters within that word. A shelf list number is needed. The shelf list number has three elements.

Examples:

Call number with author main entry and no region:

- Title : Multivariate geostatistics/ H. Wackernagel, 1995
- Class no. : 208.2
- Shelf list no. : W323
- Title mark : m
- Date : 1995
- Call number : 208.2 W323m 1995

Call number with author main entry and a region:

- Title : Expert witness guide for scientists and engineers/ A.E. Surosky, 1993
- Class no. : 760
- Region : (200)
- Shelf list no. : S976
- Title mark : e
- Date : 1993

- Call number : 760(200) S976e 1993

Call number with title main entry and a region:

- Title : China's energy and mineral industries edited by J.P. Dorian, 1989.
- Class no. : 403
- Region : (610)
- Shelf list no. : C442
- Date : 1989
- Call number : 403(610) C442 1989

The first element, an uppercase letter, is taken from the first letter of the first word of the main entry. The second element, a three digit number, is taken from Library of Congress shelf listing tables. The final element is the title mark taken from the title, or in case of a title main entry, from the next distinctive word in the title.

Dates in Call Numbers

Current classification policy has a date added to the end of monographic call numbers. In previous years a date was used only for successive editions. The date is usually taken from the imprint. Call numbers for congresses, however, use the date of the congress rather than the year of publication.

Example

Multi volume sets that are published with different edition dates for various volumes are classified without a date. Call numbers that would duplicate an earlier edition that was published in the same year are made unique by adding a, b, c, etc., to the date for successive versions.

Monograph with date:

- Title : Estimation of building vulnerability.../ G.C. Hart, 1988.
- Class no. : 240.2
- Shelf list no. : H377e
- Date : 1988

Congress with date:

- Title : Mineral resources of Russia: diamonds and gold: proceedings of the Second
- International Symposium "Mineral Resources of Russia" : held 1994, St.
- : Petersburg (published 1995)
- Class no. : 401(570)
- Shelf list no. : I573m
- Date : 1994

Size in Call Numbers

Due to restricted space at the Reston Library, publications are grouped according to size. The sizes are:

- Octavo — up to 28 cm.
- Oversize (quarto) — 28.1 to 33 cm.
- Folio — 33.1 to 46 cm.
- Superfolio — 46.1 up

Prior to July 1999, oversize materials were designated by the addition of a lower case letter in front of the shelf list number: q (oversize), f (folio) or ff (superfolio). These designations are no longer used. Instead, shelf location is indicated using a size designation label above the call number.

Translations

Translations by Publishing Houses

Translations by publishing houses are given the call number of the original with a capital letter representing the language of the translation added to the end of the title mark. If the bibliographic information of the original is unknown the call number is based on the bibliographic information of the translation. A capital letter is added to the end of the title mark for the language of the translation.

Example

• Original	:	Wirbellose Tiere der Vorzeit/ U. Lehmann.
• Call number	:	610 L528W
• Translation	:	Fossil invertebrates/ U. Lehmann.
• Call number	:	610 L528wE

Translations by USGS Translators or Translation Services

These translations are not classified or cataloged. Instead, they are kept in folders in the library's Translation file.

Restricted Material

All reports with the note: "for administrative use only," "for official use only," or similar notes are treated as restricted materials and designated by a "RESTRICTED" label above the call number. Prior to July 1999, restricted materials were designated with a * (star) in front of the classification number.

Example:

• Title	:	Mineral summaries
• Note	:	"for official use only"
		Restricted
• Call no.	:	403(271) M562 1990

9

Library Collection Development

COLLECTION DEVELOPMENT

The Working Group on Libraries set up by National Know-ledge Commission (2007) emphasized for collection building based on the information needs of users. In its recommendations the Group added "To fulfill its role in the present and changing context, each library must have a well-rounded collection relevant to its user community". A balanced and need based collection, adequate to meet the present as well as future information needs of users depends upon a well prepared collection development policy. Library staff of ten colleges responded that they had prepared and were following collection development policy, while staff of remaining 09 libraries responded otherwise. It was very disappointing to find that none of the libraries had any written guidelines for collection development.

WHO MAKES SELECTION OF SUBJECT RELATED BOOKS

Subject books are meant to meet the curriculum based information needs of users and enable them to explore the concerned subjects in depth. Library staff was asked to give ranking in order of preference to the different authorities mentioned in Questionnaire-I, according to their role in selection of subject books.

Table. Selection of Subject Related Books

Sr. No.	Persons who Select Books	Scores	Ranking
1.	Teachers	66	01
2.	Principal	60	02
3.	Library Committee	43	03
4.	Librarian	39	04
5.	Others (students and college management)	15	05

Sum total of the scores assigned to different options on the basis of ranking given by librarians reveals that teachers occupied the leading role in selection of subject books, followed by the principals and library committees respectively. Librarians attained the fourth position in order of ranking for subject related document selection, while others (students and college management) earned least scores.

GENERAL AND REFERENCE COLLECTION

As in case of subject books, scores have been assigned to the different authorities involved in selection of general and reference collection also, which are tabulated below:

Table. Selection of General and Reference Books

Sr. No.	Persons who Select Books	Scores	Ranking
1.	Teachers	62	01
2.	Principal	60	02
3.	Librarian	45	03
4.	Library Committee	43	04
5.	Others (students and college management)	05	05

Table shows that teachers have earned the highest scores in selection of general and reference collection too. Principals and librarians were given second and third preferences, while library committees and others attained fourth and fifth positions respectively. Analysis of the responses given in tables makes it clear that the teachers and principals played a leading role in selection of subject related as well as general and reference collection.

DOCUMENT SELECTION TOOLS

Scores have been assigned to the various document selection tools listed in questionnaire-I on the basis of preference ranking given by librarians. Rank '1' was given the highest score '8' followed by others in descending order of 1 score at each stage.

Table depicts that teacher's suggestions have earned the highest scores as sources of document selection, while publisher's catalogues and student's suggestions earned the second and third position respectively. Book reviews and other bibliographical tools were given least ranking as document selection tools.

Table. Document Selection Tools

Sr. No.	Sources of Book Selection	Scores	Ranking
1.	Teachers' Suggestions	132	01
2.	Publishers' Catalogue	101	02
3.	Students' Suggestions	71	03
4.	Books on Approval	54	04
5.	Book Sellers' List	42	05
6.	Book Exhibitions	40	06

7.	Book Reviews	16	07
8.	Other Bibliographical Tools	11	08

COLLECTION OF LIBRARIES

Among three components of libraries *i.e.,* collection, staff and readers, collection occupies the key position. It is collection which determines the use of a library. Collection is a wider term covering books, periodicals, microforms, electronic form docu-ments, etc. Information was gathered about the nature and size of collection of libraries under study.

TOTAL BOOK COLLECTION

Responses received about the total collection of libraries were arranged into different ranges of 5000 each. It is evident from table that majority of the libraries under study *i.e.* 10 (52.63 per cent) possessed 15,000-25,000 volumes, while 04 (21.06 per cent) libraries had 10,000-15,000 books. Only two GCE libraries crossed the figure of 30,000 volumes. The UCE library had less than 5000 volumes due to its recent origin in 2001. The GCE were found rich in collection size than GACE and UCE. Main factor affecting this was that GCE received recurring grants for reading material from both the University Grants Commission (UGC) and the State Goverment, while GACE got grants for library from UGC only.

The NCTE (2007 and 2009) require each college to have a minimum 1000 titles and 3000 books for B.Ed. Course and minimum 2000 titles for M.Ed course in libraries to get recognition. The UCE had less than 5000 volumes though it was offering both B.Ed. and M.Ed. courses. The NCTE (2007 and 2009) further mentioned that a library should add 200 titles annually wherever B.Ed. course is being run. In addition it requires annual addition of '100 quality books' where M.Ed. course is also being run. It has been found that libraries of only two GACE were fulfilling the NCTE norms for M.Ed. course.

Table. Total Book Collection of Libraries

Sr. No.	Total Number of Books Possessed	No. of Libraries	%
1.	0-5000	01	05.27
2.	5000-10000	02	10.53
3.	10000-15000	04	21.06
4.	15000-20000	05	26.31
5.	20000-25000	05	26.31
6.	25000-30000	—	—
7.	More than 30000	02	10.52
	Total	**19**	**100.00**

TEXT BOOK COLLECTION

Table shows the textbook collection of libraries of colleges of education in Punjab.

Table. Text Book Collection of Libraries

Sr. No.	Number of Text Books Possessed	No. of Libraries	%
1.	0-4000	06	31.58
2.	4000-8000	07	36.84
3.	8000-12000	03	15.79
4.	12000-16000	03	15.79
	Total	**19**	**100.00**

Table reveals that majority of the libraries had 4000-8000 textbooks. Six libraries had less than 4000 volumes and 03 possessed 8000-12000 textbooks. Three libraries had 12000-16000 volumes of textbooks. It is evident from the table that textbooks constitute a large part of the total collection of libraries.

REFERENCE COLLECTION

A good reference collection is the soul for sound reference service. It has been observed that all libraries maintained separate reference parts. Responses received about the strength of reference collection are tabulated below.

Table. Reference Collection of Libraries

Sr. No.	Number of Reference Books Possessed	No. of Libraries	%
1.	0-200	02	10.53
2.	200-500	05	26.31
3.	500-1000	02	10.53
4.	1000-1500	03	15.79
5.	1500-2500	03	15.79
6.	More than 2500	04	21.05
	Total	**19**	**100.00**

Table depicts that 05 (26.31%) libraries possessed 200-500 reference volumes, while other 05 had 500-1500 books. About 21.05 per cent libraries had more than 2500 volumes in reference parts.

In majority of the libraries, the reference collection was found to be satisfactory in proportion to their total collection. It was noticed that though the libraries of two GCE were richest in their total collection, still libraries of 04 GACE had more volumes in reference parts.

BOOK BANK

Fifteen libraries (78.94 per cent) had book banks to help poor and needy students, while remaining 04 did not. Out of the 15 libraries, 14 maintained separate book bank parts, while a librarian shared that they did not have any separate book bank part, but lend books to needy students for the full session from text books part. Table furnishes the number of volumes in book banks of 14 libraries.

Table. Size of Book Bank Collection

Sr. No.	Number of Books in Book Bank	No. of Libraries	%
1.	0-500	04	28.58
2.	500-1000	04	28.58
3.	1000-2000	03	21.42
4.	2000-3000	01	07.14
5.	More than 3000	02	14.28
	Total	**14**	**100.00**

Table discloses that out of 14 libraries having separate book bank parts, 08 had less than 1000 volumes in their respective book banks. Four libraries had 1000-3000 books and 02 possessed more than 3000 volumes. It was learnt that majority of the libraries added only gifted books to book banks.

NON-BOOK MATERIAL

Non-book material constitutes an important source of information. The NCTE also requires libraries to have electronic publications (CD-ROMs) in collection. But, it has not gained the desired momentum in the libraries of colleges of education. It was found that only 09 libraries had non-book material in meagre quantity. Out of these, seven libraries possessed a few CD's and one had cassettes that came free with books. Another library had approximately 400 maps.

DISSERTATIONS

Out of 15 colleges running M.Ed. course, libraries of 13 had dissertations. Eight libraries possessed less than 300 dissertations and 03 had 300-400 titles. Two libraries possessed more than 400 dissertations.

Number of the dissertations possessed by libraries varied according to the year of starting M.Ed. course. The University College of Education, Bathinda and SDS College of Education, Lopon (Moga) started M.Ed. courses during the academic sessions 2006-07 and 2007-08 respectively. Libraries of both of these colleges did not have dissertations.

PERIODICAL LITERATURE

Periodical publications serve the purpose of both information and recreation. These include journals, magazines and all other publications, which are issued at regular intervals.

JOURNALS

Journals are the subject specific periodicals, usually containing primary information. Table represents data about the number of journals on subscription of libraries.

Table. Number of Journals on Subscription

Sr. No.	Number of Journals	No. of Libraries	%
1.	0-10	04	21.05
2.	11-20	10	52.63
3.	21-30	03	15.79
4.	More than 30	02	10.53
	Total	**19**	**100.00**

Table reveals that majority of the libraries forming 52.63 per cent were subscribing to 11-20 journals. Three libraries had 21-30 journals on subscription, while 02 libraries were subscribing to more than 30 journals. Only one library subscribed 02 international journals. A goverment aided college library was subscribing to merely two journals. The NCTE (2007) has prescribed for B.Ed. and M.Ed. colleges to subscribe to a minimum of 10 and 15 journals respectively. But libraries of 02 colleges offering B.Ed. course and 03 colleges offering M.Ed. course in addition to B.Ed. also did not meet these standards. NCTE (2009) provided revised norms regarding journals for M.Ed. course. It requires each library to have subscription to at least one international publication.

BACK VOLUMES OF JOURNALS

Back volumes of journals are the vital sources of information for furtherance of research. All the libraries except one had back volumes of journals.

Table. Back Volume of Journals

Sr. No.	Number of Volumes	No. of Libraries	%
1.	0-100	08	44.44
2.	100-200	03	16.67
3.	200-400	03	16.67
4.	More than 400	03	16.67
5.	No Response	01	05.55
	Total	**18**	**100.00**

Table depicts that 08 (44.44 per cent) out of a total 18 libraries having back volumes of journals had less than 100 back volumes, while 03 (16.67 per cent) had 100-200 volumes. Three libraries possessed 200-400 volumes, whereas other three libraries were having more than 400 back volumes of journals. One librarian had not specified the number of back volumes of journals available in library. Survey brought to notice that back volumes of journals were not properly organised as six libraries had loose issues, while in 03 libraries these were partially bound.

MAGAZINES

In addition to journals, libraries provide general magazines to users for reading. Majority of the of libraries *i.e.,* 13 (68.42 per cent) were subscribing to less than 20 magazines, while 04 had 21-30 magazine titles on subscription. Two libraries were making available more than 30 magazine titles for users.

NEWSPAPERS

Sometimes, newspapers contain information not available from other sources. Fifteen libraries were subscribing to 05-10 newspaper titles, whereas two had 05 or less newspapers on subscription. A library was subscribing to more than 10 newspapers daily in English, Punjabi and Hindi.

LIBRARY BUILDING

Libraries are dynamic institutions which continue to grow in terms of collection, staff and readers. In order to tackle the resultant growth it becomes necessary to house a library in an independent, functional and modular building. Keeping in view the significance of library building, query was made to ascertain whether libraries have their own independent buildings. Responses revealed that only one goverment aided college library had an independent building used exclusively for library purpose. The remaining 18 libraries were housed in buildings forming part of college premises. During visit, it was observed that library of GHG Khalsa College of Education, Gurusar Sadhar was sharing building with canteen. Library was located on first floor while canteen was sited on ground floor, causing disturbance to library users. Majority of the libraries *i.e.* 07 (36.84 per cent) were housed in single rooms, while 06 (31.58 per cent) libraries had two rooms each. Three libraries consisted of 04 rooms and one had more than 05 rooms.

It was astounding to find during visit to Khalsa College of Education, Mukatsar that a teacher was taking class in library. When asked, assistant librarian shared that it was a usual practice. That majority of the libraries were housed in one or two rooms, which can not be considered sufficient for effective functioning of libraries. The NCTE (2007 and 2009) norms about library building need to be revised. These require each college to have "a library-cum-reading room.'

SEPARATE READING ROOM

A separate reading room with sufficient seating capacity and free from disturbance is the essence of all types of libraries. Survey revealed that only 05 (26.31 per cent) libraries had separate reading rooms for users, while in remaining libraries chairs were arranged within stack area. Similarly, five libraries had separate librarian's offices to perform the documentary work. In remaining libraries these were in the form of tables or cabins in corners of libraries.

USERS' VISIT TO LIBRARIES

Libraries exist to meet the information needs of users. The strength of users, their information needs and subjects of study, etc. greatly influence the resources and services of libraries. Table reveals the average number of visitors to libraries.

Table. Average Number of Visitors to Libraries

Sr. No.	Number of Visitors	No. of Libraries	%
1.	0-40	03	15.79
2.	40-80	06	31.58
3.	80-120	06	31.58
4.	More than 120	04	21.05
	Total	**19**	**100.00**

It is evident from the table that 06 (31.58 per cent) libraries were being visited by 80-120 users and other six libraries were visited by 40-80 users everyday. Four libraries were visited by more than 120 users daily on an average. In three libraries less than 40 users were visiting a day. The number of daily visitors to libraries varied due to variation in the students' strength with colleges.

SEATING CAPACITY

A library is supposed to provide adequate seating arrangement to users for reading inside library premises. Following table reveals the seating capacity of libraries.

Table. Seating Capacity for Users

Sr. No.	Number of Visitors	No. of Libraries	%
1.	0-25	03	15.79
2.	26-50	08	42.10
3.	51-75	03	15.79
4.	76-100	04	21.05
5.	More than 100	01	05.27
	Total	**19**	**100.00**

Table shows that majority of the libraries had seating capacity for 26-50 users, while 04 libraries could accommodate 76-100 users at a time. Three libraries had less than 25 seats each for users. A library had seating arrangement for more than 100 users. Six libraries had separate seating arrangement for M.Ed. students, while libraries of remaining 09 colleges offering M.Ed. course did not have such facility. Ten libraries had separate seating arrangement for teachers.

The NCTE (2007) prescribed for each college to provide seating arrangement in libraries for at least 25 per cent of their B.Ed. students and for 10 students of M.Ed. course, but 08 libraries did not meet this requirement. NCTE (2009) has revised norms regarding seating capacity of libraries for B.Ed course. It requires libraries to have seating arrangement for at least fifty per cent of B.Ed students. Only one library had drinking water facility for users. Similarly, Library of DAV College of Education, Abohar had toilet facility for faculty members. Students were not allowed to use that.

COLLECTION DISCOVERY SERVICE

A client wishing to access ADEPT must first know what libraries and collections exist. For this reason the ADEPT architecture has been extended with a central *collection discovery service*: a registry of known collections and a search capability that allows clients to find relevant collections.

CENTRAL REGISTRY

Any distributed system must provide some kind of entrance or starting point for clients. Completely decentralized systems such as the World Wide Web and Gnutella eschew any central architectural artifact in favour of non-architectural mechanisms (*e.g.*, word-of-mouth).

For ADEPT's purposes, we believe it is simpler, and sufficiently manageable and scalable, for there to be a central registry of known collections. The ADEPT collection discovery service (CDS) provides such a registry. A middleware server coming online registers itself with the CDS, at a well-known address. Thereafter the CDS periodically (*e.g.*, daily) retrieves the collection-level metadata for each of the middleware server's collections. (The "update frequency" field in the collection-level metadata might be used someday to suggest appropriate polling frequencies.) A middleware server that fails to respond after some interval (*e.g.*, a week) is considered defunct.

There can be more than one CDS we anticipate collection discovery services oriented around domains or user communities such as the National Science Digital Library (NSDL).

A middleware server may register itself with any number of collection discovery services. The CDS registry is sufficient for finding collections, but as a complete solution it scales very poorly. Given little or no information about collections, a client wishing to find information in the system can do so only by querying every collection every time. The unworkability of this approach was demonstrated by an early version of the FGDC Clearinghouse. Visitors to the Clearinghouse web site in 1999-2000 were presented with a simple list of collections (*sites* in Clearinghouse parlance) with no context other than a name (*e.g.*, "Southwest Data Centre Clearinghouse"). Additional information about sites could only be obtained manually and individually. (The Clearinghouse has since improved its interface to include a preliminary collection identification phase.)

Collection Relevance

The CDS harvests, stores, and indexes collection-level metadata for each known collection. ADEPT has specified a content standard for this metadata. The portions of the standard relevant to this discussion include:

- Spatial histograms indicating the geographic coverage of the items in the collection. A spatial histogram is a two-dimensional histogram whose domain is the Earth's surface, and in which a cell value indicates the number of collection items that.
  - Have a value for the Geographic location bucket, and
  - Whose value overlaps the cell. A graphic rendering of a spatial histogram is shown in Figure. The data structure computed and stored is an Euler histogram, which is a slight variation of a simple histogram that supports range searching.
- Analogous to the spatial histogram, temporal histograms indicating the calendrical coverage of the collection. Specifically, a temporal histogram is a one-dimensional histogram whose domain is calendrical time, and in which a cell value indicates the number of collection items that.
  - Have a value for the Date bucket, and
  - Whose value overlaps the cell. Again, the histogram is an Euler histogram.
- The controlled vocabularies used to categorize items in the collection, and, for each vocabulary term, the number of items in the collection relevant to the term.

If a vocabulary is a thesaurus (that is, supports broader/narrower relationships between terms), the counts reflect the specificity of the terms. So, for example, if "images" is a broader term for "photographs", then the number of images includes the number of photographs. The CDS allows clients to rank collections by each of the above three quantities. For example, a client specifies a spatial or temporal query in the form of a geographic region or time period, and the CDS returns a (possibly truncated) list of the known collections ranked by the number of items each collection has that spatially or temporally overlap the query region.

A vocabulary query takes the form of a single vocabulary term, and ranking of results is by the number of items associated with the term. Conjunctions of queries are discussed under Limitations, below.

It should be noted that the CDS's query language is essentially a subset of middleware's query language, *i.e.*, the query language used to query individual collections. Thus a client can formulate a single query that can be used to, in effectively one step, both identify relevant collections and subsequently search for items within those collections.

Scalability

Evaluating a query region against an Euler histogram takes constant time.

The histograms and item counts amount to only a few kilobytes per collection, and thus can all be stored in primary memory. We therefore anticipate that the CDS can easily accommodate tens of thousands of collections, and answer queries with reasonable speed, without having to resort to more sophisticated indexing and querying techniques.

Limitations

There are several limitations to our approach to collection discovery. First, the CDS, as described above, cannot perform joined queries. For example, consider the query "Find collections that are likely to contain aerial photographs of Southern California taken in the 1930s."

The CDS can rank collections by the numbers of items relevant to Southern California; by the numbers of items relevant to the 1930s; and by the numbers of aerial photographs. But it cannot rank collections on the joint condition because the underlying statistics are gathered independently.

Currently we approximate joint conditions by assuming that the statistics are linked. Under this heuristic, a collection with lots of aerial photographs and good coverage of the 1930s is presumed to contain relatively many aerial photographs taken in the 1930s. We are exploring new data structures that explicitly capture joint statistics and yet are still compact and easy to compute. Second, the CDS relies on binary statistics: an item is either relevant or it is not.

A world map drawn on the back of a napkin thus has the same spatial relevance as a high-resolution, multiterabyte dataset with worldwide coverage. We are working on incorporating resolution (specifically, minimum feature size) as a way of approximating information density. (*I.e.*, the dataset has much higher information density than the napkin, and thus would rank higher.) Ideally, one could constrain both minimum feature size *and* information density after all, there are times when one indeed wants the napkin and not the dataset.

Third, the CDS is not especially effective for collections that are not well discriminated by geographic space, calendrical time, or controlled vocabulary terms, or which contain items that lack the metadata supporting such discrimination. A possible solution may be to augment the CDS with an approach based on word frequency, such as that used in STARTS.

COLLECTION DEVELOPMENT AND MANAGEMENT POLICIES

The libraries are now functioning as Information or Knowledge Centers, resource centers, which disseminates required pinpointed information to the users. Libraries collect the information published in various forms *e.g.* books, periodicals, thesis, patents etc. and organise it in helpful sequence. The heart of the library is in its collection. The main purpose of the collection is to serve the needs of users and organisational aims in better ways. Libraries have to develop the collection keeping in view the users need and demands and hence the collection development in the library must be proper.

Traditional Libraries have some set of rules framed for the collection development but not operative, but now due use of ICT, revolutionary changes have been observed in the library practices including collection development. The framed rules are not appropriate and suits to the changing practices and hence majority of the libraries in the developed countries have formulated the collection development policies to build the proper and useful collection in the libraries which supports to the needs of the users. Similarly the change in format from print to digital made the issues to develop new policies or to amend the existing policies to suit the environment.

In digital media acquisitions the process is different due to change in format and pricing structure as compared to previous methods followed in libraries. Collection development is the main activity of any library and hence librarians are now focusing more in this area. To maintain the proper collection in libraries there is a need to develop policies or amend to the existing to suit the emerging trends in publications and acquisition methods. The increase in digital media publication and usage the collection development policies for the digital information resources are required to be developed.The process of the collection development covers selection and de-selection of the resources.

Collection development or management involves activities like collection management programme, collection development policy statement, collection assessment, funding and budgeting, selection and de-selection, preservation, and resource- sharing projects. It is very clear from the statement made by Verzosa that collection development process is a complex process involving various activities but its advantages are more to have a proper collection.

WHAT IS COLLECTION DEVELOPMENT

The purpose of collection development pointed out by Melvil Dewey was to provide 'The best reading for the largest number at the least cost'. ALA defined a very suitable definition for collection development as "A term which encompasses a number of activities related to the development of the library collection, including the determination and coordination of selection policy, assessment of needs of users and potential users, collection use studies, collection evaluation, identification of collection needs, selection of materials, Planning for resource sharing, collection maintenance and weeding."

ALA Glossary State that "Library Collections will contain all types of registered information, including printed materials of all formats, audio-visual materials, visual material, materials used with computers, graphs and three-dimensional materials and ways to access the electronic information" Harold Libraries Glossary defined "collection developments as the process of planning a stock acquisition programmed not simply to cater for immediate needs but to build a current and reliable collection over a numbers of years to meet the objectives of the services." These definitions clearly indicate the need of collection development in information growing age. If libraries need to provide qualitative services then qualitative collection is to be made available in the library irrespective of forms and formats.

WHY PROPER COLLECTION DEVELOPMENT

Collection of the documents in the library is the prime task as it is the power house of information resources. There are many factors involved to have proper collection development like

- Information explosion and Information overload
- Limited and shrinking library budgets
- Increasing users demands for pinpointed qualitative information resources due to specialisation
- Multiple forms and formats of the information resources including digital
- Increase in prices of documents all the times
- Shift in demand of users from collection based services to information and access based services
- More usage of Internet based e-documents

Since digital, internet resources, databases and e-publications are increasing and simultaneously the use in academic and special libraries are also increasing continuously. Growth in literature made necessary to manage proper collection.

Objectives and Purpose of Collection Development

The main objectives and purpose behind collection development are:

- Fulfill the user needs by proper collection
- To support the teaching learning and research endeavors
- Periodically review the collection for weeding
- To provide nascent and relevant information
- To acquire the best and useful literature to the core group of the users

Collection Development policies allows the library personnel's to develop proper collection and based on this value added services can be provided to the users. The purpose of the collection development policy is to provide guidelines for day to day acquisition and withdrawal decisions, resource allocation and long range planning of collection needs keeping in mind the library mission, activities, organisational needs and interest etc.

TECHNIQUES FOR PROPER COLLECTION DEVELOPMENT

For proper collection development for any library, a detailed written collection development policy is necessary. The policy clearly specifies the organisational requirements, goals and the user needs in specific. The Library committee formed for the proper development and progress of the library consist of the expert members from the various faculties who can contribute in formulating the proper collection development and designing the policies. It is also necessary to look in to the policies formulated by the other libraries and the policies prepared by LC and ALA etc. Library collection development policy should be in clearly spelt out in a written form.

The American Library Association's collection development policies assumed that a written collection development policy is a desirable tool that enables selectors to work with greater consistency towards defined goals. The following aspects need to be considered basically while developing policy:

- Users needs and demands
- Review the organisational needs and objectives
- Review the standard, core, border and peripheral subject areas
- Conduct use and users studies for user behaviour and need analysis
- Try to cover the sources which disseminate maximum access to current information in the area
- Take the help of techniques like citation analysis, impact factor, bibliometrics and scientiometrics studies, information audit, information behaviour of users etc
- Resource Sharing practices be initiated at various level including consortium
- Evaluation techniques must be adapted
- Trial access for the databases for certain period and get the feedback from the users before subscription
- Initiate the OA and IR project for protecting IP of organisation
- Analyse strengths and weakness of the collection regularly
- Apply management techniques for quality procurement

Many libraries have developed collection development policies but these are informal in nature and no concrete policies are developed except larger organisations. The collection development policy is required due to multidisciplinary subjects, procurement of epublications. Policy is a guideline to act on. To prepare a policy for any library a review of different standard collection development policies becomes useful to draft a policy.

REVIEW OF EXISTING COLLECTION DEVELOPMENT POLICIES

The basic elements while formulating the collection development policy for any library was discussed in the conferences also and the output presented in the National Conference on 'Putting Knowledge to Work: Best Practices in Librarianship" 1-2 May 2009 151-152 highlighted following issues.

- *Organisational Objectives*: The nature of the organisation, its function, objectives and the purpose must be considered at the initial level.

- *Users*: It is necessary to review the needs of the users of the library especially from the organisation, their main area of concern, projects under taken, information resources covering the general aspect about the stream as well as the specialised needs of the users in the area of research. Real and potential needs of the users must be covered.
- *Level of collection*: The collection may satisfy the needs of the experts as well as a common man whose interest is to read for the entertainment and knowledge addition. (Maslow's need based triangle). There is a need to focus on the current and future needs of the organisations.
- *Subject Coverage*: It is necessary to fix the core subjects in which organisational collection must be deep and updated. The peripheral subjects can be developed based on the priority as well as need based collection or even can be shared with other organisations (Resource Sharing). Hence collection assessment must be evaluated based on the area and subjects of core importance.
- *Type of Information Sources*: While selecting the information recourses it is necessary to provide the access to the literature published in the area which is covered by the secondary information sources. It is necessary to provide maximum access to the users rather than owning the information resources. To make the collection economic on demand acquisition can also be preferred in case of peripheral area or can be obtained from ILL.
- *Budget*: Allocation of the budget must be proper and as per the usage. The budget of any library is not adequate to get all the literature published and hence policies must be fixed keeping in mind the usage and cost effective factors. Resource sharing activity will also help in reducing the expenses in case of peripheral research area.
- *Forms in which material must be acquired*: It is necessary to fix the form in which documents can be acquired. A policy stating the forms (print, digital, non print etc) to be procured must be detailed. However the acquisition must always be cost effective to adjust in the budget allocated.
- *Services provided*: Many libraries provide services to the users from the organisation as well as from different institutions. For this purpose the acquisition must be qualitative.
- *Users and use studies at frequent Intervals*: It is necessary to evaluate the usage of the acquired material. If the material is less used it must be weeded or stacked in parallel.
- *Policies for the preservation of the resources*: Preservation of the literature is the objective of the library. The heritage of the knowledge is useful for the future generation and hence modern tools and techniques may be used.

IFLA POLICY FOR COLLECTION DEVELOPMENT

The IFLA suggested following points in its collection development policy:

- Must be a written Policy covering procedure for selection, de-selection planning (future), public relations, weeding, retaining, preservation etc
- Covers general, narrative and subject profiles
- Use of collection evaluation methods
- Use of collection depth indicators
- Language (English, Primary and predominantly used as per need and country language)
- Policy implementation and revision

The first elements of a collection development policy will be a mission statement of the library, the purpose of this policy and the audience to whom it is addressed. General area covers current focus or also retrospective acquisitions; the resource types (monographs, periodicals, theses, gray literature, maps, etc.); languages; formats (printed, non-print or electronic); special sources of funding (a grant or gift from a donor); the policy regarding gifts and any special policies regarding maintenance (weeding, discarding, preservation) of the collection; and size of the collections. Collection evaluation is based on quantitative and qualitative measures:

- Quantitative Measures reveal size, age, use, costs and other numeric data. Examples of quantitative measures include inventory, or shelf list measures to determine actual title or volume counts, by segment or subject area. Median age or similar measures indicate the currency of the materials. Amount expended for acquisitions in a segment or subject area per year illustrates the ongoing commitment to develop that area. Percentage of titles owned by a library when compared to a standard list shows the breadth and depth of the collection. Use statistics (including internal library use and ILL) are both collection and client-centred.
- Qualitative measures are obtained through subjective evaluation and involve the professional judgement of librarians, appraisal from subject experts, or the opinion of customers. These techniques include impressions of the condition, character and appropriateness of a section of the collection. Another qualitative technique is the judgement made by comparison of one subject in the collection to a similar subject in another library, or to a subject bibliography.

Collection depth indicators indicated are: current collection level, acquisition commitment and collection goal. Indicators define out of scope, minimum information level, basic information level, study and instructional support, research level, comprehensive level etc Each institution, including its community and other constituents, is unique. Therefore, its policy statements will be unique. The policy statements should reflect this particular library and the community it serves.

ALA POLICY

ALA covers following standard elements in its policy developed for academic libraries (College)

- *Standards* 1: Mission, Goals, and Objectives of institution
- *Standard* 2: Collections: including print materials in all formats, audiovisual materials, sound recordings, materials used with computers, graphics, and three dimensional materials. A formula is also presented in terms of collection development in the policy
- *Standard* 3: Organisation of materials: Library collections shall be organised by nationally approved conventions and arranged for efficient retrieval at time of need. The processing methods need to be applied for this purpose.
- *Standard* 4: Staff: The staff shall be of adequate size and quality to meet the library's need for services, programmes, and collection organisation. A staff formula is also presented in the policy
- *Standard* 5: Services: The library shall establish, promote, maintain a range and quality of services that supports the academic programme of the institution and encourage optional library use.
- *Standards* 6: Facilities: The library building shall provide well-planned, secure and adequate housing for its collections and personnel; secure space for users and staff, and space for the provision of services and programmes. A formula is also presented to calculate the space for per vol/Per Sqft.
- *Standards* 7: Administration: The college library shall be administered in a manner which permits and encourages the fullest and most effective use of available library resources.
- *Standard* 8: Budget: The library director shall have the responsibility for preparing, defending, and administering the library budget in accord with agreed upon objectives. These standards provide the guideline for formulating the policy.

UNIVERSITY GRANT COMMISSION (UGC) COLLECTION DEVELOPMENT POLICY

The UGC policy stated following points for collection development:

- Library Committee and its constituents (Chairman, member secretary, members, student representative)
- Library Collection norms based on courses, students and faculty
- Technical Processing.
- Library Finance

- Library Services
- Library Personnel
- Physical Facilities

AICTE COLLECTION DEVELOPMENT POLICY FOR ENGINEERING COLLEGE LIBRARIES

All India Council for Technical Education (AICTE) has formulated norms or policy for development of library collection including number of titles and their volumes, number of national and international journals including e-resources made available through INDESTAICTE. The main elements covered with formulas are:

- Collection of Books and Journals (Print Reading Material)
- Collection of Electronic Resources (e-journals and e-books etc)
- Library Personnel and Library Building

LIBRARY OF CONGRESS. COLLECTION DEVELOPMENT POLICIES

The Library's Collection Development Policy is a guide for materials to be added to the Library's permanent collections. The Collection Policy Statement (CPS) governs the Library's collection development and acquisition efforts. The statements implement the Library's responsibilities to serve. The policies provide a plan for developing the collections and maintaining their existing strengths.The highlighted points in to this policy are:

- *Collecting Levels*: Out of scope no need to buy, minimum level, basic information level, instructional level, research level, comprehensive level
- *Collection Overviews*: Scope, research strength,
- *Selection Guidelines for Electronic Resources*: Evaluate contents, add value, server reliability, judicious use of multimedia, adherence to copyright and fair use guidelines, provision of links to source for the plug-in-software, organisation and ease of navigation, presence of search and help features, procurement of Standard Fee based resources with permanent retention.

From the analytical study of the collection development policies it is understood that minimum components to be considered are:

- *Selection*: Covers purpose (free or purchased) teaching, learning, research and needs of staff and students; responsibility (Staff and librarian), Format (Print or digital), Language, special collections
- *Allocation of resources*: Considerations based on need based requirements and on demand procurement and provide more access to information than possession.
- *Collection maintenance*: Retention policies considering usage, main stack, parallel stacking, compact storage, weeding, retro-conversion etc are properly applied for better management and reduction in cost.

- *Preservation*: Rare and useful collection is to be retained for longer use and needs proper preservation manual or converting to digital
- *Access*: open access or authority permitted to consult in case of rare and confidential.
- *More use of e-publications*: The print media is shifting to e-publications and databases and more use is observed in the present generation.
- *Network based resources and consortium arrangement*: These are also to be considered while planning collection economically
- *Resource sharing and IR initiatives*: Open access and IR and resource sharing initiatives need to be considered

There is a need to develop proper collection in different forms. Collection development policies are to be framed for digital collection also as these documents may increase in the collection including acquisition and resource sharing policies.

The policies need to be revised regularly. Policy supports to customer-focused needs, so that library users have access to current, relevant and authoritative information in their preferred format.

Bibliography

A.A.N. Raju: *Facets of Library and Information Science*, Ess Ess Publications, Delhi, 2012.

Ajit Singh: *Siwatch Encyclopedic Dictionary of Library and Information Science, Vols. I to III*, Shree Publishers, Delhi, 2010.

Beales, G.: *The Evolving Roles of Information Professionals in the Digital Age*, Long Life Publication, New Delhi, 2003.

Bertozzi, S.: *Special Libraries,* Pune Publication, Maharashtra, 2006.

Bhupendra Narayan Singh: *Encyclopaedia of Library and Information Science in the Digital Age Vols. I to III*, Anmol Publication, Delhi, 2011.

Bloom, B. S.: *Key Concepts in the Architecture of the Digital Library,* Concept Publishing Company, New Delhi, 2003.

Hey, A.: *Issues of Libraries in the Digital Era,* University of Chicago Press, Chicago, 2006.

Hunt, M.: *Electronic Journals: Promises and Challenges in Indian Academic Libraries,* Guru Nanak Dev University, Amritsar, 2006.

K.G. Rastogi: *Acquisition and Collection Development in Library Science*, Alfa Publications, Delhi, 2006.

K.G. Rastogi: *Reference Services in Library Science*, Alfa Publications, Delhi, 2006.

Krishan Kumar And Jaideep Sharma: *Library And Information Science Education In India*, Har-anand Publications, Delhi, 2009.

M.A. Khan: *Indexing and Documentation in Library Science*, Sarup Publications, Delhi, 1996.

Menzies, E. P.: *The Electronic Document and its Impact on the Information Chain Professions*, Kogan Page, London, 2000.

Mukherjee, N.: *Digital Libraries: Principles and Practice in a Global Environment,* Concept Publication, New Delhi, 2005.

Poonam: *HRD in Library and Information Science*, ACE Books, Delhi, 2010.

R L Sehgal: *Designing and Evaluation of Research in Library Science (2 Vols-Set)*, Ess Ess Publications, Delhi, 1998.

R. K. Krishnan: *The Five Laws of Library Science*, Centrum Press, Delhi, 2013.

R.C. Chakravarthy and P.R.S. Murthy: *Information Technology and Library Science*, Pacific Books International, Delhi, 2012.

S. Yadagiri and R.K. Pavan Kumar: *Library Automation: Perspectives and Challenges*, Swastik Publications, Delhi, 2013.

S.K. Chaudhary: *Library Networking*, A.P.H. Publications, Delhi, 2011.

S.K. Sangma: *Cataloguing Rules in Library Science*, Centrum Press, Delhi, 2013.

S.R. Das: *Modern Encyclopaedia of Library Science (5 Vols-Set)*, Arise Publications, Delhi, 2006.

T. Bala Theresa, C. Ratna Kumari and B.A. Rani: *Information Technology and Library Automation*, Commonwealth Publications, Delhi, 2011.

T.R. Sanjiv Reddy and Shyamgopal Verma: *Library Science and Information Technology*, Pacific Books International, Delhi, 2012.

Thapar, R.: *The Impact of Digital Reference on Librarians and Library Users*, Oxford University Press, New Delhi, 1994.

V.G. Choukhande: *Information Needs and Information Seeking Behaviour : Library and Information Science Research*, Shivneri Publication, Delhi, 2008.

Vaishali Khaparde: *Advancement in Library and Information Science*, Ess Ess Publications, Delhi, 2012.

Index